Riot and Revelry in Early America

Riot and Revelry in Early America

★ ★ ★

edited by

William Pencak   Matthew Dennis   Simon P. Newman

The Pennsylvania State University Press
University Park, Pennsylvania

Library of Congress Cataloging-in-Publication Data

Riot and revelry in early America / edited by
William Pencak, Matthew Dennis, Simon P. Newman.
p. cm.
Includes index.
ISBN 978-0-271-02141-6 (cloth : alk. paper)
ISBN 978-0-271-02219-2 (pbk. : alk. paper)
1. Festivals—United States—History—18th century. 2. Parades—United States—History—18th century. 3. Riots—United States—History—18th century. 4. Popular music—United States—History—18th century. 5. United States—Social life and customs—To 1775.
I. Pencak, William, 1951- .
II. Dennis, Matthew, 1955- .
III. Newman, Simon P., 1960- .
GT4803 .C76 2002

394.26973—dc21   2001036462

Copyright © 2002 The Pennsylvania State University
All rights reserved
Printed in the United States of America
Published by The Pennsylvania State University Press,
University Park, PA 16802-1003

It is the policy of The Pennsylvania State University Press to use acid-free paper for the first printing of all clothbound books. Publications on uncoated stock satisfy the minimum requirements of American National Standard for Information Sciences—Permanence of Paper for Printed Library Materials, ANSI Z39.48–1992.

FRONTISPIECE: Charles Willson Peale, "Benedict Arnold and the Devil," woodcut, 1780. From Francis Bailey's *The Continental Almanac*. Courtesy of The Metropolitan Museum of Art, New York. Bequest of Charles Allen Munn, 1924.
In 1780, after General Benedict Arnold—who had formerly commanded the American troops occupying Philadelphia—attempted to betray his new post (West Point, New York) to the British, he was burned in effigy in a Philadelphia procession reminiscent of rough music. In this woodcut, the devil torments the two-faced effigy as Arnold himself is seen fleeing to a British ship in the background.

For Alfred F. Young and in memory of William D. Piersen

Contents

Introductions

1. Introduction: A Historical Perspective
   William Pencak 3

2. Introduction: A Folklore Perspective
   Roger D. Abrahams 21

Riot and Rough Music

3. Skimmington in the Middle and New England Colonies
   Steven J. Stewart 41

4. The Rise of Rough Music: Reflections on an Ancient New Custom in Eighteenth-Century New Jersey
   Brendan McConville 87

5. Crowd and Court: Rough Music and Popular Justice in Colonial New York
   Thomas J. Humphrey 107

6. Play as Prelude to Revolution: Boston, 1765–1776
   William Pencak 125

7. Rough Music on Independence Day: Philadelphia, 1778
   Susan E. Klepp 156

Revelry

8. White Indians in Penn's City: The Loyal Sons of St. Tammany
   Roger D. Abrahams 179

9 The Eighteenth-Century Discovery of Columbus: The Columbian Tercentenary (1792) and the Creation of American National Identity
Matthew Dennis 205

10 American Women and the French Revolution: Gender and Partisan Festive Culture in the Early Republic
Susan Branson and *Simon P. Newman* 229

11 African American Festive Style and the Creation of American Culture
William D. Piersen 255

12 The Paradox of "Nationalist" Festivals: The Case of Palmetto Day in Antebellum Charleston
Len Travers 273

Contributors and Acknowledgments 297

Index 299

Introductions

1

Introduction: A Historical Perspective

William Pencak

It is impossible to think about American history without riot and revelry coming to mind. From the Boston Massacre to the Los Angeles riots that protested the beating of Rodney King, and from the Fourth of July celebrations in 1776 that toppled statues of King George III to the cheering of millions who hailed returning Gulf War veterans in 1991, "the people out-of-doors" not only witnessed history, but made it. This volume, which arose from a conference on Festive Culture in Early America sponsored in Philadelphia by the American Philosophical Society and the McNeil (then Philadelphia) Center for Early American Studies in April 1996, seeks to bring to life how, what, and why Americans protested and celebrated "roughly" (in both senses of the word) from 1750 to 1860—that is, from Revolutionary times to the Civil War.

Between November 17 and 20, 1747, during a war with France, hundreds if not thousands of people in Boston seized some officers of a visiting British fleet and held them hostage. They were protesting what they considered illegal impressment of sailors from ships in the harbor for service in the Royal Navy, and they hoped to trade the officers for the release of the unfortunates who had been taken. While British Commodore Charles Knowles eventually freed some of the men, after first threatening to blow up the town, this crisis—the greatest riot in Boston before the Stamp Act—inaugurated a debate over the nature of popular protest that still continues today. "Our Province in a peculiar manner requires some more severe acts against Riots, Mobs, and Tumults," wrote physician William Douglass.

The Boston Town Meeting attempted to avoid responsibility for actions of a crowd that included many townspeople. Boston's inhabitants expressed their "utmost Abhorrence of such Illegal Criminal Proceedings," which they blamed exclusively on "Foreign Seamen Servants Negroes and other Persons of Mean and Vile Condition."[1]

One voice dissented from the cover-up. Within two months of the riot, the first antiwar newspaper in America, the *Independent Advertiser,* was published by a group of political outsiders that included the twenty-five-year-old Samuel Adams. This group opposed Massachusetts' exertions against the French as both economically disastrous and downright murderous, and expressed outrage that "the sober sort, who dared to express a due sense of their injuries, were invidiously represented as a rude, low-lived mob." Elsewhere, the newspaper responded to Douglass's charges by affirming that the mob was no mob, but rather "an Assembly of People drawn together upon no other Design than to defend themselves."[2]

The proper role of "the people out-of-doors" in American public life has never been resolved. Forty years later, Samuel Adams led the hardliners who wanted not only to put down but also to hang the leaders of what became known as "Shays's Rebellion": "In monarchies the crime of treason and rebellion may admit of being pardoned or lightly punished, but the man who dares rebel against the laws of a republic ought to suffer death." I call attention to the name pinned on this event because the farmers of western Massachusetts who closed courthouses and proposed changes in the Massachusetts constitution emphatically did not consider themselves rebels. They believed they were patriots, following the example of Adams himself in protesting taxes of which they and their representatives—who found attending the eastern-dominated legislature in Boston difficult—disapproved.[3]

The metamorphosis of Samuel Adams from crowd leader to champion of law and order reflects scholarly debate that still exists concerning the nature of early American crowds. Adams's opinion of colonial disturbances and crowd mobilization during the preliminaries of the Revolution has been seconded by historian Pauline Maier. She maintains that during the colonial era the "mob"—which historians now dignify as "the crowd," to avoid the very slur Adams complained about in 1747—enjoyed a quasi-legal and respectable existence. Maier writes that colonial mobs carefully selected targets and limited violence: "They served the community where no law existed, or intervened beyond what magistrates thought they could do to cope with a local problem." In keeping with Americans' image of their revolution as respectable and conservative, the crowds that resisted the British killed no one, and specifically targeted the shops and residences of offending individuals in the ten years separating the Stamp Act riots and the Battles of Lexington and Concord. The casualties, as in the "Boston Massacre," occurred largely among those who protested. Only during the Revolution itself, as loyalists battled patriots, did crowds become violent and acquire a negative reputation.[4]

Beginning in the 1960s, however, some historians argued otherwise. Influenced by protests of that decade, New Left historians, such as Jesse Lemisch, Staughton Lynd, Dirk Hoerder, and Alfred F. Young, insisted that even if people of different classes appeared in the same crowds, the agendas of sailors (always an important element in colonial ports), African Americans (a sizable contingent among seaman as well as a presence in the cities), and the less well-to-do were different from the agendas of their leaders in the upper classes. They wanted to reform society in a more democratic direction, not merely remove obnoxious grievances and pro-British officials. They were indeed "Foreign Seaman Servants Negroes Boys and Others of Mean and Vile Condition" who frequently took the lead in revolutionary politics, forcing their putative betters to adopt increasingly radical positions.[5]

Whatever their opinion on the class dimension and socially radical intentions of colonial and revolutionary crowds, historians have generally failed to examine these factors from the perspective of traditional crowd protests that employed "rough music" against those who violated community norms. Before the chapters published in this volume by Steven Stewart, Thomas Humphrey, Brendan McConville, and Susan Klepp, no scholarly collection or monograph has dealt with early American "rough music" in detail. Stewart's pioneering but unfinished dissertation, written in the late 1970s, has been used by Alfred Young and Paul Gilje in their discussions of colonial rioting, but until now there has not been much more. European historians—for instance, Natalie Zemon Davis, E. P. Thompson, and David Underdown—have done better.[6]

"Rough music," also known as "skimmington" in England and "charivari" in France, occurred when a community took the law into its own hands against a deviant, who was beaten, roughed up, or run out of town. A public procession usually climaxed the event. The playing of real, rough music, such as banging on drums and pots and pans, gave the practice its name. It is impossible to say when rough music became frequent in the colonies. Before the 1730s there were few newspapers, and incidents in rural areas, if there were any, have not survived in any accessible historical records. All we can say is that rough music in the form of skimmington first began to be noted regularly beginning in the 1730s, when colonial society was exhibiting the strains of conflict between increasingly cosmopolitan, anglicized elites and a localist populace defending traditional sexual morals and community norms.[7] Early manifestations of rough music hint at the disruptions that were just around the corner: the New Hampshire riots over masts reserved for the Royal Navy in 1739; the Stono slave revolt in South Carolina the same year; the Great Awakening; the Massachusetts land bank crisis of 1739–41; the raucous Philadelphia election of 1742; and the perhaps imaginary lower-class/slave New York "Conspiracy of 1741." All these events pitted cosmopolitan religious, political, or mercantile elites against locally oriented communities. Similarly, Bostonians improvised variations on rough music to bring down the governing elite of Massachusetts in the 1760s. Formal revolutionary bodies and informal crowds did likewise to secure the Revolution from loyalists, who retaliated in kind.

While skimmington occurred in various colonies—and many more instances doubtless went unreported—it is especially noteworthy that most of the cases we know of occurred in New York. One reason for that may be simply that New York Attorney General John Tabor Kempe took excellent notes, which have survived. But New York had always been known for a contentious population in which members of different groups lived in close proximity and thus were especially prone to offend one another.[8] New England, on the other hand, maintained a fairly homogeneous society outside of Rhode Island—where two skimmingtons occurred, in addition to one just outside the factious community of Boston and another in Attleborough, a town Rhode Island disputed with Massachusetts. In the South, conflict pitted a well-defined, plantation-studded tidewater against an equally distinct yeoman backcountry. Pennsylvania Quakers preached and practiced a pacifism that terminated in sectional strife pitting the three oldest, Quaker-dominated counties against the Scots-Irish/German frontiersmen. But in New York, all sorts of people lived side by side: great proprietors and tenants, yeomen of different ethnicities, a large number of African Americans, and even many Indians from different societies, among them the Iroquois, the Mohawks, and the Mahicans. Unencumbered with the moral mission of either Pennsylvania or New England, New York's commercial culture and turbulent development were reflected in its numerous skimmingtons, some of a political nature that Thomas Humphrey explicitly relates to landed disputes over land ownership.

New Jersey, also disputatious, merits its own detailed discussion of rough music in this volume. Not coincidentally, all the rough music Brendan McConville reports occurred in northern New Jersey, formerly East Jersey, the half of the province most similar to New York. As in New York, heavily tenanted proprietary estates prevailed in northern New Jersey, whereas western or southern New Jersey gravitated commercially toward Philadelphia and resembled Pennsylvania with its Quaker presence and freehold farms.[9]

Pennsylvania, which had an extremely high crime rate in the colonial era, also witnessed at least four recorded instances of rough music, two of which Steven Stewart notes and two of which are considered by Susan Klepp in this volume. During the Revolution, crowd violence accelerated. In this collection, Klepp reports a case in which lower-class and middle-class revolutionaries mocked the European hairstyles and fashions flaunted by both the elite Whig women and loyalist women in Philadelphia. Elsewhere, Thomas Slaughter has discussed two incidents when Philadelphia women attacked and killed other women suspected of witchcraft. These murders occurred in 1776 and 1787, the very years in which the Declaration of Independence and the Constitution were adopted. In 1779, six people were also killed in a Philadelphia riot known as "the Fort Wilson incident," and another seventeen to nineteen people were "dangerously wounded" when a protest against wealthy men who could avoid military service got out of hand. The Revolution disrupted Pennsylvania's formerly hegemonic Quaker rule and instituted one of the most contentious state political systems in the new nation. If the diverse population in the Middle Colonies made possible the first approximations of the nation's future political parties, in which competing factions campaigned for support among different groups in the hope of harmonizing them, it also accounts for the numerous social divisions, of which rough music was evidence, that exploded outside the bounds of politics.[10]

As with other crowd actions in colonial America, skimmingtons reflected people's willingness to take the law into their own hands in order to eliminate threats to well-being or moral norms. The real culprits, the crowds believed, were the individuals who flouted legitimate communal values. Women were able to reverse the gender hierarchy to punish immoral men, and freeholders and tenants challenged obnoxious landowners, judges, and merchants. Remoteness from authorities who could enforce the law against deviants (and also against crowds) was one factor that led to incidents of rough music, but not the only one. Most rough music took place in rural areas, such as the Hudson Valley and North Central New Jersey, but other instances occurred in New York City, just outside Boston, and in Philadelphia. Because governmental authority lacked the force and tradition that sustained it in Europe, colonial officials in North America were unable to command the respect and fear of authority that characterized European hierarchies in the eighteenth century.

Class conflict was another precipitator of rough music, which an outraged community inflicted either on members of a cosmopolitan elite (merchants, in at least two cases) or on marginal members of the community, such as a homeless victim in New York. The crowd practiced a "moral economy" (like that which E. P. Thompson found in England), in which outraged community members stepped in to punish those who have transgressed communal norms but were either protected by or fall beyond the reach of law enforcement.[11] An anglicized elite that was unconcerned with or unable to enforce traditional, especially sexual, morality was drawing apart from a populace that insisted that family and local norms be respected. In rough music, then, we see the germ of crowd violence—such as tarring and feathering of loyalists, including members of the same elite—a violence that was to occur much more frequently and turn deadly during the American Revolution. Examining crowd violence in Boston from 1765 to 1775, I look, in my chapter, at rough music in conjunction with other activities of the sort John Huizinga has termed "play," to show how the protesters rehearsed symbolically, as theater, the new forms of government and ideas they would articulate explicitly only once the Revolution had begun.[12]

Rough music did not disappear when the Revolution ended. Bryan Palmer has found hundreds of instances in the rural United States and Canada well into the twentieth century—including a brutal form known as whitecapping, which involved flogging moral offenders.[13] Yet as the Revolution approached, violence in America became more politicized, more deadly, and more reflective of the social divisions that rough music only mildly foreshadowed. As Thomas Slaughter cogently notes, much of this violence occurred at the margins of white settlement.[14] Bloody frays between the "Regulators" and the government of North Carolina; the Paxton Boys' massacre of peaceful Conestoga Indians near Lancaster, Pennsylvania, in 1764; the boundary disputes between Pennsylvania and Maryland, and between Pennsylvania and Connecticut settlers claiming the Wyoming Valley; and the land riots in New York, New Jersey, and the future state of Vermont—all were far more violent than the activities initiated by the urban crowds on which Pauline Maier primarily focuses. If the American Revolution began with restrained violence in the cities designed to resist British taxation, the class, intercolonial, and racial violence that had become endemic throughout the colonies in the years after 1750 intensified once the war was under way. As historian John Murrin points out, the American Revolution was more of a civil war than the Civil War itself,[15] for—except in the border states, the mountains of eastern Tennessee and West Virginia, and New York City during the draft riots of 1863—two coherent sections fought each other while easily suppressing internal resistance. In the Revolution, on the other hand, loyalist and revolutionary partisans battled each other throughout the nation.

Despite the American success against Great Britain, the new nation found it difficult to persuade its diverse citizenry to coexist peaceably within a legal framework. "Rebels" in Pennsylvania violently protested federal taxes with what are known as the Whiskey Rebellion of 1794 and in Fries's Rebellion of 1799. (The word "rebels" appears in quotation marks because those involved considered themselves to be merely protesting unjust taxes.) Philadelphians mobbed African Americans who tried to retain the right to vote, Bostonians set fire to a convent where Catholic immigrants were trying to educate their children, and abolitionists in both North and South took their lives in their hands if they spoke out against slavery. African Americans conspired against their masters in Gabriel's Rebellion, Denmark Vesey's Rebellion, and Nat Turner's Rebellion. Dueling became an acceptable means for upper-class men to settle disputes, as did wrestling matches that could end in eye-gouging or castration for the lower orders. Groups of desperadoes thought nothing of invading Florida, Mexico, Nicaragua, Cuba, or lands in Georgia guaranteed by treaty to the Cherokee Indians. Fatalities in riots became common, reaching more than one hundred in the New York City draft riots of the Civil War.[16]

Historian Paul Gilje has offered the best explanation for the transition from the limited, communally acceptable violence of the colonial period to the more murderous form that became more frequent during the new republic. The colonial ideal of localities as communities sharing a coherent civic identity in which everyone had a place in a hierarchical order gave way to a more democratic and egalitarian society. But that new society incorporated racial, ethnic, religious, regional, and other such loyalties, in addition to a national identity, where, for example, white Northern Protestants considered African Americans, the Irish, Roman Catholics, and eventually Southern secessionists to be un-American elements unworthy of the benefits of citizenship. Even traditional festivals, such as New Year's Eve celebrations in New York, featured tensions that arose from these separate allegiances and became deadly brawls. Furthermore, in the nineteenth century, government's traditional positive task of promoting the common good through moral and economic regulation came to be transformed into the negative one of remaining theoretically neutral and serving as arbiter between competing groups of people.[17]

In consequence, a host of institutions and reform movements arose in the early nineteenth century to quell democracy run amuck. As society became even more fragmented between such groups as employers and laborers, immigrants and the native-born, or southerners and northerners, the "Second-Party System" of the Whigs and Democrats developed to unite people of all sorts under their banners. Penitentiaries (or reformatories) replaced the simple jail and were intended to cure as well as punish the criminal. The temperance movement blamed liquor for the prevailing disorder, while the women's movement that overlapped it stressed the need for the civilizing influence of women in political life. Sunday schools were created to socialize children. Required attendance at common schools developed to educate the young systematically for conservative citizenship, replacing the part-time schools children had attended, when they could be spared from family farm chores.[18]

The Second-Party System, which pitted Andrew Jackson and the Democrats against Henry Clay and the Whigs, provided political stability in the midst of social violence from the early 1830s until sectionalism overcame nationalism in the 1850s. The parties united sections and classes through "machines" run by "bosses," which (usually peacefully) fought for power at the polls. Unlike the "First-Party System" of Federalists and Jeffersonian Republicans, who dueled for control of the government from 1790 until the 1810s, the competitors in the Second-Party System had come to understand the concept of a legitimate opposition. Whereas Hamilton and Jefferson understood only "factionalism," in which all partisanship represented close to treasonable opposition—not to another party but to the republic itself—the partisans of Jackson and Clay realized that both sides had much to gain from healthy competition. Social tensions could be lessened as men of different classes and regions joined in a struggle for office against a similarly composed coalition.[19]

What both party systems had in common, however, was the extensive use of parades and public celebrations as a means of *creating*—and not just reflecting—national unity, obtaining support, and overcoming divisions. Beginning in the 1780s, elite groups sought to mobilize people through public spectacles. Parades honored the ratification of the Constitution, the signing of the Declaration of Independence, Washington's Birthday, the victories of the French in their Revolution or of the Americans in the War of 1812, and the return of Lafayette in 1824. These occasions permitted leaders to orchestrate displays of patriotism in order to instill a sense of loyalty in a populace that rarely experienced the federal government directly except through the post office. Parades and the "perpetual fêtes" that French Minister Edmond Gênet observed became the principal means of popular participation in public life. Songs, banners, floats, orations, and theatrical pageants dotted the calendar and linked local public spaces throughout the land to political and national events, while simultaneously providing entertainment and patriotic education.[20]

The chapters by Roger Abrahams and Matthew Dennis in this volume show how Americans in the new nation resurrected mythical heroes to serve as symbols of unity. A Philadelphia fishing club composed of well-to-do men named itself the "Sons of St. Tammany" in honor of the Indian chief who had supposedly signed the first "treaty" with William Penn (itself almost certainly a mythical event, as no copy has been found[21]), peacefully ceding the land for the earliest settlement of Pennsylvania. During the revolutionary era, "White Indians" had resisted greedy landlords in the backcountry and the landing of British tea in Boston, but urban whites in the early republic disguised themselves as Indians to promote fraternity, have a good time, and celebrate holidays. The symbolic nationization of the Indian by commemorating the alleged donation of land to William Penn legitimated the disappearance of real Indians and made the authority of the new state seem unquestionable and ancient. And the neutralization of the Indian, his transformation from savage to "saint," mirrored what the national elite hoped civic celebrations would accomplish for a potentially obstreperous populace.[22]

In the long run, Matthew Dennis explains, Christopher Columbus, the first European to conquer Indian territory, was a far more enduring symbol than the Pennsylvania chief who had made a treaty with the world's only pacifist society. Because Americans knew little about the real Columbus, he served as a convenient empty vessel into which different parties and regions could pour their own notions of what the new nation should be doing. The new world that Columbus discovered became the prototype for the new republican world Americans hoped the United States would inaugurate, paradoxically through a conquest similar to Columbus's own achievement. More places in the United States are named after Columbus than anyone, except George Washington, and the new nation almost took the name Columbia.[23]

Early American nationalism, however, was not opposed to regionalism, partisan politics, sectionalism, and relationships of class, race, and gender, but it was tied to them. For instance, by 1800 Fourth of July parades became Democratic-Republican holidays, and Washington's Birthday celebrations became Federalist preserves.[24] Susan Davis has written of how working-class Philadelphians, unhappy about required militia service and unable to join the upper-class volunteer companies that purchased fancy uniforms and staged elaborate functions, protested by electing a half-witted hunchback colonel of their regiment and following him around town. Their mockery led to the end of compulsory militia service.[25] David Waldstreicher has shown that Jeffersonian Republicans escorted French Minister Edmond Gênet on a nationwide tour, in effect countering the triumphal journeys President Washington had undertaken to cement support for the new nation and his administration.[26] These two books in general explain that although members of the working class, women, and African Americans who were dissatisfied with their lot in society could not hope to obtain full citizenship, they could temporarily take over public space and transform parades from civic celebrations to statements of criticism. Crowds transformed what were supposed to be rituals of nationalism into protest demonstrations by those who felt excluded from a republic dominated by white middle-class and upper-class males.

In the present volume, Susan Branson and Simon Newman demonstrate that both Federalists and Jeffersonians appealed to women to observe, applaud, and ultimately participate in their various festivities. The Revolution had spurred debate about the position of women in the new republic, and many people of both sexes and parties had accepted a new role for women as the republic's guardians of moral virtue and the educators of its children.

However, the more assertive examples of women during the French Revolution, and the writings of Britain's Mary Wollstonecraft, encouraged some women to demand political influence and even full citizenship. As a consequence, parties soon relegated women to the sidelines—without, however, stifling the issues that eventually led to the women's rights movement.[27]

William Piersen shows in his chapter that African Americans too were adept at using European holidays for their own purposes. While borrowing somewhat from such Euro-American holidays as Christmas, Easter, and Election Day, the celebrations of Jonkonnu, Pinkster, and Negro Election Day incorporated African rituals and symbols to a far greater extent. Just as rioting came into disrepute among elite whites, who tried to channel lower-class energies into civic festivals, the new nation's small African American elite discouraged raucous demonstrations as harmful to the respectability they sought for their people.[28] They did not, however, as Shane White has shown, reject African nationalism, but rather redirected it into print and politics.[29]

At least one local elite also found American nationalism itself wanting. Long before the rest of the South, South Carolinians were contemplating secession. Len Travers's chapter shows that these disunionist sentiments took symbolic form beginning in the late 1820s. The state replaced Independence Day with Palmetto Day, June 28, as its principal holiday, to celebrate the fact that the week before the Declaration of Independence was signed the spongy palmetto logs that fortified Charleston absorbed the cannonballs of a British fleet and repulsed the invaders. The rise of Palmetto Day accompanied the Nullification Crisis of 1828, as well as fears about William Lloyd Garrison's radical abolitionist movement, which emerged in 1831 almost simultaneously with Nat Turner's slave rebellion. Elsewhere in the United States, however, nationalism and sectionalism usually reinforced rather than contradicted each other. No one, for instance, could question Robert E. Lee's nationalist credentials until the moment when, with great difficulty, he chose Virginia as his country over the United States. To this day, southerners see no contradiction in flying Confederate-inspired state flags alongside the Stars and Stripes.[30]

The chapters in this collection provide the general reader with colorful tales from America's past, but they also illuminate several issues that are of concern to historians and others who think about the nature of our national heritage. First and perhaps foremost, they seriously call into question a major theory of early American politics. The propensity of both rural and urban folk to riot explodes the notion that the "lower sort" deferred to their "betters" and largely allowed them to manage colonial political and economic life, a point Michael Zuckerman has powerfully argued. To be sure, in some places this was true, as in Tidewater Virginia, where planters like George Washington dominated the House of Burgesses with little opposition. But elsewhere, the deference that did exist was largely "performative," as Robert Gross has pointed out. Outwardly, laborers and farmers respected the merchants and landowners who employed them, bought their products, and loaned them money. But they were equally capable of voting them out of office, closing the courthouses where suits for debt were heard, or destroying their houses—if they put their private interests above those of the community.[31]

The festivities of the early republic orchestrated by the elites in their turn raise doubts about the historical successor to deference—namely, consensus history. Not only did elites have to go to great lengths to create a national spirit, essentially bribing and propagandizing the masses with rum and roast oxen at elections, if not with bread and circuses, but the masses frequently refused to be bought. Women, African Americans, South Carolinians, and working people modified, disrupted, or created counterfestivities that were highly political acts reflecting alternative visions of the social order.

Taken collectively, the chapters in this book permit a measure of reconciliation between scholars who describe crowds as unified community responses that deal with moral or political delinquents, and those who think they reflect class tensions between groups competing for legitimacy. At the margins of settlement in America, as in European folk culture, rough music began as a means of dealing with those who violated traditional expectations of family behavior—adulterers and wife beaters, for example. Then during the revolutionary era, such practices became politicized and were deployed against landlords and loyalists. In the cities, relatively little rough music occurred until the revolutionary crisis, when tarring and feathering loyalists, hanging them in effigy, or pelting their houses with excrement transformed the urban populace into a political force to be reckoned with on a regular basis.

The chapters also powerfully confirm the critics of Jürgen Habermas who have objected to his romanticization of the "bourgeois public sphere" that arose in the eighteenth century. Writing about eighteenth-century Europe, Habermas correctly pointed out that through coffee houses, voluntary associations, taverns, newspapers, and public prints accessible to a literate middle-class public, ordinary individuals began to take an interest in and participate in public life. In the context of the Enlightenment, the rationality of a political argument offered in the public sphere came to matter more than the authority of the source (for instance, a king or a priest) from whence it came. However, although extremely useful for explaining eighteenth-century political upheaval, Habermas's theories have their limitations. While opening doors to middle-class and upper-class white males, the new public sphere closed them to women, the poor, and the nonwhite. The old regime had recognized such people as dependents who had a certain place in a patriarchal society. Now, as "equals," their inferior social position could be attributed to their group's collective lack of rational faculties as a class, a race, or a gender. Furthermore, politicization had its downside—the mass mobilization of the French Reign of Terror or Napoleon's armies, to cite two examples.[32]

As with Habermas and his critics, the chapters in this book deal with different questions than those that historians were addressing in the 1960s and 1970s, which perhaps explains why Stewart's work was ahead of his time. Instead of mustering evidence from crowd activity to help in understanding such political phenomena as the causes of the American Revolution or the meaning of Jacksonian Democracy, these scholars are primarily concerned with discovering how people who do not write "traditional texts" are actually the "authors" of riot and revelry. To be sure, many of these incidents shed light on traditional political history, but the main concern of the present chapters is to discover what, in fact, moved early Americans to participate in rough music or societal rituals. As such, this volume contributes to the study of popular culture and to the semiotic reading of "texts" and "discourses" that express mentalities that appear on the streets or in the woods and that articulate what remains unspoken in the pages of political tracts or religious sermons.

Most of these mentalities, for all their democratic rhetoric, have been profoundly exclusionary. "The people" usually means "people like us." Hence, the most zealous advocates of democracy in America argued that a woman's place was in the home and that her nature was emotional, not reasonable. They opposed the emancipation and education of slaves, blamed the poor for their poverty, and pursued national expansion at the expense of "inferior peoples," who, they believed, had to be civilized or removed "for their own good." That women and African Americans resisted these imposed definitions is strongly evident in Piersen's and Branson's chapters. The chapters on "rough music," too, show the willingness of the urban and rural poor to demonstrate against their "betters" when their interests failed to coincide.

Yet we should also remember that elites also claimed the streets. They orchestrate the parades and set the issues that arise. Furthermore, as with the heads of antiabolitionist crowds in the 1830s, the defenders of "100 percent Americanism" during the Red Scare of 1919–20, and the attempted repression of dissent during the Vietnam War, "gentlemen of property and standing" took the lead in combating what they viewed as illegitimate efforts by a national movement to challenge their local rule.[33] They did so again in repressing unionization in the working classes throughout the late nineteenth and early twentieth centuries, and in opposing the civil rights movement in the 1960s. Some limited their opposition to words, others condoned or instigated the violence such words provoked. By insisting that the only legitimate "American" community was defined by moral conformity and geographical contiguity, they of course denied the reality on which their very existence depended—that of a complex national and world economy. This was as true when northerners were indirectly benefiting from the profits of slavery in the nineteenth century as it is today, when opponents of equal rights for recent immigrants have no trouble benefiting from the labor of those they condemn.

Informal, popular justice exercised by a community can be a powerful agent for collective liberation, but it must be exercised against people who are perceived as threats from the outside or as agents of moral rot boring away from within. Can we applaud the destruction of Thomas Hutchinson's house in September 1765 by an enraged mob of Bostonians who would undoubtedly have killed him if he had not acceded to his daughter's pleas to escape? Yet without such acts of intimidation, there would have been no American Revolution. The Tories were supposedly conspiring to destroy their country's liberties, even though they had collectively demonstrated their loyalty through peaceable behavior and considerable public service. And many Tories who did not leave the country in time were persecuted or killed.

Must we therefore conclude that no group achieves liberty except at the expense of "an-other"? For example, Edmund S. Morgan brilliantly demonstrated in *American Slavery, American Freedom* that if Africans had not become a viable supply of cheap labor, the poor whites of Virginia would not have been freed from tenancy to work for themselves.[34] Would the American middle class enjoy its privileged life or liberty without clothes from Sri Lanka, electronics made in China, and the labor of an abundance of poorly paid workers within its borders? Vigilante action at home, like intervention abroad, betters the lot of some at the expense of others. Whether justifications appear reasonable or contemptible depends on what "facts" one chooses to leave out of the rationalization offered.

When exercised by those claiming to speak for "the" community, crowd action becomes the iron fist in the velvet glove of the "tyranny of the majority" that was diagnosed in the new republic so astutely by James Madison in *Federalist* 10 and by Alexis de Tocqueville in *Democracy in America*. E. P. Thompson has reminded us that "the rituals of rough music and charivari, transposed across the Atlantic, contributed not only to the good-humored 'shivaree' but may also have given something to lynch law and the Ku Klux Klan."[35] Such acts, in fact, represent some sort of local majority—and if they do, does that make them right? America has a long tradition of vigilante "justice" that is still with us today as inner-city gangs, bombers of abortion clinics, gay-bashers, and rural militiamen claim to represent rather than transgress American values. And they are right, in a way. We cannot choose to remember only the savory parts of our history, for there are those whose tastes are different. If we call for the revival of our revolutionary tradition or a return to the intentions of the founding fathers (the Samuel Adams of 1747 or of 1787?), we need to remember that crowd punishment of deviants outside the bounds of law is as American as "mom," for women played their music as roughly as men. And, as Klepp's chapter shows, attempts to create a patriotic culture that excluded some and exalted others through political spectacles began with independence itself.

This volume is unusual in that it offers two Introductions, not just one. My Introduction is written from the perspective of history. The Introduction by Roger Abrahams, which follows as Chapter 2, reflects the concern folklorists have with the persistence of tradition and emphasizes the *continuity* of rough music and revelry rather than the revolutionary potential that historians are anxious to find. Relying on a different scholarly literature, Abrahams offers an alternative interpretation that shows how historians and folklorists can learn from one another.

Introductions

Notes

1. *Independent Advertiser,* February 8, 1748 (available in microfilmed newspapers in Clifford Shipton, ed., *Early American Imprints* [Worcester, Mass.: American Antiquarian Society, 1959]); Boston Town Meeting Records, in *Boston Record Commissioners' Reports,* 31 vols. (Boston, 1880–1902), 14:127.
2. *Independent Advertiser,* December 5, 1749, and February 8, 1748.
3. William V. Welles, *The Life and Public Services of Samuel Adams,* 3 vols. (1865; reprint, Freeport: Books for Libraries Press, 1969), 3:246. See also William Pencak, "Samuel Adams and Shays's Rebellion," *New England Quarterly* 62 (March 1989), 63–74.
4. Pauline Maier, *From Resistance to Revolution: Colonial Radicals and the Development of American Opposition to Britain, 1765–1776* (New York: Knopf, 1972), 3.
5. For a comprehensive discussion of the "New Left" historians with bibliographical references, see Alfred F. Young, "American Historians Confront 'The Transforming Hand of Revolution,'" in Ronald Hoffman and Peter J. Albert, eds., *The Transforming Hand of Revolution: Reconsidering the American Revolution as a Social Movement* (Charlottesville: University Press of Virginia, 1995), 346–493.
6. Alfred F. Young, "English Plebeian Culture and Eighteenth-Century American Radicalism," in Margaret D. Jacob and James R. Jacob, eds., *The Origins of Anglo-American Radicalism* (London: Allen & Unwin, 1984), 185–212, relies on Stewart. Young, in turn, is used by Paul A. Gilje, *The Road to Mobocracy: Popular Disorder in New York City, 1763–1834* (Chapel Hill: University of North Carolina Press, 1987), 20–21, 40, 43, 65, 67, 99, 108, 182, 254. See also Paul A. Gilje, *Rioting in America* (Bloomington: Indiana University Press, 1996), 16, 29, 47, 81; Natalie Zemon Davis, "The Reasons of Misrule: Youth Groups and Charivari in Sixteenth-Century France," *Past and Present* 50 (February 1971), 41–75; David Underdown, *Revel, Riot, and Rebellion: Popular Politics and Culture in England, 1603–1660* (New York: Oxford University Press 1985), esp. 99–103; E. P. Thompson, "'Rough Music' or English Charivari," *Annales* 27 (March–April 1972), 285–312. A more extensive version of this article appears as chapter 8 of Thompson's *Customs in Common: Studies in Traditional Popular Culture* (New York: W. W. Norton, 1993).
7. For Anglicization, see especially John M. Murrin, "Anglicizing an American Colony: The Transformation of Provincial Massachusetts" (Ph.D. diss., Yale University, 1966); and Rowland Berthoff and John M. Murrin, "Feudalism, Communalism, and the Yeoman Freeholder: The American Revolution Considered as a Social Accident," in Stephen Kurtz and James Hutson, eds., *Essays on the American Revolution* (Chapel Hill: University of North Carolina Press, 1973). For increasing levels of social disorder and class conflict in mid-eighteenth-century America, see the collections edited by Alfred F. Young, *The American Revolution* (DeKalb: Northern Illinois University Press, 1976), and *Beyond the American Revolution* (DeKalb: Northern Illinois University Press, 1987).
8. Patricia U. Bonomi, *A Factious People: Politics and Society in Colonial New York* (New York: Columbia University Press, 1972).
9. Peter Wacker, *Land and People: A Cultural Geography of Preindustrial New Jersey Origins and Settlement Patterns* (New Brunswick, N.J.: Rutgers University Press, 1975); Brendan McConville, *"Those Daring Disturbers of the Public Peace": Agrarian Unrest and the Struggle for Political Legitimacy in New Jersey* (Ithaca, N.Y.: Cornell University Press, 1999).
10. In addition to the incidents discussed by Stewart and Klepp below, Paul Gilje, *Rioting in America,* 49, has uncovered evidence of a wife-beater punished with a beating of his own in Philadelphia in December 1753 (citing the *New York Gazette & Weekly Post-Boy,* February 12, 1753); Thomas P. Slaughter, "Crowds in Eighteenth-Century America: Reflections and New

Directions," *Pennsylvania Magazine of History and Biography* 115 (January 1991), esp. 31–33; Patricia U. Bonomi, "The Middle Colonies: Embryo of the New Political Order," in Alden T. Vaughan and George A. Billias, eds., *Perspectives on Early American History: Essays in Honor of Richard B. Morris* (New York: Harper and Row, 1973), 63–92. For crime in Pennsylvania, see Jack D. Marietta and G. S. Rowe, "Violent Crime, Victims, and Society in Pennsylvania, 1682–1800," *Explorations in Early American Culture* 3 (1999), 24–54 (or vol. 66, supplemental issue of *Pennsylvania History*).

11. E. P. Thompson, "The Moral Economy of the English Crowd in the Eighteenth Century," *Past and Present* 50 (February 1971), reprinted in *Customs in Common*, 185–258.

12. See Young, "English Plebeian Culture and Eighteenth-Century American Radicalism"; and Peter Shaw, *American Patriots and the Rituals of Revolution* (Cambridge, Mass.: Harvard University Press, 1981).

13. Bryan Palmer, "Discordant Music: Charivaris and Whitecapping in Nineteenth-Century North America," *Labour/Le Travailleur* 3 (1978), 5–62.

14. Slaughter, "Crowds in Eighteenth-Century America," 30–33.

15. "From Jamestown to Desert Storm: War and Society in America," unpublished paper delivered at the Penn State History Department Colloquium, November 3, 1998.

16. See, among many sources, Thomas P. Slaughter, *The Whiskey Rebellion: Frontier Epilogue to the American Revolution* (New York: Oxford University Press, 1986). On Fries's Rebellion, see the various articles in a special issue of *Pennsylvania History: A Journal of Mid-Atlantic Studies* 67 (Winter 2000) (guest co-editor Simon Newman). See also Don Carlos Seitz, *Famous American Duels* (1929; reprint, Freeport: Books for Libraries Press, 1966); Elliot J. Gorn, *The Manly Art: Bare-Knuckles Prize-Fighting in America* (Ithaca, N.Y.: Cornell University Press, 1986); John Hope Franklin, *The Militant South* (Boston: Beacon Press, 1956); David Grimsted, *American Mobbing, 1828–1861: Toward Civil War* (New York: Oxford University Press, 1998); Richard Maxwell Brown, *No Duty to Retreat: Violence and Values in American Society* (New York: Oxford University Press, 1991); Iver Bernstein, *The New York City Draft Riots* (New York: Oxford University Press, 1990).

17. Gilje, *Rioting in America*, 63–64; Gilje, *Road to Mobocracy*, 255.

18. Michael Meranze, *Laboratories of Virtue: Punishment, Revolution, and Authority in Philadelphia, 1760–1835* (Chapel Hill: University of North Carolina Press, 1996); David Rothman, *The Discovery of the Asylum: Social Order and Disorder in the New Republic* (Boston: Little, Brown, 1971); Eleanor Flexner, *Century of Struggle: The Women's Rights Movement in America* (Cambridge, Mass.: Belknap Press of Harvard University Press, 1959); Anne Firor Scott, *Making the Invisible Woman Visible* (Urbana: University of Illinois Press, 1984); Joseph R. Gusfield, *Symbolic Crusade: Status, Politics, and the American Temperance Movement* (Urbana: University of Illinois Press, 1966); Michael B. Katz, *The Irony of Early School Reform: Educational Innovation in Mid-Nineteenth-Century Massachusetts* (Cambridge, Mass.: Harvard University Press, 1968).

19. The classic work is Richard Hofstadter, *The Idea of a Party System: The Rise of Legitimate Opposition in the United States, 1780–1840* (Berkeley and Los Angeles: University of California Press, 1969).

20. The best recent works on this subject are Susan G. Davis, *Parades and Power: Street Theater in Nineteenth-Century Philadelphia* (Philadelphia: Temple University Press, 1986); David Waldstreicher, *"In the Midst of Perpetual Fêtes": The Making of American Nationalism, 1776–1820* (Chapel Hill: University of North Carolina Press, 1997); Simon P. Newman, *Parades and Politics of the Street: Festive Culture in the Early Republic* (Philadelphia: University of Pennsylvania Press, 1997); Matthew Dennis, *Red, White, and Blue Letter Days: Identity, Public Memory, and the American Calendar* (Ithaca, N.Y.: Cornell University Press, 2001).

21. J. William Frost, " 'Wear the Sword as Long as Thou Canst': William Penn in Myth and

History," *Explorations in Early American Culture: A Supplement to Pennsylvania History* 4 (2000), 13–45.

22. See also Philip Deloria, *Playing Indian* (New Haven: Yale University Press, 1998).

23. See also Claudia Bushman, *America Discovers Columbus: How an Italian Explorer Became an American Hero* (Hanover, N.H.: University Press of New England, 1992).

24. David Hackett Fischer, *The Revolution of American Conservatism: The Federalist Party in the Era of Jeffersonian Democracy* (New York: Harper & Row, 1965).

25. Davis, *Parades and Power*, chaps. 3–4.

26. Waldstreicher, *"In the Midst of Perpetual Fêtes,"* 133–36.

27. Mary Beth Norton, *Liberty's Daughters: The Revolutionary Experience of American Women, 1750–1800* (Boston: Little, Brown, 1980); Linda Kerber, *Women of the Revolution: Intellect and Ideology in Revolutionary America* (Chapel Hill: University of North Carolina Press, 1980).

28. Roger D. Abrahams, *Singing the Master: The Emergence of African American Culture in the Plantation South* (New York: Pantheon, 1992); William D. Piersen, *Black Yankees: The Development of an African American Subculture in Eighteenth-Century Massachusetts* (Amherst: University of Massachusetts Press, 1988); idem, *Black Legacy: America's Hidden Heritage* (Amherst: University of Massachusetts Press, 1993); Sterling Stuckey, *Slave Culture, Nationalist Theory, and the Foundations of Black America* (New York: Oxford University Press, 1987).

29. Shane White, " 'It Was a Proud Day': African Americans, Festivals, and Parades in the North, 1741-1834," *Journal of American History* 81 (1994), 13–51, and with Graham White, *Stylin': African American Expressive Culture from Its Beginnings to the Zoot Soot* (Ithaca, N.Y.: Cornell University Press, 1998).

30. See Drew Gilpin Faust, *The Creation of Confederate Nationalism: Ideology and Identity in the Civil War South* (Baton Rouge: Louisiana State University Press, 1988).

31. Michael Zuckerman, "Tocqueville, Turner, and Turds: Four Stories of Manners in Early America"; John M. Murrin, "In the Land of the Free and the Home of the Slave, Maybe There Was Room Even for Deference"; and Robert A. Gross, "The Impudent Historian: Challenging Deference in Early America," all in *Journal of American History* 85 (June 1998), 13–42, 86–97.

32. For Habermas and his critics, see Craig Calhoun, ed., *Habermas and the Public Sphere* (Cambridge, Mass.: MIT Press, 1992); Joan Landes, *Women and the Public Sphere in the Age of the French Revolution* (Ithaca, N.Y.: Cornell University Press, 1986); Mary P. Ryan, *Women in Public: Between Banners and Ballots, 1825–1880* (Baltimore: Johns Hopkins University Press, 1990), esp. 10–13.

33. I analyze this persistent behavior in "Legality, Legitimacy, and the American Middle Class," in my book *History, Signing In: Studies in History and Semiotics* (New York: Peter Lang, 1993), 219–35.

34. Edmund S. Morgan, *American Slavery, American Freedom: The Ordeal of Colonial Virginia* (New York: W. W. Norton, 1975).

35. Thompson, *Customs in Common*, 530–31.

2

Introduction: A Folklore Perspective

Roger D. Abrahams

The chapters that make up this collection focus on a great range of intense and apparently spontaneous popular activities in early America. Entered into freely and with vigor, these activities tested the limits of civic authority even when sponsored by the government or by local elites. By now, the work of E. P. Thompson, Natalie Davis, Charles and Louise Tilly, Alfred Young, and many others has uncovered so many instances of this kind of tumultuous behavior that the collection in this book represents case studies of already well-established historical patterns that have served social historians well in getting at the local dynamic features of life as the culture of the working class and yeoman has been uncovered.[1]

There are so many of these reports, in fact, that we could lose sight of what propelled scholars in the 1950s and 1960s to carry out these studies in the first place. At that time, the popular media were just beginning to take note of marches, sit-ins, and other political displays. Scholars throughout the humanities and social sciences rearranged their research priorities, consciously seeking to uncover the origins of such popular public activities. Thoughtful researchers on the political left provided a basis for understanding the origins of radical practices through street action. To accomplish this, however, it was necessary to develop a new body of data about the daily lives of laborers, artisans, and the politically volatile mercantile class. But, Edward Thompson has noted, as this new body of data became available it was necessary to surmount the barrier of apparent triviality—"those aspects of a society which appear to contemporaries as wholly 'natural' and matter-of-course." Thompson assured his audience that these reports "often leave the most imperfect historical evidence." On the other hand, he argued that there was a need "to discover unspoken norms" by examining episodes and situations that were not typical. A riot sheds light on the tranquil periods, and a sudden breach of deference enables us to better understand the deferential habits that were broken. This may be true equally of public and social conduct, and of more private, domestic conduct.[2]

As a folklorist, I have found the efforts of these early historians of special interest to me because they drew deeply on the reservoir of popular life that had been detailed by the amateur folklorist-antiquarians, whose study of traditional and folk practices had been consigned to the category of vulgar errors for a century or two and had not been given the respect of scientists.[3]

Indeed, this mid-twentieth-century generation of historians was so successful in dignifying riots and grassroots fracases that such events came to be viewed as not at all unusual. This new consciousness of past resistance activities took on the appearance of normality in the stories of how nationhood in New World regimes was achieved, and especially the United States. For it was in America, as Alfred Young showed so vividly, that the practice of tarring and feathering, cobbled together from English practices of rough justice, was invented. American scholars have had little problem accepting this perspective. In America, said Young, as opposed to England, "plebeian culture seems to have carried people farther. Ordinary people went through riots to revolution, from direct action to democratic organization. New movements invented traditions. If we would understand the outcome, we need more attention to the processes of the[ir] transmission, retention, recovery and transformation."[4]

Skimmingtons, rough music, shivaree, tin-panning, belling, riding the rail, raising a ruckus, locking out or locking in—all are terms for crowds of people coming together in riotous and sometimes destructive assemblies. The performing groups engaged in such activities have equally bumptious names: belsnicklers, mummers, guisers, calithumpian bands, reflecting the pure joy of having fun at times of seasonal or life passage. Such events are notable for using objects and "props" that are used up by the time the revelry is over. Often they draw attention with that most ephemeral of all sensory data, loud noise. Bonfires, torches, candles, and firecrackers and other noisemakers are the most obvious of the self-consuming artifacts deployed at these moments. Everyday objects, like pots and pans, or brooms and sheets, are also employed out of their usual contexts, as are bird's nests, leaves, grasses, or other "natural" coverings, which become the materials cobbled together for their costumes.

The chapters in this book describe many of the spontaneous and tumultuous events that arose from the challenges of living in a frontier society—the distance between the frontier and seats of commerce and government, the difficulty of establishing clear title to the improved land, lack of ownership of land on which the settlers have come to rest, the sense of social estrangement that arises when the center of power making life decisions is so far removed both geographically and experientially. Conditions that call for quick social and political action cannot be responded to by authorities as quickly as the settlers want: the distance to the cosmopolitan centers of power, and the problems of communication over long distances, are simply too great. The result: a seemingly spontaneous but organized protest in the form of a parade or a house attack or a riot.

Because even formal religious or civic ceremonies draw on crowds and on the same devices as the more apparently spontaneous proceedings, there is always the possibility that play or some other kind of inversive activity will break out. Such proceedings draw on both solemn and hilarious motives in equal measure in the special worlds of riotous assembly or formal ritual. All these high times, in which the social act of coming together creates its own world and its own rules, draw on the same vocabulary of celebration.

These extraordinary gatherings involve taking both physical and social risks. When people come together outside the usual regulations, and with license to ceremonialize and to play, various kinds of disorder are likely to arise. This risk is often channeled, in fact, in the creation and elaboration of games and other playfully confrontational activities. Risk, in the company of a mood elevation, elicits the kinds of high spirits that are so fully illustrated in the present collection.

The work of social historians in the last third of the twentieth century points out that this kind of rambunctious behavior was one dimension of popular culture in early modern Europe. This is not to say that such behavior was absent in even earlier times; in the late Middle Ages, for example, practices of this sort were characteristic of guilds and confraternities. Pageants and parades in both periods were used not only as part of seasonal festivals but also as ways to display and enhance the power of the nobility or the monarchy. And the celebration of consumption lies at the heart of processions held in honor of monarchs, especially as they were involved in imperial schemes that added to the paraphernalia of power display. But the Royal Progresses and other elaborate Grand Processions so deeply associated with the power of the kingship were altered as more republican forms of government were introduced into the state apparatus of early modern European nations.[5]

Simon Schama, discussing the changeover of display activities from monarchies to republics regarding such festivities in the Low Countries, notices:

> Republics . . . if born in austerity, . . . invariably flourish amidst pomp, . . . an aldermanic rather than regal [display], consistent with the public adjuring of the rites of monarchy. It may have little in common with court mystique in which the aura of the god-prince is veiled, . . . republican pomp is no less grandiose. It is public rather than secluded, bombastic rather than magical, didactic rather than illusionist. . . . It offers participation and loyal huzzahs rather than bowed heads and awed prostration. Yet it, too, is a device for the appropriation of power.[6]

Consider this: Even on the Plymouth Plantation the appointed guardian of the settlement, Miles Standish, would not leave the encampment without arraying in parade his six or seven soldiers led by a drummer and a horn-blower.

As this collection and other recent works on American social history attest, these small social dramas involving vigilante actions, kangaroo courts, whitecapping, and calling out the posse comitatus all signaled that there was a shared sense of dislocation from the metropolitan authorities.

America as a nation, by tradition, was born in such assemblies. As early as the 1750s, broadside sketches and songs satirized life in the colonies. The song "Yankee Doodle" carries a nonsensical name (like callithumpian or skimmington bands) and made fun of the settlers and their rough-and-ready style of assembling. This tune and the verses associated with it float in and out of the lives of Americans from that time well through the Revolution, and from it Americans took the name by which they are known worldwide, "Yankees."

The earliest versions of "Yankee Doodle" reveal the youthful enthusiasm of colonial life, a casual celebration of clearing, sowing, and harvest, and a defense of property and rights. It is a song about how young men strut and prance when they get a little grog in them, times when they play at soldiering together, sticking feathers in their hats and making swell officers of themselves and getting a good laugh out of it. The song itself wanders from one kind of frolic to another. Commonly the song began with a topsy-turvy stanza commenting on the goings-on at a cornhusking frolic, where the young men showed off, throwing the ears one way and husks another, turning cartwheels, wrestling, drinking, and trying to find red ears of corn that gave them license to kiss the girls.

> Corn cobs twist your hair off
>   Cart wheel frolic round you.
> Old fiery dragon carry you off,
>   And mortar pestle pound you.
>
> Husking time is coming on
>   They all begin to laugh, sir—
> Father is a coming home
>   To kill the heifer calf, Sir.

And later, a stanza comments:

> Now husking time is over
>   They have a deuced frolic
> There'll be some as drunk as sots
>   The rest will have the colic.

Other stanzas make fun of the ragtag boys that show up on Election Day and at other times when the voluntary militia is called out, making plain just what the feather in the cap meant, for that was the way in which a captaincy was taken on in jest, by tradition.[7]

Is this a song about a new nation and its earliest ways of expressing a frontier and egalitarian enthusiasm? Or is it simply a record of how these new Americans redirected the agricultural enterprise from the Old World Harvest Home—celebration that now extols an egalitarian ethos? Old World country ways are thus revived in a new and distinctively cheeky American spirit.

In the apparently spontaneous and raucous gestures, this rough music is in dramatic contrast to those royal pageants and civic ceremonies that are strategically planned and executed as exhibitions of power. Equally tumultuous, official pageantry is highly programmed, prepared for and executed by those in command. Yet the same sort of display devices are employed: drums and cannons, bonfires, pennants, parades, and elaborate and often ridiculous costumes.

Between the prodigious pageantry of the theater-state and the "antic and horrible" festivities that "make night hideous" and fill days with clamor lie a number of less extravagant display events. These festivities, celebrations, and entertainments exhibit the deepest resources of any group's creativity, producing significant memorable and reportable moments. The more ritualistic and ceremonial the event, the greater the tendency to use these moments to find clues to collective memory and meaning in past performances. Festivities are the embodiment of the history of movement and settlement. Within each person and each community of celebrators reside unexplored memories, things actively forgotten except when they come under threat. In the face of shared hazard, ceremonies—especially the apparently spontaneous ones, lit from within—give free rein to the most social impulses of individuals. Each time a skimmington or a riot occurs, it takes on a life of its own, out of accumulated feelings of social disruption already apparent within a community. Much of the wealth and creative energy of a community is expended both in the most ceremonial activities and in the most topsy-turvy ones.

This collection of essays testifies to the apparent spontaneity of such events, which are usually cobbled together by groups of people in the face of some injustice or some other more broadly social sense of alienation. This appearance of spontaneity is just as much a matter of custom as the grotesque costumes and eccentric behavior of the participants. The vocabulary of public display emerges as a congeries of forms and routines used in a wide variety of settings.

In the late nineteenth and early twentieth centuries, traditional displays of this sort were an important feature of folklore study. Throughout Europe, at the center of the study of traditions stood the various seasonal festivities, on which points of passage local historians and scholars focused, accumulating arguments and producing studies aimed at synthesizing these seasonal passages as they were practiced "for time immemorial"—such masterworks as Sir James George Frazer's *The Golden Bough* and Arnold Van Gennep's *The Rites of Passage* are prime examples of this. The globalizing arguments of Frazer and Van Gennep, however, have been eclipsed by the more tightly circumscribed ethnographic and distributional analyses that have come into fashion in the last century. The Frazerian perspective, arising from a strong connection with European (especially Mediterranean) points of yearly passage, has not maintained a hold on those interested in situated and experienced high-intensity events. The intellectual baggage and the dulling sense of too-easy generalizations has caused this perspective to go out of favor. Van Gennep's work, based on not-dissimilar materials assembled in his *Manuel de folklore français contemporain,* has had greater durability. Van Gennep's notions of the rites of passage are still viable in the interpretive apparatus on ritual states throughout the world and in the ethnographic reports of the second half of the twentieth century.[8]

Until the new cultural history was strongly informed by these ethnographic reports, historians had forsworn using such traditional materials because of their perceived ephemeral character. These are events in which costumes and other devices of display are endowed with power and meaning for the day and then thrown away, or put back in the storeroom for use next year. As mentioned, their ephemerality makes them seem transitory, because they use disposable and often self-consuming devices to seize the moment and produce an intense if fleeting experience. And yet as enactments drawing on collective memory, in festive and ritual format, the past is put at the service of present needs. Indeed, many pasts are contained in the intensity of the festive moment, only some of which invoke traditions and relate to the folkness of the community. Others refer to particulars of the historical experience of those parading. Little wonder that folklorists, anthropologists, and historians have each found their way to this body of traditions, conducting their own archaeological investigations of these sedimented cultural performances.

In the recent drift toward interdisciplinary study, public display events are receiving extensive attention from folklorists and, more recently, historians. In this they are joined by scholars in other disciplines; literary and art historians and anthropologists have cast light on these collective forms by which a community celebrates itself and proclaims its ideal values to the spectators. In the programmatic working out of the procession, the pageant, or the parade, in its combination of ceremonial elaboration in speeches, in musical performances, and in dance, these scholars find lapidary representations of community rendered in such self-conscious and highly spelled out formulations that they reap a harvest of understandings. The licensed play of the festival moment encourages both the ceremonial elevation of those in power and the inversion of the social order through a stylized set of activities that involve both dressing up and cutting up.⁹

In the 1960s and 1970s, carrying out ethnographic fieldwork with advanced technological apparatus made it possible to record such events so that complex forms and vital experiences could receive appropriately rich rendering. Under the impact of structuralist thinking, symbolic anthropologists and ethnographers of communication and performance wrote a series of profound works on the symbolic processes contained with specific rituals and festivals. They demonstrated that the cultural productions of all groups, if approached with sensitivity, can reveal complexities as great as any of the masterworks of written literature.¹⁰

Historians as well as folklorists have been looking anew at how display activities such as parading or mobbing might help us understand the thoughts and actions that animate the everyday life of a people. The displays themselves promise quick and concrete insights into the symbolic system of a community. The intensity of the occasion, and the power of invoking meaningful pasts within the confines of the events, encourages a hermetic idealization of festive forms of the group that has chosen to represent itself from within. The mirrors that reflect inwardly within the event must be made into windows into the outside world, if that world is to understand what the experience of such assemblies means to those involved.

These public displays are not usually heavily programmed or rehearsed. Some of the most effective are even contrived to appear to be improvised at that moment. Their attractiveness stems from their apparent spontaneity and their ragtag costumes and willy-nilly (and often confrontational) behaviors. While considerably smaller in scale, these traditional outbreaks embody many of the same socially inversive motives as Carnival, and in a this they are in contrast to the ceremonially stylized power pageantry of the theater-state. Indeed, the two kinds of display are often juxtaposed even within the same community, as in the various "Doo-Dah Parades" that have sprung up in the United States as inversion of more official civic pageants. Susan G. Davis's study of parades and counterparades in nineteenth-century Philadelphia shows that this has been an American tradition for some time. Because of this mixture of forms and motives, any community is capable of operating on a number of symbolic levels at the same time, and in a way that players and audience can respond on many levels at the same time.[11]

Certain conventional figures emerge at the heart of these events involving serious play. Leaders are elevated along with their court, even when they are anointed only for the festive times. Clowns, fools, people dressed as animals, and animals dressed as people are also common, to say nothing of the wildmen dressed in leaves and bird's nests, and the various other masked figures representing the half-world of the spirits. Of these, none is more important for the proceedings than the exotic figures who represent significant outsiders. Often clothed in the garb of an ancient enemy of the people (such as the Moors after the Crusades throughout Europe), these figures are both enormously attractive and fearsome. In parades and pageants, they are among the most attractive of the figures, and also among the most dreadful. In each domain, either in homelands or hinterlands, uncivilized figures emerge as distinct from those living with good manners and civic responsibility. Cast as being backward, tradition-bound, or behind the times, they are old-fashioned and less refined. At home, the resident aliens were called "peasants" in early modern Europe, later taking the more honorific term "folk." In the outposts of civilization, strangers were called "savage" or "primitive."[12]

In more informal revels, these scare figures become mischief makers. These entertainments are widely reported under a variety of names that announce their helter-skelter organization and tactics: as callithumpian bands or skimmington riders, the players mumble their lines and rush their speeches, which are often delivered in distorted voices or through a voice-altering mask. This role-playing occurs most commonly in the form of bands of luck-visit mummers (or belsnicklers, the German term used by early Pennsylvanians), who carouse during holiday times. They have license to beg, coerce, trick, entertain, and on rare occasions to heal sick individuals or the community as a whole.[13] As these groups come to the door or gate, they announce themselves by making noise or formal speeches that proclaim their purpose in coming. Commonly they stage a fight that is stylized around speeches or a dance and escalates the proceedings to near mayhem. They take a formal leave and are recompensed in a symbolic way for their visit.

Drawing on court records and other official documents, historians have uncovered many scenes of such mummery throughout Europe. Now informed by ethnographic details drawn both from observation and from local memorial traditions, folklorists have returned, once again, to these materials.[14] The interdisciplinary movement has some distance yet to travel, as evidenced by the fact that the two disciplines have not joined forces in casting light on these materials. Historians have recovered some of the political and social messages contained in certain of the mobbing practices as they were employed at particular times and places, finding in them clues to movements of resistance within specific polities. Folklorists, of course, see in these figures a thread leading to a very ancient past, and to a kind of society in which the community provided its own entertainment. In this, they share the sense of nostalgia often reported by members of the performing community itself, the players and the audience who themselves know well that this is the old way of playing. This sentiment commonly accompanies traditional revelries when they have been consciously maintained. That this nostalgic note resonates through the work of social historians as well may not be so self-evident. By casting these scenes in terms of the moral economy of the populace, historians have idealized the notion of "the crowd," seeing in such gatherings evidences of a protorevolutionary group formation.[15]

Neither folklorists nor historians have addressed the largest question involved in these representations: how to get at possible meanings when masking of this sort takes place. In these traditional displays, repeatedly, the figures that are played (and the singing, dancing, and speech-making that are stimulated) are not simply the product of the imagination. They are based on figures who have entered into the historical experience of the group doing the playing, as when the play of "The Moors and the Christians" is replayed on the Feast of Corpus Christi throughout Iberia and the Hispanic New World. In such cases, playing the role of the "other" can also mean becoming the enemy. But more than this, in such imitation these "others" are represented in distinctly ambivalent and ambiguous ways. They are endowed with the power of the uncivilized outsider as they are rendered in a positively attractive manner. It is evident that addressing such questions takes us beyond the usual domains of both folkloristics and social history and into semiotics.

The ongoing project of reviving the materials of tradition, then, has involved the efforts of many disciplines working in a number of different geographic areas and cultural traditions. In the process, riddles, proverbs, and traditional systems of belief, as well as these folk mobbings, no longer are viewed as simply the unaccountable fragments of past traditional practices at a particular historical moment. Historians began to pay serious attention to folklore materials of this sort as the new cultural history developed. Discussing this change, one of those most deeply involved, Robert Darnton, has noted that "after generations of struggle to discover 'what actually happened' " during specific historical times, "historians have learned to cope with documentary problems. And if they want to understand what a happening actually is" for those who participated or looked on, historians "can take advantage of the very elements" that in the past have distorted our reading or reports derived from hearsay or from journalistic accounts. The goals of historical writing have been altered in an attempt to arrive at greater understandings—not of what happened when, but of how people acted and reacted in the ordinary world. As a result, today "we can read a text . . . not to nail down all the whos, whats, wheres, and whens of an event but rather to see what the event meant to the people who participated in it."[16]

And as Darnton and others of this persuasion have shown, the chance records of traditional performance and celebration are prime resources for this historical reconstruction.[17] This intellectual enterprise extends far beyond the confines of any one profession to that interdisciplinary cohort sometimes referred to as "cultural critique." Those language and cultural philosophers, anthropologists, folklorists, and social, literary, and art historians have all joined in describing specific cultural formations with regard to how they come to be produced or "invented" in response to historical conditions. This group addresses the very idea of culture as a manifestation of the rationalization of bourgeois nation-states through bureaucratic consolidation at home and through colonial expansion abroad. Performance and celebration can either support or disrupt this process.[18]

By questioning the basic premises of all disciplines and, in the process, recognizing the contingent character of their practices, folklorists and historians now find common ground in studying everyday display events. As overtly constructed worlds, public displays make no claims to mirror the real world. They deal only in pomp and in play. They are complicated cultural operations that are of greatest interest to scholars who deconstruct them to discover underlying social reality.

With other human sciences, the writing of folklore and history had come to be studied as a cultural accomplishment rather than a revelation of truth. Both disciplines have acknowledged that they emerged as parts of larger sociopolitical and intellectual situations and are equally affected by Western biases. Perhaps even more important, a number of historians have begun to address their materials in terms that are especially conducive to a fruitful conversation between the disciplines. One such historian, Greg Dening, has pursued a situation in which different peoples confront each other across a cultural divide. He discusses the reactions of as many of those involved as he can discover, his special insights deriving from the interactions between Tahitians and Europeans. At the center of his response to the variations in perspective is the insight that historians are like other people who tell each other stories, seizing on fragments of the past for whatever the present purposes may call for. "Storytellers, mythmakers, gossipers, sculpt events with choice words and fine dramatics and pass them on by word of mouth so that their histories are embellished by each occasion of their telling," Dening keenly observes. Describing the writing of history in this manner is to cast it into the terms usually drawn on by folklorists. Says Dening, glossing this metaphor further, "Participants in the event choose a genre—a diary, a letter, a poem, a newspaper to clothe their interpretation of what has happened. . . . These relics of experience—always interpretations of experience, never the experience itself—are all that there is of the past. Historians never confront the Past, only the inscriptions that the Past has left. History is always interpretation of interpretation, always a reading of a given text."[19]

The materials of folklore are also derived from chance recordings made of relics of the past that wander into the present through the power of memorial apparatus. Owning up to the contingent and sometimes arbitrary character of these fragments that preserve memory constitutes the most important recent development in understanding lived experiences. Perhaps we might say that much of folklore and social history, then, involves the discovery of these fragments and how societies make relics of them—that is, how societies endow them with preternatural meanings (for instance, the Boston Tea Party as preserved in folklore and memory). Acknowledging the process by which societies reflexively construct memory now characterizes the mutual attempt by historians and folklorists to make some sense of the past.

Imitation may mean a great many things, especially in public display activities. When imitation is carried out at public assemblies, the motives can be as disparate as veneration and mockery, sometimes at the same moment. From the records we have about the "White Indians," it is difficult to ascertain how much of the actual events emerged in the spirit of tomfoolery and how much was deadly serious. Motives are seldom unmixed or unmitigated, especially when people imitate styles of dress, talk, eating, singing, and dancing. Even the most mocking performance has an aesthetic dimension. And when a moment is socially defined as licentious or playful, the mixture of motives is all the more complicated and explosive.

The playfulness of masquerading, emerging as a way of practicing political resistance, confounds common understandings of the ways in which political and social changes are brought about. Nonetheless, it is clear that in all these festive activities serious cultural business is being transacted. In festivities a community comes together to experience life intensely. All symbolic forms at such moments are endowed with meanings that are especially powerful. Festivals are commonly held at those points of passage in the year when a group undergoes release most fully. Insofar as the masks that are put on and the roles that are played are often derived from figures that are regarded as the enemies of culture at all other times, the social motives being played out become all the more complex.

In a commercial culture these holiday techniques of masking and of display have spilled over into popular entertainments and displays of resistance to the official worlds. Indeed, it is precisely through festive entertainments like parades and civic pageantry that one can begin to posit the existence of a culture developed within a market-driven polity in the towns and cities. This commercially inspired culture might be studied in the same manner as both folk and elite groups, through the development of their own traditional modes of self-representation.

Surveying the impact of the strange and marvelous creatures that Europeans discovered in the New World, Howard Mumford Jones described the attractions and the terrors of the images that were sent back home: "The New World was filled with monsters animal and animals human; it was a region of terrifying natural forces, of gigantic catastrophes, of unbearable heat and cold, an area where the laws of nature tidily governing Europe were transmogrified into something new and strange. Terror and gigantism have their attractiveness. . . . The Renaissance image of the New World was compounded of both the positive and negative elements which attract and repel."[20] This terror and gigantism became socially useful as

Americans developed the details of their own style and social organization. The attractive features began to outweigh the fearsome ones, at least as far as the invention of useful roles to take on in early display activities.

Americans discovered a sense of social unity in Indian life, at least on the level of the achieved community. The "White Indians" of Maine announced "We all won [one] brother" as they dressed up and acted as Indians in resistance to what they regarded as the introduction of class attitudes in their lives.[21] This was certainly the message carried by the Boston "Mohawks" as well. In the face of a perceived foe, they appeared to invent traditions—when they were actually availing themselves of an already well-known and customary means to endow adopted practices with the sense of being "as old as time." If the colonists and settlers saw themselves as rejecting the old European decadent traditions, they found in the New World materials to draw on that seemed to be even earlier and closer to the earth, "older than the Flood."

This instantly archaic factor is only one of the ways in which such moments encourage the intense involvement of the participants. All the other devices of display and ceremony, and even ritual, encourage the creation of an instant community on which community assembly is predicated. All riots, parades, processions, and skimmingtons rely on this shift of energy and focus from the everyday. In the resulting symbolically enriched environment, both the deep past and the emerging present are served. New symbols arise out of old vocabularies in the responses of the moment.

That this invention was both a historic process and a folkloric one is manifest. Such cases demonstrate the usefulness of bringing the insights of historians and folklorists together as they bear on occasions in which public display events are invented. Folklorists, studying these activities in terms of their continuity with a kind of timeless past, hone in on the vocabulary and the motives of traditional practices. Historians encountering these materials find in these activities techniques of cultural invention that are central to understanding how social forces manifest themselves in organizations of volunteers as they invent themselves, even as they enter into mobbing activities. When these perspectives are brought together with the insights of cultural criticism, one can recognize the immense amount of cultural production accomplished in the most mundane social activities. By understanding the display events as highly intensified political activities as well as heated-up semiotic constructions, a deeper understanding of the uses and reuses of traditional practices may be achieved. This interdisciplinary effort brings us closer to being able to see how celebrations can help us understand more fully the ways in which cultural imitation across boundaries operates. This is all the more important as the plural character of culture itself is discovered and rediscovered under particular circumstances throughout the world. The science of humankind demands a broader theory of how new cultural productions are launched that draws both on the most archaic forms and on an appropriation or invention of new forms arising from the coming together of different peoples.

These remarks are based in part on my article "History and Folklore: Luck Visits, House-Attacks, and Playing Indian in Early America," in Ralph Cohen and Michael S. Roth, eds., *History and . . . Histories Within the Human Sciences* (Charlottesville: University of Virginia Press, 1995). Thanks to the University of Virginia Press and the editors for permission to reprint. I appreciate the assistance and guidance of Bob St. George at all stages in helping to work out this argument. I also thank Rhys Isaac, Shane White, Simon Newman, Cynthia Van Zandt, Tom Slaughter, and Michael Zuckerman for counsel leading to a larger understanding of this phenomenon during this period; Richard Dunn and the members of the Wednesday Brown Bag group at the Center for the Study of Early American History; the Ethnohistory Seminar at the University of Pennsylvania; Ron Baker at Indiana State University, for inviting me to give the Joseph Schick Lecture, at which I presented an early version of this argument; Caroll Smith-Rosenberg and Michael Roth, for informed and enthusiastic readings along the way; and my wife, Janet, earlier on, for the hard editing.

Notes

1. The works of Thompson and Davis are discussed by Susan Desan, "Crowds, Community, and Ritual in the Work of E. P. Thompson and Natalie Davis," in Lynn Hunt, ed., *The New Cultural History* (Berkeley and Los Angeles: University of California Press, 1989), 47–71. There are a number of interviews in *Visions of History*, by MARHO—The Radical Historians Organization, ed. Henry Abelove (New York: Pantheon Books, 1983), including those with Thompson, Davis, and Eric Hobsbawm, which discuss the political involvements of these figures.
2. E. P. Thompson, "Folklore, Anthropology, and Social History," *Indian Historical Review* 3, no. 2 (1977), 251.
3. The English conversations on this subject are detailed in Richard M. Dorson, *The British Folklorists: A History* (Chicago: University of Chicago Press, 1968). See also Philippa Levine, *The Amateur and the Professional: Antiquarians, Historians, and Archaeologists in Victorian England, 1838–1886* (Cambridge: Cambridge University Press, 1986).

4. Alfred F. Young, "English Plebian Culture and Eighteenth-Century American Radicalism," in Margaret C. Jacob and James R. Jacob, eds., *The Origins of Anglo-American Radicalism* (Atlantic Highlands, N.J.: Humanities Press, 1991), 206.

5. Peter Burke, *Popular Culture in Early Modern Europe* (New York: Harper Torchbooks, 1978), provides an overview of the literature on popular cultural entertainments and eruptions throughout Western Europe. He documents the change in attitudes toward these entertainments in the section called "The Triumph of Lent." Edward P. Thompson, his students, and his followers have drawn on events of this sort, teasing out their political implications. See Thompson, *Customs in Common* (New York: The New Press, 1993), and also Bob Bushaway, *By Rite: Custom, Ceremony, and Community in England, 1700–1889* (London: Junction Books, 1982); David Cressy, *Bonfires and Bells* (Berkeley and Los Angeles: University of California Press, 1989); and the recent encyclopedic work of Ronald Hutton, *The Stations of the Sun: A History of the Ritual Year in Britain* (New York: Oxford University Press, 1996).

6. Simon Schama, *The Embarrassment of Riches: An Interpretation of Dutch Culture in the Golden Age* (Berkeley and Los Angeles: University of California Press, 1988), 221–22.

7. J. A. Leo Lemay, "The American Origins of Yankee Doodle," *William & Mary Quarterly*, 3d ser., 33 (January 1976), 435–64.

8. Sir James George Frazer, *The Golden Bough*, 3d ed., 12 vols. (London, 1908); Arnold van Gennep, *The Rites of Passage*, trans. Monika B. Vizedom and Gabrielle L. Caffee (Chicago: University of Chicago Press, 1960).

9. The movement is surveyed in Hunt, ed., *New Cultural History*, 1989.

10. The books that had the greatest impact during this period included Victor W. Turner's *The Forest of Symbols* (Ithaca, N.Y.: Cornell University Press, 1967), *The Ritual Process* (Ithaca, N.Y.: Cornell University Press, 1977), and *Dramas, Fields, and Metaphor: Symbolic Action in Human Society* (Ithaca, N.Y.: Cornell University Press, 1974); and Clifford Geertz's series of articles included in two collections, *The Interpretation of Cultures* (New York: Basic Books, 1973) and *Local Knowledge* (New York: Basic Books, 1983).

11. Susan G. Davis, *Parades and Power: Street Theater in Nineteenth-Century Philadelphia* (Philadelphia: Temple University Press, 1986), esp. 73–112.

12. The foundational arguments here arise from the reading of the literature of travel resulting in the perception (and creation) of the Other. Important arguments here are Margaret T. Hodgen, *Early Anthropology in the Sixteenth and Seventeenth Centuries* (Philadelphia: University of Pennsylvania Press, 1964); Ronald L. Meek, *Social Science and the Ignoble Savage* (Cambridge: Cambridge University Press, 1976); Johannes Fabian, *Time and the Other: How Anthropology Makes Its Object* (New York: Columbia University Press, 1983); and James Boon, *Other Tribes, Other Scribes* (Cambridge: Cambridge University Press, 1982). An especially useful overview of the subject written from the perspective of the cultural critique is Arjun Appadurai, "Afterword," in Appadurai, Frank J. Korom, and Margaret A. Mills, eds., *Gender, Genre, and Power in South Asian Expressive Traditions* (Philadelphia: University of Pennsylvania Press, 1991).

For the range of use of callithumpian in the United States, see *Dictionary of American Regional English*, ed. Frederic G. Cassidy (Cambridge, Mass.: Belknap Press of Harvard University Press, 1985–). See also Hans Kurath's *A Word-Geography of the Eastern United States* (Ann Arbor: University of Michigan Press, 1949), fig. 182, "Serenading." Kurath includes other terms, mapping their deployment: horning (horning bee); chivaree; calathump or calathumpian band; skimerton or skimelton; belling; bull banding; and tin panning. For an insightful study of a local callithumpian tradition used for political commentary, see Davis, *Parades and Power*.

13. This healing function is described in detail in Gail Kligman, *Calus: Symbolic Transformations in Romanian Ritual* (Chicago: University of Chicago Press, 1977). For the role of luck in healing the sense of community, see Martin J. Lovelace, "Christmas Mumming in England: The House-Visit," in K. S. Goldstein and N. V. Rosenberg, eds., *Folklore Studies in Honour of Her-*

bert Halpert: A Festschrift (St. John's, Newfoundland: Memorial University Press, 1980); and Henry Glassie, *All Silver and No Brass: An Irish Christmas Mumming* (Philadelphia: University of Pennsylvania Press, 1975).

14. Key works here include, in addition to the above, Emmanuel LeRoy Ladurie, *Carnival in Romans,* trans. from the French by Mary Feeney (New York: Braziller, 1979); *Le Charivari: Actes de la Table Ronde Organisée à Paris* (April 25–27, 1977), ed. Jacques Le Goff and Jean-Claude Schmitt (Paris, 1981); Charles Tilly, "Charivaris, Repertoires, and Politics," working paper, Ann Arbor, Michigan, 1980.

15. In this regard, see esp. Young, "English Plebian Culture and Eighteenth-Century American Radicalism."

16. Robert Darnton, *The Kiss of Lamourette: Reflections in Cultural History* (New York: W. W. Norton, 1990), 342–43.

17. Here the work of Natalie Zemon Davis and E. P. Thompson, mentioned above, and the studies included in Robert Darnton, *The Great Cat Massacre* (New York: Basic Books, 1984), illustrate both the usefulness and the restrictiveness of this kind of historical writing dealing with the materials of tradition.

18. Tradition and authenticity in this critical literature have been shown to be anchoring terms in bourgeois ideology. Many studies have recently emerged detailing the invention of traditions. See here *The Invention of Tradition,* ed. Eric Hobsbawm and Terence Ranger (Cambridge: Cambridge University Press, 1983). Ranger himself has pointed to the strange reception of the work by folklorists and historians in "The Invention of Tradition Revisited: The Case of Colonial Africa," in Terence Ranger and Ofumeli Vaughan, eds., *Legitimacy and the State in Twentieth-Century Africa* (in press). In a related argument, homelands have been described as "imagined communities" in Benedict Anderson's *Imagined Communities: Reflections on the Origin and Spread of Nationalism* (London: Verso, 1983). Both terms, "inventing" and "imagining," at first glance make the process of national culture-building seem imposed, unnatural, propagandistic, spurious by its very character; the construction of a history based on the power of such inventions does not conform to "the facts." No matter how much intellectual pleasure the demystification attending the revelation that these are inventions may produce, one cannot ignore that these social constructions were successful in bringing about a sense of shared culture and community sufficient to rationalize politically the idea of the nation. It seems important to question just how imagined or invented such specific cases are, when they are demonstrably regarded as authentic and real by the participants and their subsequent interpreters.

19. Greg Dening, *The Death of William Gooch: History's Anthropology* (Honolulu: University of Hawaii Press, 1995), 27.

20. Howard Mumford Jones, *O Strange New World: American Culture, the Formative Years* (New York: Viking Press, 1964), 70.

21. Alan Taylor, *Liberty Men and Great Proprietors: The Revolutionary Settlement of the Maine Frontier* (Chapel Hill: University of North Carolina Press, 1990), 184.

Riot and Rough Music

Skimmington in the Middle and New England Colonies

Steven J. Stewart

[EDITOR'S NOTE: This chapter is a revised version of an underground classic on which Alfred F. Young drew heavily in his article "English Plebeian Culture and Eighteenth-Century Radicalism," in Margaret Jacob and James Jacob, eds., *The Origins of Anglo-American Radicalism* (London: George Allen & Unwin, 1984), 185–212. Stewart's article is based on work he did between 1973 and 1981 for an unfinished Ph.D. dissertation. He then went on to a distinguished career as a history teacher at Abington (Pennsylvania) High School, from which he is now retired. When he presented a small portion of his dissertation at the conference on festivals and rituals hosted by the Philadelphia Center for Early American Studies in April 1996, the depth and importance of his research astounded the audience. His was the first major effort by an American scholar to look on this side of the Atlantic for acts of crowd violence comparable to the "rough music," "skimmington," and "charivari" that Natalie Z. Davis, David Underdown, and E. P. Thompson have investigated in their pathbreaking investigations of popular culture in early modern Europe. What follows is a distillation of the original research from Stewart's dissertation. I have edited Stewart's work to preserve intact all his documentary evidence as well as his important conclusions. I believe it is important, for historiographical as well as historical memory, that those who read this chapter recognize the extent of Stewart's originality of thought as well as the depth of his research. Hence, my own Introduction to the present volume, Chapter 1, has only minimal discussion of the historical works that Stewart treats in more detail, whereas my editing of Stewart's essay only occasionally cites works that appeared after 1980 that might provide useful supplemental information. Also, while Stewart's dissertation was divided, as customary, into chapters, I separated the cases of "rough music" by incident to make it easier to trace and classify them. Like any dissertation, Stewart's required revision. Although what follows is not the book that ought to have evolved, I hope it conveys the essence of a major work of scholarship that, thanks to Alfred F. Young's sponsorship, is finally making an impact two decades after its completion. —William Pencak]

Introduction

Evidence of the practice of skimmington begins to appear in the Middle and New England colonies of British North America in the early 1730s. In this variation of English "rough music," or French "charivari," members of a community rode the offender around town on a rail, usually for some breach of sexual conduct. They hoped thereby to humiliate him or her publicly and force the offender to leave the area. Evidence of skimmington in unpublished accounts, court records, and newspapers suggests that skimmington was employed to offset lax law enforcement for moral turpitude. The judicial authorities, from local constables and justices of the peace to provincial supreme courts, were unwilling or unable to prosecute sexual offenders as they coped with increases in more serious crimes. As the gentry who held many of these positions became more anglicized and refined, the populace adopted skimmington in an attempt to enforce and preserve traditional Protestant morality.

But skimmington was more than just punishment for adulterous or abusive husbands. Agents of greedy landlords, people suspected of carrying diseases, and loose women were among those who felt the wrath of the communal will. The class, religious, and sectional conflicts that emerged in the decades before the Revolution also resulted in crowd actions. Borrowing from skimmington, mobs directed tarring and feathering and public humiliation against Crown officials, who like tyrannical husbands were seen as cruel and unfaithful to their proper function.

The *Oxford English Dictionary* in 1933 defines "skimmington" as "a ludicrous procession formerly common in villages and country districts, usually intended to bring ridicule or odium on a woman or her husband in cases where the one was unfaithful or ill-treated the other." The word is believed to have come from the "skimming ladle" that could be used by a wife to beat her spouse.[1]

Violet Alford traces the history of skimmington back to the first century B.C.E. It was most prominent in southern England, where it was called "rough music." In France, similar instances were called "charivari." In both countries, the term referred to a crowd, often disguised and under cover of darkness, that would gather to express its displeasure against a perpetrator of a repugnant act, by means of a formalized ritual of riding the victim around on a pole. The "rough" music made by bells, horns, drums, and kitchen utensils, and accompanied by shouting and singing, drew a crowd and focused attention on the culprit. Although the goal of these crowds was to punish alleged offenders, they rarely wanted to kill or maim, preferring instead to force them to either behave properly or leave the community.[2]

Alford found that rough music had several stages. First, a crowd gathered and beat on pots and pans, blew whistles, and rang bells. In a second, more serious stage, the offender was seized and ridden around on a ladder or a pole. (In some cases an effigy was substituted.) If a donkey was used for the ride, the victim faced the tail and was forced to hold on to it as a sign of his disgrace. Finally, the unfortunate was obliged to witness—or, if a spouse-beater, sometimes experience—a public reenactment of the repugnant conduct, followed by a mock judgment and sentence, which was usually expulsion from the community.[3]

Bryan Palmer and Natalie Zemon Davis thoroughly researched the charivari in nineteenth-century North America and early modern France, respectively. Palmer finds that wife-beaters were seldom victims of this ritual, but that violators of expected marriage norms—wealthy old men wedding much younger women, married men who impregnated single women, cuckolded husbands, unwed mothers, and adulterers—were the most frequent candidates. Davis demonstrates that charivari's main purpose was to guarantee community survival. The limited availability of marriage-age females meant that any match that had little or no chance of producing children, such as that between an older woman and a younger man, might invite a charivari. Domineering wives were another target. Davis shows that whereas the charivari declined in the expanding cities of sixteenth-century France, the practice continued in rural areas.[4]

In England, E. P. Thompson noted that in preindustrial times rough music was directed primarily against husband-beaters; a wife was expected to be chaste and an obedient wife and mother, not a dominating shrew. But by the nineteenth century, punitive action began to shift more against wife-beaters. Thompson speculated that increasing mobility during the Industrial Revolution meant that women were much more likely to leave their places of birth when they married, losing the protection of their families, especially fathers and brothers. As no laws formally protected a beaten wife, communities imposed rough music.[5]

The arrival of rough music in North American is obscure. William S. Walsh maintains that the practice of charivari was brought over by French settlers of Louisiana and the Canadian provinces, where it became known as "shivaree." Bryan Palmer records a charivari in Quebec on June 28, 1683, in which a young widow remarried only twenty days after her husband had died. The bishop intervened and threatened those who participated with excommunication. But Palmer finds no other instances during the seventeenth and eighteenth centuries.[6] As for the British colonies, Palmer could find only two examples before the mid-eighteenth century. In 1675, a group of ship's carpenters in Boston paraded a fellow worker when he refused to complete the required seven-year apprenticeship before applying for work on his own. Nine defendants admitted guilt and were fined. And in 1705, Andrew Lawton of the same town received a raucous midnight serenade for carrying on a protracted and open adulterous affair.[7]

In British North America, skimmingtons began to occur more frequently in the 1730s. At that time, an increasingly cosmopolitan elite became less interested in enforcing laws against adultery or domestic violence. As David H. Flaherty writes, "The growing leniency in punishments for fornication in all the colonies as the seventeenth century progressed bore testimony to the increasing tolerance for sexual deviance in the New World and the slackening commitment to the strict enforcement of a moral code.... Sexual acts that were illegal and immoral but not harmful to anyone [besides the parties immediately involved] did not have a high priority."[8] Just as David Underdown notes that skimmington most characterized the most conservative rural parts of England that resisted Puritan reforms, mid-eighteenth-century colonial rural communities or the urban lower classes resorted to rough music to punish offenses against morality that their betters chose to ignore.[9]

Case One: Spouse Abuse in Ridgefield, Connecticut

The earliest instance of skimmington not mentioned by Bryan Palmer that I have been able to find occurred in Ridgefield, Connecticut, on December 17, 1733. One William Drinkwater had been abusive to his wife in some unspecified way, and when neighbors tried to intercede on her behalf he responded by "proving quarrelsome." In return, the town's women tied him to a cart and beat him on the back with rods until, in endeavoring to get away, Drinkwater pulled his arm out of joint. Being whipped in such a manner was a standard colonial punishment for crimes like violent assault. After being untied, Drinkwater complained to a number of magistrates, "but all he got by it was to be laughed at." He then moved with his family to New Milford in Orange County, New York, in the dead of winter, approximately forty-five miles across the Hudson River. A report from his new home stated: "He proves a good Neighbor and a loving Husband. A remarkable Reformation arising from the Justice of the good Women!" A man considered a troublemaker by the entire community, represented by its women and its magistrates, had been successfully removed.[10]

Case Two: Wife Abuse in London

The next year, 1734, the *New York Weekly Journal* printed a story about rough music from England that may have inspired colonial mimesis. It concerned a tailor who, failing his wife sexually, symbolically beat her with a yardstick instead, perhaps in response to her taunts.

> It seems [he] had been very sparing of one instrument, but very liberal of his Wooden Yard about his Wife's Back and shoulders. [He] gave such offence to the good Women of that Neighborhood by his Behaviour that they resolved NEMINE CONTRADICENTE [unanimously] to toss him in a Blanket. The magnanimous taylor for some time defied them; but when he actually saw the Blanket brought forth, and a fixt Resolution in the Countenances of the Amazons, he thought it time to retreat Accordingly he mounted to the top of his House, and lock'd himself up in his Garret, from whence he held a Parly with the Enemy; but was a length so pro-

voked by the Insults of the Ladies, that he came rushing down among them with one of his Yards in the Hand, threatening terrible Revenge upon them; but them regardless of his Stick and his Threats immediately hussled him into a Blanket, where ten or a Dozen of them tossed him to some tune, in the open Street, to the great Satisfaction of a vast Multitude of Spectators, and this we hear did a great deal of Good among the other TOYLERS in the Neighborhood, as well as to the tayler we speak of, for not being able to show his Head, he has sat very close to his Work ever since.[11]

As in the Connecticut case, where local officials approved of rough music, this report from England suggests that while women may have instigated the punishment, they could not act without at least the tacit approval of the men of the community, who would have constituted a good part of the "vast Multitude of Spectators." Noteworthy is the Latin phrase "Nemine Contradicente," used to signify unanimity in contemporary courts of law and legislative bodies. It conferred on women at least a quasi-legitimacy, much as the officially sanctioned medieval French "courts of love" studied by Peter Goodrich, through publicly humiliating pronouncements, symbolically permitted noble women to condemn heartless men to lives without love.[12] And if the tailor was not expelled from his residence, he was nevertheless obliged to lay low to escape the taunts that would inevitably follow a man chastised by women.

Case Three: Wife Abuse in Chester County, Pennsylvania

Six months after the news from London, women near Philadelphia also took revenge on behalf of a battered wife:

We hear from Chester County, that last Week at a Vendue held there, a Man being unreasonably abusive to his Wife upon some trifling Occasion, the Women form'd themselves into a Court, and ordered him to be apprehended by their Officers and brought to tryol: Being found guilty he was condemn'd to be duck'd 3 times in a neighboring Pond, and to have one half cut off, of his Hair and Beard (which it seems he wore at full length) and the Sentence was accordingly executed, to the great Diversion of the Spectators.[13]

Unlike the whipping at the cart's tail performed by the Connecticut women, a punishment for which men and women were both eligible, Chester County's females explicitly reversed the gender hierarchy by inflicting on a man a penalty reserved primarily, if not exclusively, for women. Again, the crowd assumed the trappings of formal justice and received approbation from "Spectators," who included males.

Case Four: Out-of-Town Adultery in Boston, Massachusetts

More than a year later, on October 23, 1736, it was the turn of Boston women to punish two young men known for committing adultery:

> One Ezekiel N-d-m of this town, and another Young Man that formerly lived with Mr. P-R F-N's of this town, was going over to Roxbury, to see their Mistresses, were met between the fortifications and the Gallows by a Troop of young Ladies or Female Foot Pads, who instantly surrounded them and attacked them, but EZEKIEL by reason of his very long legs soon stradled out of their Reach, but left the other unhappy young Man a sacrifice to their Rage, who immediately seized him, and threw him down to the Ground, and some holding him fast, the others strip'd down his Breeches and whip'd him most unmercifully; but EZEKIEL got off without any Damage, saving he was very much affrighted.[14]

A new perspective on rough music appears in this report from Boston as reprinted in the *New York Weekly Journal*. On the one hand, the action of the women seems to win approval. In a town with just under three thousand adult males, it would be fairly easy to identify the guilty Ezekiel given the initials of his surname, and either ostracize or reduce him to a figure of public mockery. By twice capitalizing his name, the writer goes overboard in identifying him. Yet the women are also termed "Foot Pads" (members of a crime ring) rather than given the dignity of a court. Perhaps the best way to reconcile these perspectives is to conclude that whoever wrote the story simply thought that all concerned had contributed to a hilarious situation and believed that his audience too would get a good laugh. Noteworthy also is the manner of punishment: the man who was caught was not whipped on his back, but spanked in the manner of a child. Mention of the youth of both the men and the women recalls Natalie Davis's insight that many French charivaris were performed by youths whose informal organization helped to constitute an early modern, age-specific culture about which we know little.[15]

If other skimmingtons occurred during 1730s and 1740s, they have yet to be discovered. Their number began to increase, however, in the 1750s, especially in the turbulent provinces of New York and New Jersey beset with land riots against proprietors bent on collecting what were deemed unreasonable rents. In this disorderly situation, provincial officials attempted to prosecute perpetrators of rough music, but usually with little success.

Case Five: A Merchant in Poughkeepsie, New York

For example, on April 24, 1751, New York Attorney General Richard Bradley presented the king's case against Jeremiah Hunt, his wife, and eleven others for contempt, riot, and disturbing the peace. The skimmington had taken place that January 29, at Poughkeepsie in Dutchess County. Bradley related how "joining with themselves and diverse other malfactors and disturbers of the peace . . . unknown and disguising themselves in order that they might not be known . . . with force and arms . . . unjustly unlawfully routously and in a noisy and turbulent manner wickedly did ride Skimmington about the house of one Isaac Marks." Marks, a merchant, complained of the fences surrounding his house being torn down, and of the "Great Terror Scandal & Grievous damage of him." Bradley sought to set a strong example to others of like mind by prosecuting.[16]

We do not know why Marks was the butt of rough music, but that he was of high social standing (whereas almost all the rioters were tenants, almost certainly farmers) may explain why Bradley prosecuted the offenders rather than sympathizing with them. Nevertheless, not only did the crowd include both men and women, but two of those accused, Michael and Ambrose Vincent, owned large tracts of land. Only one of the rioters, Able Simpson, appeared to have a prior court record, having paid a fine for assault in 1747. The accused hired an attorney, V. Crannel, who appeared for them on three occasions before New York's Supreme Court. After the case was postponed three times by mutual consent, it was dropped in 1752 after Attorney General Bradley died. The repeated postponement suggests that the evidence was not convincing on either side.[17]

Case Six: Adultery and Alleged Prostitution in New York City

A March 1754 riot over a case of sexual misconduct in New York City itself, however, merited the attention of New York's new attorney general, William Kempe. Led by Mary Allison, wife of apothecary William, a crowd consisting of about a hundred people—of whom eight other women and two men were identified—pursued one Gertrude Wilson. One James Jackson provided an eyewitness account:

> On Friday the first of March . . . as he was returning home from a ride . . . coming through one of the gate[s] in the Stockade Fence, he saw a Woman run and a Mob of Boys after her . . . came up a little woman, whom he . . . understood to be the Wife of Dr. William Allison and [she] called the woman [being chased] . . . a whore, and said that she was a pocky whore, and she had taken away her husband from her and bid her go home to her bulluc[. T]hat Mrs. Wilson . . . answered and said I have no bulluc at Home nor am I more a whore than you are nor so much, I will make you suffer for this usage.[18]

Mrs. Wilson sought refuge in a house, but a German doctor named Hendrick Suydam (showing his professional solidarity with the cuckolded Dr. Allison), Ephraim Lockwood, David Robinson, and others went into the house to get her out, all the while encouraging the crowd to abuse her. When she emerged, they threw dirt and pennies at her, probably mocking her as one who received money for sex. Mrs. Wilson then fled to another house, from which she was again ousted. Jackson then heard Robinson trying to excite the crowd "by crying out several times Mob the Whore—Mob the Whore." He also noted one John Christie in a nearby house "looking and laughing." Mrs. Wilson finally escaped into a third house, at which time Jackson rode away.[19]

The identifiable members of the crowd were indicted in the April 1754 term of the New York Superior Court. Besides Mary Allison, Dr. Suydam (also spelled Sidam), and Lockwood and Christie, for whom no occupations were given, these included Mary Woolsey; Jane Robinson, a single woman; Mary Muchlowain, a spinster; David Robinson and John Wilks, both victuallers; and Joseph Higginbotham, a mariner. Mathew Woolsey and one Ernest August Jacobus Printz Van Tollinsel were not identified further. All were charged with employing sticks, stones, and other weapons in an assault that lasted more than an hour, and with being "Rioters Routers and Disturbers of the Peace."[20]

Fragmentary evidence suggests that a judgment was reached on April 24, 1755. Nine of the eleven defendants were convicted; the fate of the other two is unknown. Six pleaded guilty, three pleaded not guilty. All were fined, but the amounts and whether they were ever paid remain unknown.[21] We can only speculate that here justice may truly have been done on behalf of a woman, perhaps a prostitute or an adulteress, with punishment inflicted on a crowd led and in considerable part composed of respectable citizens who had forgotten their station in life. On the other hand, we do not know the status, or the "connexions," of the enigmatic Mrs. Wilson who provoked such fury. We do know, however, that prosecutions were undertaken in colonial New York only if someone paid for them, so unless Attorney General Kempe dipped into his own pocket or was so sure of his case that he expected to recoup his losses from the fines, either Mrs. Wilson or someone sympathetic to her financially supported her suit against some pillars of the community.[22]

Cases Seven Through Nine: Two Mysteries and a Homeless Victim

Skimmington rarely led to successful prosecution. For example, nothing was done when two yeomen farmers, Joseph Smith and Philip Scheffer of Westchester, complained that on January 21, 1757, George Cronkheight, David Williams, James Travers Jr., Hezekiah Travers Jr., and Johannes Miller, also yeomen, had rioted in front of Smith's house at Courtlandt's Manor. The riot begin around two o'clock in the morning and lasted about three hours. In company with many unidentified persons, the accused, "allegedly armed with Clubs, and Staves Fiddles French Hornes & making hidious and umber noises," contributed to "the great disturbance and terror of the said Joseph Smith."[23]

The popular legitimacy such actions enjoyed may be sensed in two letters to New York Attorney General William Kempe imploring him not to prosecute them for rioting. That the riots in question went unreported and we know nothing about them suggests that an unknown number of incidents of rough music must forever be lost to history. The first letter, from one Samuel Strongham, claimed that he was new to the area and that "the mob they black'd me by violence & then I wipt it off again as well as I could want [but] went with them." Strongham was implying that he was singled out for prosecution because in his unsuccessful attempt to leave the crowd he made himself identifiable. In a second letter an Elijah Dean claimed that he had indeed blackened his face to participate in a riot, "but I did not know it was any Break of Law—and I did no man any damages."[24] Communally sanctioned intimidation of miscreants—which could be extended to witnesses—was legitimate if not legal. Dean perhaps thought he was simply engaging in fun and games, much like the crowds that rioted on Pope's Day every November 5 in Boston.[25] Added to the fact that many rioters were disguised beyond recognition, successful prosecutions were nearly impossible.

That blackface rather than a mask was the preferred disguise suggests that there was a racial element in the rioting. Because British colonists considered blacks especially prone to crime and disorderly behavior, it was easy to scapegoat them when a community preferred not to accept responsibility, and possible punishment, for its actions. For instance, following the great Boston impressment riot of November 17–20, 1747, the town blamed the unrest on "Foreign Seamen Servants Negroes and other Persons of Mean and Vile Condition." While lower-class people probably started the riot and pushed it further than town leaders wanted to, the entire community participated in taking British officers hostage and intimidating Governor William Shirley into negotiating for the release of sailors pressed into the navy. It was most useful to be able to blame all the trouble on those routinely branded as unruly rather than risk possible punishment for attacking the British navy in time of war.[26]

A letter of 1764 from William Kempe's son and successor, John Tabor Kempe, provides an almost heartbreaking instance of why prosecutions for riot were futile. John Kempe responded to an unknown recipient: "I received yours brought by Mackensie. I have examined him and find he has been much beaten. But the story he relates I think is incredible he says they would beat him because he would Sleep in the Highway. Nevertheless it may be true of some people in your County [Westchester] who often act upon very extraordinary motives."[27] It appears that a badly beaten homeless person who had been the target of some inhabitants of Westchester was discovered by a respectable person who sent him to Kempe in the hope that justice might be done. Kempe could not decide whether the story was true, but he did realize the hopelessness of pursuing the matter. As poverty and vagrancy increased in the mid-eighteenth-century colonies, communities expelled poor strangers, meanwhile trying to care for poor locals as inexpensively as possible. It appears that Mackensie, a member of this despised group of strolling poor, was given a particularly nasty "warning out."[28]

Case Ten: Adultery and Interracial Sex in Rye, New York

For a February 28, 1758, incident at Rye in Westchester County, the high rank of the rough musicians, rather than the low status of their target, prevented prosecution. A distinguished justice of the peace who lived in Rye, Ebenezer Kniffin, wrote to Attorney General William Kempe at the request of the victim, Hezekiah Holdridge, stating: "A certain number of people [took Holdridge] from a tavern in Rye and carried him on a rail which they call riding the Scimiton for their reasons of so doing I am informed he took a woman from Rye and went to Long Island and there remained for some time and returned again to Rye and brought her into his own house with his wife and being guilty of the same fact which I suppose to be undoubtedly true, I thought it proper to give your honor a full information as I understand the case."[29] Yet if Holdridge hoped that Kniffin would help him achieve satisfaction, he was mistaken. The justice of the peace confirmed that adultery was the reason for the punishment. Holdridge himself then wrote complaining that sixteen of his neighbors "riotously assembled together and assault him, beat him, abused him, burnt his hair, and shamefully used him and afterwards put him on a rail and carried him along the streets and after through [threw] him off, and laid hold of him and forced him to walk with him [them] near two miles abusing him all the way." What Holdridge sarcastically termed a "criminal conversation" with Rachel Johnson had provoked the "Scimiton," after which "abuse they left him in great danger of his life."[30]

Twenty-nine residents of Rye disputed both Kniffin's account and Holdridge's charges. Sixteen "honored inhabitants," five identifying themselves as "esquire," signed a single letter to Attorney General Kempe characterizing Holdridge as "a man of scandalous character attacking his loose behavior with women and by Report . . . as his having too much familiarity with other men's wives is true."[31] A second letter with thirteen additional signatures was even more damaging to Holdridge. The signatories admitted that had they participated in the skimmington but maintained that they did not "put him in peril of his life." They justified their conduct, charging:

> Holdridge went from this town with another man's wife to Long Island. Left his own wife . . . in a suffering condition who in his absence applied to the Churches aid and for relief. . . . Holdridge returned to Rye had the impudence to carry his strumpet to his own house there they would go to bed together leaving his wife. . . . But this is but a small part of his own actions. . . . Since he first came to this town hath (caused) by his wicked practices two or three families (black as well as white) . . . being separated. . . . And the reason that a number of us got together was to show our resentment of such wicked behaviors . . . so scandalous in a Civil Society . . . we had no other design but to show him and his strumpet but we failed in that (tho so we intended) in being so bold to complain and we assure you he was not anyways hurt and we can [by] . . . credible evidence prove. We could enumerate too many particulars of his wicked life and actions but refer that to further opportunity if your honor desire it.[32]

Holdridge had done more than commit adultery. His desertion of his wife had added to the town's charges for poor relief. His fornication had disrupted families and violated racial taboos. He was indeed a menace to "civil society." Some of those justifying the skimmington included the sons of the town's Congregational and Presbyterian ministers—the latter, John Smith, who had received George Whitefield at his church in 1740, was a personal friend of Jonathan Edwards. Also petitioning against Holdridge was William Willett, father-in-law of Alice Colden, daughter of New York Lieutenant-Governor Cadwallader Colden and brother of Westchester County Sheriff Isaac Willett. Other signatories included two constables, five justices of the peace, one judge of the court of common pleas, and a former army major.[33] Holdridge's case was hopeless.

Case Eleven: Adultery in Warwick, Rhode Island

Although New York then as now enjoyed a reputation for turbulence, skimmingtons occurred elsewhere too. The diary of Samuel Tillinghast of Newport recorded a skimmington that occurred in Warwick, Kent County, Rhode Island, about August 25, 1759.[34] Jonathan Clarke, a Newport goldsmith and known adulterer, went to visit the "strumpet (he keeps and has kept a long time)" in Warwick. His "Doxey" was staying at the home of a William Greene when, according to Tillinghast,

> the young men of the town being appraised of it, beset the house, took Clarke a bed and carried him off in his shirt to a tavern a mile distance, there clothed him, then provided a horse, mounted him and carried him the town over, from house to house, till next morning, sun a hour or two high, attended with many sorts of music, viz. drums, violins, horns, shells, pumking vine [pumpkin], and a near thirty cowbells, with acclamation and Loud Huzzah. In the conclusion carried him back to Greene and discharged him—I wish that all others that deserve it, were served like manner, . . . before they discharged the prisoner made him acknowledge he was well-used, very gently-treated if he don't go off is promised another visit.

Clarke, a wealthy man in Newport, was satisfying his lust out of town, much to the consternation of Warwick's young men, who either could not afford comparable companionship or perhaps even had moral objections to such goings-on. In any event, perhaps Clarke's status prevented him from suffering more than fear, humiliation, a headache, and a warning to stay out of Warwick. The incident went unreported in local papers. If it were not for Tillinghast's diary, it would remain unknown.

Case Twelve: Adultery and Death in Attleborough, Massachusetts

On the other hand, a skimmington in 1764 in Attleborough, Massachusetts, nine miles north of Providence, Rhode Island, led to death. Jonathan Sheppardson Jr., a cordwainer and father of eight, was charged by his neighbors with "an unlawful correspondence with a young woman who he had for some time entertained in his house." In response, "a number of men who lived near him, and were acquainted with his way of life, formed a resolution of punishing him for his domestic misdemeanors and as the most suitable method to render his behavior contemptible they concluded to mount him on a wooden horse, and ride him Skimmington, as mark of indignity." Sheppardson, however, "being resolutely bent on defense, and charging his gun with a design to shoot any who would dare to molest him," held them off. The crowd retired to wait for a more opportune time.[35]

It came ten days later. As Sheppardson returned from his cow pasture with a load of firewood, thirty or forty men surprised him. Simeon Washburn of Rehoboth, a neighboring town, had come up to lead the "ride" along with Sheppardson's neighbor, Benjamin Ide Jr. Sheppardson again resisted, drawing "a long sharp knife from a sheath he had fixed in the inside of his coat" and warning the crowd, some members disguised in blackface, to back off. Ide rushed and seized him, but "Sheppardson instantly cut him across one of his arms to the bone, and then while clenched together, gave the knife a violent thrust into his kidnies." Another of the company, who attempted to assist Ide, received a bad cut, and a third came up and swore he "would lose his life but he would take away the bloody weapon, and being a stout fellow, he actually got it away, but was so terribly wounded in the contest that his life is despaired of."[36] The stout man survived, but Ide died about fifteen minutes later.

At last seizing Sheppardson, his assailants proceeded to vent their anger and carry him "some distance on a rail." When they learned of Ide's death, "which greatly intimidated them, . . . they immediately dispersed and fled, lest a discovery who they were should involve them in the difficulties their conduct had subjected them to." Besides the question of responsibility for Ide's death, they may have been aware of the 1751 Massachusetts "Act for Preventing and Suppressing Riots, Routs, and Unlawful Assemblies," which stipulated that "if twelve or more, being armed with clubs or other weapons, did not disperse after warning they would forfeit all their lands and tenements, goods and chattels . . . be whipt thirty-nine stripes on the naked back . . . suffer one years imprisonment, and once every three months receive the same number of stripes."[37]

In any event, no one came forward to testify against Sheppardson, who had immediately surrendered himself to a justice of the peace at Taunton, the seat of Bristol County. A jury of inquest agreed that "Benjamin Hyde [Ide], jun. was slain by Jonathan Sheppardson, jun. after a violent manner."[38] Although not convicted, Sheppardson moved out of town shortly after his wife bore a child on February 27, 1765. He became one of the first settlers of Templeton, Massachusetts, about sixty miles to the north, although his family was prominent in Attleborough and had lived there since 1694.[39]

Ide also came from an influential town family. Coincidentally, his wife, Abigail, was also expecting a child at the time of the riot. Ide was not entirely innocent of sexual misconduct himself, for he must have wasted no time getting Abigail pregnant after his father died on March 31, 1752, leaving him "all my housing and lands, all cattle, sheep, horses, and all out of doors goods." Abigail gave birth to a daughter, Betty, on December 27, scarcely three months after they were married on September 16.[40] The younger Ide's sudden death precipitated nine years of litigation over a substantial estate valued at £258 by members of his family, which suggests that the Ides were not the most pleasant folks to be around, either.[41]

The Attleborough riot illustrates how difficult it is to generalize about skimmington. Unlike several of the previous incidents, the rioters appeared to be male, and exclusively so. Whereas other riots involved resentment against strangers, such as men who went philandering in other towns or a homeless man, here two solid inhabitants clashed in a town close to a major city and easily within reach of the authorities. Newspapers were quick to cite the event as an example of increasing lawlessness, urging their readers to report crimes to the authorities rather than taking the law into their own hands. A letter from Taunton was reprinted in both Newport and Providence:

> Tis to be hoped the sorrowful occurrence which happened at Attleborough, as mentioned in the Public Prints, and for which Mr. Sheppardson is now confined here, will put a check to such lawless and outrageous proceedings, which have late been very frequent in this part of the County. considering not only that it is the grossest violating of civil society to punish any person unheard, but also fatal disasters may attend the perpetration of them; If these persons whose indignation is so kindled would take half the pains to observe their neighbors bad conduct as they do to punish it, at the expense of the public peace, they might furnish the Authority with sufficient evidence for conviction, by which they would serve the public, and

gratify their own resentments, and at the same time be free from the fatal disasters, and legal punishments that attend SKIMMINGTON RIOTERS.[42]

The author's mention of "very frequent" riots included several in Boston: one on Coronation Day in 1762 and three in 1764. Fences were torn down on Beacon Hill; a militiaman was freed by a crowd as he was suffering the uncomfortable punishment of riding the wooden horse; and a boy was killed by being trampled under one of the carts bearing the Pope's effigies, over which the North and South End crowds were fighting on November 5.[43] Fears of rioting were not limited to New England. On November 8, 1764, a New York paper termed the Attleborough incident a "catastrophe [that] will no doubt prevent riding Skimmington for the future, and may be a warning—that the pursuit of even good designs, by irregular and unlawful methods may be attended with the most fatal consequences."[44]

Case Thirteen: A "Bad House" in Fishkill, New York

New York itself had provided another skimmington almost simultaneously. On October 31, 1764, in Fishkill, nine miles south of Poughkeepsie, nine people and "divers unknown unlawfully riotously and routously assembled and gathered themselves together . . . to break and enter upon . . . [the] dwelling house of Elizabeth Clarke." A poor widow who was spending time with Benjamin Vandervort, Clarke had a reputation, which she claimed was undeserved, for keeping a "bad house" and "entertaining servants." After returning from a wedding party, which suggests they had been drinking, the revelers stopped by Mrs. Clarke's for some of the gingerbread she baked by trade. Finding her and Vandervort together, perhaps in bed, they stripped her, beat him, and took him for a skimmington ride. For half an hour, to the "great disturbance and terror" of the couple, "the crowd did beat wound and ill-treat . . . and put other wrongs to them."[45]

At least three members of the victims' families, Clarke's son William and John and Jacob Vandervort, were present. John reported that William made a futile effort to spirit away "Benjamin Vandervort & carried him prisoner" for his own safety. When William advised the crowd to desist "they damned cursed him & called him a Damned Drunkened Rascal and said they had a commission to do it." Benjamin testified that one James Higby "damned & laid hold of him seized him assaulted him out of the House . . . kicked him . . . whipped him . . . dragged him out of the House." Vanderwort was "scared," Attorney General John Tabor Kempe's emphasized. Vanderwort also saw them tear "the wrappes off Mrs. Clarke almost down to her shoes." William testified that when the crowd seized his mother "she cried Murder her gown they tore off broke some of her Buckels and Bruised her side very much." He also reported that he "heard whips" and Benjamin's screams of "for God sake let me go."[46]

A member of the crowd, A. Ludlow, denied any violence was committed. He admitted that the crowd came "some small distance from the House and turned their horses and Jingled Bells blowed horns and went away, came again & did the same, came a third time. . . . They all went in—did not see any Body lay hold on Benjamin Vandervort, did not see any Blows given to any Body." Jacob Vandervort corroborated the three visits and also heard stones being thrown at the house.[47]

Another visit followed. On November 2, five of the original nine, two others, and "diverse unknown" persons returned. They sprang upon Elizabeth and William Clarke as they walked along the road near her house. "With a force and arms that is to say with stiks stones clubs and other offensive weapons and accompanied with dogs . . . did . . . set on [William and] excite a large dog . . . pursue chase and worry . . . beat wound and ill-treat . . . and [inflict] other wrongs" on him.[48]

This fracas apparently started over a challenge to a fight, although who challenged whom remains in doubt. According to Stephen Brinkerhof, "William Clarke had sent a challenge to Peter Johnson to come fight him that evening, . . . that Johnson was going to fight and that they heard the Skimmington people were together, and they went to see fair play that Johnson should not be hurt."[49] Apparently Clarke was a tough customer if Johnson needed a crowd to protect him: he had not only stood alone trying to rescue Vandervort the night before, but may have been the William Clarke convicted of assault in Dutchess County in 1775 and 1778.[50] A witness sympathetic to Clarke, however, reported that it was Johnson who had "challenged Clarke & stopped to fight him—but Clarke retired. . . . Johnson challenged him again . . . but Clarke deferred fighting . . . seeing the group of these people was afraid of them." Perhaps hoping to provoke William, or to force him to honor his challenge if he was backing out, Johnson "held a Club over Mrs. Clarke's Head, threatened to knock her brains out, and greatly abused her by words." William sought refuge inside his mother's house, but "Abraham Lent came to fetch the damned Son of a Bitch back & said let us have our revenge of him . . . and pursued him & seized him by the Nose & Twisted it til the Blood run violently." Another rioter, Peter Janse, "came up & spit in his face and thrust his Fist under his nose & threatened to be the death of him." Clarke still tried to get into the house, but Andrew Mich "set a dog upon him, who followed him, & seized him by the Breeches & Hair of his Head." All the while the crowd pursued him, until a second group of people rescued him. Richard Van Wyck had heard Brinkerhof was gathering the "Skimmington people" and had organized the second party to break up the fight.[51]

What was going on at the Clarkes? A poor widow who consorted with servants, entertaining them, at the very least keeping them from their duties, perhaps permitting drinking and prostitution, and baking gingerbread as a front? A son with a reputation for quarrelsomeness who may have served as her bouncer but who was intimidated by a crowd accompanied by a hunting dog? The evidence hints that "yes" is the answer to these questions, but of course is too scanty to prove it. The outcome of the skimmington reveals that Mrs. Clarke's enemies were local notables who, as in the case of New York City's Gertrude Wilson a decade earlier, had to be brought to justice by the provincial attorney general. A local justice of the peace who tried to indict them was himself indicted by the grand jury "for breach of Duty."

Knowing the rioters' connections, Mrs. Clarke feared that *she* would be prosecuted and dragged into court. In fact, she had either heard rumors that she had been indicted—perhaps spread to force her out of the area—or confused them with the charge against the justice who had sought to prosecute the rioters:

> I was at court here [Fishkill] on New Year's day and being informed the rioters against me was to endeavor to prove something to the Grand Jury. I know not what in order to get me indicted . . . they turn me off and told me there was nothing against me but as I have creditably been informed since, the jury found an indictment against me and also against my son for I know not what and I am a poor widow and the snow so exceedingly deep that I can not come to New York this Court but hope nevertheless to be ready at what

time you shall command my anything to the SKIMMILTONERS—the judges . . . being against me and sideing with the rioters being their relations. . . . Moreover I heard say the rioters swore as evidence to this court that I have kept a bad house (entertaining servants) which I can sufficiently disprove.[52]

Elizabeth Clarke was perhaps referring to the grand jury when she said "the judges," for it was they who charged the local justice of the peace, William Humphrey, "for breach of Duty in his Office of Justice to witt, for taking five recognizances of persons in this county, to witt, Isaac Lent, Abraham Lent, Jun., Andros Mick, Korick Myers, and James Higbie. Since the Last Court returnable this January Sessions and hath not returned the recognizances in This court which we conceive was his duty to do, We therefore do present him guilty of a misdemeanor and Desire the court to put this in form—Lewis Tappan foreman."[53] The local elite intended to teach Humphrey a lesson. They apparently persuaded him one way or another that he could not effectively prosecute the rioters. Because he failed to follow up on his recognizances, he was technically accused of not doing his duty whereas his real crime was attempting to do it.

Why Humphrey took such an interest in the fate of the Clarkes is also a mystery. He appears to have quarreled with the local elite before and may have sought revenge. He may well have funded the Clarkes' prosecutions of their assailants, assuming they were as poor as Elizabeth claimed. Humphrey, in fact, had written to John Tabor Kempe's father, William, justifying his conduct in a similar situation eleven years earlier: "I am always willing to submit to better judgement well knowing that i am not a Judge of the Law, but I Act as near as I can and as much as possible for the Peace of his Majesty's subjects, Also knowing when parties go with complaints they seldom fail to make a plain storey on their own side."[54]

Humphrey was not about to accept defeat. Like the Kempes and other royal officials, he perceived himself to be the agent of an imperial system at least theoretically trying to control lawless colonists. But this did not make him popular with a local elite when he did not legitimize their extralegal actions. Explaining these circumstances, he wrote a (missing) letter to Attorney General Kempe, who responded by endorsing Humphrey's conduct:

> I received yours with regard to the first I hope you will bind over the others to the Supreme court for I observe there are but seven

offenders yet bound—with regard to your last letter, I have to inform you that you acted right in returning the Recognizances to the Supreme Court and that you would have done wrong had you returned them to the Court of Sessions in your County—I am greatly surprised therefore that the Grand Jury should think of indicting you for doing what you was obliged by law to do, and for which you would have been punishable if you had not done . . . be pleased as soon as possible to send me a copy of it [the indictment] certified by the Clerk of the Court, and if I find it to be such as you are informed it is, I will immediately cause a NOLI PROSEQUI [no one to be prosecuted] to be entered on it, Be pleased also to inform me whether any of those Rioters were indicted at your Sessions, and which of them, and send me a copy of those indictments that I may so proceed that Justice be done.[55]

The Dutchess County elite made a mistake when they defied Humphrey, for now they had to tangle with Kempe and New York's highest bench. For the first riot, carpenter James Higby, tailor John Van Vleck Jr., miller Korah Myers, and yeomen Andrew Mick [Mich], Jonas Schooner, Lanah Vandewater, and Daniel Hausbrook were indicted. For the second riot, all of these seven except Hausbrook were also indicted, along with yeomen Isaac Lent and Peter Johnson.[56] Most of the defendants were of Dutch ancestry, as indeed were most people in the Hudson Valley, but by the 1760s dealings between them and the English, including men like Higby and Johnson, were common.[57] Significant, however, in a region where most people were tenant farmers on great estates, is that the rioters were identified as craftsmen or yeomen—that is, men who owned their own farms. They would probably have employed the servants they angrily accused Mrs. Clarke of entertaining, and would have had enough clout with the local authorities to prevent prosecution on that level.

In fact, they probably were able to ensure that they received only the mildest of penalties. Although on June 11, 1765, a jury convicted all the defendants except Van Vleck and Hausbrook, fines of a mere six shillings, eight pence were imposed on five of the rioters—Higby, Lent, Johnson, Mick, and Myers—on July 31 by Judges David Jones and Robert L. Livingston.[58] It is tempting to speculate that as members of major landholding families themselves (Jones on Long Island, Livingston in the Hudson Valley) they sympathized more with the local establishment than with either the suspected denizens of a "bad house" or with officials who represented a government that had suddenly begun to offend the provincial elite by imposing taxes and cracking down on violations of commercial legislation. At any rate, perhaps the irony of his leniency was not lost on Livingston in 1766 when his family required British troops to put down land rioters on their own estates.[59]

Case Fourteen: Wife Abuse in Newark, New Jersey

On July 11, 1765, a New York newspaper recalling the deadly rough music in Attleborough, Massachusetts (Case Twelve), also noted:

> A like affair we hear has lately happen'd at Newark, only that is has not yet attended with any fatal consequences, which however should be a warning to all persons concern'd in such unlawful enterprises—Such another company of disciplinarians, disguised with black'd faces, a few days ago seized a man of that place, who was known to be jealous of his wife; and upon suppositions that his jealousy was injurious to his wife, they gave him a severe whipping, and left both of them tied all night.[60]

Here rough music was performed by men at the county seat. Perhaps they tied the man and his wife together to encourage more intimate relations and less jealousy.

Case Fifteen: Adultery and Sexual Assault in New York City

On August 22, 1766, Dorothy, wife of merchant William Tongue, assaulted Elizabeth, wife of another merchant, James Patterson. With the assistance of four female slaves and one black man, Tongue cut off Patterson's clothes, held her down on her back, beat her with a broomstick, and threatened to kill her with a knife, only refraining, she claimed, because he did not know "where to conceal the Damned Body." Tongue then gagged Patterson with a handkerchief so she would not scream during the following ordeal: "At first pitch with a spoon and afterwards more from an old saucepan was put into the private parts of said Elizabeth Patterson and . . . the said Dorothy Tongue did prepare and put on said private parts a Plaster of hot pitch and coyan pepper spread on leather." Tongue appeared before New York's Supreme Court of Judicature at the October term, 1766, to answer charges. An adulterous relationship between Elizabeth Patterson and William Tongue was probably the reason for this appropriate if brutal mode of punishment. Elizabeth Patterson produced seven witnesses, including Dr. John Charleton, to appear on her behalf. However, there is no record of the disposition this case, which involved two substantial women of the second-largest city in British North America. Rough music was by no means practiced exclusively by the lower orders in sites removed from the courts of justice. Like the Jacksonian crowds described by Leonard Richards, prominent people sometimes led attacks on deviant inhabitants.[61]

Case Sixteen: Adultery and Castration in Shrewsbury, New Jersey

On April 18, 1768, a New York newspaper reported: "One Mr. ——— of that Place, being plied with strong Liquor by three Females, till he was much intoxicated, they then proceeded very deliberately to deprive him of his Manhood by C——n, which they effectively performed. The crime he was charged with, was for depriving his Wife of Favours that he bountifully lavished upon his Neighbours. The Operators were his Wife, his Wife's Mother, and one other Woman. He is in a fair Way of recovering, and the Women are all in Custody."[62]

No record of prosecution or punishment survives this horrible retribution for philandering.

Case Seventeen: Extramarital Sex and Possibly Aborted Rough Music in Ulster County, New York

On the night of July 13, 1768, four yeomen, Micah Lewis, James Hays, James Brisby, and Samuel Perkins, all disguised with blackened faces, appeared at the home of Barbara Lyneall of Newborough. Lyneall, a spinster, spied the men as she approached her house on the way back from a visit to Mr. Knowlton, who was perhaps her lover. Lyneall called out to inquire who was there, and someone responded, "A parcel of friends." Only too late did she realize their faces were blackened. She later accused all four of striking her, tearing off her handkerchief and necklace, and severely bruising her neck. She recalled that Samuel Perkins put the necklace in his pocket while the others tore off her petticoat. Brisby then threatened her with his ax and "a very indecent posture"; he was shirtless at the time. But for some reason she was neither raped nor further mistreated—perhaps her cries attracted rescuers who frightened the men away.

We can only speculate what really happened. Although there is a record of Lyneall's complaint, no evidence survives of a trial or verdict. It is possible that the men were punishing Lyneall for an affair with Knowlton, but perhaps rape, robbery, or both was the intention. Robbery seems a doubtful motive because they were yeomen—freeholding farmers. They may have wanted to deprive her of a necklace she had received for sexual favors. Brisby's obscene gesture may have indicated that they were jealous that the wealthy Knowlton was enjoying the favors of a woman they desired.[63]

Case Eighteen: The Merchant with Measles, East Hampton, New York

In the decade after the Stamp Act of 1765, rough musicians creatively adapted skimmington to serenade British officials and their loyal American supporters. These groups seemed clearly to have violated the "moral economy" of local communities far more than a wife-beater, adulterer, or prostitute, who only threatened a particular locality's stability or moral scruples, not the freedom and social order of all the colonies.[64] But obscure instances of rough music became entangled with revolutionary developments in the 1770s and illuminate how imperial and individual violations of local norms were perceived to be analogous.

Epidemics of measles were leading causes of death in colonial America in 1713–15, 1729, 1736, 1739–41, 1747–48, 1759, and 1772–73. Colonists were conversant enough with medical theories of contagion that if the arrival of a stranger coincided with an outbreak, he would be a plausible scapegoat if he displayed a reasonable approximation of the disease's symptoms.[65] Such was the fate of Ebenezer Dayton, a merchant from Brookhaven, New York, who was known as a peddler of glassware, cloth, and earthenware in central and eastern Long Island.⁶⁶ The pious Dayton saw no conflict between business and religion. He had previously been a schoolteacher in Newport, Rhode Island. Dayton had approached that job as a sacred calling, having "determined to consecrate my whole life time and labour" as "the rising generation's devoted . . . and very humble servant." He must have been fairly successful, for he claimed that he published in 1769 "A Serious Poem" at the request of his students, "calculated to excite exalted ideas of virtue, and raise their detestation of vice, and so help regulate their conduct in life." This "Concise Poetical Body of Divinity" intended to promote "Christian knowledge, Godly devotion, and real piety" followed a month later.⁶⁷

But between 1769 and 1772 something happened to Dayton. He may have retained some semblance of piety, for on June 28, 1772, he attended church in East Hampton, Long Island, after selling his wares there. But he had given up teaching and writing moralizing poetry and had become a fairly successful merchant with a sarcastic wit. After he contracted measles, despite warnings to isolate himself, he continued to do business, even appearing in church.

Leaving East Hampton the following day, June 29, he was pursued by three men: Aaron Isaacs Jr., Barnabas Mulford, and Jeremiah Hedges. Two or three miles west of town these men caught up with Dayton as he was riding in his one-horse cart. Even though the proximity of an infected person was known to cause measles, they asked Dayton to return to town and acknowledge that he had caused the outbreak of measles there. When he refused, a fourth man, Anamias Mulford, who had just arrived, tried to turn Dayton's horse around. Dayton fired his pistol as a warning, whereupon Mulford took out his own and cocked it next to Dayton's horse's head. Thus persuaded, Dayton returned to East Hampton, where around nine or ten o'clock in the morning the group was met by Captain Henry Parsons, Samuel and Steven Russell, and a crowd summoned by a drum beaten by Henry Chatfield and then Merry Parsons.⁶⁸

Upon arrival in East Hampton, Chatfield held the bridle of Dayton's horse as he led the procession to Samuel Bewell's house. Bewell persuaded Dayton to surrender his pistol before the procession moved on to the house of Nathan Conklin. By this time twelve people had assembled, although not spontaneously. Elisha Mulford Sr. later deposed that "he met Daniel Hedges who told him they were going to mob Dayton, and asked him for rotten eggs." The crowd used the eggs to pelt Dayton. When he attempted to escape from his cart, Anamias Mulford pummeled him to the ground, but later Dayton fled into Conklin's house.

Dayton stayed as Conklin's unwilling guest until that evening as a crowd of between fifty and a hundred gathered. Conklin treated him civilly, providing him with liquor and, presumably, food. When it became dark, Dayton asked to see Colonel Abraham Gardiner, whom he hoped would help him, but Gardiner had joined other members of the local elite in orchestrating the proceedings against Dayton. Gardiner was prosecuted for participating in the riot, along with two of the town's eleven other trustees, David Fithien and Daniel Hedges. Five trustees had the same surnames as other rioters: John Chatfield, Esq., Steven Hedges, Samuel Parsons, and Henry and Jeremiah Dayton.[69] Gardiner told Dayton that his only hope was to provide written acknowledgment that he had brought the measles, but Dayton's confession for some reason failed to satisfy the colonel. When the crowd heard Gardiner announce "That won't do," it loudly repeated the phrase. Gardiner then wrote another document for Dayton to sign. When Dayton refused again unless he could add his own postscript, Gardiner warned him he would have to "abide the consequences."[70]

At this point Conklin suggested that Dayton, who was understandably feeling ill, go to the house of Henry Dayton, perhaps a relative. Although he claimed to be too sick to go, Aaron Isaacs and Ezekial Mulford, Dayton's uncle, began carrying him there. But Isaacs suddenly let Dayton fall, stating, they "were no horse." At this point, John Davis led Dayton to Jeremiah Hedges, who provided a rail, exclaimed that the prisoner "would never get out of town alive," and threatened to "take him limb from Joint." When Job Mulford tried to stop the crowd, he was ordered to desist or else join Dayton on his ride. Job was then chased from the scene by Barnabas, yet another Mulford, and Hedges. Dayton called on Conklin to safeguard his purse, which contained much money and important papers. Conklin refused. Dayton's punishment thus came only reluctantly after negotiations over his confession to a community in which he had friends and relatives broke down.

By the time the skimmington did start, the crowd was truly incensed. Not only did one Mulford chase another, but a Dr. Samuel Hutcheson, who happened to arrive in town, was "struck by the mob" when he tried to stop it from putting Dayton on the rail. Earlier in the day, he had left the village and "tried not to see" the proceedings, but he could not avoid them when he returned again at nightfall.

A number of eyewitnesses described the ride. Jehiel Howel testified that Ezekiel Mulford and Aaron Isaacs called for the rail. They then saw Dayton "several times lifted up, and thrown down upon the ground. They said they would carry him to the Swamp and duck him. Dayton looked pale and ill." Aaron Isaacs Sr. noted, "They rode Dayton on a rail, [he] was often up and down, upon his last fall he cried out exceedingly that he was hurt." Joseph Avery related that afterward Dayton told him that "they attempted to ride him on a Rail that they threw him off of."

Attorney General John Tabor Kempe summed up the ride: "[The crowd] did again beat wound and ill-treat and did violently cast and throw [him] on the ground ... did drag [him] along the ground and divers times did lift up put and carry [him] astride on a pole did then and there divers times together with the pole throw [him] from a great height—suddenly and with violence to the ground by reason whereof the said Ebenezer Dayton was not only sorely bruised but hurt so that his life was in great danger."[71]

Finally, the crowd carried Dayton to the frog pond, ducked him, and left him in the road like a "dead man, crying murder." Only Colonel Gardiner's intervention caused the ride to end. But when he spoke softly to Dayton and offered to take him home, Dayton responded "no." The exasperated Gardiner replied that then "he might lie there and rot," whereupon Dr. Hutcheson and Job Mulford took Dayton to Hutcheson's house. The unchastened Dayton swore that "the people would pay for it."

The crowd cared more about the fate of Dayton's pocketbook than his physical well-being. Hutcheson and Job Mulford searched the road for the pocketbook with a lantern, finding nothing. They then searched Dayton's person and found no money, except a small sum in his breeches. While they wished to punish Dayton, they did not want to be accused of robbery; it seems they wanted to make sure Dayton was not hiding the money and claiming it was lost. They were also searching fruitlessly for a doctor's receipt proving Dayton had had the measles, which suggests that Dayton had claimed he had it and carried it in the pocketbook. The next morning, Jeremiah Conklin arrived with news that he had found the pocketbook. It was empty. When Dayton claimed that he had lost £100, Joseph Avery noticed that he "was to[o] ill to lay down and very hoarse."

Two doctors from Brookhaven were summoned to examine Dayton in his wretched state. Dr. Gilbert Smith confirmed his fears that he had suffered "a rupture" (a hernia) during the ride, "in the scrotum, not the groin," and predicted that "the low weight of bowels will enlarge it." Dayton's reply, that he had not been born with the hernia and "he would not have it for a great deal of money," indicates the sarcasm he had expressed earlier toward those who wished him well, an attitude that provoked the ride in the first place. Dr. Daniel Wiggins, who had previously treated Dayton for smallpox in 1771, allowed that he "may be propped up but the least excessive coughing or even talking will make it [the scrotum] fall again."

John Tabor Kempe wasted no time in pursuing the case. As early as July 20, George Muirson, the sheriff of Suffolk County, had received his orders to serve warrants in a suit already labeled "Ebenezer Dayton vs. Henry Parsons & 16 Others," including Colonel Gardiner, three Mulfords, two Conklins, and a Daniel Dayton. The defendants were charged with trespass, three separate counts of assault and battery, false imprisonment, and damages to Dayton's horse, goods, and reputation as a merchant. A writ from the Supreme Court issued on August 1 commanded the seventeen accused men to appear at the county courthouse in Southold on September 23.[72]

Through their attorney, Thomas Hicks, the seventeen pleaded not guilty on September 4. But it seems they hoped to avoid a trial. On receipt of the court date, Hicks forwarded to Kempe an affidavit signed by Justice John Chatfield, undoubtedly a relative of at least two of the accused, certifying that Aaron Isaacs Jr., a material witness, would be out of the colony on business until September of the following year. A second letter notified Kempe that yet another witness, Job Willet, was in Connecticut and was not expected back until after September 25. Kempe set the trial back a year until September 29, 1773,[73] but he feared that his case would collapse as witnesses for one reason or another left the jurisdiction. To ensure that the trial would in fact take place, on May 2 Kempe ordered the sheriff to seize and hold the seventeen defendants plus three new ones—Daniel and Eleazar Conklin and David Osborne—until the trial date. Whether the men were in fact jailed for nearly four months, or whether Kempe was content with their signed promise to appear at the trial, is unknown. What appears certain is that Dayton was perhaps not as desperate as he seemed to be, since either he or Kempe had to cover Muirson's fees of £41.10s for processing the warrants to seize the men, and it is unlikely that Kempe would do so out of his own pocket.[74] It is also possible that Dayton had powerful friends—perhaps the New York merchants with whom he did business—and may have owed them some of the money, which he hoped to recoup with a successful prosecution.

Kempe prosecuted the case vigorously. He received numerous depositions from people in East Hampton and the Brookhaven area, where Dayton had been raised.[75] The four key issues were whether money was stolen from the missing pocketbook, whether the riot had damaged Dayton's business, the nature of Dayton's injuries, and whether he in fact had the measles. All the issues were intertwined, for Dayton lost not only the money he carried with him but also at least some of his credit and ability to do business, as he needed the money to pay his creditors. Furthermore, if the skimmington had reduced a healthy man to a chronically ailing one, it was of course relevant in calculating the damages.

The missing money was considered first. Drs. Samuel Hutcheson and Gilbert Smith testified that three days before the riot Dayton had with him £44.9s.6d he intended to deliver to one L'Hommedieu in the East Hampton area. William Wright of Brookhaven increased the figure to £56 from old debts Dayton recently collected. (Were he in fact returning home after several years' absence to make his creditors pay up, Dayton's unpopularity would have yet another component.) But a father and son from Brookhaven, Josiah and Hugh Smith, disagreed. Josiah claimed that Dayton told him he had sent £70 or £80 off to his own creditors in New York just before the riot. After the skimmington, when Dayton asked Josiah if he remembered the conversation, Josiah replied that he did, and Dayton "desired him to keep it secret, saying it might hurt him." Hugh Smith was even more damaging. He testified that Dayton had sent some £240 to New York. After the riot, Dayton had said that Hugh was mistaken: "He had not said that he had sent the money, but that he collected so much to send . . . he desired him not to give his evidence for that it would do him more damage than all the evidence they had . . . against him." Yet another Smith, Isaiah, testified that while Dayton had lost only about £46 or £47 he had advised him "to put in all the damages he could make." Dayton estimated his losses at about £200. This suggested to Isaiah that Dayton was padding the bill, for he also claimed that the crowd "did not get all money he had—that one of his pocket books was in his chest."

Supporting Dayton was William Wright, a man Dayton had hired to sell goods for him. He believed that while Dayton had intended to send the money to New York to be credited to his account at the firm of Watts and Murray, he could find no man trustworthy enough to carry it. There is at least some plausibility in Dayton's claim, because his credit collapsed after the riot. Three city merchants, John Murray, Jacob Watson, and Nathaniel Roe Jr., testified, in Watson's words, that Dayton "was in good credit before. He has been trusted little since and done little business. . . . Before this his payment was better than most of his customers."

Next an effort was made to estimate the loss the riot had caused Dayton's business. Dayton tried to prove distress by showing that after the riot he could no longer use the services of William Wright, a man he had hired to handle his surplus business for £25 a year, for Dayton had little trade remaining. He even had to borrow £30 from Wright to pay for a barrel of rum or molasses that arrived, and quickly spent the £20 Wright had collected in his absence: "he was pressed by his creditors, he had not money to send them." Wright's testimony casts a more sympathetic light on why Dayton was touring Long Island collecting old debts, and also why he may have felt obliged to share knowledge of his financial situation with so many old acquaintances he was pressing for cash. Yet we should not be too sympathetic, for Dayton had either plenty of cash, convertible assets, or wealthy connections, which enabled Kempe to prosecute his case.

As with Gertrude Wilson and the Clarkes, victims of skimmington who had substantial assets or powerful friends stood a far better chance of justice (or revenge) than marginal members of society. Challenges to local mores from below could be squelched with far more impunity than challenges by those who had support from above. This may explain why a broad spectrum of colonial society was willing to turn its ire against a British and an anglicizing elite that was perceived as intrusive and immoral, even at the price of risking disorder from marginal elements that were considered equally threatening to localist autonomy.

Dayton's calculation of his loss increased as time went on, which may or may not suggest dishonesty. Wright notes that Dayton spent several days trying to figure out the sum, and James Moger, with whom Dayton boarded, testified that Dayton at first estimated his loss at £100, then at £200. It is plausible that Dayton needed time to calculate exactly what he had or had not sold, and how much damage was done to his business by his injuries. Another factor was the injury his horse sustained in the riot.

Later, when his hernia did not heal (Moger noted that thenceforth "he usually carried his hand in his groin"), Dayton also wanted compensation for suffering and loss of income. When Major William Smith of Brookhaven urged him to accept a compromise, Dayton responded: "The lowest he would take, he said, [was] £3 or £4,000." Dayton said he had been "greatly abused, but it was of a private Nature which he would tell him if he kept it secret. At length he said they had burst him by turning him over a Rail—that he was disabled from getting his living."

The question of the extent to which the hernia disabled the already ailing Dayton was the third issue the court considered. Several witnesses testified that before his injury, in addition to his peddling, Dayton had been a strong and dependable farm worker, plowing fields and pitching hay, but could not perform manual labor thereafter. Isiah [*sic*] Moger related that a month before the riot he and Dayton had been exercising, hopping and jumping. But "a month after he came back" to Brookhaven, Moger "challenged him to run [and] Dayton declined [saying] the time had been he could run with him, but now he could not run without a jacket and breeches." This statement shows he could not run at all, for Moger swore that afterward he never ran or jumped and was very lame. Samuel Thompson noted that while Dayton had had a similar condition at the age of eight, his "mother made trusses and bandages for him—Has often heard his mother say since she cured him—Never heard him complain of it afterwards tho—he has seen him every week during his life."

The final factor in the lawsuit was whether Dayton had the measles, and what this meant for his overall case. On the one hand, making a man with measles ride skimmington may have aggravated his injuries. On the other hand, if he had willfully carried the disease into a church it might decrease any moral basis for his case. Jehiel Howel testified that Dayton "was very ill" the day before the riot. David Mulford swore that Dayton told him that he would not have identified his own uncle Ezekiel Mulford as a rioter "had he not when he was sick of the measles come to him and abused him." Henry Dayton, with whom Ebenezer Dayton often boarded, revealed that Ebenezer in fact had been sick at his house with the measles for ten days. Dr. Samuel Hutcheson, who had attempted to help Dayton during and after the riot, confirmed the illness: "Before the riots and while plaintiff told him he had a sum about him which he had rec[eive]d from Dr. Gilbert Smith for L'Hommedieu and that he was afraid his having the measles would prevent his paying it as soon as L'Hommedieu expected it." Dr. John McLean also swore that Dayton had told him he had the measles and desired him to keep it a secret, since people would not trade with an infected man.

Nevertheless, Dayton found witnesses to swear that he had had measles as a child but in any event carried medicines that would prevent its recurrence. Furthermore, he argued that he had repeatedly been exposed to measles, had not been reinfected, and considered himself immune. Finally, he argued that during the last seven years he had suffered periodically from a consumptive cough, for which he claimed doctors treated him when the cough reappeared in East Hampton. Yet he refused to accept McLean's diagnosis and heed his warning not to go out among the people.

The preponderance of evidence suggests Dayton was willfully carrying the measles infection, which gave the East Hampton skimmington some legitimacy. Yet Kempe went ahead with the trials in the fall of 1773, charging the defendants with three incidents of assault and battery. First, they had allegedly vigorously pursued Dayton, thrown eggs and cocked a gun at him, pinioned him, and brought "him back in triumph to the Mob collected in East Hampton." Second, they had carted him around town and pelted him with "stones, rotten eggs, and other filth." Third, they were accused of taking him out of Conklin's house, riding him on a rail, "throwing him frequently down with violence," and ducking him. In addition, Kempe piled on numerous other charges: for false imprisonment, for confining Dayton to Conklin's house for twelve hours, for damages to his horse and his goods, for loss of money, for injuries sustained to his body, and for damages to him as a trader and to his subsequent loss of credit.[76]

Kempe, perhaps influenced by the prominent New York merchants with whom Dayton traded and to whom he owed money, placed special emphasis on the last charge. He argued that Dayton "is greatly hurt in his credit in as much that divers persons had & will refuse to credit or trust him with goods in the way of his business as they used to . . . and to his damage of £1000," a round number that was clearly a guess. Kempe maintained that if Dayton could not personally travel and handle the large farming accounts on which his trade in goods depended, the farmers would be unwilling to trust him for the normal length of time in matters of buying and selling such commodities as wheat, rye, corn, flax, seed, beef, and pork.[77]

The £1,000 exceeded by about fourfold Dayton's tangible, estimated losses: £24 for his horse, £16 for his goods, £44.9s.6d for lost money from Gilbert Smith, an additional £56.18s.1d from collected debts, and £118.12s.5d for goods sold on the trip. Kempe accepted the story that Dayton had more than £200 in his pocketbook. He also believed Dayton was entitled to receive damages for pain of body, pain of mind, the hernia, and the scandal of the skimmington ride and its effects on his reputation in the future. Long Island historians B. F. Thompson and Nathaniel S. Prime, writing in 1839, and Henry Hedges, following their lead in local publications of 1889 and 1897, assert that Dayton won a £1,000 judgment, an average of £50 each from the twenty defendants. The actual trial record and judgment, however, do not survive. The head of the Chatfield clan had to sell his residence, Chatfield Hill, to pay his son's share.[78]

Whether Kempe hoped to tack on an additional £157.12s.2d in court costs or whether these would come out of Dayton's settlement is not certain. These expenses included a bill of £30 to two lawyers—£25 to Richard Morris and £5 to Samuel Jones—for the trial, which indeed took place on September 29, 1773. Kempe also billed Dayton £2 for consultation and advice before commencing prosecution in 1772, another £2 for putting off the trials, £3 for consulting with the two lawyers for two days prior to the trials, £10.12s.10d to pay the clerk of the court, and various miscellaneous expenses, most notably £41.10s for paying the sheriff to serve subpoenas, and £2.3 to each of forty-three witnesses.

It seems clear that the East Hampton crowd, like so many in colonial America, saw nothing wrong with punishing someone who flagrantly threatened community well-being. Only the fact that Dayton had more clout and persistence than most victims, or the less likely possibility that Attorney General Kempe had seized a golden opportunity to either make money, do justice, or punish some political opponents, led to a successful prosecution. Furthermore, unlike the members of the Bostonian elites who were mobbing Tories at the same time, East Hampton was far too small a community to successfully resist the weight of the Crown.

Despite the Crown's intervention on his behalf, Dayton became a fierce patriot during the American Revolution. In 1775 he joined a militia company, and in 1776 he was the clerk of the Coram Committee of Safety, the town in which he married Phebe Smith forty-eight days after the riot and where he settled down. Forced to flee with his family to Bethany, Connecticut, when the British occupied Long Island after chasing Washington's army out of New York, Dayton became a successful privateer against the British at sea and a raider against the Tories on Long Island.[79]

Yet both sides mistrusted Dayton, considering him an enemy agent and smuggler. On March 14, 1780, Long Island Tories raided his home in Bethany, thoroughly ransacking the house and stealing £450 in gold and silver before being captured by Connecticut militia a few days later. At the trial that convicted the Tories, they implicated Dayton as one of their own, in effect branding him a traitor and a spy. But he published affidavits attesting to his loyalty and to his success as a merchant before the British came to Long Island in August 1776. The court ruled in his favor, and he "received judgement awarding him, in the aggregate, many thousands of pounds" for his services and to compensate for the slanders.

It is tantalizing but inconclusive to speculate that rumors of Dayton's disloyalty were spread by the friends and families of those who had suffered in his earlier lawsuit, or by those who had felt the sting of his sharp tongue and perceived its inconsistency with his religious principles. In addition to resisting taxation and tyranny, the American Revolution was supposed to show how virtuous communities could serve as models for a corrupted world. It is therefore understandable that many doubted that Dayton—who could selfishly imperil his neighbors' lives, insultingly refuse to confess this grievous fault, and with the help of British authorities sue even members of his own family over such a just chastisement—could ever serve any cause greater than his personal interest.

Case Nineteen: All in the Family: John Jay and Skimmington in Hempstead, New York

Members of the Seaman and Birdsall families of Hempstead, Long Island, had intermarried on numerous occasions. We do not know why on November 13, 1773, shortly before the Boston Tea Party, Benjamin Birdsall and a crowd of nine men dragged John Seaman from his dinner table and greatly abused him on the road outside his house. At first they dragged him through mud and water, and finally they carried him about on a rail. Several times they threw him to the ground, bruising him severely. They also dragged him repeatedly through a large puddle of dirty water. The crowd finally took him home, by rail, after about an hour's sport.[80]

Unlike other skimmingtons, the action against Seaman divided the community, instead of uniting it against a deviant. Birdsall invited Bean Seaman, whose relationship with John was unclear, to join the crowd. But he refused, as did Jacob Jackson, who witnessed the event. Seaman's brother Zebulon tried to aid him, but Birdsall ran out of the crowd and "fell foul of him and abused him," forcing him to return home. Two female Seamans, Martha and Mary, helped Seaman clean off the dirt and close his shirt after the tumult. The records of Attorney General Kempe, who Seaman hired as his attorney, note fifteen more potential witnesses but provide no further details.

But Seaman never received his day in court, unless the records have disappeared. Kempe most likely dropped the case as the worsening imperial crisis occupied him, or perhaps the litigants settled informally. The nearly two-year delay in judgment reads like a farce. Someone came up with a bold plan to forestall Seaman's suit. On January 17, 1774, Kempe received a letter delivered by Samuel Jackson that read: "Sir please stop action against Benjamin Birdsall for we have agreed to leave the matter [informally]. . . . Sir: I am your humble servant John Seaman." Kempe suspected a ruse, but was unsure, for he penned a reminder to himself "to write Mr. John Seaman to know if he has dropped his actions ag[ains]t Benjamin Birdsell."[81]

But Kempe did not inform Seaman until March 2 that he either had to write in his own hand or inform Kempe in person to halt the proceedings. He then requested a prompt reply as to whether Seaman wanted the case to continue. Seaman responded on April 5 that he did, but not until October or November 1774 did Kempe indict Birdsall on two counts of assault and one of trespass, alleging that the riot was committed without "reasonable cause" and that Seaman was very bruised and hurt.[82]

Justice continued to move slowly. Only on May 5, 1775, did Birdsall's attorney, John Jay, enter a plea of not guilty on his behalf. Seaman was getting nervous. On June 21, he reiterated to Kempe that he still wanted to proceed against Birdsall; fearing that others might be misrepresenting him, he disavowed any actions or statements not made personally by him. Seaman expressed the hope that his case would be heard the next time the Supreme Court sat at the circuit seat of Jamaica. Seaman was heartened when in mid-August a trial date was set for September 6, 1775. He expressed his pleasure through a letter to Kempe hand-delivered by Silas Smith, whom he recommended as a good source on the actual details of the skimmington. But four days before the trial was scheduled, Kempe wrote to Jay and called it off. No record remains of any further action.[83]

It is tempting to read events of the American Revolution into this family feud in a small Long Island community. Assuming Seaman may have been a loyalist (his will is abstracted in the volume for 1780–82, when the British still occupied the area) who hired the Crown's attorney, and Birdsall a patriot who hired a leading if conservative revolutionary, then both the skimmington and the false representation of Seaman make sense. The crux of the American case against Parliament, which if Seaman was a loyalist he may have denied, was that the British legislature's claim to represent the colonies was illegitimate. What better way to teach a Tory such a lesson than to follow up a skimmington with a letter falsely representing his wishes? And what more appropriate a date—September 1775, when New York revolutionaries were preparing to supplant the royal government and launch an invasion of Canada—for all parties concerned to take their disputes out of court and, most probably, onto the battlefield of revolution.

Conclusion

In works published in 1968 and 1971, respectively, John Demos and David H. Flaherty ask for more research into extralegal means of social control in colonial America. Demos shows that the punishable offense of fornication had been prosecuted in seventeenth-century New England, but that in the eighteenth century "such prosecutions seem to have been steadily more rare and finally to have ceased altogether." This "suggests a falling away from restrictive standards of sexual morality." The increase in skimmingtons in the mid-eighteenth century indicates that many inhabitants and communities still adhered to traditional morality but that enforcement by the formal authorities was no longer effective. Demos suggests that more research is needed before we can conclude that the community condoned fornication, or that the middle and late-eighteenth century became the most "free" period in our history.[84]

Flaherty in turn argues that laws concerned with enforcement of morals failed in a setting where law and morals were consciously intertwined. In the seventeenth century, British North America tried to enforce morality through laws passed by secular government. Many of these laws went unenforced, such as the death penalty for adultery in Massachusetts. Flaherty proposes:

> The upholding and enforcement of morality by extra-legal means was by contrast relatively successful. . . . Alternative methods of social control existed and have always prevailed in Western society to make up for deficiencies in official legal processes. . . . Particularly

in the realm of sexual morals, communities developed a self-generating form of social control over the behavior of the populace. Small population units living in relative intimacy and collective isolation from other villages induced conformity of behavior in the majority and discouraged conscious imitation of deviant behavior.[85]

One extralegal method used during the eighteenth century in British North America was the skimmington ride. It was employed in Massachusetts, Rhode Island, Connecticut, New York, New Jersey, and Pennsylvania in a form similar to the examples of rough music and charivari researched by scholars of European history. The procession, the accompanying antiphony of musical instruments, the insults, the taunts, and the carrying of the victim on a rail all demonstrate that the form of skimmington in the colonies followed French and English practices.

The incidences of skimmington discussed in this chapter suggest that the victims of crowd violence had been flouting society's morals for some time. A continuing refrain seems to be the presence of phrases such as "a noted adulterer" or "an unlawful [sexual] correspondence." The people who enacted the skimmington had long endured the misconduct of their neighbors before they reached consensus that the conduct must cease. A single fact often galvanized the crowd into action. For example, Hezekiah Holdridge left his wife in a suffering condition to commit adultery, and then had the temerity to bring his mistress into his house with his wife. Jonathan Sheppardson Jr. also brought his mistress home.

A number of factors led to the revival of the skimmington ride in the mid-eighteenth-century colonies. Foremost was the shift from traditional to modern forces. Family, marriage, the economy, law, and government were becoming more secular. As provincial government tended to seek mere law and order rather than strict moral regulation, rural communities especially were faced with threats to the moral standards they refused to abandon. For example, in Ridgefield, Connecticut, William Drinkwater, a skimmington victim, was unable to obtain redress from the local magistrates. Many people there believed secular and moral law should continue to reinforce each other, leading Connecticut officials to realize they could not use the criminal law to punish the rioters, which would require a trial by a jury of the vicinage.[86] Aware that they could escape punishment, the inhabitants turned to skimmington.

The behavior of colonial law enforcement officials also bears mention. Historian Michael Zuckerman notes that constables did not seek their positions, were often chosen against their wishes, and had little ability to challenge the community that selected them by making unpopular arrests. Their only authority sprang from the voluntary compliance of the inhabitants.[87] Local constables often witnessed skimmingtons, but not one made an arrest; the victim had to seek redress at a higher level. Nor did constables assist in obtaining witnesses or aid in the prosecution. Where they were not part of the crowd, they clearly acquiesced in the crowd's actions.

Neither did other local officials such as town supervisors and council members act effectively to help skimmington victims or prosecute their attackers. In East Hampton, New York, three of the town's twelve supervisors were charged with participating in the riot, while five others appear to have been related to the rioters. Even justices of the peace failed to intervene. The exception is Justice William Humphrey of Fishkill, New York. Despite his bumbling efforts, the victims received justice, but mainly because of the efforts of New York's attorney general. In Rye, New York, local justices supported the skimmington crowd rather than the victim. David Flaherty stresses the importance of justices of the peace in setting the moral tone of colonial communities: "Their enthusiasm or lack of interest in the enforcement of morals was a crucial point in the system."[88]

Although New York's attorney generals Richard Bradley, William Kempe, and John Tabor Kempe sought to prosecute the crowd members who had violated the law, they were severely limited by two factors. First, they needed an adequate supply of information to establish a case, subpoena witnesses, and proceed to trial. This proved impossible when the lower levels of law enforcement did not cooperate. Another limitation was the requirement that the attorney general pay for the costs of prosecution himself, until he could obtain compensation from the victim. This limited the chances that justice could be obtained if the victim had little money, or if the attorney general felt the chances of conviction were slim and not worth his attention.

A comparison of these examples of rural crowd violence with studies of urban crowds results in some striking observations. As Douglas Greenberg points out, "riots in rural areas required far more planning and organization than those in cities. There were no ready and available crowds in New York's outlying counties, neither transportation nor communication was very good. . . . Since careful planning was required, cold calculation almost certainly played a more important role than spontaneous response to an inherently emotional situation."[89] Premeditation and planning are apparent in the incident that occurred in Attleborough, Massachusetts. The crowd was so well organized that when an attempt at skimmington went awry they reorganized and tried again ten days later. They succeeded then in riding their victim out of town. In East Hampton, participants collected rotten eggs the day before. In Hempstead, a passerby was asked if he wanted to participate (he refused). For people to get together, use force, and enact a skimmington required great determination. Yet although more skimmingtons occurred in rural areas, Boston and New York City also were the scene of skimmingtons.

Skimmington rides, then, were used in the absence of other effective agencies of government. The crowd members agreed that they were acting on behalf of what was good and just. In eleven incidents—eight skimmington rides, two attempted rides, and one case of other rough music—the crowd behaved as though a community consensus existed against wrongs they loathed. Michael Zuckerman notes that in rural areas the crowd "was most clearly the ultimate expression of a community consensus, for no mob could have existed for more than a moment in those towns without the toleration of the people." Douglas Greenberg concurs: "There really was not much that government could do if citizens were intent upon resisting the law. . . . It was dangerous enough to apprehend just one offender. New York society in the eighteenth century simply lacked the resources to resist such disorder."[90]

In only three instances studied were acts of violence punished by the legal authorities. One was the case involving Mary Allison in 1754 in New York City; the other two occurred in Fishkill and East Hampton, New York. In five others, crowd members were formally charged and prosecution was begun, but never carried through to conviction. In Attleborough, Massachusetts, no witness came forth despite a participant's death and appeals from the newspaper. In Poughkeepsie, Rye, and Hempstead, New York, the defendants were charged but trials were never held. In the Cortlandt Manor rough music, only a deposition was taken.

Skimmington, then, was used at a time when those responsible for law enforcement did not take action against those who violated the community's moral standards. Instead, the crowds resorted to extralegal violence. The community clearly publicized its resentment in a universally familiar method, with the understanding that it taught a moral lesson. In France or England, charivaris or rough music succeeded when the victim removed himself from the community. In the colonies, the primary goal of removal was achieved in all cases where the results are known, with the exception of Ebenezer Dayton. In that case, vindication through the legal process may have lessened the humiliation of the skimmington ride and allowed him to continue his business in the community afterward.

Skimmington helps us to see what eighteenth-century British North American communities valued, what they condemned, and what could not be enforced through the formal authorities. Skimmingtons, which could range from merriment to brutal violence, provided an outlet for the community. The terrified victim, fearing his life was about to be ended, heard the din of raucous noise and music, listened to the taunts of the crowd, and endured a ride that must have seemed endless. He was certainly aware that his neighbors loathed both him and his behavior. Although the victim learned his lesson too late, the moral would be apparent to others who were contemplating similar behavior.

As colonial communities continued their concern with immorality, the use of traditional skimmington is not surprising. If anything, as Bryan Palmer shows, it persisted and occurred frequently along with other forms of rough music (especially "whitecapping," or whipping) into the twentieth century in both Canada and the United States, because federal and state authorities were too weak and too distant to respond to community outrage, especially in rural areas.[91] But as elite officials in the late colonial era became more anglicized and more remote from rural townships (and psychologically estranged from the artisans and mechanics who composed urban crowds), they shifted from a concern with upholding public morality to prosecution of such crimes as theft, acts of personal violence, and having a disorderly house. The court records afford a glimpse of an America growing so fast that the legal authorities could not keep up with the society's desires and needs. Into this breach stepped the community, using traditional although extralegal means to defend its standards and integrity. The North and South Carolina Regulators, land rioters throughout the northern and middle colonies, and urban revolutionary crowds would do likewise.

Notes

1. *The Oxford English Dictionary*, 12 vols. (Oxford: Oxford University Press, 1933), 9:143.
2. Violet Alford, "Rough Music or Charivari," *Folklore* 70 (December 1959), 505–18.

3. Bryan D. Palmer, "Discordant Music: Charivaris and Whitecapping in Nineteenth-Century North America," *Labour/Le Travailleur* 3 (1978), 5–62. The author is indebted to Bryan Palmer for providing him with a copy of this article.

4. Natalie Zemon Davis, "The Reasons of Misrule: Youth Groups and Charivaris in Sixteenth-Century France," *Past and Present* 50 (February 1971), 41–75.

5. E. P. Thompson, " 'Rough Music' or English Charivari," *Annales E.S.C.* 27 (March–April 1972), 285–312, based on an English translation provided courtesy of Joan Tomei. A more extensive version of this article appears as chapter 8 of Thompson's *Customs in Common: Studies in Traditional Popular Culture* (New York: The New Press, 1993).

6. Willliam S. Walsh, *Handy-Book of Literary Curiosities* (Philadelphia, 1911), 149; Palmer, "Discordant Music," 17–18.

7. Ibid.; Richard B. Morris, *Government and Labor in Early America* (New York: Columbia University Press, 1946), 147.

8. David H. Flaherty, "Law and the Enforcement of Morals in Early America," in Donald Fleming and Bernard Bailyn, eds., *Law in American History* (Boston: Little, Brown, 1971), 229.

9. David Underdown, *Revel, Riot, and Rebellion: Popular Politics and Culture in England, 1603–1660* (New York: Oxford University Press, 1985), 102.

10. *New York Weekly Journal*, December 31, 1733, 1.

11. *New York Weekly Journal*, November 4, 1734, 2.

12. Peter Goodrich, *Law in the Courts of Love* (London: Routledge, 1996).

13. *Pennsylvania Gazette*, April 10–April 17, 1735, 4; *New York Gazette*, April 28, 1735, 4; *New York Weekly Journal*, May 5, 1735, 4.

14. *New York Weekly Journal*, November 8, 1736, 3.

15. Davis, "The Reasons of Misrule."

16. Minute Book of the Supreme Court of Judicature, 1750–54, Plk 813, New York City Hall, Records Room, Manhattan County, New York (hereafter cited as MBSCJ-NY), October 16, 1750, to January 19, 1754. Four names are in the charge. Marks had numerous lawsuits against customers who failed to pay for merchandise, but no rioters were former or future litigants, although they may well have been friends or family members. Ancient Records, Dutchess County Court House, Poughkeepsie, New York (hereafter cited as AR-DCCH). For the years 1751–58, see numbers 2301, 2302, 2341, 2425, 2433, 2434, 2501, 2552, 2635, 2682, 2766, 2801, 1883, 2923, 2978.

17. Clifford M. Buck, comp., "Resume of Deeds in the Area of Original Beekman Patent," Typescript, Dutchess County, New York, c. 1970: John Amy, nos. 533, 1243, 1282; John de Longe, nos. 169, 174, 533, 962, 1059, 1135; Jeremiah Hunt, nos. 628, 1089, 1109; Isaac Marks, nos. 14, 17, Witness to Land Transaction of Estate of "Col. Gilbert Livingston," done by Robert G. and Henry Livingston, April 16, 1751, pp. 3–4; Michael Vincent nos. 221, 248, 479, 628, 771, 792, 794, 839, 844, 851, 856, 872, 874, 882, 927, 935–39, 941, 986, 1005, 1038. Michael Vincent (b. 1720 or 1721) owned large amounts of land that he, in turn, leased out; he married Ruth Hunt, probably a relative of Jeremiah Hunt, another rioter, and Ambrose Vincent married Dorothy Hunt, sister of Michael's wife Ruth. For genealogical information, see Anna M. Buck and Clifford M. Buck, *The Buck Family* (n.p.: 1959), 8, 10. For Simpson's conviction, see AR-DCCH, no. 316, March 2, 1747. Simpson was jailed, "discharged with fee paid—good behavior." See MBSCJ-NY, April 24, 1751, 45; August 3, 1751, 68; and October 24, 1751, 93, for appearances in the case. Omitted here is a brief analysis of a case of rough music from Elizabeth, New Jersey, reported in the *Pennsylvania Gazette* for December 26, 1752. Brendan McConville discusses it more fully in his chapter in this volume.

18. John Tabor Kempe Papers, New-York Historical Society, hereafter cited as Kempe Papers, Box G-L, Deposition of James Jackson, n.d. William Kempe succeeded Richard Bradley as Attorney General in November 1752. He served until his death in July 1759 and was succeeded

by his son, John Tabor Kempe, who became a loyalist and served, including under the British occupation, until 1782.

19. Ibid.

20. Kempe Papers, Kempe Charges, Box A–B, MBSCJ-NY, April 25, 1754, 42; Plk 816, see also Plk 975. Unlike the Minute Book cited in note 16, volumes in this collection from 1754 onward are found in the Surrogates Court, Manhattan Hall of Records.

21. Ibid., April 24, 1755, 156, Plk 816. Julius Goebel and T. Raymond Naughton, in *Law Enforcement in Colonial New York* (New York: Columbia University Press, 1944), 192, claim that twelve people were found guilty. Curator Joseph Van Nostrand of the Manhattan Hall of Records was unable to find the sources they used. For law definitions, see John Bouvier, *Bouvier's Law Dictionary and Concise Encyclopedia*, 3 vols. (St. Paul: West Publishing Co., 1914), 1:418, 3:2852; and Henry Campbell Black, *Black's Law Dictionary* (St. Paul: West Publishing Co., 1968), 107, 262, 1151. Invaluable assistance was provided by attorneys James Schildt and Richard Link in unraveling legal records.

22. Goebel and Naughton, *Law Enforcement in Colonial New York*, 734, 747–48, write that in New York "the Attorney General would either be out of pocket or he would have to find some means of compensation" for his efforts. "The Supreme Court did not pursue a policy of ordering confinement until such charges were paid." The Attorney General had no salary. Kempe had to resort to fees, private practice, or influence in government spheres to acquire land at nominal costs. See Catherine S. Crary, "The American Dream: John Tabor Kempe's Rise from Poverty to Riches," *William & Mary Quarterly*, 3d ser., 14 (April 1957), 176–95, esp. 180–81.

23. Deposition of Joseph Smith and Philip Scheffer, n.d., Kempe Papers, Box P–U.

24. Samuel Strongham to William Kempe, February 22, 1754, and Elijah Dean to William Kempe, February 22, 1754, Kempe Papers, Box 4, folder marked "Miscellaneous Letters and Legal Papers."

25. For Pope's Day, see article by Alfred Young cited in Chapter 1, note 6, of this volume, and his "Pope's Day, Tar and Feathers, and Cornet Joyce Jr.: From Ritual to Rebellion in Boston, 1745–1775," paper presented at the Anglo-American Historians Conference, Rutgers University, New Brunswick, New Jersey, 1973; and Peter Shaw, *American Patriots and the Rituals of Revolution* (Cambridge, Mass.: Harvard University Press, 1981), esp. 190.

26. John Lax and William Pencak, "The Knowles Riot and the Crisis of the 1740s in Massachusetts," *Perspectives in American History* 10 (1976), 106.

27. Letter from J. T. Kempe to [unknown], July 17, 1764, Kempe Papers K–P, Box I, folder marked "Abrahams–Browne."

28. Robert Cray, *Poverty and Poor Relief: New York City and Its Rural Environs, 1700–1830* (Philadelphia: Temple University Press, 1988).

29. Letter from Ebenezer Kniffin, March 2, 1758, Kempe Papers, Box G–L. Kniffin "was a man of means and influence . . . was Justice of the Peace, 1755–69. Lived opposite the Episcopal Church . . . [had] a farm of 90 acres." Charles W. Baird, *History of Rye* (n.p., 1871), 418. A subsequent letter dated April 18, 1763, from Kniffin to J. T. Kempe attested to the character of one Captain James Holmes of Bedford, Kempe Papers, Box H.

30. Letter from Hezekiah Holdridge, March 7, 1758, Kempe Papers, Box G–L. Holdridge's case is discussed at greater length by Thomas Humphrey in this volume, but as his interpretation is somewhat different, it is instructive to have them both appear.

31. Letter from "Subscribers, Honored inhabitants of Rye," March 10, 1758, Kempe Papers, Box G–L. None of the sixteen was among those accused by Holdridge.

32. A different Letter from "subscribers," March 10, 1758, Kempe Papers, Box G–L. Of the thirteen signatures nine—Robert Bloomer, Abraham Lyon, Ezekiel Merrit, Joseph Merrit, Robert Merrit, Solomon Purdy, Joseph Sherwood, John Slater, and Joseph Williams—were among those accused by Holdridge.

33. The Kniffin, Purdy, Brown, Wetmore, Merritt, and Lyon families, four of whose members Holdridge accused, were prominent among the twenty-nine inhabitants of Rye who subscribed to a ferry to Oyster Bay, Long Island, started in 1739. Some of these families had originally settled Rye in 1663. See Marilyn E. Weigold, "Rye to Oyster Bay Ferry" (1975), pamphlet in possession of Rye Historical Society, Rye, New York, 8; and Baird, *History of Rye*, 78, 83. For the clergy, see Book of the Vestry Men and Churchwardens of the Parish of Rye, New York, 1710–1795, 132; William F. Dornbusch, *Index of Wills, Rye, Mamaroneck, Harrison*, 1967, 237; and Ellen Cotton McKay, *A History of the Rye Presbyterian Church* (Lancaster, Pa., 1957), 36–37, 52. For other notables, see Thomas J. Scharf, *History of Westchester County*, 2 vols. (1886), 2:662–63; Robert Bolton, *History of Westchester County*, 3d ed., 2 vols. (New York, 1905), 1:xvi; and New-York Historical Society, *The Letters and Papers of Cadwallader Colden*, vol. 9: *Additional Letters and Papers, 1749–1775* (New York, 1937), 136, 156.

34. Samuel Tillinghast Diary, September 13, 1759, Newport Historical Society, Newport, Rhode Island.

35. *Providence Gazette*, October 27, 1764, 3; *Boston Post-Boy & Advertiser*, November 5, 1764, 2; *New York Gazette & Weekly Post-Boy*, November 8, 1764, 2.

36. See newspapers cited in note 35. All report the same story. "Ide" is the correct spelling of the name, although it was reported in the newspapers as Hyde or Hide. See Systematic History Fund—Vital Records of Attleborough to 1850 (1934), 154, and the pamphlet "Ide Family Genealogy," 4, manuscript at Old Bay Colony Historical Society. Two Boston newspapers (the *Boston Gazette & Country Journal*, October 29, 1764, and the *Boston Post-Boy & Advertiser*, October 29, 1764, and July 22, 1765) erroneously reported that Simeon Washburn had also died in the riot. Perhaps Washburn was one of the wounded, for he continued to buy and sell land after the incident and personally appeared in county court at Taunton to sign a land deed on October 31, 1765. See Bristol County Land Records, Probate Court, Taunton, Massachusetts, Grantor vol. 50:136 (hereafter BCLR).

37. *Providence Gazette*, October 27, 1764, 3; *Massachusetts Province Laws, 1750–1751*, 544–46. Goebel and Naughton, *Law Enforcement in Colonial New York*, did not uncover any evidence of 1 George I c.5, the Riot Act of 1714, being used in New York. They felt it was "a necessary condition to a prosecution of the rioters as felons" in England. "Colonial officials treated English statutory precedents as if they were the equivalent of the common law precedent which they were free to imitate." Despite the absence of the Riot Act, officials still referred to them as "riots" composed of "rioters" (ibid., 122–24). Although a violation of the Act was a felony in England, the colonies used their own statutes as the basis for indictments for riot.

38. *Newport Mercury*, November 8, 1764, 3. The name of the justice could not be found. It could have been King's Attorney Samuel White or any of the following: George Leonard Sr. or Jr., Ephraim Leonard, or James Williams. See *History of Bristol County* (Philadelphia, 1883), 891. For Samuel White and Ralph Davol, see *Two Men of Taunton* (Taunton, Mass., 1912), 65, 150, 153; and *Providence Gazette*, October 27, 1764, 3.

39. Francis Wayland Shepardson, "The Shepardson Family," paper delivered at the Old Bay Colony Historical Society, Taunton, Massachusetts, August 15, 1912, 1–10 (on deposit there); BCLR Grantor 49:184, December 31, 1764. The Shepardsons left sometime between the birth of their child on February 17, 1765, and the opening up of new grants in Templeton on September 25, 1765. Shepardson, "The Shepardson Family," 8. See also Hamilton D. Hurd, *History of Worcester City, Massachusetts*, 2 vols. (Philadelphia, 1889), 1:125. Shepardson had subsequent dealings in Attleborough. In April and May 1766, two legal actions were taken on his behalf. A warrant was served against Jedidiah Freeman for nonpayment of two notes due Sheppardson in August and December 1764, for £5.16s and £6.13s.4d. In May the court ruled Freeman had to pay up by October 1766. May 1766 term, Inferior Court of Common Pleas Records, vol. 8 (1762–67), 322, housed at Bristol County Court House, Taunton, Massachusetts.

40. Shepardson, "The Shepardson Family," 8; Records, Town of Attleboro, 1699–1777, 44; and *Vital Records of Attleborough to 1850 and Town of Attleborough I. (1695–1844)*, 45, last two at Attleboro Public Library. Will of Benjamin Ide Sr., March 30, 1752.

41. Inventory of estate of Benjamin Ide Jr., August 14, 1765, 19:95–97. See also Complaint of Joseph Barnard, husband of Elizabeth Ide, daughter of Benjamin, November 20, 1773, in Bristol County Probate Records, Probate Building, Taunton (division accomplished March 13, 1773), 24:328–29; Vital Records of Attleboro to 1850, 496, Attleboro Public Library.

42. *Newport Mercury,* November 9, 1764, 2; *Providence Gazette,* November 10, 1764, 2.

43. Dirk Hoerder, "Mobs and People: Crowd Action in Massachusetts During the Revolution, 1765–1780" (Ph.D. diss., Free University of Berlin, 1971), 111–13.

44. *New York Gazette & Weekly Post-Boy,* November 8, 1764, 3.

45. Ibid.; Plk 341, January 19, 1765, Hall of Records, Manhattan County, New York; Letter from Mrs. Elizabeth Clarke, January 1765, Kempe Papers, Box C–F.

46. Kempe Papers, Box G–L, "Riot & Assault 31 Oct. 1765" (date is in error; it should be 1764).

47. Ibid.

48. H. R. Parch. 140, B4, January 19, 1765, Manhattan Hall of Records.

49. Kempe Papers, Box G–L, "Riot & Assault 31 Oct. 1765 [1764]."

50. AR-DCCH no. 8139, 10465 for the assaults.

51. Kempe Papers, Box G–L, "Riot & Assault 31 Oct. 1765 [1764]."

52. Letter from Mrs. Elizabeth Clarke, January 1765, Kempe Papers, Box C–F.

53. Letter from Lewis Tappan to John Tabor Kempe, January 1765, Kempe Papers, Box G–L.

54. William Humphrey to William Kempe, September 12, 1754, Kempe Papers, Box M–Q.

55. John Tabor Kempe to William Humphrey, January 14, 1765, Kempe Papers, Box G–L.

56. Kempe filed all the charges on January 19, 1765, Plk 341 and H. R. Parch. 140 B4, Manhattan Hall of Records. Lanah Vandewater could also have been Lewis.

57. See Joyce Goodfriend, *Before the Melting Pot: Society and Culture in Colonial New York, 1664–1730* (Princeton: Princeton University Press, 1975).

58. Plk 806, June 11, 1765, Manhattan Hall of Records. MBSCJ-NY 1764–67 (Rough), 81, Manhattan Hall of Records, July 31, 1765. At least Dutchess County Court Records show no previous convictions for Higby, Johnson, Mick, Myers, or Schooner. Isaac Lawson (nos. 663, 3780), Peter Lawson (no. 97), Abraham Lent (no. 7709, 8015), Isaac Lent (no. 6752), and Daniel Hausbrook (nos. 8068, 9682) were all involved in minor civil litigation, mostly nonpayment of debts. Numbers refer to cases at AR-DCCH.

59. Of numerous sources on New York land riots, see Edward Countryman, *A People in Revolution: The American Revolution and Political Society in New York, 1760–1790* (Baltimore: Johns Hopkins University Press, 1981), esp. 47–55; and Thomas Humphrey, "Agrarian Rioting in Backcountry New York: Tenants, Landlords, and the American Revolution in the Hudson Valley" (Ph.D. diss., Northern Illinois University, 1996).

60. *New York Gazette & Weekly Post-Boy,* July 11, 1765, 3. There is no record of the riot in the New Jersey Historical Society or in the Essex County Hall of Records, both in Newark.

61. Kempe Papers, Kempe Charges, Box P–U. There is no record of the case in the Manhattan Hall of Records. For comparable crowds led by leading citizens, see Leonard L. Richards, *"Gentlemen of Property and Standing": Anti-Abolition Riots in Jacksonian America* (New York: Oxford University Press, 1970).

62. *New York Gazette & Weekly Mercury,* April 18, 1768, 2. No record exists of any women in custody being released on bail for this crime in the "Bail Records: 1733–1770," file no. 305 in Monmouth County Hall of Records, Freehold, New Jersey.

63. Kempe Papers, Deposition of Barbara Lyneall, October 21, 1768, Box G–L. There is no record of this case in the Manhattan Hall of Records.

64. See especially the works of Young, Shaw, and Hoerder cited in editor's introduction to this article and in notes 25 and 43.

65. John Duffy, *Epidemics in Colonial America* (Baton Rouge: Louisiana State University Press, 1971), 164–78; conversation with Dr. William Truscott, August 4, 1981, Lansdale, Pennsylvania.

66. Much misinformation exists about the "Dayton Measles Affair." Three historians of Suffolk County have erroneously dated it as occurring after the Revolution: Benjamin F. Thompson, *History of Long Island* (New York, 1839), 198; Nathaniel S. Prime, *History of Long Island* (New York, 1845), 173; and Henry P. Hedges, *A History of the Town of East Hampton* (Sag Harbor, 1897), 195–96. They also state that the famous Aaron Burr was Dayton's lawyer. Mary-Jo Kline, editor of the Burr Papers, stated that Burr could not have been involved as he was not a lawyer and only sixteen years old in 1772. For Dayton (1744–1802), see *Dictionary of American Biography* (New York: Charles Scribner's Sons, 1928), 3:314–15. In 1772, Dayton resided in Coram, New York, not Bethany, Connecticut, where he later lived. He was not just a "peddler of geegaws," but a well-to-do merchant who had given up teaching and started a successful business.

67. Hervey Garrett Smith, "Patriot Peddler," *Long Island Forum* 38 (April 1975), 67; Ebenezer Dayton, "A Serious Poem," May 18, 1769, no. 11233, and "A Concise Poetical Body of Divinity," June 23, 1769, no. 11232, both in Charles M. Evans, *American Bibliography* (Chicago: Blakeley Press, 1903–34), on microfilm in Clifford K. Shipton, ed., *Early American Imprints* (Worcester, Mass.: American Antiquarian Society, 1959).

68. All the information in this case, except where otherwise noted, comes from fifty-six depositions in the Kempe Papers, Box BSW 4.

69. No kin relationship between Ebenezer and Henry Dayton has been proven, although one is possible.

70. Henry P. Hedges, *Records of the Town of East Hampton* (New York, 1889), 4:228–29 (April 7, 1772).

71. See the case marked "Ebenezer Dayton vs. Henry Parsons and 16 Others," June 19, 1772, in Kempe Papers, Box BSW 4 (hereafter cited as Kempe Charges).

72. Those charged were Henry Parsons, Merry Parsons, Samuel Russell, Stephen Russell, Anamias Mulford, Ezekiel Mulford, Barnabas Mulford, Jeremiah Conklin, Jacob Conklin, Henry Chatfield, Lewis Chatfield, Daniel Hedges, Jeremiah Hedges Jr., John Davis, Abraham Gardiner, David Fithien, and Daniel Dayton. Thomas Hicks to J. T. Kempe, September 4, 1772; John Chatfield to Kempe, September 16, 1772, Kempe Charges. See also the following item in Surrogates Court, Manhattan Hall of Records: George Muirson to J. T. Kempe, HR Pleadings Plk 18.

73. Manhattan Hall of Records, HR Pleadings Plk 18. The three additional names were subsequently dropped from charges. J. T. Kempe to Thomas Hicks, August 16, 1773, Kempe Charges. "Minutes of the Supreme Court of Judicature," April 21, 1772–January 17, 1776, SC7, 110, mentions on July 31, 1773, that the upcoming Circuit Court was to be held at Southold on September 29, Paul Klapper Library, Queens College, Queens, New York. The Circuit Court records have not been located and probably do not survive.

74. George Muirson to J. T. Kempe, July 20, 1772, Kempe Charges.

75. Kempe Pre-Trial Notes, Kempe Papers, Box BSW 4.

76. Despite the lack of Circuit Court records, all of Kempe's correspondence corroborates that a trial was held on that date. There is no record of any trial in "Supreme Court Records, 1660–1840," Suffolk County Court Records, County Center, Riverhead, New York; Kempe Charges and Kempe Pre-Trial Notes, Kempe Papers, Box BSW 4.

77. For the cost of the trial and damages paid, and information in this and the next two paragraphs, see Kempe's Bill in Kempe Charges, especially Richard Morris and Samuel Jones to J. T. Kempe, November 26, 1773, and Kempe Pre-Trial Notes, Kempe Papers, Box BSW 4. In the bill, Kempe itemized the financial damages to Dayton, and arrived at a total bill. He felt additional compensation was owed Dayton for other damages, but never wrote out a bill for them.

78. See sources cited in note 66 above. Hedges (*A History of the Town of East Hampton*, 195–96) indicates that a guilty verdict had been passed on a Chatfield whose father had to raise money to pay his fine by selling the family estate, Chatfield Hill, on the main road from East Hampton to Sag Harbor.

79. For information on Dayton's role in the Revolution, see H. G. Smith, "Patriot Peddler," 67; Frederic G. Mather, *The Refugees of 1776 from Long Island to Connecticut* (Albany, N.Y., 1913), 326, 992; Orville Ackerly, "Ebenezer Dayton: A Revolutionary Character" (1903), typescript at the Suffolk County Historical Society, Riverhead, New York; *Riverhead News,* July 18, 1903, 2; T. L. Montgomery, ed., *Pennsylvania Archives,* 5th ser., vol. 1 (Harrisburg, 1906), 652–53; Elizabeth J. Lines, *Bethany and Its Hills* (New Haven, 1905), 24; Israel P. Warren, *Chauncy Judd; or The Stolen Boy* (New York, 1874), 281–82 (for an account of a young boy kidnapped by the raiders); Ebenezer Dayton, "Affidavit," Long Island Collection, Queens Borough Central Library, Jamaica, New York (typescript), provided courtesy of David Erhardt of that library.

80. Genealogical records indicate marriages between the Seaman and Birdsall families both before and after the riot. See Mary T. Seaman, *The Seaman Family in America* (New York, 1928), 59–60, 81, 84; and John Seaman's Will in *New-York Historical Society Collections—Abstracts of Wills, 1780–1782,* vol. 10 (New York, 1901), 222. Other members of the crowd were Joseph Birdsall, Samuel Seaman, Pearcy Pool, Richard Totten, Anthony Wright, William Powell, Thomas Powell, and Jacob Pratt. See Kempe Charges, Kempe Papers, Box BSW 7, which contains Charges, Notes, and Depositions. This is the source for all information about the riot not otherwise noted.

81. Letter from (pretended) John Seaman to J. T. Kempe, January 17, 1774. Kempe supposed it was written by Birdsall, Kempe Papers, Box BSW 7; Kempe Notes, Box 4.

82. J. T. Kempe to John Seaman, March 2, 1774; Seaman to Kempe, April 5, 1774, Kempe Papers, Box BSW 7.

83. John Jay to J. T. Kempe, "received" May 5, 1775; John Seaman to Kempe, June 21, 1775; Kempe to Jay, August 21, 1775, and September 2, 1775. All in Kempe Papers, Box BSW 7. There is no record of this case in the Manhattan Court of Records or the "Minutes of the Supreme Court of Judicature, April 21, 1772–January 17, 1776," SC 7, Paul Klapper Library, Queens County, Queens, New York.

84. John Demos, "Families in Colonial America: An Exercise in Historical Demography," *William & Mary Quarterly,* 3d ser., 25 (January 1968), 56–57.

85. Flaherty, "Crime and Law Enforcement," 222, 245–46.

86. Ibid., 232–33, 245, 246, 248.

87. Michael Zuckerman, *Peaceable Kingdoms: New England Towns in the Eighteenth Century* (New York: Knopf, 1970), 86–87.

88. Flaherty, "Crime and Law Enforcement," 223.

89. Greenberg, *Crime and Law Enforcement in Colonial New York,* 148.

90. Ibid., 161; Zuckerman, *Peaceable Kingdoms,* 245.

91. Palmer, "Discordant Music."

4

The Rise of Rough Music

Reflections on an Ancient New Custom in Eighteenth-Century New Jersey

Brendan McConville

"We hear," reported the *New York Weekly Post Boy* in 1752, "that an odd Sect of People have lately appeared [at Elizabethtown, New Jersey] who go under the Denomination of Regulars." The group numbered "near a Dozen," who "dress themselves in Women's Cloaths, and painting their Faces, go in the Evening to the Houses of such as are reported to have beat their wives." The group would grab the abuser, "strip him, turn up his Posterior, and flog him with Rods most severely, crying out all the Time, Wo to the Men that beat their Wives." "It seems," continued the *Post Boy* correspondent, "that several Persons in that Borough (and tis said some very deservedly) have undergone the Discipline, to the no small Terror of others, who are any Way conscious of deserving the same."[1]

The behavior of the Elizabethtown Regulars was representative of a body of Anglo-American customs known collectively as "rough music." These customs functioned as a popular extralegal means of policing the boundaries of political, social, and sexual normalcy in early modern society. This chapter examines the uses of rough music in eighteenth-century New Jersey. At least four communities—Elizabethtown (1752), an unnamed town (1753), Newark (1765 and 1770), and Bound Brook (1770)—reported repeated incidents of these customs in the period between 1750 and 1776. Specifically, it is my contention that in New Jersey rough music seems to have been most common in areas settled by New Englanders; that rough music was used primarily against adulterous and abusive men; that rough music became more common after 1750 as the society experienced a period of disorder; and that some among the American gentry interpreted rough music as a threat to their authority, a challenge that became explicit when revolutionary crowds used these customs against royal officials.

There is no detailed study of rough music in colonial America, perhaps because so many historians have accepted without question that the predominance of Calvinism in New England and the Middle Colonies inhibited the transfer of English plebeian culture to North America. Only recently have a few scholars begun to examine the appearance of English plebeian customs in eighteenth-century America, and they rely heavily on English studies to interpret the few incidents of rough music that have come to light.[2] However, a preliminary comparison of rough music on both sides of the Atlantic indicates that the radically different social conditions in the American colonies significantly altered the use and meaning of the customs.

Recent studies of rough music in England reveal an array of extrainstitutional rituals intended to confine sexuality (particularly female sexuality) within marriage, maintain gender boundaries, and uphold the rigid patriarchy of premodern society.[3] Convention dictated that men should rule forcefully in their homes and that couples should confine sexuality within marriage. Common people (often young men) used noise, processions, physical intimidation, and, in some cases, brutal violence to inform individuals or couples that their behavior had violated customary or common law. In Devon, troublemakers witnessed bloody, ritualistic "stag hunts" that ended outside their own homes. In Wiltshire, "wooset-hunters" paraded night after night in noisy procession past the dwellings of adulterous couples. In some areas, young men performed rough music, beating wooden spoons on tins outside the bedchambers of newlyweds whose premarital relationships had a whiff of scandal. And throughout England, scolds and cuckolds found themselves tied to poles and dragged through the streets while children hurled filth at them. Called "riding the stang" in the north of England, this custom was also known as "riding the wooden horse" and "riding skimmington."[4] At least one study suggests that communities singled out scolds in particular because they disrupted the normal workings of a patriarchal society.[5] English common folk routinely used rough music to uphold the pillars of patriarchy when reality failed to reflect convention.[6]

Forms of rough music successfully crossed the Atlantic by 1700 and were part of a colonial popular culture that was more traditional and thus more tumultuous than historians have previously imagined.[7] Consider, for example, the "throwing of the stocking" at the 1736 nuptials of a Baptist couple of New England descent in Monmouth County, New Jersey. This custom, part of the broader family of activities labeled "rough music" by historians, celebrated marriage. "In the after part of the day," wrote Jonathan Holmes, one of the guests, "I went unto John Boords . . . it being wedding times there." A frolic followed the ceremony, at which "the young folks was a Showing tricks" in a colonial Puritan version of a French charivari, the custom of playfully (usually) tormenting newlyweds.[8] "The Groom and the Bride," wrote the amused Holmes, "Luckely Slipt into bed, and fastened the doore." But in a house filled with guests determined on playful torment, the new couple were far from safe. "Some notice was given," wrote Holmes "of the matter before the groom was gott to bed. Some indeavoured to peep but the females hindred us with a Seeming desire to have all to themselves & that while the groom was undressing."

The guests soon hatched a plan to break into the wedding chamber: "Some said that they would open the door and Se if the brid was rightly put to bed and would throw the stocken." The locked passage blocked them until "after some time the wind rose . . . that drew the window Shett opne & a person jumpd in and opened the doore, then all hands in a seeking the brides stocking which after a while I found in my hand & an other I found under the bed nere where the good order logg lay."[9] Not one to let an opportunity pass, Holmes "then [took] to throwing the Stocking of her Some threw I threw and hit the brides nose, which made a lafter, and of her we had done I saluted the bride and bid the couple not to forget fulfilling the first commandment."[10] The stocking-throwers upheld, with humor, the rule that sexual expression be confined to marriage.[11] They supported, rather than challenged, the bonding of the couple, albeit in a manner designed to embarrass as much as to encourage. The guests' behavior at this Monmouth County wedding suggests that colonial popular culture was more lively than historians have previously suspected.

After 1750, rough music rituals considerably more violent than the throwing of the stocking were performed in the New Jersey towns of Newark, Elizabethtown, and Bound Brook as local plebeians sought to maintain order in their society. The newspaper accounts through which we know about these incidents of rough music are relatively sparse in their descriptions—we are uncertain even of the number of incidents—but the accounts do suggest patterns of change in the use of the custom, and the broader factors that encouraged the rise of rough music. Important differences distinguished colonial perceptions of good order from those of English society, differences that explain why rough music developed a new character in New Jersey, and indeed throughout much of British North America.

The transplanting of rough music to North America changed one key aspect of its use. In New Jersey, and apparently in other colonies as well, violent and adulterous husbands, rather than scolds or cuckolds, became the primary targets of rough music.[12] That was the case in Newark, Elizabethtown, and Bound Brook. The influence of Calvinism, particularly in its Puritan form, may best explain this change. In the areas of New Jersey populated by New Englanders, rough music was a means of upholding community values. Gangs of men ostracized excessively violent or adulterous husbands when other means of controlling them weakened under the stress of change.

From the sixteenth century onward, Puritan preachers dedicated to creating a godly society tried to alter traditional gender relationships. Ministers inculcated in women the belief that good wives should obey their husbands. In the ideal Puritan family, sober and levelheaded men would not need to use violence to control their wives, and neither spouse would engage in adultery.[13] The Great Migration helped turn these beliefs into the dominant ethos of a new society

Calvinism and the migration to New England encouraged other changes that further delegitimated domestic violence. In particular, New England Puritanism transformed a popular culture that had hitherto been filled with images of violent and unruly women. While the degree to which American Puritans suppressed folk belief has been exaggerated, Puritans frowned on the bawdy folktales that depicted evil stepmothers or cuckolding wives ruling whimpering husbands.[14] The suppression of such longstanding popular beliefs weakened the view that women connived to control men and therefore had to be violently dominated. Similarly, the scarcity of a genre of English popular crime literature that often portrayed women murdering men contributed to a reconceptualization of gender relationships in the New England colonies in the seventeenth century.[15]

Clearly, women remained subordinate and violence against women sometimes gained official sanction, as in the sporadic witch trials of that century.[16] But generally the pulpit had begun to replace the rod as a legitimate tool of controlling women.

Demographic realities may well have reinforced these changing perceptions. During the first decades of settlement, considerably more men than women lived in New England, although the ratios were not nearly as skewed as they were in the Chesapeake.[17] These unbalanced sex ratios may have encouraged restraint in the behavior of men toward women in the formative years of the New England colonies, much as male behavior toward women temporarily changed in the seventeenth-century Chesapeake.[18]

The laws of the New England colonies embodied these changed beliefs. Women could and did go to court if their husbands beat or otherwise abused them. Spousal abuse or adultery might well be punished with fines, whippings, or even the dreaded scarlet letter.[19] It is far from clear whether this modified patriarchy actually improved the overall position of women in the Puritan colonies or merely reconstructed patriarchal oppression. Certainly women continued to suffer domestic abuse. However, New Englanders perceived that all disorder needed to be controlled, not just that perpetrated by domineering women. To Puritans, violent husbands seemed to be as serious a threat to a godly society as scolds, and the legal system tried to control unruly men.[20]

As migrants from Puritan New England settled much of New Jersey, it is not surprising that they brought with them the laws and customs of the colonies to the north, including those governing domestic violence. Beginning in the 1660s, New Englanders established settlements across northern and eastern New Jersey, and their descendants dominated numerous communities in the colony well into the eighteenth century.[21] New Jersey's legal code paralleled that of New England, although that cultural influence was tempered somewhat by the presence of Scottish, Dutch, and Quaker populations.[22] When New England Puritans founded the town of Newark in 1666, their leaders declared that the people of the new community would be governed by "such orders and Law whilst they are settled here by themselves as they had in the Place from whence they came."[23] While court records for seventeenth-century New Jersey are relatively sparse, we do know, for example, that in 1694 Doctor Henry Greenland appeared in the Middlesex Court of quarter sessions on behalf of his daughter Frances to complain that she had been abused by her husband, Daniel Brynson. The case illustrates that violent husbands were subject to legal sanction in the colony during the seventeenth century.[24] These values were still preached in New Jersey in the 1750s.[25] Esther Edwards Burr, daughter of one important New England Calvinist preacher, and wife of another, recalled hearing a sermon entitled "Husbands love your Wives; and let the Wife see that she reverence her husband."[26] These norms were part of an ethos brought from New England that would inform and even encourage the use of rough music against violent men.

By the mid-eighteenth century, New Jersey had begun to visibly change, and these changes seem to have encouraged domestic violence and institutional weakness.[27] The rise of rough music at Newark, Elizabethtown, and Bound Brook was one of the responses to these changes. It is unclear exactly how the rough-music gangs were formed or why they choose to perform rough music the way they did. But the broader conditions that encouraged their actions are apparent.

It is impossible to understand the rise of domestic abuse and the subsequent rise of rough music in response to it apart from profound changes in the colony's legal system. Throughout the first three-quarters of the eighteenth century, the colonial bench and bar underwent a dramatic transformation that was accelerating in the 1740s just as rough music seems to have become more common. The untrained judges and part-time lawyers of the seventeenth century, who were usually drawn from the local community and thus familiar with local values, were gradually replaced by professionally trained gentlemen lawyers. These men introduced a more complex legal code and a highly stylized ritual system modeled on that of London's Inns of Court. This anglicization of the legal system was itself connected to the introduction of a more authority-driven, hierarchical notion of patriarchy that alienated a significant portion of the yeomanry in the northern colonies. A recent study of women and the law in Connecticut demonstrates that one effect of these changes was that battered and abused women gradually lost their ability to seek legal redress, and I believe that the same was true in all the British colonies, particularly those north of Pennsylvania.[28]

An intense period of violence over property rights was weakening New Jersey's royal legal system at the very time these broader changes in the working of the bench and bar were occurring. The inability of the colony's population to agree on the origins of property rights led to decades of diffuse violence punctuated by a violent upheaval that began in 1745 and continued for seven years.[29] The people of the towns of Newark and Elizabethtown (both of which saw rough-music gangs in the 1750s and 1760s) were leaders in this prolonged struggle against the gentry's property claims. The gentry-dominated courts ceased to function for periods during the property upheaval.[30] In June 1755, Esther Edwards Burr of Newark wrote: "To day the Court sets. There has not been a Supream Court held in this County this seven years till now."[31] The idea of a unified society where the legal system represented collective values never truly recovered from the breakdown of the 1740s and 1750s.

The rise of rough music cannot be understood merely as a product of changes in the legal system or the property disputes. There were other changes at work that would weaken traditional behavioral controls and perhaps encourage men to turn to rough music to control domestic violence. The shared spiritual faiths that bound the communities together in the seventeenth century declined in the eighteenth century. As early as 1705, aggressive missionaries from the Society for the Propagation of Gospel in Foreign Parts (SPG) planted Anglican churches in East Jersey's New England towns, and these attracted the colony's emergent patricians. The older Congregational, Presbyterian, and Baptist churches slowly came to be dominated by common people, a trend greatly accelerated by the Great Awakening, which itself split these congregations.[32] The resulting religious and social polarization weakened the religious codes that had played such an important role in maintaining the fabric of community life. A map of Newark town lots prepared in 1776 suggests the degree of bitterness and division caused by religious change, for it lists landowners by religion, graphically portraying the spiritual and geographic polarization of the community.[33] The authority of Puritan churches had been significantly weakened, and as a result church censure was increasingly ineffective as a means of encouraging acceptable behavior. As watchfulness collapsed, a host of social problems arose, including an apparent rise in domestic violence.[34]

The growth of anonymous commercial networks may also have encouraged domestic violence, if the experiences of one East Jersey family are any indication. In that family, the purchase of tea sets, and tea consumption by the wife, was interpreted by her often drunken husband as a challenge to his authority.[35] He met this challenge with violence, and members of the community responded to his abusive behavior with rough music. "I have," wrote his battered wife in 1753, "for some Years past borne, with uncommon Patience, the lashes of an ill-natur'd Husband." He "made it a Practice, to stay at a Slop-Shop till he had drowned his Senses in Rum, his Darling Delight, and then poor I must stand clear." The wife's tea sets, an increasingly common consumer good of the period, became part of the battleground where the tension between the couple and the changes in the broader society met. "The merciless Wretch," complained his bitter wife, "wou'd spare neither my Tea Cups or Saucers to throw at my Head, besides whipping me." She sarcastically remarked that "he always had Compassion on the Rum Glasses . . . and tho' we have had but two of those Glasses for these Eight or Ten Years . . . they have liv'd to see as many Dozen of Tea Cups and Saucers broke over my Head." The husband tried to force her to drink tea out of the rum glasses, but she refused, "his destroying of 'em has brought me so low, that I have no more Apparel than I at present have on, and I will have Tea Cups and Saucers if I pawn my very Shift; for I must own I love Tea as well as he loves Rum." Only the intervention of a group of "Regulators" using rough music saved her from more beatings. "My Case," she wrote "being happily nois'd abroad, induced several generous young Men to discipline him. . . . They have regulated my dear Husband, and the rest of the bad ones hereabout."[36]

Consumption of luxury goods significantly altered gender relationships in colonial America, but the contours of these changes is still clear. In this case, the transformation of the home into a setting for the heavily ritualized consumption of tea may have been perceived by the husband as a threat to his control of his wife and his domestic environment. While not strictly feminine, the attendant ritual of teatime provided women with an opportunity to gather groups of friends to talk, gossip, and no doubt in the case of this particular New Jersey wife, to complain about an abusive husband.[37] Such groups provided a counterbalance to the masculine, tavern-centered culture where this abused woman's husband consumed large quantities of rum. Rum glasses thus became symbolic of an older, more masculine set of social assumptions, which appeared to be under assault by commercial forces that were encouraging a feminization of some aspects of society, as represented by the importation of tea and tea sets into America.[38]

Two results of these broader changes were an apparent increase in domestic violence and a corresponding increase in rough music after 1735.[39] In January 1736/7, Jonathan Holmes, a man of New England descent, calmly recorded a visit with "J. Reids—with John Stanley Bowne & Andrew

McCoy & drank sider. . . . I heard of a fashion that was in their parts to Whip the women. John MacConnen whiped his wife in 4 or 5 days twenty times, John Tyler, William Terry and John Rogers was not so apt to whip their wives although they did sometimes."[40] In 1755, Esther Edwards Burr of Puritan Newark reported the flight of Mary Ogden Banks from an abusive husband. "She was in," Burr reported, "to bid me farewel and said she was ruened soul and body, and cryed as if her heart would break, and I cry'd two." Burr was disgusted by such abuse, and she thanked heaven that "it was not my portion to be Bound to such a Beast, Nay Devil he is more like."[41] In 1774, the wife of John Ludeman of Newark complained to the New York newspapers of the "unnatural and beastly usage" she received from her husband, which had occasioned her flight to New England. While this woman used standard legal language, she closed her letter with a request for "all of those who are interested in virtue" to "avenge my injuries, which call load for vengeance, and bring him to public shame."[42] This sort of literary evidence is hardly conclusive about levels of abuse in the parts of eastern New Jersey settled by New Englanders, but it does suggest that domestic violence (and adultery) were problems, that contemporaries recorded them as such, and that in these cases traditional social institutions were unable to deal with the abuse.

The chronological and geographic distribution of rough-music incidents strongly suggests a connection between the broader changes in the society and the use of forms of vigilante violence to combat a perceived breakdown of order in the family. Rough-music gangs became active around 1750, and a considerable (though indeterminate) number of rough-music incidents occurred for certain in the towns of Newark, Bound Brook, and Elizabethtown in this period. All these communities were originally settled by New Englanders, and all were enmeshed in the violent property disputes. A 1753 letter to the *Pennsylvania Gazette* from an Elizabethtown wife declared that she had fled her husband's home because "her life was in danger from the ill usage she received from him,"[43] while an account of rough music in East Jersey in the same year depicted a husband "drowned . . . in Rum" beating his wife until a band of Regulators intervened and whipped him.[44] The chronology of rough music provides further evidence of a relationship to the property disputes. Rough music erupted in these towns first between 1750 and 1755 and then again between 1765 and 1770. The former period was one of widespread rioting, while the latter coincided with renewed rioting over property ownership and a general economic crisis caused by a shortage of paper money.[45] When formal institutions faltered, custom became a primary means of maintaining order in some New Jersey communities.

The behavior of many of the rough-music gangs strongly suggests a self-conscious usurping of institutional authority, particularly of the legal system, in localized efforts to stem domestic violence. In East Jersey the law called for punishment of adultery by divorce, banishment, and, most common, whippings. Traditionally, adulterous men received thirty-nine lashes, as under Mosaic law,[46] and the rough-music gangs seemed to have adopted a crude version of this ritual of punishment. It was usual for the Regulars at Elizabethtown to assault an adulterous or abusive husband, "strip him, . . . and flog him most severely."[47] In 1753 an East Jersey wife complained of a husband "whipping me" until a band of "Regulators" violently corrected his behavior.[48] Twelve years later, Newark Township's "Disciplinarians" whipped a husband they thought overly jealous, only to turn on his wife and her lover after discovering that her husband's fears of adultery were well grounded.[49] At Bound Brook in 1770, rough music against violent men reached a dramatic climax when a group whipped William Daniel to death after he had mistreated his wife.[50] By adopting whipping, the form of punishment used by the legal system, the rough-music gangs emulated, and in a sense even supplanted, the courts.

The same general pattern of rough music appeared in other parts of the northern colonies, suggesting that the change in behavior of New Jersey's rough-music gangs was in part tied to broader transformations in British North America. Violent or adulterous husbands were the targets of rough music in other eighteenth-century colonies as well.[51] In the 1760s, New York City, Rhode Island, and Attleborough, Massachusetts, saw violent and unfaithful husbands receive whippings at the hands of rough-music gangs.[52] The widespread geographic distribution of the redirected custom suggests that many factors worked to transform the use of rough music in America, but in the case of New Jersey the persistence of Puritan values in some towns best explains this change.

Ideally, a shared faith, submission to authority, and the placing of corporate interests before the interests of the individual bound Puritan (and indeed all premodern) communities together. But by the 1740s, community life had grown factional and disjointed as changes in the legal system, rioting, religious schisms, and consumption combined to weaken the institutional structure of the society. When the legal system faltered, some Jerseymen used rough music to try to reestablish the integrity of the modified patriarchy in which they lived.

Colonial rough music was intended to preserve an existing order. By using rough music to discipline men who stepped over accepted boundaries of behavior, Jerseymen reaffirmed those boundaries and their own understanding of the appropriate working of patriarchy. But as the broader context in which they acted changed, their actions took on new meanings.

In a world where the king was the symbolic father of the political family, anything that denied or usurped the power of the patriarch was potentially subversive. Rough music had many potential meanings, depending on the specific context. As it became more common in a changing social and political world, the latent antipatriarchal character of rough music became more apparent, and patricians began denouncing such rituals.[53] The advent of the imperial crisis led to the overt politicization of rough music, as crowds threatened local magistrates with the wooden horse and other forms of ritualistic abuse. By 1770, observers among the gentry saw these rituals as part of the broader challenge to imperial authority. What began as a customary effort to reinforce existing norms became symptomatic of a contest over whose notions of normalcy would predominate in the colony.

Patrician fears about rough music grew not out of the perception that it represented disorder but rather from the recognition that it represented a vision of justice independent of their control. New Jersey's largely Anglican and Quaker gentry emerged as a coherent social group only after 1710.[54] As they struggled to impose their hierarchical social vision on an unruly society through an increasingly anglicized court system, they became suspicious of anything that challenged that vision.[55] Rough-music rituals did exactly that, expressing popular perceptions of justice based on the Puritan heritages of the New Jersey towns.

The gentry's increasing anxiety about rough music can be traced through their published reaction to the East Jersey incidents between 1750 and 1770. The correspondent who reported rough music in Elizabethtown in 1752 treated the incidents in a lighthearted manner, wishing only "that in order for the more equal Distribution of Justice, there wou'd arise another Sect, under the Title of Regulatrixes who should dress themselves in Men's Cloathes, and flagilate the Posterior of the Scolds."[56] Such tolerant and apolitical attitudes were all but absent by 1770.

The turn toward condemnation of rough music proceeded slowly at first. A report in 1753 indicated that some elements in the society, almost certainly among the gentry, felt threatened by the rise of rough music. "Prudence Goodwife" reported that some people wanted to see the Regulators arrested for whipping her drunken, tea-hating husband. "Tho' there are some," wrote the woman, "that are afraid of whipping their Wives, for fear of dancing the same Jigg; yet I understand, they are not afraid of making application to have those dear Regulators indicted."[57] A writer commenting on the actions of the Newark "Disciplinarians," who performed rough music in 1765, declared their actions "unlawful Enterprises" that should cease immediately. The Newark gang, this writer insisted, would cause "fatal Consequences" if they did not stop. He immediately connected the activities of the gang to an incident of rough music in Rhode Island where the intended victim of a skimmington killed one of his attackers and "dangerously wound[ed] one or two more."[58] This critic saw rough music in New Jersey as signifying a general crisis of order. In 1770, rioters at Newark supposedly threatened to make the magistrates of that town ride skimmington.[59] What had seemed an anomalous farce in 1752 easily crossed the line and became a threat to the political authority of the gentry twenty years later.[60]

While it is impossible to derive precise motivations from actions alone, the transformation in the plebeian performance of rough music indeed suggests a challenge to the gentry on some level. Whereas the Regulars at Elizabethtown (1752) and the Disciplinarians at Newark (1765) performed rough music in disguise at night, the Bound Brook "Regulators" of 1770 and the Newark crowd of the same year whose members tried to make the magistrates ride the wooden horse appeared during daylight without disguise. The regulating gangs competed vigorously and ultimately openly with the legal system, and the gentry accordingly saw them as a threat.

The full political potential of rough music remained unrealized, for as long as these rites were directed against abusive husbands and philandering spouses. When common people began to threaten members of the gentry with rough music as punishment for perceived transgressions against the common good, however, the political potential and meaning of rough music became suddenly and dramatically apparent. The crowd action at Newark in 1770 in which a mob threatened to make magistrates ride the wooden horse illuminated this transition. The threatened rough music challenged a legal decision that awarded ownership of thousands of acres in the Newark interior to the Board of Proprietors of Eastern New Jersey, only the most recent in a succession of land title disputes that plagued colonial New Jersey. By threatening the magistrate with the wooden horse, the crowd seemed intent on correcting the behavior of the officials rather than displacing them. In this context, the wooden horse appeared to be a tool of tradition rather than subversion.

Yet the overt politicization of rough music can be seen in the same incident. The Newark "Liberty Boys," as the crowd called itself, consciously identified themselves with the New York Sons of Liberty. They insisted that they acted to defend their "Liberty and Property" as part of the broader Whig resistance to tyranny, thus integrating traditional customs and rituals of misrule into the symbolic system of a radical political movement.[61] Moreover, the people punished the court rather than reinforcing or supplanting it in the punishment of wrongdoers. In this context, rough music became subversive. The earlier adaptation of rough music for use against abusive domestic authority figures allowed for the easy use of the custom by the Whig political movement, a movement whose world view was shaped by a powerful antihierarchical political ideology.

The adaptation of a host of plebeian social customs to political ends seems to have occurred across the northern colonies after 1764. Alfred Young, Gary Nash, and Dirk Hoeder demonstrate how the drive to organize popular political support for resistance to the Stamp Act in Boston redirected and politicized the rituals associated with Pope's Day processions, shifting the emphasis away from their traditional anti-Catholic tendency and instead using the customs to protest the arbitrary use of power.[62] Indeed, as both Young and Peter Shaw have suggested, the latent antipatriarchal tendencies in plebeian rituals became apparent as resistance to imperial authority grew in the decade or so before 1776.[63]

The transformation of rough music from a social to a political phenomenon sheds light on the shadowy but important process through which personal experience and social perceptions become political attitudes. It may well be that an increase in domestic violence and general disorder gave republicanism (with its potent streak of antipatriarchal rhetoric) its appeal among some plebeians.[64] The breakdown of order that prompted rough music, the performance of the rituals themselves, and the increasingly hostile reactions of the gentry perhaps raised questions in plebeian minds about the ordering of society and the authority of the gentry themselves. While this process of politicization is poorly understood at present, further study of rough music in particular and plebeian culture more generally in eighteenth-century America may well tell us more about what common people believed they were fighting for in the Revolution and how they came to hold these beliefs. And while this chapter, with its limited geographic parameters and source base, can only suggest lines of inquiry, a more extensive examination of rough music in eighteenth-century America might illuminate how a host of changes—in law, gender relations, folk customs, politics, and religious life—were interrelated and acted to transform the society.

Rough music took on new direction and a new meaning when it was transplanted to New Jersey, tempering rather than expanding the authority of fathers and husbands in their families. After 1750, rough music became rather more common as disorder eroded institutional restraints on personal behavior. At first, common people turned to rough music to combat domestic violence when the court system failed to intervene. However, the latent subversion of a custom that limited patriarchal authority became ever more apparent during the imperial crisis as revolutionary crowds used rough music to intimidate and discipline imperial officials. As in so many other aspects of eighteenth-century life, European ideas and traditions became subversive in the American environment.

Notes

1. William A. Whitehead et al., ed., *Documents Relating to the Colonial, Revolutionary, and Post-Revolutionary History of the State of New Jersey* (*Archives of the State of New Jersey*, 1st Series, 1–42 [New Jersey, 1880–1949]) (hereafter cited as *NJA*), vol. 19: *Newspaper Extracts*, 3:225–26. For a New England episode where men dressed like women in order to engage in extralegal action, see Laurel Thatcher Ulrich, *Good Wives: Image and Reality in the Lives of Women in Northern New England, 1650–1750* (New York: Vintage Books, 1991), 195. Why men dressed as women is open to conjecture. The most prevalent explanation is that because the common law treated violent women differently (and allowed for greater latitude, because they were "only women"), men assumed this identity when engaged in extralegal action. The question of cross-dressing in the early modern period is complex. For the beginnings of a discussion, see Vern Bullough and Bonnie Bullough, *Cross-Dressing, Sex, and Gender* (Philadelphia: University of Pennsylvania Press, 1993); Kristina Straub, *Sexual Suspects: Eighteenth-Century Players and Sexual Ideology* (Princeton: Princeton University Press, 1992); and Peter Stallybrass, *The Politics and Poetics of Transgression* (Ithaca, N.Y.: Cornell University Press, 1986).

2. By far the best of the American studies is Alfred Young's "English Plebeian Culture and Eighteenth-Century American Radicalism," in James R. Jacob and Margaret C. Jacob, eds., *The Origins of Anglo-American Radicalism* (London: Humanity Books, 1991), 184–212. Young sees rough music becoming more common after 1750 and argues for a broad transfer of English plebeian culture to American shores in the latter half of the eighteenth century, in part because of growing disorder in American society. Other studies that address colonial rough music in-

clude Richard Maxwell Brown's "Violence and the American Revolution," in Stephen G. Kurtz and James H. Hutson, eds., *Essays on the American Revolution* (Chapel Hill, N.C.: Institute of Early American History and Culture, 1973), 81–120; Pauline Maier, *From Resistance to Revolution* (New York: W. W. Norton, 1972), 3–26; and Peter Shaw, *American Patriots and the Rituals of Revolution* (Cambridge, Mass.: Harvard University Press, 1981), 204–33. Also useful is Bryan Palmer's "Discordant Music: Charivari and White Capping in North America," *Labor/Le Traveilles* 1 (September 1978), 5–62.

3. For the best discussions of rough music in early modern England, see David Underdown, *Revel, Riot, and Rebellion* (New York: Oxford University Press, 1985), 100–103, 106, 110–11, 216, 265, 279; Martin Ingram, "Ridings, Rough Music, and Mocking Rhymes in Early Modern England," in Barry Reay, ed., *Popular Culture in Seventeenth-Century England* (New York: St. Martin's Press, 1985), 166–97; David Underdown, "The Taming of the Scold," in Anthony Fletcher and John Stevenson, eds., *Order and Disorder in Early Modern England* (New York: Cambridge University Press, 1985), 116–36; and E. P. Thompson, *Custom in Common* (New York: The New Press, 1991), 467–538. For Thompson on the conservative social character of rough music until the end of the eighteenth century, see ibid., 524. Thompson (516–31) goes on to argue convincingly that various types of rough music were adapted to political and industrial protest in the nineteenth century. A number of other studies have examined the use of similar customs in Europe. The best known of these are Natalie Davis, "Women on Top" and "The Reasons of Misrule," essays in her *Society and Culture in Early Modern France* (Stanford, Calif.: Stanford University Press, 1985), 97–151; and Peter Burke, *Popular Culture in Early Modern Europe* (New York: Harper & Row, 1978).

4. Thompson, *Custom in Common*, 467–75, 482. "Skimmington" seems to derive its name from a type of wooden ladle used to beat on pots during rough music processions. Underdown, "The Taming of the Scold," 116.

5. Susan D. Amussen, "Gender, Family, and the Social Order, 1560–1725," in Fletcher and Stevenson, eds., *Order and Disorder in Early Modern England*, 196–217.

6. Underdown, *Revel, Riot, and Rebellion*, 100–101.

7. For a deeper discussion of this culture, see Young, "English Plebeian Culture," 185–212; and Shaw, *American Patriots and the Rituals of Revolution*, 177–231.

8. Davis, "The Reasons of Misrule," 97–123.

9. Exactly what the "good order logg" was is unclear.

10. April 25, 1737, Diary of Jonathan Holmes, Holmes Family Papers, New Jersey Historical Society (hereafter referred to as NJHS). I believe this is actually a reference to the saying "Be fruitful and multiply," but that is just a guess.

11. John D'Emilio and Estelle B. Freedman, *Intimate Matters* (New York: Harper Trade, 1988), 16–26, discuss the ways in which colonial society tried to confine sexuality to marriage.

12. The question arises, What was done to scolds in North America? and in New England? John Murrin has brought a court case to my attention from Essex County, Massachusetts, in 1768 in which a women, Luce Pernah, was brought to court for nightwalking, scolding, and general disorderliness. This incident is recorded in Essex Sessions, 1764–77, pp. 152–64. Alice Morse Earle, writing one hundred years ago, indicated that the ducking of scolds was common in the middle and southern colonies but not in New England, a generalization I agree with; see Alice Morse Earle, *Curious Punishments of Bygone Days* (Chicago, 1896), 11–28. Earle goes on to maintain that New Englanders used cleft sticks and gags to punish scolds (101–5).

My claim that rough music was primarily directed against men should not be understood as a blanket statement. I have no doubt that scolds were the subject of popular derision and that from time to time they were the subject of different kinds of rough music. Murrin also pointed out a case from Essex, Massachusetts, where two mariners (sailors?) had assaulted a Marblehead widow, carried her on board their ship, ducked her several times (nearly drowning her), then painted her face and carried her ashore. Was she a scold? a prostitute? It is unclear. Essex Sessions, 1761–78, March 30, July 13, and December 28, 1762. Tom Humphrey, "Agrarian Rioting in Backcountry New York: Tenants, Landlords, and the American Revolution in the Hudson Valley" (Ph.D. diss., Northern Illinois University, 1996), has brought to light two more cases of rough music against women, in New York City, in which women dressed as men assaulted a woman they called a "whore" and cried out "Mob the whore!" It is worth noting that all three of these cases occurred in ports, reinforcing the idea that the ports were a place of popular cultural transmission and popular cultural transformation. James Jakson Deposition, March 1, 1754, New York City; The King agt Dorothy the Wife of William Tingue, October 22, 1766, in New York Supreme Court, J. T. Kempe Papers, Unsorted Lawsuits, NYHS. But the majority of cases of rough music we know about seem to be directed against abusive men, with a minority directed at adulterous husbands and couples. The same shift occurred in Europe in the late eighteenth and the early nineteenth centuries. See Thompson, *Customs in Common*, 508–14, 522, 529–30; and Davis, "Women on Top," 150.

13. Carol Karlsen, *The Devil in the Shape of a Woman* (New York: W. W. Norton, 1987), 160–66, gives a good brief account of the transformations worked by Puritanism on gender roles and the paradoxes of the supposed transformation. For the decline in legal protection for women, see C. Dallett Hemphill, "Women in Court . . . Salem, 1636–1783," *William & Mary Quarterly* 39 (January 1982), 164–75. English Puritans generally frowned on the excessive use of force by fathers in families. For a stimulating discussion, see Susan Amussen, " 'Being Stirred to Much Unquietness': Violence and Domestic Violence in Early Modern England," *Journal of Women's History* 6 (Summer 1994), 72.

14. Roger Thompson, *Sex in Middlesex: Popular Mores in a Massachusetts County, 1649–1699* (Amherst: University of Massachusetts Press, 1986), 112.

15. Susan Amussen, "Being Stirred to Much Unquietness," 72. David Hall, *Worlds of Wonder, Days of Judgment* (Cambridge, Mass.: Harvard University Press, 1989), 52, suggests that this sort of crime literature, as well as other "popular" literature, became more common in New England in the late seventeenth century.

16. Karlsen, *Devil in the Shape of a Women,* gives the best discussion of gender relations in New England and how they related to the witchcraft accusations. Other useful studies include Paul Boyer and Stephen Nissenbaum, *Salem Possessed: The Social Origins of Witchcraft* (Cambridge, Mass.: Harvard University Press, 1974); and John Putnam Demos, *Entertaining Satan: Witchcraft and the Culture of Early New England* (New York: Oxford University Press, 1982).

17. Mary Beth Norton, "The Evolution of White Women's Experience in Early America," *American Historical Review* 89 (June 1984), 598–99. Karlsen, *Devil in the Shape of a Woman,* 202–6, suggests, accurately, that the evening of sex ratios in the latter part of the century significantly altered women's status and options.

18. Lois G. Carr and Lorena S. Walsh, "The Planter's Wife: The Experience of White Women in Seventeenth-Century Maryland," *William & Mary Quarterly* 34 (October 1977), 542–71.

19. Young, "English Plebeian Culture," 191.

20. Ibid., 190. Like abusive husbands, scolds were prosecuted in the courts of New England and elsewhere. For a brief discussion of New England scolding, see Thompson, *Sex in Middlesex,* 122, 125–26. For a discussion of gossip and defamation in Maryland, see Mary Beth Norton, "Gender and Defamation in Seventeenth-Century Maryland," *William & Mary Quarterly* 44 (January 1987), 3–39; for slander in Virginia, see Clara Ann Bowler, "Carted Whores and White Shrouded Apologies: Slander in the County Courts of Seventeenth-Century Virginia," *Virginia Magazine of History and Biography* 85 (October 1977), 411–26.

21. Edward Paul Rindler, "The Migration from the New Haven Colony to Newark, East New Jersey: A Study of Puritan Values and Behavior, 1630–1720" (Ph.D. diss., University of

Pennsylvania, 1977); John Murrin and Rowland Berthoff, "Feudalism, Communalism, and the Yeomen Freeholder: The American Revolution Considered as a Social Accident," in Kurtz and Hutson, eds., *Essays on the American Revolution*, 273–76; *Collections of the New Jersey Historical Society*, vol. 6: *Records of the Town of Newark, New Jersey* (Newark, N.J., 1864), 1–3 (hereafter cited as *Newark Town Book*); Edwin Hatfield, *History of Elizabeth, New Jersey* (New York, 1868). It is also possible that the Dutch of East Jersey were involved in rough music. They shared the Calvinism of the Puritans and certainly felt alienated from the norms of the predominate, English-speaking society. The study of the transmission of Dutch popular culture to the colonies is still developing.

22. We know of several instances in West Jersey where abusive husbands were dragged into court by their victims (although it is unclear under what law they were charged). Because West Jersey was dominated by Quakers and was for a time a separate province, this is far from conclusive evidence for East Jersey; we are unsure even what laws were in force in the seventeenth and eighteenth centuries, as the legal code was repeatedly modified, adding Quaker, Scottish, and Dutch influences to the body of laws, but I believe that both local laws and custom protected women from what was considered excessive violence. It is also possible that violent men were prosecuted under laws designed to restrain drunk and disorderly men. H. Clay Reed and George J. Miller, *The Burlington Court Book* (Washington, D.C.: Historical Publishing Co., 1944), 152, 177, 248; William Starr Myers, ed., *The Story of New Jersey* (New York: Lewis Historical Publishing Co., 1945), 53. For an account of the response of a Jerseyman of New England descent to eighteenth-century domestic violence, see Jonathan Holmes Diary, January 28, 1736–37, Holmes Family Papers, NJHS. Holmes suggests, as I have indicated elsewhere in this chapter, that chronic domestic violence was alien to New Englanders but common among the Scots and Scots-Irish.

23. *Newark Town Book*, 4.

24. George J. Miller, *Ye Olde Middlesex Courts* (Perth Amboy, N.J., 1932), 46.

25. For a recent discussion of domestic violence in eighteenth-century London, see Margaret Hunt, "Wife Beating, Domesticity, and Women's Independence in Eighteenth-Century London," *Gender and History* 4 (Spring 1992), 10–33.

26. Carol F. Karlsen and Laurie Crumpacker, eds., *The Journal of Esther Edwards Burr, 1754–1757* (New Haven: Yale University Press, 1984), 96.

27. The literature that describes the New England town and its decline from the unity of the early seventeenth century is vast and well known. See Kenneth Lockridge, *A New England Town* (New York: W. W. Norton, 1985), 93–164; and Boyer and Nissenbaum, *Salem Possessed*; Philip Greven, *Four Generations: Population, Land, and Family in Colonial Andover, Massachusetts* (Ithaca, N.Y.: Cornell University Press, 1970), 175–258. For more recent studies that address the same themes, see Richard I. Melvoin, *New England Outpost* (New York: W. W. Norton, 1989), 267–75; and Fred Anderson, *A People's Army* (New York: W. W. Norton, 1985), 3–62. For a modern examination of one of New Jersey's New England towns, see Rindler, "The Migration from the New Haven Colony."

28. Brendan McConville, *"These Daring Disturbers of the Public Peace": The Struggle for Property and Power in Early New Jersey* (Ithaca, N.Y.: Cornell University Press, 1999), esp. chap. 6; Cornelia Hughes Dayton, *Women Before the Bar: Gender, Law, and Society in Connecticut, 1639–1789* (Chapel Hill, N.C.: Institute of Early American History and Culture, 1995).

29. McConville, *"These Daring Disturbers of the Public Peace."*

30. Ibid., 81–125, 126–28, 282–328.

31. Karlsen and Crumpacker, eds., *Journal of Esther Edwards Burr, 1754–1757*, 125.

32. Nelson Burr, *The Anglican Church in New Jersey* (Philadelphia: Church Historical Society, 1954), 489–553. Thompson, Brinton-Coxe Historical Abstracts, Historical Society of Pennsylvania. Missionary Letters, Letterbooks, The American Mission, SPG, Microfilm, New York

Historical Society, The Records of Trinity Anglican Church, Newark, N.J., New Jersey Historical Society.

33. For a discussion of the role of watchfulness, particularly by women, in maintaining the Puritan social order, see Ulrich, *Good Wives,* 101–3. See also map 139A, C-8, Map of Newark 1776–80, Map Collection, New Jersey Historical Society.

34. Young, "English Plebeian Culture," 190–92.

35. T. H. Breen, " 'An Empire of Goods': The Anglicization of Colonial America," *Journal of British Studies* 25 (April 1986), 467–99.

36. *NJA,* 19: *Newspaper Extracts,* 3:324–27. This letter, signed by "Prudence Goodwife," is tightly styled and may well have been written by a member of the gentry sympathetic to those using rough music to halt the flood of domestic violence. The letter is something of a mystery, having no name signed to it and no location being given for the activities of the Regulators described. But I have employed the letter as evidence because I believe it accurately reflects both the causes and the consequences of rough music in New Jersey.

37. Rodris Roth, "Tea-Drinking in Eighteenth-Century America: Its Etiquette and Equipage," in Robert Blair St. George, ed., *Material Life in America, 1600–1860* (Boston: Northeastern University Press, 1988), 439–62, esp. 439–41, 453.

38. For an interesting discussion of tea, gender, and popular culture in the British Atlantic, see Jane Grey, "Gender and Plebeian Culture in Ulster," *Journal of Interdisciplinary History* 24 (Autumn 1993), 251–70. For a interesting aside on the role of the tea set in gender conflict, see the 1774 letter of Thomas Kearney, John Provost, and Coonradt Hendricks to *Rivington's New-York Gazetteer,* where the authors described the dissolution of the marriage of Anna and Paul Vandervoort when he seized her goods and property from a previous marriage to serve his own ends. According to the three authors, as he took his leave of her, Paul Vandervoort seized all of her movable property, but as he departed he turned and handed her "one tea cup and saucer." Clearly, this was meant as an insult of some sort, perhaps related to her consumption patterns. *NJA,* 29: *Newspapers,* 10:131.

39. I have considered the possibility that the reason we know nothing of rough music in the earlier period is that the sources that recorded such activity are sparse or nonexistent. But it does seem that there was a surge in plebeian activity in the period after 1750; the evidence from other colonies suggests the same pattern. See Young, "English Plebeian Culture," 182–212. If rough music was infrequently used before the middle of the eighteenth century, then how did it survive and how was it revived? These daunting questions have no final answer, but several possibilities present themselves. The imperial wars in North America encouraged the transmission of some aspects of British plebeian culture to North America. The British army used the wooden horse (strapping a man to a log) as a form of punishment. The demands of empire brought more and more British soldiers to America, who served alongside militia units. Certainly, colonial militia saw rough music used to discipline British troops during the Seven Years' War, and while they did not like it when British officers attempted to discipline provincials with the wooden horse, they may have carried the custom home and used it against unruly men. Alice Walker Earle indicates that the custom was commonly used in the British army in colonial America and became a common punishment in the Continental Army. For a discussion of the military's use of the wooden horse, see Anderson, *People's Army,* 125–26; Young, "English Plebeian Culture," 190; and Earle, *Curious Punishments of Bygone Days,* 128–32. Earle goes on to suggest that the wooden horse came to be a common punishment meted out by courts in New England for a number of crimes, but this seems to have occurred during and after the Revolution.

The arrival of new waves of migrants from Britain in the eighteenth century may also help explain the emergence of rough music. Massive numbers of North Britains (Scots, Scots-Irish, and those from the north of England) flooded into the middle colonies. Like all migrants, they brought extensive cultural baggage with them, including the practice of using rough music (called "riding the stang" in the north of England) against aggressive men. If they continued to do so in North America, it seems possible that others appropriated the usage to their own ends; such usage was uncommon in the south of England. E. P. Thompson discusses this use of rough music in the north of England in *Customs in Common*, 492–93. For the North Britain migration, see David Hackett Fischer, *Albion's Seed* (New York: Oxford University Press, 1989), 605–782.

Newspapers and broadsides might also have served as conduits transferring plebeian culture from Britain to America. Since rough music was reported in the newspapers, and newspapers and other printed materials were becoming more common in the eighteenth century, it seems possible that print became the medium for the transference of rough music from one area of the British Atlantic to another.

40. January 28, 1736/7, Jonathan Holmes Diary, Holmes Family Papers, NJHS.

41. Karlsen and Crumpacker, eds., *Journal of Esther Edwards Burr*, 110.

42. Ibid., 475–76. The irony, perhaps intended, was that by writing to the newspapers she delivered the public humiliation she called for. The relationship between print culture and popular culture, particularly rituals of humiliation, is a complex one; clearly print culture provided new ways of humiliating people in front of huge audiences.

43. *Pennsylvania Gazette*, January 23, 1753, no. 1257.

44. *NJA*, 19: *Newspaper Extracts*, 3:324.

45. Ibid., 126–28, 282–328.

46. Preston W. Edsall, *Journal of the Court of Common Right and Chancery of East New Jersey* (Princeton: Princeton University Press, 1937), 124.

47. *NJA*, 19: *Newspaper Extracts*, 3:225–26.

48. Ibid., 324–27.

49. Ibid., 24: *Newspaper Extracts*, 5:565–66.

50. Ibid., 27: *Newspaper Extracts*, 7:10–11.

51. For the overwhelmingly masculine identity of the targets of rough music, see Young, "English Plebeian Culture," 190.

52. Brown, "Violence and the American Revolution," 120; *Newport Mercury*, November 9 and 12, 1764.

53. For the broadest discussion of the plebeian/patrician split, see Gordon S. Wood, *The Radicalism of the American Revolution* (New York: Knopf, 1992). For a detailed and stimulating discussion of the hostility between plebeians and patricians in one colony, see Edward Countryman, *A People in Revolution: The American Revolution and Political Society in New York, 1760–1790* (Baltimore: Johns Hopkins University Press, 1981), 5–98. E. P. Thompson, David Underdown, and Alfred Young have all demonstrated that, in certain contexts, rough music could be transformed from a means of maintaining a traditional social order into a tool of popular political protest. See Thompson, *Customs in Common*, 516–26; Underdown, *Revel, Riot, and Rebellion*, 110–11; Young, "English Plebeian Culture," 204–6.

54. Thomas L. Purvis, *Proprietors, Patronage, and Paper Money* (New Brunswick, N.J.: Rutgers University Press, 1986), 66–74, discusses the gelling of the gentry in New Jersey and their dominance of the colony's political system in the eighteenth century.

55. There is no modern study of the bar in New Jersey, but several other colonies have received recent scholarly attention. See John Murrin, "The Legal Transformation: The Bench and Bar of Eighteenth-Century Massachusetts," in Stanley Katz and John Murrin, eds., *Colonial America* (New York: McGraw Hill Press, 1983), 540–72; Milton M. Klein, "The Rise of the New York Bar: The Legal Career of William Livingston" and "Prelude to Revolution in New York: Jury Trials and Judicial Tenure," in *Politics of Diversity* (Port Washington, N.Y.: Associated Faculty Press, 1974), 129–77; and A. G. Roeber, *Faithful Magistrates and Republican Lawyers: Creators of Virginia Legal Culture, 1660–1810* (Chapel Hill, N.C.: Institute of Early American History and Culture, 1981). Perhaps one way of thinking about the Anglicization of the legal

system is to see it as an attempt to impose one sort of patriarchy on a society or societies where patriarchy had undergone significant modification. It is unclear, because of the character of the sources, whether the late eighteenth-century gentry were less vigorous than the earlier, less professionally trained magistrates in punishing violent men.

56. *NJA,* 19: *Newspaper Extracts,* 3:226.
57. Ibid., 324–27.
58. Ibid., 24: *Newspaper Extracts,* 5:565–66.
59. Ibid., 27: *Newspaper Extracts,* 3:11.
60. Ibid., 4:54.
61. Ibid., 8:66.
62. Alfred Young, "Pope's Day, Tar and Feathers, and 'Cornet Joyce, jun.,' From Ritual to Rebellion in Boston, 1745–1775," unpublished paper cited in Gary Nash, *The Urban Crucible* (Cambridge, Mass.: Harvard University Press, 1986), 165; Dirk Hoerder, "Boston Leaders and Boston Crowds, 1765–1776," in Alfred Young, ed., *The American Revolution* (Dekalb: Northern Illinois Press, 1976), 239–45.
63. Shaw, *American Patriots,* 184–86, 188–90. Shaw focuses on how Joyce Jr., an officer who participated in the execution of Charles I, became an effigy figure in the Pope's Day celebration. In the early 1770s, a figure dressed as Joyce Jr. began to preside over the intimidation of public officials in Boston. Young, "English Plebeian Culture," 194, also discusses Joyce Jr., seeing in him an effort to establish elite control over tarring and feathering, while Shaw sees him as an encourager of tar and feathers as well as other sorts of ritual punishment. Shaw, heavily influenced by psychoanalytic theory, explores the patricidal aspects of the rituals used by the revolutionaries.
64. *NJA,* 27: *Newspaper Extracts,* 8:54–55.

5

Crowd and Court

Rough Music and Popular Justice in Colonial New York

Thomas J. Humphrey

In early March 1768, Hezekiah Holdridge walked into the small rural town where he had lived with his wife and children. Word of his return spread through the town quickly, and he was shortly confronted by a small crowd of laborers, yeomen, and blacksmiths who intended to teach him a lesson. The crowd seized Holdridge, abused and beat him, and even "burnt his Hair." When they tired of that punishment, the crowd tied him to a rail, probably a long piece of rough hewn lumber, hoisted him in the air, and carried him through the streets of the town, taunting him and encouraging other townspeople to join them. After a few hours of such punishment, the crowd untied Holdridge and let him climb off the rail, but they forced him to walk two more miles through town so everyone who had missed the earlier events could harass him at their leisure.

The crowd had beaten Holdridge and ridden him around town on a rail because he had abandoned his wife and children and married another woman in a nearby town.[1] The attack on Holdridge offers a classic example of rough music employed by members of a community to punish others in their community for violating acceptable standards of behavior. What makes this instance of rough music fascinating is that this classically European rite occurred in Rye, New York, where townspeople used controlled but no doubt frightening violence to humiliate and punish Holdridge for breaching the boundaries of normative behavior for married men in the community. Further, the crowd of townspeople probably attacked Holdridge because they knew local officials and local courts would not punish him for his transgressions.[2]

Colonial New Yorkers drew on the European tradition of rough music to correct members of their community who behaved improperly or who violated established codes of conduct. Crowds of New Yorkers also built on these traditional methods of punishment to check the political and economic ambitions of men whose actions threatened the best interests of the community in the 1750s and 1760s. As in Boston and in Philadelphia, European traditions of rough music colored rituals of resistance in New York during the imperial crisis in ways that historians are only now beginning to appreciate. At the same time, an examination of crowd violence illuminates different aspects of crowd actions and violence in colonial New York that may well be applicable to similar subjects in other colonies. The leaders of crowds who employed rough music usually emerged from among the members of the crowd, and not from other ranks in society. These crowds used violence to punish their targets painfully, but violence and the threat of violence—terror—were used to intimidate and frighten potential transgressors. Thus, crowds inflicted violent punishment publicly so everyone in the community could see the effects of deviant behavior, and crowds used the threat of future violence to coerce members of the community to conform to normative standards of behavior within that community. Sometimes crowds used only terror to compel victims to abide by the community's requests and, while no physical harm befell the victim, the fear that compelled them to obey the crowd was based on the crowd's ability both to impart fear of violence and to inflict that violence. This chapter puts the rites of violent political and economic crowd resistance and rebellion of the 1750s and 1760s into the broader context of traditional European-style rough music.[3]

Crowds used the rites of rough music irregularly, forcing historians to extrapolate from the few extant accounts and, unofficially, sometimes rioting against official rule of the community. The rough music involving Hezekiah Holdridge, for instance, was typical in both its causes and execution of rough music as practiced in Europe. Crowds of men from the "lower sort," with leaders who emerged from their ranks, loudly and usually violently punished people who violated the community's standards of acceptable conduct. In some cases of rough music, the crowd placed people on a rail or an ass, or in a cart, and ushered them through the streets of the town, hurling garbage and stones at them and calling them names associated with their deviant behavior. Sometimes, the crowd further humiliated their victim by placing the unfortunate person backward on the rail or the ass. Noise, singing, and music often accompanied the activities and were powerful forces in the creation of what was for the victim a terrifying ritual that could turn horrifically violent at any moment. Worse, victims often knew, as did the crowd, that the experience would end with some form of physical punishment inflicted by the crowd on the person targeted for violence. When violence was not used explicitly, or used metaphorically, the rite of rough music was still a terrifying event for the victim because there was real potential for real violence. Whether symbolic or brutally real, violence was countenanced by those who believed that it served and protected the best interests of the community. Once crowds punished their victims and reestablished rules of behavior, they usually let them return to their houses and families.[4]

In much the same way that the attack on Holdridge constituted a classic case of men participating in and leading rough music, an assault on a Mrs. Wilson by an angry group of "boys" in 1754 suggests that women also organized crowds for rough music when they discovered other women behaving improperly. In March that year, a group of "boys" chased Mrs. Wilson through the streets of New York City. When they caught their victim, one member of the crowd stepped forward and called Wilson a "pocky whore" for seducing her husband. Wilson faced the ire of a local crowd because she, a married woman, was suspected of having an affair with one or more of the married men in the community. Like Holdridge, she had violated standards of appropriate behavior for married women in that community, and in doing so threatened the stability of the households of her neighbors. The "boy" who stepped forward first was Allison Williams, the wife of a doctor in the city. By calling her a "pocky whore," the "boys" (who were evidently women dressed as boys probably to escape detection by local authorities) deemed Wilson unattractive as a result of the scarring often associated with smallpox. They may have also been insinuating that Wilson suffered from the venereal diseases that often afflicted prostitutes. The crowd continued to pelt Wilson with rocks and insults, forcing her to find refuge among the residents of the neighborhood. When she knocked on the first door she came to, the inhabitants refused to let her in and pushed her back out in front of the angry crowd. Male spectators encouraged the women to continue their assault, and one of the crowd yelled out "Mob the whore, mob the whore!" Wilson, who maintained that she was no "more a whore" than any of her attackers, eventually found refuge in a house a few blocks from the place where the crowd first confronted her.[5]

The gendered differences in the crowds that assaulted Holdridge in Rye, and Wilson in New York City, suggest some of the prescribed gender roles of their culture. Perhaps the gendered divisions between the two groups resulted from an English Puritan perception of gender roles in the household and in the community, which held that women were responsible for the moral and spiritual development of the family. As Cornelia Hughes Dayton correctly points out, policies used to create a Puritan society in the British North American colonies in the eighteenth century reduced the power men wielded over women and "undercut men's sense of sexual entitlement to women's bodies." Men in that community may well have left to women the discipline of an adulteress. Although few if any New Yorkers were Puritans in the 1750s, European Protestant women also freed themselves from some of the control and power of male clergy to interpret Scripture themselves and to use their newly found religious knowledge to redefine and enforce moral behavior in their households. Such women may have considered it their duty to maintain the moral standards of other women in their community, in order to assert and to preserve their newly won authority over different aspects of their households.[6]

Women not only punished other women but also sometimes helped punish men like Holdridge. In some cases, such as those in Chester County and in Boston discussed by Steven Stewart in this volume, women even led crowds in rough music. Women took such roles because anyone who committed adultery threatened the socially and culturally defined order of married men and women in a world in which men so clearly dominated women. The patriarchal social and political hierarchy found ready equivalents in the power structures of the family and the household, and women needed to preserve the order of their households and, as a result, the actions of other women. In that patriarchal hierarchy in which power was gendered, a married woman's reputation depended on her sexual conduct and that of her husband. Women, to that end, punished adulteresses because women could best reestablish and reinforce appropriate sexual conduct of married women in their community, but women also assaulted adulteresses in an effort to maintain as much control over their own lives, husbands, and households as possible.[7]

Where the crowds that attacked Holdridge and Wilson sought to correct social misbehavior, political and economic protesters throughout the Hudson Valley employed similar rites of rough music to voice their discontent. When Stamp Act rioters in Albany and rural rebels in the southern portion of the Hudson Valley confronted members of the community who had in some way violated appropriate standards of behavior, these crowds drew on their shared cultural tradition of rough music to enforce proper conduct and punish the offenders. These offenders incurred the wrath of angry neighbors because they had jeopardized the well-being of people in that community. The political and economic agendas of the people who mounted these protests, however, transformed the events themselves. The participants infused the classical incantation of rough music with new political and economic meaning. Yet we see in these actions the power and persistence of early modern European forms of rough music used by crowds who were laying the groundwork for a new society and culture.[8]

Henry Van Schaack became one of the primary targets of Stamp Act protesters in Albany, New York. The British Parliament had passed the Act in 1765 in order to generate revenue in the British North American colonies and to help defray the costs of colonial administration. The Stamp Act dictated that colonists buy the appropriately stamped paper to carry out any activity outlined in the Act and included legal, church and commercial documents, playing cards, books, and newspapers. The Act would have affected nearly every colonist at some point in his or her life, but it struck particularly hard at the urban colonial merchant elite, who conducted the majority of the legal activity and business in the colonies. A local official would have to distribute paper and collect the tax.[9] Many of the leading merchants, lawyers, and powerful landlords in the northern Hudson Valley opposed the Act on the mutually reinforcing grounds of political principle and economic self-interest. One of these men, Robert R. Livingston, believed the Stamp Act the most "injurious and . . . impolitick Act ever a Kings Scoundrel invented." In Albany, attorney Abraham Yates echoed that sentiment, declaring that the Stamp Act "appears to us as Odious." Yates was one of a crowd of about fifty who confronted Van Schaack at a local tavern in Albany in January 1766 because rumors were swirling around town that he had volunteered to be a tax collector and a distributor of stamped paper. The men met with Van Schaack to convince him, or coerce him if necessary, to abide by the wishes and interests of the community by surrendering his position as distributor and collector. When these rebels strove to convince Van Schaack to give up his post, they were attempting to preserve levels of appropriate economic and political behavior in their community in much the same way that the people who punished Holdridge and Wilson endeavored to maintain standards of social behavior.[10]

On January 4, 1766, a crowd of men formally invited Henry Van Schaack to meet them at Thomas Williams's tavern in Albany City. The invitation was as much a demand as a request, and, recognizing the crowd's threatening behavior, Van Schaack invited several of his friends to accompany him. When he opened the door to the tavern, Van Schaack and his friends were greeted by a crowd of forty to fifty men who cheered him loudly three times, banging their mugs and cups on the tables as they sang out their praises. They greeted Van Schaack so enthusiastically and positively because, by accepting their invitation, he showed his commitment to the community. They recognized and rewarded him for his effort to conform to their desires, and in doing so these men acknowledged Van Schaack for the rest of community they represented, who also detested the Stamp Act. Earlier in the evening at taverns throughout the town, people had gathered to voice their objections to the Stamp Act and its supporters, and the people in the taverns had selected representatives to meet later with Van Schaack at Williams's tavern. After a few minutes of cheering, a delegate from the crowd stepped forward and informed Van Schaack that the crowd had learned he had applied for the position of distributor of stamped paper. Van Schaack assured them that he "never made any such application," but his disavowal did not satisfy the crowd at all. The men at the tavern then demanded that Van Schaack swear an oath that he had never applied for the job and that he never would. For his part, Van Schaack refused to take the oath, and he tried to leave, but John Vischer and several others blocked the door. These men more fiercely implored Van Schaack to take the oath. He again refused, but was allowed to leave while the committee debated another course of action.

Approximately one hour after he returned home, Van Schaack was again summoned to attend his opponents at the tavern. That Van Schaack, badly shaken by his earlier encounter, immediately complied with the demand indicates the crowd's power and legitimacy as representatives of the community. The same group greeted Van Schaack with cheers that turned into derisive jeers. Van Schaack believed that the men were now quite drunk and dangerous, and they threatened him "very much" as they again demanded that he swear he had not applied for the office of distributor of stamped paper. He again refused and again went home.

On the following evening, Van Schaack learned that the same crowd had again gathered at Williams's Tavern. While the crowd would have settled for Van Schaack's publicly sworn oath to renounce his rumored application for the post of distributor of stamped paper the previous evening, the crowd was now in an ugly mood and wanted Van Schaack to suffer physically for scorning their desires. When he discovered the crowd's much more violent intentions, a frightened Van Schaack sought assistance from local magistrates—who offered protection, tellingly, only if Van Schaack took the oath in accordance with the crowd's demands. Van Schaack responded that he would take the oath if all the freeholders and magistrates in Albany took the same oath, but the magistrates refused. The magistrates were unwilling to take the oath themselves, either because they would have been denying their oath to the king to uphold the law or because some of them may have applied for the job of stamp tax collector. While these men certainly wanted to avoid the peril Van Schaack faced, they did not want to break their oath with the king or to purposely put themselves in the way of an angry crowd. As a result, the magistrates' refusal to stand against the crowd and with Van Schaack forced Van Schaack to face that angry crowd alone.

After several hours of drinking at the tavern, the crowd left to compel Van Schaack to take the oath they had proposed the night before. The people who had sent their representatives to Williams's Tavern the previous night now joined the smaller crowd, and approximately four hundred people marched the streets of Albany to protest the Stamp Act and attack Van Schaack. As they made their way noisily through the streets, the crowd cheered Van Schaack as an honorable man, but derided him for supporting the Stamp Act. When they arrived at his house, the assembled crowd called for Van Schaack to face the crowd and take the oath. Van Schaack, however, had heard the loud crowd yelling while it was still a few blocks from his house, and he had fled to the outskirts of town, where he spent an uncomfortable and cold night in the snowy woods outside the city. Only the knowledge that his life was in imminent peril could compel Van Schaack to face the danger of spending a night outside in the woods in January. When the crowd realized the prey had fled, they resorted to destroying the windows of Van Schaack's house, then broke into the house, destroyed his sleigh, and threw most of his furniture through windows and out into the streets. The following morning, Van Schaack returned to discover the damage, and a note posted to the door of the Dutch church:

> Where as Mr. Henry Van Schaack has by general impudence and unequaled obstinacy drawn himself the Resentment of his Fellow Citizens to his Considerable Damage already, these on theretofore, to Advise him To meet the Sons of Liberty In the morning to prevent more consequences
> Signed Freedom

Underneath was another piece of paper featuring what was later described as a "gallows with a figure drawn in imitation of a man hanging"; above the gallows was written "Henry Van Schaack" and below was "The just fate of a traytor." Frightened, exhausted, and freezing cold, Van Schaack bowed to the community's desires and took the oath later that day. The crowd did not bother him again.[11]

Around the same time the Stamp Act protesters assaulted Henry Van Schaack in Albany, rural rioters in the southern portion of the Hudson Valley also drew on their shared cultural heritage of crowd action to attack agents of their landlords who were trying to evict them from their farms. Many of these people had settled on land in southern Dutchess and northern Westchester Counties and had signed long-term leases with the Wappinger Indians. Frederick Philipse, a powerful New York landlord, also claimed much of this land, and in the middle of the 1750s he and son-in-law Beverly Robinson began forcing these inhabitants to either quit the land or sign short-term leases with the Philipses. The Wappingers responded by seeking legal counsel and taking the Philipses to court over legal ownership of the land. Not surprisingly, the Wappingers did not fare well in a court dominated by the Philipses and other New York landlords. Bolstered by the promise of a favorable decision, Beverly Robinson began demanding that tenants sign shorter leases. Some of the inhabitants, however, balked at the forced lease restructuring and rebelled against what they interpreted as activities that assaulted their economic and social well-being.[12] In the late summer of 1765, Robinson and the sheriff of the county, James Livingston, began evicting the tenants who refused to sign new leases, sometimes burning them out of their houses and farms. Soon after, disgruntled rural people met to organize their response, and they selected

William Prendergast, Isaac Perry, Elisha Cole, and others to lead them in their fight for land. Prendergast, for his part, vowed to restore "Justice" and to "relieve the oppressed."[13]

In May 1766, Prendergast led approximately sixty men on a raid of Robert Hughson's farm to throw Hughson and his wife off the land. The Hughsons refused to move because Robert Hughson's wife was close to delivering their baby and could not travel. A few days later, Robert Hughson complained about the attack to his father, George Hughson, who told the story to Dutchess County Justice of the Peace Samuel Peters. In response, Peters immediately obtained writs for the arrest of the rioters, but when he and the elder Hughson ventured out to deliver the writs, they were met and captured by Prendergast and his men. The rural rioters attacked the men because they had helped Beverly Robinson and the Philipses threatened the welfare of the inhabitants of the region. After securing their prisoners, the rioters carried them to Samuel Towner's Tavern near Pawling, New York, where they tried to convince them to destroy the writs they had for the rioters. The rioters also demanded that Hughson and Peters swear to give evidence in favor of the rioters rather than continue to collect evidence against them. When both men refused, Prendergast decided to compel them.[14]

One day after the rioters had seized Peters and Hughson, they constructed a courtroom in a nearby field where they took their enemies to stand trial for maltreating rural people.[15] The rioters placed Hughson and Peters in a makeshift dock within a square of wooden rails that marked out the roughly twelve-foot-by-twelve-foot courtroom. Approximately two hundred rebels gathered around the "courtroom" as Prendergast paraded inside brandishing a cutlass and warning Peters and Hughson of their punishment if they refused to stop harassing the rioters. Prendergast determined that the rioters would ride Peters and Hughson on a rail "to the first convenient Place of mud and water, and there duck them as long as we think proper, and from thence we would take them to a White Oak Tree, and there whip them as long as we think proper, and thence take them out of the country and there kick their Asses as long as we think fit." Prendergast called for specific publicly inflicted and violent punishment in order to intimidate Peters and Hughson, which shows both the power of the rites of rough music and the strength of those who employed it. Suitably cowed, Peters destroyed the writs of eviction and evidence against the rioters that he carried, but the crowd refused to be denied the opportunity to inflict their own brand of justice on a man who had so openly threatened their welfare. For them, the courtroom drama was incomplete until they had publicly punished the agent of the landlords. So the rioters grabbed Peters, dragged him through the mud, and beat him, stopping only when Peters promised not to "take advantage of them for keeping him in Custody." After the crowd similarly tried and assaulted Hughson, the two prisoners were released.[16]

Although the rioters modeled their court roughly after traditional, institutional courtrooms, there was no impartial judge to adjudicate. Instead, the rebels set up their own courtroom as part of their rebellion against the New York landlords, who led the colony's social and political ruling class. In this country courtroom, the rioters, not the New York landlords, held the power, and Peters and Hughson, agents of the landlords, bowed their heads and spoke softly. These rural rioters also improved on traditional European-style rough music by investing it with a profound criticism of New York's social and political structure.[17]

Prendergast also invoked the tradition of the courtroom as a public place to lend credence to the riots. By co-opting the tradition of the courtroom, a place where rioters usually lost their battles with the New York landlords, the rural rioters tried to gain power in a world in which they generally held little power. Moreover, because the courtroom was a public place the rioters could persecute their enemies in a ritualized and public setting in which the entire community might watch and participate. That public and ritualized nature of courts and courtrooms also indicates that the rioters were doing more than attacking people who violated acceptable standards of behavior. As they fought to wrest some social and political power from the New York landlords, the rebels also sought to gain power in their community permanently.[18]

Beverly Robinson and the Philipses did not endure the rioters' insurgency long. In July 1766, they appealed for and received help from the British army to defeat and capture the rural rebels. Prendergast was captured a short time later and taken to Poughkeepsie, New York, under heavy guard to stand "Tryal for Misdemeanours laid to his Charge."[19] Prendergast quickly found himself in another, more hostile courtroom. The New York landlords ruled politics, and their power extended to the courts. As Peters and Hughson had faced hostile judges when they stood trial in the country courtroom just a few weeks before, so Prendergast faced equally antagonistic judges in his trial. All the justices were prosperous and powerful New Yorkers, and most owned land and rented it to tenants or were related to New York landlords. One justice, Robert R. Livingston, operated part of his family's manor and was the cousin of Robert Livingston Jr., the lord of Livingston Manor, which was a few miles north of the region where Prendergast rioted. William Smith Jr., another justice, married into the Livingston family and shared the Livingstons' distaste for rural rioters. While Smith thought his "Wife's connections with the Landlords rendered it improper that [he] should be one of the Judges" at Prendergast's trial, he stayed on the bench anyway. Another member of the court, John Morin Scott, was also acting as the Philipses' attorney in their ongoing land dispute with the Wappinger Indians over the land for which Prendergast and his followers rioted.[20]

In the Court of Oyer and Terminer in Poughkeepsie, Prendergast defended himself with help from his wife, Mehitabel Wing, a Quaker from Dutchess County. While Prendergast refuted the arguments presented by John Tabor Kempe, the colony's attorney general, Wing's behavior during the trial "attracted the Notice of the Audience" because she "never failed to make every Remark that might tend to extenuate the Offence, and put [her husband's] Conduct in the most favourable Point of View."[21] Despite Wing's powerful presence in the courtroom, the jury decided against Prendergast, and the justices returned with their sentence twenty-four hours later. The court gave Prendergast what it described as the "usual severe sentence for Treason." The judges determined that Prendergast should be taken back "whence he came and from thence shall be drawn on a Hurdle to the Place of Execution, and then shall be hanged by the Neck, and then shall be cut down alive, and his Entrails and Privy members shall be cut from his Body, and shall be burned in his sight, and his Head shall be cut off." The court further ordered that Prendergast's dead and headless body be quartered and disposed of at the "King's Pleasure." After the court read how they wanted Prendergast to pay for his crimes against the king, he "fell like a slaughtered ox," uttering a cry that melted to tears "even those least susceptival of Compassion."[22] Apparently, the court only wanted to intimidate Prendergast and other potentially insurgent rural people in the Hudson Valley, because it then recommended that the sentence be reviewed by the king. In the end, the king reviewed Prendergast's case and granted him a full pardon in December 1766. The landlords' calculated and beneficent use of their power in the courtroom proved successful for a while, and rural rebellion waned in the southern part of the Hudson Valley in the late 1760s and early 1770s.[23]

The antagonists in the battle for land in northern Dutchess County— William Prendergast and rural rioters on one side, and the Philipses and the New York landlords on the other—fought for social and political power. The rebels wanted to obtain it by owning the land on which they lived and worked, and the New York landlords wanted to preserve their hold on that power by maintaining their hold on land. To do so, they had to defeat the rioters without provoking full-scale rural rebellion. Both sides used the arena of the courtroom to announce their aspirations, but in dramatically different ways. The rioters upset the traditional order of public courtrooms by claiming the power of that institution and by putting the normally powerful in an inferior position. Their courtroom represented disorder to the landlords because the rioters wanted to overturn the society in which they lived, and they used their country courtroom as an example of that disorder. That the rioters turned their world upside down, momentarily, was in large part only apparent because they did so by co-opting the physical space and rituals of an established and ritualized institution. The landlords used their court to refute the rebels and repulse the rioters' attempts to gain power. Once they defeated the rioters in the field and captured many of the leaders, the landlords did not necessarily have to execute Prendergast physically because they had already done so metaphorically. Moreover, by asking the king to spare Prendergast, the men in power in colonial New York demonstrated their ultimate strength. They had defeated their enemy, and spared him. Thus, the New York landlords and colonial officials had used their courtroom both to defeat the rioters by prosecuting the leader of the riots and to eradicate the elements of disorder the rioters created, reifying their position at the top of the colonial society. That both these groups used the physical structure of the courtroom as the place in which to act out their endeavors suggests the fundamental nature of the court as an important public arena that people used to shape their culture and society.[24]

The trials in which William Prendergast participated, and the other examples of ritualized, violent popular justice examined in this chapter, suggest the ways in which these colonial New Yorkers preserved social and political order in their communities. They did so by invoking the European tradition of rough music during which those members of the community who felt threatened, or who saw standards of behavior undermined, attacked others in the community who the crowd thought were responsible for potentially subverting order. Ironically, these crowds often attempted to restore order to their region by momentarily turning their world upside down and by sometimes using highly ritualized institutions to attack local officials. Some of these crowds attacked their victims and co-opted official institutions precisely because the rioters and revelers knew either that officials would not address some social deviancies or that they could not participate equitably in official proceedings. These examples indicate that leaders often emerged from among the participants, that women sometimes participated in rough music, and that these crowds used terror and frightening violence to achieve their goals. Furthermore, Stamp Act rioters in Albany, and land rioters like William Prendergast particularly, blended rituals they borrowed from rough music and court procedures to make clear their aspirations based on their different notions of political and social equality. These last two examples also illustrate how rough music informed the rituals of opposition used by colonial New Yorkers during the early stages of the imperial crisis, indicating that colonists entered that crisis with dramatically different perceptions of equality and order that shaped their actions from the earliest moments of the crisis. Historians are only beginning to investigate and understand how those differences shaped the resultant conflicts.

The author would like to thank Paul Gilje, Ruth Herndon, Laurie Humphrey, Allan Kulikoff, and Alfred Young for their help with this chapter.

Notes

1. Hezekiah Holdridge's deposition to John Bull of Westchester County, New York, March 7, 1758, and a letter from some of the members of the crowd addressed to William Kempe, Attorney General of New York, March 10, 1758, both in the Lawsuits, G–L, John Tabor Kempe Papers, New-York Historical Society (NYHS). The letter to Kempe was unsigned. The rail to which Holdridge was tied probably resembled rails used by crowds in England and consisted either of a rough-hewn log or of two long, wooden planks nailed together to form a trough; the crowd would have placed Holdridge on the pointed side of the "V." See E. P. Thompson, "Rough Music," in his *Customs in Common: Studies in Traditional Popular Culture* (New York: The New Press, 1993), 479–80; and Natalie Davis, *Society and Culture in Early Modern France* (Stanford, Calif.: Stanford University Press, 1975), 302–3 n. 47.

2. For a discussion of rough music in a European context, see Thompson, "Rough Music," 467–538; David Underdown, *Revel, Riot, and Rebellion* (New York: Oxford University Press,

1985), 100–103, 110–11; Robert Darnton, *The Great Cat Massacre and Other Episodes in French Cultural History* (New York: Basic Books, 1984), 96–97; and Suzanne Desan, "Crowds, Community, and Ritual in the Work of E. P. Thompson and Natalie Davis," in Lynn Hunt, ed., *The New Cultural History* (Berkeley and Los Angeles: University of California Press, 1989), 47–71. For the transference of that tradition from England and Europe to the British North American colonies, and for the use of rails as a particular brand of punishment, see Alfred F. Young, "English Plebian Culture and Eighteenth-Century American Radicalism," in Margaret Jacob and James Jacob, eds., *Origins of Anglo-American Radicalism* (London: Allen & Unwin, 1984), 184–212; Peter Linebaugh, "All the Atlantic Mountains Shook," in Geoff Eley and William Hunt, eds., *Reviving the English Revolution: Reflections and Elaborations on the Work of Christopher Hill* (London: Verso, 1988), 195–200; and Marcus Rediker, "Good Hands, Stout Heart, and Fast Feet: The History and Culture of Working People in America," in Eley and Hunt, *Reviving the English Revolution*, 222.

Rough music was not the only cultural tradition immigrants brought with them to North America, nor was it the only traditional rite or festival that the inhabitants of the colonies adopted and changed throughout the seventeenth and eighteenth century. Another example is the Pinkster holiday, the Dutch commemoration of Pentecost, which Dutch settlers of New York celebrated in the seventeenth century approximately seven weeks after Easter. By the late eighteenth century, African Americans had made the holiday an almost exclusively African American celebration that they celebrated on the sites of the initial Dutch settlements; see Shane White, ed., "Pinkster in Albany, 1803: A Contemporary Description," *New York History* 70 (April 1989), 191–99; Donna Merwick, *Possessing Albany, 1630–1710: The Dutch and English Experiences* (New York: Cambridge University Press, 1990), 75; and White " 'It Was a Proud Day': African Americans, Festivals, and Parades in the North, 1741–1834," *Journal of American History* 81 (1994), 13–50.

3. The literature on the protests of the Stamp Act and involving the imperial crisis is rich, but these historians have stressed the importance of these protests as the incipient stages of the American revolutionary movement. See Edmund S. Morgan and Helen Morgan, *The Stamp Act Crisis* (Chapel Hill: University of North Carolina Press, 1953), 119–33; Bernard Bailyn, *The Ideological Origins of the American Revolution* (Cambridge, Mass.: Belknap Press of Harvard University Press, 1967), 99–102; Edmund S. Morgan, *Inventing the People: The Rise of Popular Sovereignty in England and America* (New York: W. W. Norton, 1988), 239; and Gordon S. Wood, *The Radicalism of the American Revolution* (New York: Vintage Books, 1992), 172–75. For other perspectives on the same events, see Dirk Hoerder, *Crowd Action in Revolutionary Massachusetts* (New York: Academic Press, 1977), chaps. 1 and 2; and Edward Countryman, *A People in Revolution: The American Revolution and Political Society in New York, 1760–1790* (New York: W. W. Norton, 1981), chaps. 1 and 2.

4. For general descriptions of rough music, see Thompson, "Rough Music," 467–538; and Davis, "Women on Top," in *Society and Culture in Early Modern France*, 150–51 n. 45. For an alternative reading of crowds who participated in rough music in New York that did not use violence regularly and that were generally led by their social betters, see Paul A. Gilje, *The Road to Mobocracy: Popular Disorder in New York City, 1763–1834* (Chapel Hill: University of North Carolina Press, 1987), 20–25. Gilje focuses on New York City and does not spend much time examining the rest of the colony in this study. See also Gilje's more comprehensive *Rioting in America* (Bloomington: Indiana University Press, 1996), esp. chap. 1.

5. James Jackson's Deposition, March 1, 1754, Unsorted Lawsuits, G–L, Kempe Papers, NYHS. While this is a case of women dressing as men, men sometimes dressed as women when they ritually punished people. See Brendan McConville, "The Rise of Rough Music: Reflections on an Ancient New Custom in Eighteenth-Century New Jersey," in this volume. See also Natalie Davis, "Women on Top," 146–49; and Laurel Thatcher Ulrich, *Good Wives: Images and*

Reality in the Lives of Women in Northern New England, 1650–1750 (New York: Vintage Books, 1991), 195. For other rioters who disguised themselves, see Alan Taylor, *Liberty Men and Great Proprietors: The Revolutionary Settlement on the Maine Frontier, 1760–1820* (Chapel Hill: University of North Carolina Press, 1990), chap. 7. Not all women or rioters felt so compelled to disguise themselves. See Barbara Clark Smith, "Food Rioters and the American Revolution," *William & Mary Quarterly,* 3rd ser., 52 (January 1991), 3–38; and Alfred F. Young, "The Women of Boston: 'Persons of Consequence' in the Making of the American Revolution, 1765–1776," in Harriet B. Applewhite and Darline G. Levy, eds., *Women and Politics in the Age of the Democratic Revolution* (Ann Arbor: University of Michigan Press, 1990), 181–226.

    6. Cornelia Hughes Dayton, *Women Before the Bar: Gender, Law, and Society in Connecticut, 1639–1789* (Chapel Hill: University of North Carolina Press, 1995), 10; see ibid., 9–14, for discussion of patriarchy in colonial America in which Dayton stresses the importance of men's "implicit endorsement" of laws and conventions that reinforced male authority in the early and middle decades of the eighteenth century. For a discussion of how patriarchy may be cultural as well as institutional, and for a more inclusive interpretation of patriarchy, see Thompson, "Rough Music," 499–505. Here I am not striving to use one interpretation, either institutional or cultural, but rather seeking to broaden our understanding of the term to include institutional and cultural meanings without abandoning the important frameworks laid out by Davidson and Thompson. For a version of this, see Ann Little, "The Politics of Patriarchy: New Haven Colony and District, 1635–1690" (Ph.D. diss., University of Pennsylvania, 1996), chap. 5.

    7. See Susan Juster, *Disorderly Women: Sexual Politics and Evangelicalism in Revolutionary New England* (Ithaca, N.Y.: Cornell University Press, 1994), 94–96; Dayton, *Women Before the Bar,* 165–73; and Mary Beth Norton, *Founding Mothers and Fathers: Gendered Power and the Forming of American Society* (New York: Knopf, 1996), 232–33. For inversion of sex roles by disorderly women, see Davis, "Women on Top," 124–51; Underdown, *Revel, Riot, and Rebellion,* 99–101; David E. Underdown, "The Taming of the Scold: The Enforcement of Patriarchal Authority in Early Modern England," in Anthony Fletcher and John Stevens, eds., *Order and Disorder in Early Modern England* (New York: Cambridge University Press, 1985), 116–35. For the tightening of patriarchal order, see Dayton, *Women Before the Bar,* 9–14 and passim; Terri L. Snyder, " 'Rich Widows Are the Best Commodity This Country Affords': Gender Relations and the Rehabilitation of Patriarchy in Virginia, 1660–1700" (Ph.D. diss., University of Iowa, 1992); Kathleen M. Brown, *Good Wives, Nasty Wenches, and Anxious Patriots: Gender, Race, and Power in Colonial Virginia* (Chapel Hill: University of North Carolina Press, 1996), chaps. 1 and 7; and Carole Shammas, "Anglo-American Household Government in Comparative Perspective," 3rd ser., *William & Mary Quarterly* 52 (January 1995), 104–50.

    8. E. P. Thompson argued that crowds in England used elements of rough music during their political and economic protests, becoming more radical because of the nature of the activity the revelers protested. While he maintained that domestic rough music was essentially conservative, politically and economically motivated rough music utilized by "radical" English "Jacobins" in the 1790s and during the movement against the Reform Bill of 1832 proved subversive. See this discussion in Thompson, "Rough Music," in *Customs in Common,* 524–25; see also a discussion of the Swing riots described by Eric Hobsbawm and George Rudé in *Captain Swing* (New York: Pantheon, 1968).

    9. See Morgan and Morgan, *The Stamp Act Crisis,* 119–33; Hoerder, *Crowd Action,* chaps. 1 and 2; Countryman, *A People in Revolution,* chaps. 1; and Wood, *The Radicalism of the American Revolution,* 172–75.

    10. Robert R. Livingston to Robert Livingston Jr., Woodstock, May 1, 1766, Livingston Papers, roll 8; Abraham Yates to Robert Livingston Jr., Albany, January 3, 1766, Livingston Papers, roll 8, 13 rolls of microflim, Franklin Delano Roosevelt Library, Hyde Park, New York (Livingston Papers). For the Livingstons' business activities, see Cynthia Kierner, *Traders and*

Gentlefolk: The Livingstons of New York, 1675–1790 (Ithaca, N.Y.: Cornell University Press, 1992), 41–43, 92–97. For taverns as places of political discourse, see Peter Thompson, *Rum Punch and Revolution: Taverngoing and Public Life in Eighteenth-Century Philadelphia* (Philadelphia: University of Pennsylvania Press, 1999).

11. The narrative and quotes are taken from "Henry Van Schaack's case representing the abuse he met with from the traitors at Albany," Albany, New York, January 1766, Unsorted Lawsuits, V–Z, Kempe Papers, NYHS. See also Abraham Yates to Robert Livingston Jr., Albany, January 3, 1766, Livingston Papers, roll 8; and the corresponding articles in the *New York Gazette,* January 20, 1766, and the *New-York Post Boy,* January 23, 1766.

12. See Governor Henry Moore to the Earl of Shelburne, Fort George, New York, December 22, 1766, in E. B. O'Callaghan, ed., *Documents Relative to the Colonial History of New York,* 15 vols. (Albany, N.Y., 1857), 7:885–86; Oscar Handlin and Irving Mark, "Chief Daniel Nimham v. Roger Morris, Beverly Robinson and Philip Philipse—An Indian Case in Colonial New York, 1765–1767," *Ethnohistory* 11 (Summer 1964), 193–246. John Tabor Kempe, New York's Attorney General, examined Nimham's complaint and issued an opinion on it on July 28, 1762, Unsorted Lawsuits, M–O, Kempe Papers, NYHS; and the "Hampton Map of the Upper Patent of Philipsburgh, 1757," no. 11068, NYSL.

13. David Akin quoted Prendergast in Lawsuits, C–F, Kempe Papers, NYHS. See also the depositions of James Covey Jr., Ebenezer Weed, and Felix Holdridge, November 23, 1765, Unsorted Legal Manuscripts, Box 1, Kempe Papers, NYHS. See also Lieutenant Governor Cadwallader Colden to General Thomas Gage, Spring Hill, September 2, 1765, *Documents Relative to the Colonial History of New York,* 7:758; and William Smith Jr. to Governor Robert Monckton, New York City, November 8, 1765, *Historical Memoirs from 16 March 1763 to July 1778 of William Smith,* ed. William Sabine, 2 vols. (New York: Arno Press, 1966), 1:30.

14. Robert Hughson's Deposition, May 27, 1766, Unsorted Lawsuits, Box 4, Kempe Papers, NYHS; Samuel Peters's Deposition, Unsorted Lawsuits, Box 4, Kempe Papers, NYHS; and the testimony of Samuel Peters and George Hughson in Mark and Handlin, "*The King v. William Prendergast,*" 179–84.

15. For descriptions of the court, see the testimony of Peters, Hughson, and Reuben Garlick in Mark and Handlin, "*The King v. William Prendergast,*" 179–85. For the use of wooden rails during instances of rough music, see Thompson, "Rough Music," 479–80; and Davis, *Society and Culture in Early Modern France,* 302–3 n. 47. For that tradition in the colonies, see Young, "English Plebian Culture," 190–92; and Fred Anderson, *A People's Army: Massachusetts Soldiers in the Seven Years' War* (New York: W. W. Norton, 1984), 124. For the use of rails in rough music in New York, see Hezekiah Holdridge's deposition to John Bull of Westchester County, New York, March 7, 1758, and a letter from some of the men who were part of the crowd that attacked Holdridge addressed to William Kempe, then the Attorney General of New York, March 10, 1758, both in Lawsuits, G–L, Kempe Papers, NYHS. The crowd attacked Holdridge because he was an adulterer. The judges of the illegal court consisted of Prendergast, Cope Covey, Elisha Cole, Stephen Harrington, Daniel Crawfoot (also Crawford), Jabez Barry, and Daniel Townshend. Peters and Hughson could not name all of their numerous attackers. See their testimony in Mark and Handlin, "*The King v. William Prendergast,*" 179–84.

16. Testimony of Samuel Peters and George Hughson in Mark and Handlin, "*The King v. William Prendergast,*" 180–85; and Samuel Peters's affidavit, June 7, 1766, Unsorted Lawsuits, P–U, Box 4, Kempe Papers, NYHS.

17. For a discussion of rough music in a European context, see E. P. Thompson, "Rough Music," in his *Customs in Common: Studies in Traditional Popular Culture* (New York: The New Press, 1993), 467–538; Underdown, *Revel, Riot, and Rebellion,* 100–103, 110–11; and Darnton, *The Great Cat Massacre,* 96–97; and Desan, "Crowds, Community, and Ritual in the Work of E. P. Thompson and Natalie Davis." For the transference of that tradition from England to

the British North American colonies, see Young, "English Plebian Culture and Eighteenth-Century American Radicalism," 184–212; and Peter Linebaugh, "All the Atlantic Mountains Shook," 195–200. In her dissertation, Ann Little argues that people in New Haven colony did not use rough music to enforce social norms because the courts effectively policed the members of the community. As courts in New Haven became occupied with other matters in the eighteenth century, Little maintains, people increasingly used rough music to punish inappropriate behavior. See Little, "The Politics of Patriarchy," chap. 5. Compare Little with Dayton, *Women Before the Bar*, 121–38.

18. According to Michel Foucault, courts consisted of the combatants, the judge who presided over the proceedings, and the physical table between the two that represented a relatively equitable place where both parties could make their arguments. He maintains that crowds did not set up courts as institutions in the sense that the official governors could establish courts, or a court system, because the actions of the crowd always pitted the crowd against their enemies. Furthermore, Foucault argues, people in rebellion needed to destroy courts because the institution contained too much of the power they were overthrowing to be useful to their rebellion. It is important that he notes, too, that the ruling class used courts to turn one part of the lower class against another. Presumably, they could exercise such power in the courts because they dominated the courts. That was certainly the case in colonial New York. What emerges from Foucault's analysis of courts as an institution is that the ostensibly impartial jurists judged only their peers impartially. When "lower sort" people appeared in court, the judges used their power against the lower sort and to disrupt the emerging collective consciousness of the lower sort. In other words, the court, for Foucault, was established with only the image of impartiality and the courts rapidly became places where one class or group confronted their opponents. Thus, in New York, the court the rioters established resembled the official court because they both were dominated by one class who used their power to oppress their opponents. See Michel Foucault, *Power/Knowledge: Selected Interviews and Other Writings, 1972–1977* (New York: Pantheon, 1980), chap. 1.

For a discussion of how land ownership helped shape people's political and economic activities, and for how property ownership dictated the structure of power in colonial New York, see Irving Mark, *Agrarian Conflicts in Colonial New* York (Port Washington, N.Y.: Friedman, 1940), chap. 2; Sung Bok Kim, *Landlord and Tenant in Colonial New York: Manorial Society, 1660–1775* (Chapel Hill: University of North Carolina Press, 1978), chap. 3; and Countryman, *A People in Revolution*, 74–85. When New York landlords did not think they could win a legal battle over property, they sometimes tried to fix the trial; see *The King agt. Dirck Swart*, January 23, 1768, Unsorted Lawsuits, P–U, Kempe Papers, NYHS. Swart was an agent of the Van Rensselaers, who owned a one-million-acre estate in Albany County, New York, and who faced serious threats to their land in the early 1760s. Swart tried to fix the jury in a case in which opponents of the Van Rensselaers challenged the boundaries of their estate. For jury trials in New York, see Klein, "From Community to Status: The Development of the Legal Profession in Colonial New York," 133–56; and Klein, "Prelude to Revolution: Jury Trials and Judicial Tenure," *William & Mary Quarterly*, 3rd ser., 27 (October 1960), 439–62. Klein's discussion focuses on the legal profession, and courts, as institutions rather than as participants or arenas of cultural and social debate.

19. *Boston Gazette*, July 14 and August 4, 1766; *New-York Mercury*, July 28, 1766; and the Geographical, Historical Narrative, vol. 707, folios 18–19, 32–33, quoted in Mark, *Agrarian Conflicts*, 148–49.

20. See the discussion of suffrage and jury service in E. Maria Becker, "The 801 Westchester County Freeholders of 1763," *New York Historical Society Quarterly* 35 (July 1951), 282–321; *Historical Memoirs of William Smith*, July 10, 1766, 34; and Prendergast quoted in G. D. Scull,

Montresor Journals, in *Collections of the New-York Historical Society* (New York, 1882), 384 (entry dated August 19, 1766).

British Parliament passed the Stamp Act in 1765 to raise revenue in the British North American colonies to help pay for colonial administration. The Act dictated that colonists buy the appropriate stamped paper to carry out any activity outlined in the Act and included legal, church, and commercial documents, playing cards, books, and newspapers. The Act would have affected nearly every colonist at one point in his or her life, but it struck particularly hard at the urban colonial elite, which consisted of the majority of lawyers and businessmen in the colonies. For a fuller explanation of the Stamp Act, and how colonists responded to it in different and sometimes dangerous ways, see Morgan and Morgan, *The Stamp Act Crisis*, 119–33; Bailyn, *The Ideological Origins of the American Revolution*, 99–102; Morgan, *Inventing the People*, 239; and Wood, *The Radicalism of the American Revolution*, 172–75. For historians who have tried to place the Stamp Act riots into a broader Atlantic world perspective, and who correctly give agency to lower sort colonists, see Hoerder, *Crowd Action*, chaps. 1 and 2; and Countryman, *A People in Revolution*, chaps. 1 and 2.

21. *Boston Gazette*, September 15, 1766.

22. Sentence quoted in *New-York Mercury*, August 18, 1766; *New-York Gazette*, September 1, 1766. See also the descriptions of the case, the verdict, and the sentence in the *Boston Gazette*, September 1 and 8, 1766. William Smith quoted in Staughton Lynd, *Anti-Federalism in Dutchess County, New York* (Chicago: Loyola University Press, 1962), 50.

23. John Tabor Kempe quoted in Mark and Handlin, "*The King v. William Prendergast*," 170–71; Kempe expressed his opinions on rural rioters in *The King v. Elisha Cole*, June 13, 1766, Sorted Legal Manuscripts, Box 2, Kempe Papers, NYHS; Governor Henry Moore to the Lords of Trade, New York City, August 12, 1766, *Documents Relative to the Colonial History of the State of New York*, 7:849–50; *Historical Memoirs of William Smith*, vol. 1, July 10, 1766, 33–34.

24. For the prospect of spontaneous crowd violence, and for ritualized violence to be captivating and entertaining, see Mikhail Baktin, *Rabelais and His World*, trans. Hélène Iswolsky (Bloomington: Indiana University Press, 1984), chap. 1. Baktin particularly writes: "One of the indispensable elements of the folk festival was travesty, that is the renewal of clothes and of the social image. Another essential element was a reversal of hierarchic levels" (81). See also Bill Buford's analysis of English soccer supporters in the 1980s in his *Among the Thugs* (New York: W. W. Norton, 1992), in which Buford concludes that "violence is one of the most intensely lived experiences and, for those capable of giving themselves over to it, is one of the most intense pleasures" (205). See also Darnton, "Workers Revolt," in *The Great Cat Massacre*, in which he notes that such an examination helps us see how "workers made their experience meaningful by playing with themes of their culture" (99).

6

Play as Prelude to Revolution: Boston, 1765–1776

William Pencak

Play, Space, and Revolution: Theory

In 1977, the philosopher Roberta Kevelson argued in *Inlaws/Outlaws: A Semiotic of Systematic Interaction* that one of the most important forces for change in human history is the interrelationship among play, artistic and intellectual creation arising from play, statutory law, and political protest. Kevelson supported her thesis by analyzing the Robin Hood ballads as the poetic form that perpetuated the tradition of outlawry emerging from the "play space" of the English forest, where Robin and his Merry Men not only defied tyranny but did it with a sense of humor. Sherwood Forest was a realm of freedom where "the emergent individual rebelled and asserted the prioritized order of personal right, communal bond, and the enormous stakes risked in the plea for justice." There the outlaw defied statutory law and established "an effective *praxis* for social change," for his rebellion created "competing orders of society and conflicting systems of law." The "Outlaw Ballad" and "Statutory Law" are "symbolic signs," the aesthetic expressions of an "agon" between, respectively, the "free" world of outlaw play space and the authoritarian realm of the king and his courts. The Outlaw Ballad stands up for both the sacred law of divine justice and the British common law guaranteeing communal and individual rights against the state and superior to profane law of the king. Out-law is egalitarian and created through interactive communication among all those who claim the right to speak; in-law is statutory, hierarchical, and handed down by decree.[1]

Kevelson's analysis is not completely original. It draws on Johan Huizinga, Charles Peirce, and Michel Foucault, although none of them linked the outlaw in his play space to the evolution of law, or showed how rebel ballads asserted a higher law than that proclaimed by statute. From Huizinga's classic study *Homo Ludens: A Study of the Play Element in Culture*, Kevelson borrows the insight that play, as a voluntary activity outside the demands of ordinary life, "is free, is in fact freedom." "Play" as used by Huizinga and Kevelson is more than fun and games; it refers to activity in a special space in which unusual behavior is tested in opposition to more institutional regulated spaces. "While it is in progress all is movement, change, alternation, succession, association, separation." Paradoxically, however, play "at once assumes fixed form as a cultural phenomenon." Play requires order, ritual, "the rules of the game"; "it creates order, *is* order," but not the mundane order of business as usual. "Into an imperfect world and into the confusion of life it brings a temporary, a limited perfection." Play occurs in "a sacred space, a temporary real world of its own, [that] has been expressly hedged off for it," from whence "it continues to shed its radiance on the ordinary world outside, a wholesome influence working security, order, and prosperity for the whole community." Hence, "the play-concept as such is of a higher order than seriousness. For seriousness seeks to exclude play, whereas play can well include seriousness."[2]

Students of the philosopher Charles S. Peirce will recognize in Huizinga and Kevelson echoes of Peirce's critique of evolution and determinism. Peirce described his work as "an onslaught upon the doctrine of necessity." He coined the terms "anancastic evolution" or "cataclasmine evolution" to deny the gradual, nonrevolutionary "progress" that so enthralled his late-nineteenth-century contemporaries. He insisted that progress came through "leaps" and "the violent breaking up of habits": "Anancastic evolution advances by successive strides with pauses in between. The reason is that in this process a habit of thought having been overthrown is supplanted by the next strongest. Now this next strongest is sure to be widely disparate from the first, and as often as not its direct contrary." Troubled times are golden moments of opportunity for the exceptional person to lead a community toward something genuinely new—which Peirce insisted came from "pure play" or "musement" rather than predictable historical forces.[3]

At first glance, Kevelson's insistence on spontaneity and play, and her approach to reality as an ever-changing kaleidoscope—that preserves constant movement and change without deconstructing the world as the kaleidoscope contains recognizable shapes, or facts, to construct shifting configurations—seem to be far removed from the theories of Michel Foucault. Foucault is most famous for showing how supposedly free societies discipline and punish their members through "micro-tyrannies" exerted by through the "capillaries of power." But he also found a way out: individuals can adopt "a strategy of struggle," appearing as "points of insubordination" who confront the powers that be and "escape." They "open a void, a moment of silence, a question without an answer, provoke a breach without reconciliation where the world is forced to question itself." Foucault calls these spaces where creativity flourishes "heterotopias," astutely noting that such "spaces" become the sites "of contestation," "of concrete freedom, i.e. of possible transformation." He therefore praised Nietzsche's "effective history," which "introduces discontinuity into our very being—as it divides our emotions, dramatizes our instincts, multiplies our body."[4] Revolution and play thus go hand-in-hand, especially in preliminary stages before things get deadly.

The Case of Revolutionary Boston

Boston between 1765 and 1776 was such a play space in which creative freedom flourished. While the content of revolutionary thought was conservative—stressing preservation of traditional colonial rights to self-taxation and government—the manner of its assertion was revolutionary. Bostonian protests contained within them the embryo of a new social order that would redefine America as a unique space of freedom in human history and condemn those who thought otherwise.

Popular protest in Boston utilized nine elements that might be considered play in Huizinga's sense:

1. Revolutionaries encouraged the involvement of boys.
2. Patriots used play as an excuse to minimize the severity of their protests, and thereby argue that the authorities' response was all out of proportion to the offenses committed.
3. Disguises and pseudonyms, including the presentation of adult rioters

as boys, were employed not only to mask identities but also to symbolize the fact that people were stepping outside their normal routines and creating new identities and a new structure of authority.
4. Humor was used to mock-punish, mock-execute, and mock-bury supporters of Britain.
5. New holidays and processions replaced older official celebrations and those sanctioned by popular custom. Some of these activities commemorated events in which the Bostonians themselves had participated, thus giving them a sense of creating a heroic, memorable society whose deeds supplanted those they had previously celebrated.
6. Much protest literature took the form of sarcastic humor.
7. Crowd activity replaced traditional symbols of law and authority with another system located outdoors in play space, or indoors as the crowd moved into enclosed public spaces from which it had hitherto been excluded. A tree was dubbed the Liberty Tree to replace the province and townhouse as the central location of symbolic authority and punishment.
8. Officials who refused to enter into dialogue with the crowd and recognize the legitimacy of its space became targets of protest. The crowd forced them to relocate to its space, thereby recasting itself as the ultimate legal and moral authority, both indoors and outdoors, since it claimed the right to locate the seat of societal judgment and call its putative betters to account there.
9. Revolutionary songs redefined America as a play space or realm of nature exempted from the stultifying constraints of the tyrannies that confined most of the world's population.

Let us see how these points help us look anew at the nature of the American Revolution.

Involvement of Boys:

1. Schoolboys appeared in Boston's very first revolutionary crowd actions, those protesting the Stamp Act in August 1765. "You would have laughed to have seen two or three hundred little boys with a flag marching in a procession on which was King, [William] Pitt, & Liberty forever, it ought to have been Pitt, [John] Wilkes, & Liberty," reported "Loyal Nine" crowd organizer John Avery Jr. concerning the August 14 protest against Stamp Master Andrew Oliver.[5] "Boys and Children" were ostensi-

bly responsible for starting the fire that signaled the riots of August 26, although "whispers from a person unknown," reinforced by physical coercion and "insult and outrage" against government officials, ensured that they were not dispersed. Later that night, when Lieutenant Governor Thomas Hutchinson's house was destroyed, "a number of boys from fourteen to sixteen years of age, some mere children, did a great deal of damage."[6]

Crowds of lads roamed Boston in the late 1760s to enforce the nonimportation agreements. On February, 22, 1770, between sixty and three hundred schoolboys, symbolically imitating the European custom of placing the severed heads of traitors on poles, placed such an effigy on a post in front of the house of Theophilus Lillie, who was openly violating the agreement. When Ebenezer Richardson, a customs informer who lived next door, tried to knock down the post, the boys began throwing sticks and stones at him. When he retreated to his house, "the boys assembled and said they were going to have a frolick," one witness reported; another noted that some men looking on laughed as the boys "carried the pageantry." Unfortunately, Richardson did not see any humor in the affair and fired on the crowd, killing one lad and wounding another. Boys aged fourteen to fifteen, "swearing and cursing," then throwing snowballs, sticks, and pieces of ice, also initiated the Boston Massacre two weeks later.[7]

"Play" Employed to Minimize Seriousness of Protests:

2. Boys served two useful purposes in the Boston crowd. First, riots in which hundreds of people threatened British officials could be dismissed as hysterical overreactions to boys at play. The prosecution's case in the Boston Massacre, for instance, rested on the assertion that "this violent attack [on the soldiers] turns out to be nothing more, than a few snowballs, thrown by a parcel of boys, the most of them at a considerable distance, and as likely to hit the inhabitants as the soldiers, . . . a common case in the streets of Boston at this [winter] season of the year."[8] Defending the soldiers who fired on the crowd, John Adams said: "We have been entertained with a great variety of phrases to avoid calling this sort of people a mob. Some call them shavers, some call them geniuses. The plain English is, gentlemen, [that they were] most probably a motley rabble of saucy boys, negroes and mulattoes, Irish teagues, and outlandish [foreign] jack

tars [sailors]. And why we should scruple to call such a set of people a mob, I can't conceive, unless the name is too respectable for them."[9] Similarly, Boston's *Gazette* played on the theme of age versus youth in lamenting the death of the boy killed by Richardson: "Inhumanly murdered, the young lad . . . last week fell a sacrifice to the rage and malice of an old offender and his abettors." John Adams commented: "The ardor of the people is not to be quelled by the slaughter of one child and the wounding of another."[10]

The Boston patriots themselves assumed the name "Sons of Liberty" or "Liberty Boys" to identify their most prominent organization. Starting on November 5, 1765, they began to join the real boys who, in Pope's Day processions, had previously taken to the streets, tormenting effigies of the Pope and the Catholic Pretender while wearing imitation bishops' miters and pretending to be "imps of the Devil."[11] Scholars Michael Wallace, Edwin Burrowes, Winthrop Jordan, and Jay Fliegelman have emphasized the patriarchal and matriarchal metaphors that were employed by both Americans and Britons to define the relationship of sons—not daughters—to a father or mother country. For the British, the Americans were ungrateful and disobedient children. They in turn, considered themselves adults ready to govern their own affairs.[12]

Rebels also called attention to their youth and that of their land in song. Dr. Joseph Warren, the lawyer who defended the British soldiers accused of the Boston Massacre and who died at Bunker Hill, wrote of "Free Amerikay," "this maiden climate" inhabited by "sons" who will some day assume the mantle of their fathers: "Some future day shall crown us the masters of the main." William Billings, Bostonian patriot and perhaps the most famous colonial American composer, wrote in "Chester" of how "Their veterans flee before our youth, / And gen'rals yield to beardless boys."[13]

Disguises and Pseudonyms:

3. Besides identifying their rebellion with youth, the patriots played other games and assumed other guises. At the Tea Party, they disguised themselves as "Mohawks"—perhaps serving notice that Indians from North America could triumph over the East India Company. The participants wore rough blankets, painting their faces and speaking in mock-Indian jargon they invented for the occasion.[14] In their pamphlets, Bosto-

nian writers identified with the common people—"Humphrey Ploughjogger" (John Adams), "Populus" (Samuel Adams)—or the community ("A Friend to the Community," "Americanus," John Adams as "Novanglus" [New England]). Classical heroes' names, such as "Mentor," "Junius Brutus," Caesar's assassin, and "Callisthenes" (Josiah Quincy), or concepts like "Vindex" and "Candidus" (Samuel Adams), were also popular. Biblical figures, including "Joshua" and "Elisha," and heroes of seventeenth-century British freedom struggles, such as "Hampden," "Sidney," and "O.C." (Oliver Cromwell), reappeared to aid their spiritual descendants. Samuel Adams resurrected Puritan minister "Cotton Mather" as well.[15]

Loyalists and patriots traded self-praise and insults through impersonation. One exasperated loyalist urged readers to spurn "yon patriot bellowing loud" and "pull off the mask" of liberty that hid the "private grudge or party rage that forms the scheme." A loyalist pamphleteer, John Mein, gave such aliases as "Johnny Dupe" to John Hancock, and "Muddlehead" to Otis, calling attention to Hancock's funding of much protest activity and Otis's increasing insanity.[16] Patriots responded in kind: Mercy Otis Warren's play "The Group" featured prominent loyalists in the guises of Hazlerod, Meagre, Hateall, Beau Trumps, Humbug, Spendall, Dupe, and Fribble.[17] The rebels symbolically took on the mantle of past greatness when James Otis appeared on the cover of Bickerstaff's *Almanac* for 1770 supported by Liberty and Hercules, who treaded a serpent under his feet. In 1774, however, Gleason's *Massachusetts Calendar* depicted Governor Thomas Hutchinson at the hour of his death with a copy of Machiavelli's works at his feet while a devil, a skeleton, a serpent, and an alligator torment him.[18] Boston crowd leader Ebenezer Mackintosh named his son Pasquale Paoli Mackintosh, thereby identifying Boston's cause with the struggle for freedom then going on in Corsica under Paoli's direction; Hutchinson, however, compared Mackintosh to Massianello, the Sicilian revolutionary whom he considered a destructive bandit.[19] Disguises and play became vehicles through which revolutionaries could identify with cosmic struggles from the Bible, antiquity, British history, and even the eternal struggle of God against the devil.

Mock Punishments, Executions, and Burials:

4. Elements of humor, frequently of a sardonic and far from harmless sort, abounded in the protests against Britain beginning with the Stamp

Act riots. Stamp Master Andrew Oliver's effigy was hung from the large elm that would become the "Liberty Tree." Attached to it was a poem: "Fair freedom's glorious cause I've meanly quitted / For the sake of pelf; / But ah! The Devil has me outwitted, / And instead of *stamping* others, I've *hang'd* myself." A devil's imp in obvious imitation of the annual Pope's Day festivities pointed a pitchfork at the effigy, while the devil himself peeped out of a boot—a pun on the name of former British Prime Minister Lord Bute (pronounced Boot), who was widely if erroneously believed to be responsible for the Stamp Act. The boot had a "Green vile" sole, which referred to Britain's current head of government, George Grenville. A crowd in a "joyous" mood gathered at the site and insisted on mock-stamping all the goods being brought into town, for the Tree was on the only road into Boston over the narrow neck that connected it to the mainland. The stamps were playfully considered "the mark of the Beast," foretold in the biblical book of Revelation. The effigies were then paraded around town, beheaded, and burned in the manner of Pope's Day figures.[20]

Similarly, when Lieutenant Governor Thomas Hutchinson's house was destroyed on August 26, the crowd went out of its way to "stamp" (the word they used) on furniture, books, and other items before destroying them: the footprints on Hutchinson's manuscript collection and the draft of his *History . . . of Massachusetts-Bay* may be viewed in the Massachusetts Archives via microfilm. The obnoxious loyalist printer John Mein (pronounced Mean) was especially vulnerable to puns on his name, as when he stood in for the Pope and was burned in effigy in 1769: "*M*ean is the man, M——n is his name, / *E*nough he's spread his hellish fame; / *I*nfernal furies hurl his soul, / *N*ine Million times from Pole to Pole."[21] These four verses also formed an acrostic using his name.

Loyalist Justice of the Peace John Murray also suffered from the crowd's humor. In 1769, when he attempted to release on bail a man who was implicated as an accessory in the beating of James Otis by a customs officer, a crowd refused to let him take depositions in the case, pulled off his wig, and carried it behind him on a pole as he was escorted out of Fanueil Hall at the head of a raucous procession. By removing the symbol of his upper-class status and mocking rather than honoring him by following him through the streets, the crowd reduced Murray to its own level.[22]

"Hillsborough treats" (or feces), named for the newly appointed British Secretary of State for the Colonies, were smeared on the houses, and in one instance the person of merchants who refused to sign the nonimportation agreements, symbolically indicating what the populace thought of them and the British goods they attempted to sell. The *Boston Gazette* was especially pleased when Thomas Hutchinson's two sons, "the TWO CHILDREN," finally signed the agreement after their shop had been repeatedly targeted.[23] In an interesting role reversal, the revolutionaries' adolescent behavior in intimidating the importers was projected onto two adult merchants whose sole claim to importance was their powerful father. And British soldiers were taunted with cries of "lobsters" or "bloody backs" to rub symbolic salt in the wounds of the brutal floggings they received.[24]

The ultimate instance of brutal yet playful revolutionary humor was the act of tarring and feathering, which made a human being resemble a chicken. The pseudonymous Joyce Jr. was captain of the "Committee for Tarring and Feathering," established in 1774 by Boston's leaders to limit such incidents only to those that were considered absolutely necessary. "Modern dress," "the American Mode," a "New England jacket," and especially "a new method of macaroni making as practiced at Boston," were euphemisms for the punishment.[25] Macaronis (from the Italian *ma carone* [my dearest one], for Italian clothes, art, and opera were cultural affectations of the contemporary British aristocracy) were dandies, London's eighteenth-century Eurotrash; tarring and feathering mocked aristocratic pretensions just as the original British words to "Yankee Doodle" (whose main character "stuck a feather in his cap and called it macaroni") made fun of Americans' efforts to imitate their "betters." Americans, of course, reversed the reversal and adopted the song as their own.[26]

Creation of New Festivities:

5. Bostonians also redefined themselves by creating new public festivals. Pope's Day itself was transformed. No longer did the North End and South End mobs battle for possession of their respective effigies. Instead, on November 5, 1765, the crowds, united behind a smartly uniformed Ebenezer Mackintosh, marched together through the streets. In a mock coronation ceremony, Mackintosh had been inaugurated as "First Captain-General of the Liberty Tree" on November 1, appropriately All Souls' Day. Accompanying Mackintosh was General William Brattle, a future loyalist but at the time a staunch patriot and commander of the province's armed forces. By placing Mackintosh at the head of the column, the mob and

the militia were equated as defenders of communal liberty (indeed, their membership overlapped considerably), and Mackintosh was granted equal symbolic generalship with Brattle. No longer did a mob dressed as shabbily as they could, and with blackened faces (although the Tea Party seems to have borrowed these customs), enter the houses of the well-to-do, practice "anticks," "demean themselves with great insolence," and break windows if their hosts refused to reward their efforts with small sums of money. Beginning in 1765, this raucous forerunner of Halloween was institutionalized as play merged into politics, and respectable inhabitants joined in the procession. Largesse was now administered through distribution of refreshments paid for by such prominent Whigs as John Hancock. Henceforth, the Pope and the Pretender were either supplanted or supplemented by images of Governor Francis Bernard and his successor Thomas Hutchinson, and other villains from both sides of the Atlantic. The newly appointed customs commissioners had the misfortune to arrive in Boston on Pope's Day 1767, to be met by a large crowd parading the usual devils, popes, and pretenders with signs on their breasts: "Liberty & Property & No Commissioners."[27] Threats of murder conveyed through symbolic execution could thus be simultaneously interpreted by their perpetrators as no more than playful public ritual.

Boston patriots annually celebrated such events as the August 14 riots and the repeal of the Stamp Act, but no commemoration was more striking than the yearly remembrance of the Boston Massacre of March 5, 1770. Each year thereafter, until 1783, elaborate tableaux and symbolic reenactments of the event preceded the Massacre Oration, in which the people were exhorted not to betray the honored dead by failing to defend their liberties. Joseph Warren's speech in 1775, some six weeks before the battles at Lexington and Concord, predicted the impending war and rhapsodized that by preparing to sacrifice themselves in the manner of Crispus Attucks and his fellow heroes, they would earn eternal salvation in establishing a country where virtue and happiness could coincide—a playground, in other words.[28] "Having redeemed your country, and secured the blessing to future generations, *who,* fired by your example, shall emulate your virtues, and learn from *you* the heavenly art of making millions happy; with heart-felt joy—with transports all your own, YOU CRY, THE GLORIOUS WORK IS DONE. Then drop the mantel to some young ELISHA, and take your seats with kindred spirits in your native skies."

Work will be finished, millions will be happy, people will go into transports and ecstasies, and there will be no more need for Elishas to battle tyranny. Little transition will be required from the "heavenly art" practiced in America to the heavenly joys of the afterlife. Warren has placed his cause and his countrymen's deeds in a long chain of heroism dating back to the Bible and extending indefinitely into the future. Ironically, he himself became one of the necessary sacrifices when he died at Bunker Hill that June. In the 1776 Massacre Oration, the Rev. Peter Thatcher took language straight out of Thomas Paine's pamphlet *Common Sense,* published that January, to reinforce the idea of America as a sacred space in which freedom, compared to a beautiful woman, can receive the erotic love denied her elsewhere:[29] "Freedom is offered to us, she invites us to accept her blessings; driven from the other regions of the globe, she wishes to find an asylum in the wilds of America; with open arms let us receive the persecuted fair . . . and when the earthly scene shall be closing with us, let us expire with this prayer upon our quivering lips, O GOD LET AMERICA BE FREE."

The "wilds" of America, out-law space, has become an "asylum"—a Sherwood Forest, a place that is both safe and wild, a play space, in other words. The outlaws have taken over, and the rest of the world has been revalorized as outside true law and God's will.

Sarcasm:

6. In the years preceding the Revolution, America was being redefined not only as a place for freedom but also as a land of play and humor, in songs and literature as well in protests and rituals. Logical argument may have been the tool of the pamphlets and speeches addressed to royal governors and Parliament, but sarcasm that often turned vicious dominated the cartoons, broadsides, almanacs, and popular literature that conveyed the revolutionary message to the general public. Take, for instance, a poem that appeared in the *Boston Gazette* on December 2, 1765:

> Spurn the Relation—She's no more a Mother,
> Than Lewis to George, a Most Christian Brother,
> In French Wars and Scotch, grown generous and rich
> She gives her dear children pox, slavery, and itch.

Humor can barely hide the fact that, even at this early stage in the colonial protests, America's relationship with Britain is placed on the level of

Britain's relationship with France—two nations that had been at war for most of the eighteenth century. All the colonies get from what is no longer their mother—the "monster" of Paine's *Common Sense* has already appeared to devour her young—is slavery and venereal disease, with the implied whoring and illegitimacy. In the Massachusetts legislature, James Otis not only denied Parliament the right to legislate for the colonies on constitutional grounds, but also morally condemned the members of Parliament who had voted to tax the colonists. All they learned at Oxford and Cambridge was "smoking, whoring, and drinking." "Button-makers, pin-makers [industrialists], horse-jockeys [nobles], courtiers, pensioners, pimps, and whoremasters" dominated the House of Commons. They wanted to violate America, treat her as a pimp would use a whore, but they had also abused and destroyed their own play space and were now seeking to do the same elsewhere. The persecuted fair maid of freedom could retain her virginity only apart from such perversions.[30]

Historians have not paid sufficient attention to the power of the identification of loyalists and the British with excrement and disgusting forms of sexual intercourse. The strength of these statements can best be realized if we recall the similar forms of protest and language that students injected into political discourse during the 1960s. Furthermore, tarring and feathering involved stripping the victim naked, turning him into a being resembling a chicken, and placing him on a rail in a manner that caused pain in his genitals—that is, symbolically robbing him of his masculinity and humanity and identifying him with a female bird known for its cowardice.

Relocation of Political Authority:

7. Massachusetts protesters placed at the center of their play space a miniature version of a natural world in the form of the Liberty Tree. The focus of public authority shifted as of August 14, 1765, from the official government buildings to the outdoors, from no longer legitimate authorities to a people who symbolically entered the state of nature every time they met to discuss their rights and protest violations against them. The tree was an old elm in a grove of trees on the only road out of Boston over the narrow "neck" that separated it from the rest of Massachusetts. It linked town and country, and it was there, rather than in the courts or at the usual sites of government, that enemies of the people were executed in effigy or forced to acknowledge the people's supremacy.

Government Officials Forced to Enter the Crowd's Space:

8. For instance, the crowd insisted that Stamp Master Andrew Oliver resign at the Liberty Tree when his commission arrived. But though Oliver had written to Britain and asked leave to resign, had promised not to execute the act in the meantime, had refused the customs commissioners' requests to issue stamps, and had even published a notice in the *Boston Gazette* that he had "taken no measures to qualify himself for the office, nor had he any thoughts of doing so" (that is, indicated his refusal of the office in no fewer than four different ways), the Sons of Liberty deemed his actions unsatisfactory. They demanded a public resignation: "N.B. Provided you comply with the above, you shall be treated with the greatest politeness and humanity. If not —!" Oliver had no objection to resigning, but aware of the symbolic importance of the place where he did so, "he sent to T. Dawes [a leading patriot whose nephew William was the other rider with Paul Revere] to desire him to interpose and at least procure leave for him to resign at the town house but after two or three consultations nothing more could be obtained than a promise of having no affront offered and a proposal to invite the principal persons of the town to accompany him." Crowd leader Mackintosh escorted Oliver in the pouring rain to the Liberty Tree, where he resigned again. It is significant that in damaging Oliver's house during the August 14 riot the crowd chose to tear down his garden fences, break his windows, and batter down his door. The barriers he had erected between himself and the crowd—symbolically, between two types of law, two visions of society—came down.[31]

Twelve days later, the first demand the mob made when it surrounded Lieutenant-Governor Hutchinson's house was that he come outdoors, speak with them, and deny he had anything to do with writing or enforcing the Stamp Act. Like Oliver, Hutchinson realized that by entering the outlaw space of the crowd he would be acknowledging its superior authority, and he termed this "an indignity to which he would not submit"; he had likewise refused repeated requests from both newspapers and private parties to state that he had not supported the Stamp Act. To prove his innocence, all he really had to do was publish some private correspondence (unearthed by Edmund S. Morgan in the mid-twentieth century) in which he opposed the Act every bit as eloquently as his political opponents.[32]

Hutchinson and Oliver both refused to speak to a crowd of people assembled outside the regular government institutions, to acknowledge such an ad hoc group as "the people," and to accept their own accountability to them. For these officials, "the people" could only speak through their legally chosen representatives, not through a self-selected group of protesters. At issue was who were "the people" and in what capacity could they be represented. In 1748, justifying the mob that resisted a massive naval impressment, a group including the young Samuel Adams argued in their protest newspaper, the *Independent Advertiser,* that it was notorious that "the sober sort, who dared to express due sense of their injuries, were invidiously represented as a rude, low-lived mob."[33] Similarly in 1765, John Adams could only deduce that Oliver and Hutchinson were in fact secret abettors of the Stamp Act—itself evidence of a scheme "to reduce the body of the people to ignorance, poverty, dependence"—because by refusing to vindicate themselves before the crowd, they showed "a contempt of that equality in knowledge, wealth, and power, which has prevailed in this country."[34] For Adams, these two high-ranking officials were no better than the average inhabitant and were obliged to speak to him as an equal.

Hutchinson's and Oliver's refusal at the time of the Stamp Act to put themselves on a plane of equality with a group they considered "rabble" in fact symbolized the manner in which a Massachusetts administrative elite—negatively signified as "pensioners," or recipients of unearned income in the form of government salaries—had been distancing itself from the people of Boston for a quarter-century. Beginning around 1740, they began to live as much as possible in suburban country houses constructed in imitation of the British gentry. Many, although not Hutchinson and Oliver, joined the Anglican church, which their compatriots spurned as a mask for popery. And the elite intermarried and socialized among themselves, becoming more and more a group that believed it was entitled to rule and receive deference.[35] The people symbolically tried to break down these barriers by tearing down Hutchinson's and Oliver's fences and entering their houses in violation of the privacy they had so carefully cultivated. They insisted not only that Oliver resign but also that he do so in a humiliating manner at a site where his authority counted for nothing vis-à-vis the Sons of Liberty.

Hutchinson, by refusing to speak to the crowd, was obliged to flee from it or suffer death. He in fact appeared willing to die, but he left his house only when his elder daughter refused to go without him. His unwillingness to communicate with the crowd except in his official role, combined with the remarks he made from the bench of the Superior Court over which he presided as chief justice the next day, explains why Hutchinson was detested. First, he stated that the distress of his family was "infinitely more insupportable than what I feel for myself." Hutchinson had antagonized the people precisely by being overly solicitous of his family in obtaining government positions for his relatives and socializing primarily with an extended kinship network. He had adopted a privatized personal life that he refused to view as incompatible with his official responsibilities. Then he apologized for the fact that he had to wear old, borrowed clothes instead of his usual judicial robes, which had been destroyed. In other words, he objected to being sartorially on a level with the crowd. He also expressed indifference to his life, stating that he did not clear his name "through timidity" and adding: "They can only take away my life, which is of but little value to me when deprived of all its comforts, all that is dear to me, and nothing surrounding me but the most piercing distress."[36] Apart from his possessions and official symbols of office, Hutchinson was saying, life was not worth living. These remarks must only have added to the hostility of a town that had suffered from protracted poverty and depression and where men were claiming that to die in defense of their liberties was a badge of honor.

Only in the official venue of the Superior Court did Hutchinson reveal his true position on the Stamp Act; he had refused to do so before what he had already deemed a new "model of government" where "the authority is in the populace."[37] In a scene that moved even his opponents, he called "GOD to witness (and I would not for a thousand worlds call my *Maker* to witness to a falsehood) . . . that I never, in New England or Old, in Great Britain or America, neither directly nor indirectly, was aiding, assisting, or supporting, or in the least promoting or encouraging what is commonly called the STAMP ACT, but on the contrary, did all in my power, and strove as much as in me lay, to prevent it." Hutchinson's lobbying occurred in private letters to influential people rather than in published or public statements, which is yet another sign of his estrangement from the evolving popular political culture. While his conduct and writings show him to be as aware as contemporary theorist Jürgen Habermas that people from a previously apolitical "private sphere" were demanding political authority, he abhorred rather than celebrated this development.[38]

The out-law crowd not only insisted that the government acknowledge the superiority of its space, or law, but also encroached on regular law space. The people entered the legislative chamber in Massachusetts for the first time in 1766, when a gallery was built to accommodate them. No longer were debates kept secret so representatives could speak their own minds without fear of reprisal. The legislators' behavior would henceforth be subject to popular scrutiny, primarily of the Bostonian protesters.[39] And during the trial of Ebenezer Richardson, the crowd encroached on the precincts of justice as well. When Chief Justice Peter Oliver charged the jury to find a verdict of justifiable homicide, his life was threatened: " 'D——n that judge, if I was nigh him, I would give it to him' [someone shouted]; but this was not a time, to attempt to preserve decorum; preservation of life was as much as a judge dared to aim at." The mob shouted out to the jury, "Blood requires blood!" and hissed the judges as they left the court.[40]

While compelling native sons like Hutchinson and Oliver to come down to their level, the Bostonians insisted that customs commissioners and British soldiers had no right to share their space at all. The customs commissioners were "warned out" of town in effigy on the day of their arrival—a practice New Englanders reserved for newcomers to let them know that if they became indigent they could not expect the community to support them. They were then actually chased out the next year by being subjected to rituals in which the crowds searched and seized *their* premises and possessions—which was a reversal of who had the formal right to intrude on others' spaces. In June 1768, in yet another case of the crowd assuming the powers of government, people assembled at the Liberty Tree and condemned and then burned a boat belonging to Customs Commissioner Harrison, following a mock vice-admiralty court proceeding. In July, Customs Commissioner Robinson's house was thoroughly searched in hopes of finding him. In a parody of the searches undertaken by the customs service for contraband, it was conducted "not by virtue of any writ of assistance, but by candle light." The crowd searched "out-houses, bales, barrels, mealtubs, trunks, boxes, packs, and packages, packed and unpacked, and in short, every hole and corner sufficient to conceal a ram cat, or a commissioner, they could find neither." (Note that the first place mentioned was the place for excrement.) The commissioners got the message and fled to the protection of the British fleet.[41]

When the soldiers came to Boston in 1768, even the provincial council tried to deny them barracks in the town, which caused their commander to quarter his troops on the Boston Common, land collectively possessed and used by the inhabitants of the town. Because some seventy soldiers had deserted, with the connivance of the people, within two weeks of arriving, sentries were ordered to be especially watchful. Bostonians balked at responding "Friend!" to the usual challenge of "Friend or Foe?" and hauled soldiers into sympathetic local courts for assault if they attempted to stop them. Given the cheapness of rum and the fact that soldiers had almost nothing to do, fights broke out between the troops and the inhabitants. The antagonism intensified when soldiers on military pay would perform unskilled labor in their spare time more cheaply than those who depended on those jobs for their entire livelihood. The fatal violent clash occurred after a year and a half, and the outcome of the "Massacre" of seven Bostonians led to fierce threats that the inhabitants of the province would join the townfolk in massacring the twelve hundred troops, which induced Governor Hutchinson to exile them to barracks on Castle William, an island in Boston Harbor.[42] The Bostonians thus symbolically fought for and won their "independence" of soldiers who remained exiled on an island from 1770 to 1774.

America Signified as "Play Space" in Song:

9. Two lyrics written in response to the Boston Massacre illustrate the redefinition of America in the song literature of the Revolution as approximating a felicitous—rather than the chaotic Hobbesian or Lockean—state of nature, a land of play, an out-law space different from the rest of the world.[43] One tune, "Unhappy Boston," straightforwardly condemned the soldiers as "fierce barbarians grinning over their prey," which accompanied the famous and false Paul Revere engraving showing soldiers firing in unison at Captain Preston's command on helpless civilians. The poet appealed to God, "a judge who can never be bribed," who "strips the murderer of his soul," to do justice if somehow the loyalists on Massachusetts' "venal courts, the scandal of the land," connived to free the accused troops, which they ultimately did on obvious grounds of self-defense. The courts, or the official law, have become the scandal of "the land," the natural society. The song opens with a lament: "Unhappy Boston, see thy sons deplore, / Thy hallowed walks besmear'd with guiltless gore." Boston is a sacred space violated by "savage bands." Britain and its soldiers are placed outside true law as barbarians who enjoy slaughter. Defining Boston as inhabited by guiltless sons, the identification of America with childhood and innocence is confirmed; its law is one with the divine, and hence true law rather than the nonlaw of the legal authorities.

The other Massacre song, "You Simple Bostonians," sarcastically yet playfully assumes the voice of British troops. The patriots falsely claimed that this tune was "much in vogue among the friends to arbitrary power," but they published it to arouse the populace against the arrogance of an army that, although stranded on an island in the harbor after the Massacre, supposedly cherished thoughts of murderous revenge. The Bostonians are labeled "simple" in order to call attention to the fact that the British did not think much of their pride in their literacy and knowledge of their rights. The colonists' identification with a more natural society than Europe is also mocked when they are called "pumpkins." "Of your Liberty Tree, I'd have you take care," is the first threat the pretended soldier-songwriter makes, but destruction of the symbol is only a prelude to the total destruction of American society: "For if that we chance to return to the town, / Your houses and stores will come tumbling down." In short, if the Americans thought having a few British soldiers in Boston was a violation of their liberty, they only had to wait for a larger fleet and army: "And to a bleak island, you shall not us drive, / In every house, you shall have three or four, / And if that will not please you, you shall have half a score." In other words, there are many more European Britons than American Britons, and they were determined to keep coming until the Liberty Tree and all it signified came down. (In fact, after Britain sent a large army to Boston in 1774 to enforce the Coercive Acts, the Liberty Tree was chopped down.)

As with many revolutionary songs, "You Simple Bostonians" put new words to an English tune—in this case, the popular "Derry Down," which is the chorus to each of four verses. It is most instructive to see what lyrics are being replaced. The English "Derry Down" began as a patriotic wartime song about a "Liberty Hall" written by George Alexander Stevens in 1757. It begins with the dismissal of "Old Homer . . . Grecians or Trojans" as "heathenish" heroes who need to be replaced by "hearts of oak"—that is, heroic, contemporary Britons, especially sailors. In the American version, it is the British who have become tyrants rather than heroes, and the indoors liberty "hall" of justice and government (a confined space) has been replaced by the out-law, outdoors "Liberty Tree," an open space. The juxtaposition is especially telling because the only "liberty hall" the British soldiers in Boston possess is the "bleak" fortification in the middle of a New England harbor. The use of "simple" Bostonians is also telling because the Bostonians had not been dismissing their classical heroes, but rather holding up a virtuous antiquity as a model to a corrupted Britain, as their pseudonyms—that is, play personae—suggested. Unlike the British "Liberty Hall," the Bostonians dismiss the "hearts of oak" rather than the classics.

But in Britain itself, a comic parody of "Derry Down" had quickly supplanted the original version. "Liberty Hall" was symbolically transformed from a symbol of British justice and civilization into George Colman's song "Lodgings for Single Gentlemen," which bemoaned that in "London, that overgrown place" there were plenty of bad, expensive lodgings, and "Will Waddle, whose temper was studious and lonely, / Hir'd lodgings that took Single Gentlemen only; / But Will was so fat, he appear'd like a ton,— / Or like two single gentlemen roll'd into one." If "You Simple Bostonians" is mocking the parody instead of, or in addition to, the original "Derry Down," "Single Gentlemen" refers to the exile of the British troops to the harbor island, to the problem of finding space for them in a land of liberty. The soldiers are thus identified with the comic, ineffectual "Will Waddle." "Waddle," of course, is the way a duck moves on the water, but in a person it implies the pathetic efforts of someone who is overweight to move from place to place. The soldiers, shifted from location to location in the course of their stay in Boston until they were exiled, were waddling indeed. The threat that they might return in greater numbers is dismissed by association of more soldiers with the overcrowding of London apartments by comic figures in the play *My Night Gown and Slippers* in which the "Derry Down" parody was sung.[44]

The greatest of the song adaptations made by the Bostonians rewrote the English patriotic tune "Heart of Oak" itself—still sufficiently famous that a British colleague could instantly recall its tune and words in 1996! Written by the great actor and playwright David Garrick in 1759 at the height of British triumphs in the Seven Years' War, it was performed in a play, titled *Harlequin's Invasion,* which revealed the utter contempt in which the British held—or pretended to hold—the possibility of a cross-channel invasion after the navy destroyed the French armada at Quiberon Bay. The song reeks of the arrogance and jingoism that maintained its momentum after the war and led to the crackdown on colonial autonomy:[45]

> Come, cheer up, my lads, 'tis to glory we steer,
> To add something more to this wonderful year;

> To honor we call you, as free men, not slaves,
> For who are as free as the sons of the waves?
>   Heart of oak are our ships,
>   Heart of oak are our men:
>   We are always ready
>   Steady, boys, steady,
>   We'll fight and we'll conquer again and again.

Further stanzas bemoan the fact that Britain's enemies are so afraid of her that they are always running away and she must pursue them even to get them to stand and fight. The song concludes with welcome anticipation of an invasion that will permit the British "to drub 'em on shore as we drubb'd 'em at sea."

There is much to unpack here. First, American colonials had a rather different experience of the connection of the British navy to freedom, as they universally detested and resisted naval impressment and frequently helped the suffering sailors to desert.[46] Second, "Heart of Oak" demonstrates that the British saw themselves as sons of liberty much as the Americans did. They too had a unique space for freedom: "the waves" of which Britain was the world's undisputed master. A drinking song sung in the play spaces of theaters and taverns, "Heart of Oak" urged men to fight, be cheerful, and praise "our soldiers, our sailors, our statesmen," all of whom were perceived as vehicles of liberty.

The American version of "Heart of Oak"—the "Liberty Song"—was written by Philadelphia lawyer John Dickinson.[47] Ironically, in light of the fact that he would oppose signing the Declaration of Independence, Dickinson mailed a copy of the song to Boston's James Otis on July 4, 1768. The lyrics and tune achieved great popularity there, manifested by two parodies that soon appeared as well. Dickinson's freemen do not define liberty through conquest, which is the only activity they undertake in Garrick's version. They answer the call not of Britain but of a "fair LIBERTY" (again, a beautiful woman) as "AMERICANS," symbolizing the intercolonial unity for which Dickinson and Otis were hoping. The Americans' heroes are not European Britains, but "our worthy *Forefathers*" who receive the "cheers" Garrick gives to the contemporary British soldiers, sailors, and statesmen, about whom the Americans had differing opinions. "To climates unknown [they] did courageously steer," Dickinson notes, indicating that the waves are not the true home of freedom, but in fact an obstacle that have to be overcome to obtain it: "Thro' oceans to deserts for freedom they came, / And dying bequeathed us their freedom and fame." Deserts, however, become revalorized as spaces where "the TREE their own hands had to LIBERTY rear'd." "Growing strong and revered," they "Cry'd" out in "transport[s]" of joy that "Our children shall gather the fruits of our pain." America is a land where men are born to freedom, as the new refrain emphasizes; "In FREEDOM we're BORN, and in FREEDOM we'll LIVE, / Our purses are ready, / Steady, friends, / Steady, / Not as SLAVES but as FREEMEN our Money we'll give."

Here, people no longer suffer, but enjoy: the Liberty Tree not only symbolizes the contemporary struggle, but also now retrospectively signifies the American experience from the beginning. The waves, or space, of British freedom have always been an ordeal for Americans—imagine being "Steady, friends, steady" on waves! The colonists needed to establish their own playground of liberty. And a playground it is, for, as a verse Dickinson sent in later as an addendum rhapsodizes, "How sweet are the labors that Freemen endure, / That they shall enjoy all the Profit, secure— / No more such sweet labors AMERICANS know, / If Britons shall reap what Americans sow." In America, labor is made sweet and transformed from endurance to enjoyment, and will remain so as long as Britons, who are now defined as a separate group from Americans, do not steal the harvest or tread on American space. Abundance leads to America's exceptional prosperity, and to Americans' belief that they were exceptionally immune to the tragedies of other nations.

However, Dickinson predicts a dire future if Americans are not "steady" in temporarily forsaking the joys of their land to sternly defend their right to maintain sole possession. "Swarms of PLACEMEN and PENSIONERS soon will appear," he predicts, "like locusts deforming the charms of the year." An enchanted land will be devoured by "swarms" of insects—a nice touch, which refers both to the author's opinion of the moral stature of British officeholders and to the biblical plagues that were but temporary obstacles to a chosen people bound for a land flowing with milk and honey. The next stanza urges unity: "By *uniting* we stand, by *dividing* we fall" (Franklin should not be given credit for everything memorable said in the eighteenth century!). After assuring his readers that heaven has blessed "each generous deed" they will perform in sacrificing for freedom, Dickinson offers them a destiny that is preferable to being mere heirs to glorious forefathers who dropped freedom in their laps. Dickinson's generation, too, can emulate the deeds of a glorious past rather than sycophantically enjoy their playground as children of heroic forefathers: "All ages shall speak with *Amaze* and *Applause,* / Of the *Courage we'll shew* in support of our laws." British North America, some two million people (one-fifth slaves plus a sizable contingent of white bound indentured servants), will be the wonder of the ages. Dickinson predicted a forthcoming war in which not British law but OUR LAWS will be defended—that is, the outlaws of the playground. "To DIE we can bear,—but, to SERVE we disdain, / For SHAME is to Freemen more dreadful than PAIN." Reputation and avoidance of unjust laws that reduce men to slaves can be achieved in opposition to the Britain that claimed to stand for "freemen not slaves" in "Heart of Oak." *You* are slaves, Dickinson is telling the British as he appropriates the song and its symbols.

Dickinson's final verse represents something of a backtracking (as this is only 1768) from the logical consequences of an argument Thomas Hutchinson saw so clearly three years earlier. The first eight verses of the song find nothing positive in Britain, extol formation of a separate identity, and define America as a space of freedom, as opposed to the slavery imposed by a British law now defined as alien, rather than the source of liberty—like the waves, it must be crossed, transgressed, to find real or out-law liberty. But suddenly Dickinson sings: "This bumper I crown for our SOVEREIGN's health, / And this for BRITANNIA's glory and wealth; / That wealth and that glory immortal may be, / If She is but *just*—and *We* are but *Free*." The last two lines reverse the apparent reversal of the first two: loyalty to Britain is conditional on Britain leaving the colonies alone. What makes Britain glorious is redefined from the conquest bragged about in Garrick's "Heart of Oak" to an imperial power that refuses to impose its laws on the unwilling. Britain, in other words, should glory in the liberty of its colonies, which replaces militancy urged in Garrick's song. But just as Garrick dares his nation's foes to try to invade Britain, Dickinson has no problem should England decide to suppress America. She has the enviable choice of remaining a playground of freedom or becoming the wonder of the world in defending it.

"The Parody" of Dickinson's song appeared in the *Boston Gazette* a little over a month after the original was published. Because the *Gazette* was Boston's leading patriot paper, the fact that the parody was supposedly written by a Tory from Castle William—that is, one of the customs commissioners who had been obliged to flee earlier that year—indicates that the patriot leadership knew taunting only inflamed their constituents with a zeal for liberty. "Come shake your dull noddles, ye pumpkins, and bawl / And own that you're mad at fair Liberty's call," the song begins, insulting the Americans' intelligence, their pride in their agrarianism, their manhood (children bawl), and their sanity in refusal to submit to the Townshend Acts—all in two lines. "Old Satan," rather than heroic planters of the Liberty Tree, is now the rebels' ancestor, and the only tree they should enjoy is Tyburn, the gallows of London.

American abundance is denied as the patriots are termed "brats and bunters"—children, that is, but obnoxious ones—who far from living in a land of plenty hope to "feather their nests" by "reaping what other men sow." America, as the British maintain, is exploiting the mother country rather than the reverse. Now it is the patriots who become insects who will "melt like the locusts when winter is near" when "red coats appear." Future ages will remember the rebels as "numskulls . . . rascals, fools, whoresons . . . the vilest banditti that swarmed." Real freedom is protection from "mobs, knaves, and villains." Here the patriots are having fun, joyously assuming in a drinking song the very criticisms loyalists made of them. They deal with contempt through parody and play.

"The Parody Parodied" of Dickinson's song appeared in the almanac published by the patriot printers Edes and Gill for 1770. It is rather more serious than the first parody, in that while condemning "Ye insolent tyrants! who wish to enthrall / Ye minions, ye placemen, pimps, pensioners, all," the king appears in the seventh of eleven verses and is the recipient of much goodwill in the hope that he can restore American liberty. The writer is certain that although "oppress'd and reproach'd, our king we implore, / Still firmly persuaded our rights he'll restore." But what if he does not? "When our hearts beat to arms, to defend a just right, / Our monarch rules there, and forbids us to fight." War in defense of liberty is already being contemplated; only the belief that a just monarch will realize that his true greatness lies in defending American rights restrains hearts that already desire to take up arms against his evil advisers, for the next stanza assures the latter that no threats "could make us submit to their chains for a day." Only lingering "affection" for Britain "prevent[s] the fierce conflict which threatens *your* [emphasis added] fall!" Americans have been sufficiently goaded into an armed struggle that they are confident they will win, and sure that their victory will bring about Britain's demise, not theirs. America's glory, of which "all ages shall speak, with amaze and applause," will be "of the prudence we show in support of our cause." The refrain defines Americans as the "sons of Freedom" who will "never surrender, / But swear to defend her, / And scorn to survive, if unable to save."

"Yankee Doodle" brought the message of the Boston streets and ballads to the Continental Army at Cambridge. The British first sang the song in the French and Indian War to make fun of the inept Americans ("doodle" means dolt), but the rebels adopted "Yankee Doodle" as a badge of honor in yet another example of revolutionary play. The most famous verses were written in 1775 by Edward Bangs, a Harvard sophomore, who mocked the "tarnal pride" of General Washington, the gaudy dress of his entourage, and a "thousand men, / As rich as Squire David." The most interesting stanza suggests that Washington and the non–New Englanders in the army were so foppish that they would make terrible soldiers and were even not real men: "The flaming ribbons in his hat, / They looked so taring fine, ah, / I wanted pockily to get, / To give to my Jemimah." But the joke is on "Yankee Doodle" himself, who some trench-diggers threatened to bury in their work: their threat "scared me so I hoofed it off, / Nor stopped as I remember, / Nor turned about till I got home, / Locked up in mother's chamber." Making fun of the expected cowardice of an inexperienced militia, but at the same time suggesting to them that the alternative is to run back to mother, Barnes is trying to shame the troops who would jocularly sing this song into defending their masculinity as an essential element of their liberty. Otherwise, they must abandon the outdoors play space of the camp for mother's chamber—an enclosed space of not-play, symbolically the security and protection offered by a mother country at the price of freedom.

"Yankee Doodle" became the tune of the Revolution, the only one to survive in the popular imagination into the twentieth century: "For every loyalist stanza there were a hundred improvised by Yankee bards."[48] One verse even became, if I can get playful, a meta-narrative in which patriots confident of victory conflate fighting, feasting, and having fun in America with the same activities in the army: "Yankee Doodle is the tune, / That we all delight in; / It suits for feasts, it suits for fun, / And just as well for fightin'."

What can we learn from examining the American Revolution from the perspectives of play and song by analogy with Kevelson's treatment of Robin Hood and the outlaw ballads? People do not move easily to reject a system of government and make a revolution. A decade before the Declaration of Independence, people in Boston were already playing at murdering their rulers and setting up a new government that met under the Liberty Tree, thereby symbolically placing themselves in a state of nature. Much like the warfare of primitive peoples, such as the Yamomamo of the Amazon or the Maring of New Guinea, where chest-slapping and arrow-dodging respectively prefigure and try to avert deadly conflict, the Revolution's history, to reverse Karl Marx's dictum, appeared first as farce and then as tragedy (or triumph).[49] In their streets and in their songs, Americans played out ideas they put into formal writing and revolutionary praxis only in 1775 and 1776. They were psychologically preparing for independence, and beginning in the mid-1760s they were playfully and symbolically declaring it. To put it in old-fashioned Puritan terms that the New Englanders would have understood, play was preparation for salvation.

In revolutionary Boston, then, under the pressure of unprecedented events in the critical decade 1765–76, there was a spontaneous creation of new and eclectic forms of political activity to accompany an emerging new form of political society. Historians can easily show similarities between the ideas of the American revolutionaries and those found in British satirical prints, European forms of rough music, Old Whig, Florentine republican, Roman classical, Puritan/biblical, or English constitutional/common law ideas. However, in the songs and protests of the streets we do not hear the language of Locke, Machiavelli, Trenchard and Gordon, Moses, Winthrop, Cicero, or Coke, or Samuel Adams's stern praise of a "Christian Sparta." While such ideas may be found in the pamphlets the elite wrote for one another and to edify their transatlantic supporters, in popular songs and protests we instead hear praise for an America where, uniquely, the chaotic state of nature is subtly transformed into the good natural society—the space of leisure, happiness, and ordered liberty. We also sense the exuberance of youth—the enthusiasm of relatively young people for a young land. The irrepressible and protean Benjamin Franklin was the exception who proved the rule: most prominent men his age were loyalists.[50]

Furthermore, the American Revolution could not have occurred unless the gap between elites and masses was bridged. It does not therefore advance our understanding of Boston's revolution, and perhaps that of other locales, to focus on class antagonisms, which are always there in some form or other, when what must be explained is how a political elite joined with a largely apolitical populace to make a revolution. To assign primary agency to leaders or followers makes as much sense as arguing whether sodium or chloride is the essential ingredient in table salt. The essence of the situation was creative interaction in new circumstances. What was remarkable was General William Brattle and Shoemaker Ebenezer Mackintosh leading a parade together, or Philadelphia lawyer Jonathan Dickinson writing the "Liberty Song" sung by artisans in the streets of Boston, or the wealthiest man in Massachusetts, John Hancock, becoming the idol of the lower sort. Until things became deadly serious with Lexington and Concord, humor, play, and song were vital in permitting new boundaries to be stretched and new rituals, political entities, and ideas to be tested. Tension and conflict could be mediated, underplayed if not shrugged off, in an atmosphere of genial male camaraderie, in a fluid environment with no predictable outcome.

The interpretation of the Revolution advanced here corresponds to the "network analysis" of social protests advanced by late-twentieth-century sociologists, an interpretation that is remarkably consonant with Peirce's and Kevelson's notions of a universe evolving to unpredictable ends through creative interaction. Societal change cannot be explained by fixed interests or statically defined social or economic groups, but only by the dynamic interaction of diverse elements in associations, informal or formal yet fluid, that bring them together. (In her book *Inheriting the Revolution: The First Generation of Americans,* Joyce Oldham Appleby argues that the early years of the new nation presented similar opportunities for personal creativity.[51]) Agendas for change are not inflexible reflections of particular positions, but emerge from a common posture of hostility that diverse groups share toward an unresponsive elite and, by extension, toward those proelite groups to whom that elite is indeed responsive.

Now that sympathetic theorists of revolution, people of the left, no longer need to justify or even consider the static and sterile self-justifications advanced by twentieth-century faux-Marxist regimes, America's revolution no longer appears anomalous. As Timothy Wickham-Crowley points out in his study of Latin American revolutions, the cooperation of intellectuals—like the young lawyers and pamphleteers in Boston and other port cities in the 1760s—and people of all classes has been required to topple successfully what he has termed "mafiacracies" or "patrimonial praetorian regimes."[52] Here a small number of families dominate leading government positions and are sustained by a military force or some equivalent, a fair approximation of the Hutchinson-Oliver group in Massachusetts and the troops that arrived to protect them. Jack Goldstone's postulation that a state fiscal crisis, alienation of the elites, and multiclass mobilization were the sources of revolution also fits the Bostonian scene—as indeed it does the classic French and Russian revolutions, in which a government becomes increasingly estranged from its subjects.[53] Conflict among revolutionary groups usually becomes prominent or dominant only when the old regime has been toppled.

Speaking in the House of Lords in January 1775, urging his fellow nobles not to send more troops to America and provoke a separation, William Pitt told this story. A person of "respect and authenticity" had stated "that these were the prevalent and steady principles of America—That you might destroy their towns, and cut them off from the superfluities, perhaps the conveniences of life; but that they were prepared to despise your power, and would not lament their loss, whilst they have—what my Lords?—their *woods* and their *liberty*."[54]

The question before us today is whether we can possess liberty with wood that has been turned into paper. Except for Yankee Doodle, America's revolutionary outlaw ballads do not linger in our heritage. They do not evoke nostalgic and romantic memories, as the English legend of Robin Hood does for an industrial power that mourns the vanished forest. For not only did Robin's American counterparts survive, they went beyond being pardoned by good King Richard: the revolutionaries supplanted the king himself. It is as though the Merry Men of Sherwood Forest had taken over England's government instead of the hearts of its people. As such, our government is now theoretically hemmed in by paper (produced from fallen trees) guarantees of liberty, by the Declaration of Independence's injunction that it exists only to protect our "life, liberty, and pursuit of happiness," and by the Constitution's Ninth and Tenth Amendments that the states and the people retain all powers not specifically delegated to the government. Our revolutionary icons are the papers that attempt to define the respective spaces of the government and the people, thereby estranging them despite the assertion that government comes from "We the People."

But can an institutionalized play space be a play space at all? Once America is defined as the land of freedom, does standing against a government that in theory exists only to support freedom become logically impossible? Samuel Adams thought so. He was the most vociferous opponent of Shays's Rebellion in Massachusetts in 1786 and 1787: "In monarchies the crime of treason and rebellion may admit to being pardoned or lightly punished, but the man who dares rebel against the laws of a republic ought to suffer death."⁵⁵ Whether freedom, and what sort, can survive in a government based on revolution that outlaws revolution is an interesting question that I shall not attempt to answer here.

Earlier versions of this chapter were presented at the Omohundro Institute for Early American History and Culture, Williamsburg, Virginia, November 1996; the University of Maryland Colloquium for Early American History, College Park, Maryland, September 1997; and the Massachusetts Historical Society, Boston, October 1997. This chapter, substantially revised from William Pencak and J. Ralph Lindgren, eds., *New Approaches to Semiotics and the Human Sciences: Essays in Honor of Roberta Kevelson* (New York: Peter Lang, 1998), 165–201, is reprinted with permission of Peter Lang. The author thanks the audiences at these meetings, especially James Axtell, James Henretta, Stephen Marini, Philip Morgan, Alison Olson, and Richard Ryerson, for helpful advice he did not always follow.

Notes

1. Roberta Kevelson, *Inlaws/Outlaws: A Semiotics of Systematic Interaction* (Bloomington: Research Center for Language and Semiotic Studies, Indiana University, 1977).
2. Johan Huizinga, *Homo Ludens: A Study of the Play-Element in Culture,* trans. R. F. C. Hull (New York: Roy Publishers, 1950), 3. For a complementary treatment of play in revolutionary Boston and additional bibliographical sources, see Robert Blair St. George, *Conversing by Signs: Poetics of Meaning in Colonial New England Culture* (Chapel Hill: University of North Carolina Press, 1998), chap. 3, "Attacking Houses."
3. Charles S. Peirce, *Lectures on the History of Science, Commonly Known as "Lowell Institute Lectures,"* in Carolyn Eisele, ed., Historical Perspectives on Peirce's Logic of Science (Berlin: Mouton de Gruyter, 1984), 150; idem, "Lessons from the History of Sciences," in Charles Hartshorne, Paul Weiss, and Arthur Burks, eds., *Collected Papers of Charles S. Peirce,* 8 vols. (Cambridge, Mass.: Harvard University Press, 1931–58), 1:109 (references to this collection are customarily cited as *CP* followed by volume and then paragraph number); idem, "Evolutionary Love," *CP* 6.312–14; idem, "A Neglected Argument for the Reality of God," *CP* 6.455–56. For a discussion of Peirce's approach to history, see my "Charles Sanders Peirce, Historian and Semiotician," *Semiotica* 83, no. 3/4 (1991), 311–32.
4. Michel Foucault, *The History of Sexuality,* vol. 1: *An Introduction* (New York: Pantheon, 1978), 89; idem, "Two Lectures," in Colin Gordon, ed., *Power/Knowledge: Selected Interviews and Other Writings, 1972–1977* (New York: Pantheon, 1980), 96; idem, *Discipline and Punish: The Birth of the Prison* (New York: Pantheon, 1977), 31, 194; idem, "Afterword: The Subject and Power," in Hubert L. Dreyfus and Paul Rabinow, eds., *Michel Foucault: Beyond Structuralism and Hermeneutics* (Brighton: Harvester Press, 1982), 224–26; Thomas R. Flynn, "Foucault and the Spaces of History," *Monist* 74 (April 1991), 165–87. For a general discussion of Foucault's

historical theory, see my "Foucault Stoned: Insanity Reconsidered, and History," *Rethinking History* 1, no. 1 (1997), 35–55.

5. John Avery to John Collins, August 19, 1765, in Ezra Stiles, *Extracts from Itineraries and Other Miscellanies of Ezra Stiles* (New Haven: Yale University Press, 1916), 435–37.

6. *Boston Post-Boy*, September 2, 1765; *Boston Newsletter*, September 5, 1765; Peter Shaw, *American Patriots and the Rituals of Revolution* (Cambridge, Mass.: Harvard University Press, 1981), 191–93.

7. John Adams, *Legal Papers*, ed. L. Kinvin Wroth and Hiller Zobel, 3 vols. (Cambridge, Mass.: Harvard University Press, 1965), 2:396–99, 420.

8. Ibid., 3:92, 108, 114–15.

9. Ibid., 3:266.

10. *Boston Gazette*, February 26, 1770; Adams, *Legal Papers*, 2:400.

11. Shaw, *American Patriots*, 190; Alfred F. Young, "English Plebeian Culture and Eighteenth-Century American Radicalism," in Margaret D. Jacob and James R. Jacob, eds., *The Origins of Anglo-American Radicalism* (London: Allen & Unwin, 1984), 185–212.

12. Edwin Burrowes and Michael Wallace, "The American Revolution: The Ideology and Psychology of National Liberation," *Perspectives in American History* 6 (1972), 167–306; Winthrop D. Jordan, "Familial Politics: Thomas Paine and the Killing of the King," *Journal of American History* 60 (September 1973), 294–308; Jay Fliegelman, *Prodigals and Patriots: The American Revolution Against Patriarchal Authority* (New York: Cambridge University Press, 1982).

13. Oscar Brand, *Songs of '76: A Folksinger's History of the Revolution* (New York: M. Evans, 1972), 43, 147.

14. Benjamin W. Labaree, *The Boston Tea Party* (New York: Oxford University Press, 1964), chap. 7; Dirk Hoerder, *Crowd Action in Revolutionary Massachusetts* (New York: Academic Press, 1977), 257–64; Alfred F. Young, "George Robert Twelve Hewes, 1742–1840: A Boston Shoemaker and the Memory of the American Revolution," reprinted in *In Search of America: The William & Mary Quarterly, 1943–1993* (Williamsburg, Va.: Institute of Early American History and Culture, 1993), 258–60.

15. I have culled these names at random by leafing through Arthur M. Schlesinger, *Prelude to Independence: The Newspaper War Against Britain, 1764–1776* (New York: Knopf, 1956); and Philip Davidson, *Propaganda and the American Revolution* (Chapel Hill: University of North Carolina Press, 1944).

16. Schlesinger, *Prelude to Independence*, 142, 106.

17. John Adams, *Works*, ed. Charles Francis Adams, 10 vols. (Boston: Little, Brown, 1850–56), 10:99.

18. The image of Hutchinson is reprinted in my *War, Politics, and Revolution in Provincial Massachusetts* (Boston: Northeastern University Press, 1981), 195.

19. George P. Anderson, "Ebenezer Mackintosh: Stamp Act Rioter and Patriot" and "A Note on Ebenezer Mackintosh," Colonial Society of Massachusetts, *Publications* 26 (1927), 15–64, 348–61; Thomas Hutchinson to Thomas Pownall, March 8, 1766, reprinted in Edmund S. Morgan, ed., *Prologue to Revolution: Sources and Documents on the Stamp Act Crisis, 1764–1766* (Chapel Hill: University of North Carolina Press, 1959), 125.

20. Davidson, *Propaganda*, 175–77; Shaw, *American Patriots*, 8–13.

21. Shaw, *American Patriots*, 17; Hoerder, *Crowd Action*, 207–8, 227.

22. Hoerder, *Crowd Action*, 207–8.

23. Ibid., 227.

24. Adams, *Legal Papers*, 3:86.

25. Young, "English Plebeian Culture," 194.

26. For a thorough discussion of the origin and transformation of "Yankee Doodle," see Irwin Silber, ed., *Songs of Independence* (Harrisburg, Pa.: Stackpole Books, 1973), 69–80.

27. Shaw, *American Patriots,* 16, 188; Hoerder, *Crowd Action,* 117–18.

28. Hoerder, *Crowd Action,* 185; Robert Middlekauff, *The Glorious Cause: The American Revolution, 1763–1789* (New York: Oxford University Press, 1982), 157; Shaw, *American Patriots,* 17.

29. Davidson, *Propaganda,* 197–98.

30. New England Papers, 2:91, 96–98, Sparks Manuscripts, vol. 43, Houghton Library, Harvard University.

31. Edmund S. Morgan and Helen M. Morgan, *The Stamp Act Crisis* (Chapel Hill: University of North Carolina Press, 1953), 163–72, 179–80, 368–69.

32. Josiah Quincy, ed., *Reports of Cases Argued and Adjudged in the Superior Court of Judicature of the Province of Massachusetts Bay Between 1761 and 1772* (Boston, 1865), 173; Thomas Hutchinson, *History of the Colony and Province of Massachusetts Bay,* 3 vols. (Cambridge, Mass.: Harvard University Press, 1936), 3:88; *Boston Evening Post,* August 19, 1765; *Boston Gazette,* August 26, 1765; Edmund S. Morgan, ed., *Prologue to Revolution,* 122, 126; Edmund S. Morgan, "Thomas Hutchinson and the Stamp Act," *New England Quarterly* 21 (1948), 461–92.

33. *Independent Advertiser,* February 8, 1748, and December 5, 1749; John Lax and William Pencak, "The Knowles Riot and the Crisis of the 1740s in Massachusetts," *Perspectives in American History* 10 (1976), 163–214.

34. Adams, *Works,* 2:167.

35. William Pencak and Ralph J. Crandall, "Metropolitan Boston Before the American Revolution," *Proceedings of the Bostonian Society, 1977–1985,* 55–77; John M. Murrin, "Anglicizing an American Colony: The Transformation of Provincial Massachusetts" (Ph.D. diss., Yale University, 1966); Rowland Berthoff and John M. Murrin, "Feudalism, Communalism, and the Yeoman Freeholder: The American Revolution Considered as a Social Accident," in James Hutson and Stephen Kurtz, eds., *Essays on the American Revolution* (Chapel Hill: University of North Carolina Press, 1973), 256–88.

36. Quincy, ed., *Reports of Cases,* 170–73.

37. Morgan, ed., *Prologue to Revolution,* 124.

38. Jürgen Habermas, *The Structural Transformation of the Public Sphere* (Cambridge, Mass.: MIT Press, 1989).

39. Samuel Alleyne Otis to [unknown], June 17, 1766, Otis Papers, vol. 2, Butler Library, Columbia University.

40. Adams, *Legal Papers,* 2:405.

41. Young, "George Robert Twelves Hewes," 256; Shaw, *American Patriots,* 188.

42. John Shy, *Toward Lexington: The Role of the British Army in the Coming of the American Revolution* (Princeton: Princeton University Press, 1965), chap. 7; Hiller B. Zobel, *The Boston Massacre* (New York: W. W. Norton, 1970), esp. chaps. 12 and 16 (see 206–11 for threats to massacre soldiers).

43. Brand, *Songs of '76,* 20–22.

44. W. Chappell, *The Ballad Literature and Popular Music of Olden Times* (London, 1855), 677.

45. Ibid., 715–17; Noted on these pages: James Boswell, Samuel Johnson's biographer, when visiting Corsica, remarked that the inhabitants asked him to sing an English song and he sang "Heart of Oak." "Never did I see men so delighted with a song as the Corsicans were with 'Heart of Oak.' 'Coure di querco!' cried they, 'Bravo Inglese!' It was quite a joyous riot. I fancied myself to be a recruiting sea-officer—I fancied all my chorus of Corsicans aboard the British fleet."

46. See Lax and Pencak, "The Knowles Riot," and William Pencak, *America's Burke: The*

Mind of Thomas Hutchinson (Lanham, Md.: University Press of America, 1982), chap. 2, for Hutchinson's lifelong, principled opposition to the practice.

47. John Dickinson, *Political Writings, 1764–1774*, ed. Paul Leicester Ford (Philadelphia, 1895), 421–32, has the text of the song and both parodies.

48. Silber, ed., *Songs of Independence*, 80.

49. John Keegan, *A History of Warfare* (New York: Knopf, 1993), 94–102.

50. See my *War, Politics, and Revolution*, chap. 8, for the case of Massachusetts.

51. Cambridge, Mass.: Belknap Press of Harvard University Press, 2000. Mustafa Emirbayer and Jeff Goodwin, "Network Analysis, Culture, and the Problem of Agency," *American Journal of Sociology* 99 (May 1994), 1411–54, has an excellent summary of this literature. See also Roger Gould, "Multiple Networks and Mobilization in the Paris Commune, 1871," *American Sociological Review* 56 (December 1991), 716–29; and idem, "Trade Cohesion, Class Unity, and Urban Insurrection: Artisanal Activism in the Paris Commune, 1871," *American Journal of Sociology* 98 (January 1993), 721–54. I thank Kurt Seidel for calling my attention to this important body of work, cited here and in the next two notes.

52. Timothy P. Wickham-Crowley, *Guerrillas and Revolution in Latin America: A Comparative Analysis of Insurgents and Regimes Since 1956* (Princeton: Princeton University Press, 1992).

53. Jack A. Goldstone, Ted Robert Gurr, and Farrokh Moshirir, eds., *Revolutions of the Late Twentieth Century* (Boulder, Colo.: Westview Press, 1991). For a good discussion of such approaches to revolution, see Jeff Goodwin, "Toward a New Sociology of Revolutions," *Theory and Society* 23 (December 1994), 731–66.

54. William Pitt (Earl of Chatham), speech in House of Lords, January 20, 1775, reprinted in Max Beloff, ed., *The Debate on the American Revolution*, 3d ed. (Dobbs Ferry, N.Y.: Sheridan House, 1989), 191–92.

55. William V. Welles, *The Life and Public Services of Samuel Adams*, 3 vols. (1865; reprint, Freeport: Books for Libraries, 1969), 3:246.

7

Rough Music on Independence Day: Philadelphia, 1778

Susan E. Klepp

During the celebration of the second anniversary of American independence on July 4, 1778, a crowd action occurred in Philadelphia that was designed to enforce a particular moral vision of the community. A playful mob of radical men, many of them foot soldiers, marched a scruffy woman with elaborately dressed hair around town to the accompaniment of a drummer and cheering onlookers. They finally stopped at the tavern where fashionable men and women had gathered for an exclusive ball. There the rowdy men and outlandish woman drove home their satirical message on the folly of the latest women's fashions—those ever higher, elaborately decorated, and expensive hairstyles that some American women copied from European aristocrats. Most incidents of rough music are known only from a single reference to a parochial dispute, but this episode touched a raw nerve in revolutionary America, sparking comment throughout the newly independent states. It acquired national significance as members of the political and social elite sought to contain the damage wrought to their reputations by responding in their letters and diaries to this rebuke by radical commoners.[1]

Long hair had been associated with masculine strength since the days of Sampson and Delilah, but in the 1770s it was elite women who no longer bound and covered their tresses. They loosened, teased, padded, and decorated their hair to add a foot or more to their stature, towering above men. While elite women accentuated their long hair when they appeared in public, it might be significant that elite men were shaving their heads in order to don elaborate curled and powdered wigs, sometimes constructed from women's hair.[2] They sported hair, but it was false. The fashions in hair offended traditional gendered expectations but were embraced enthusiastically by many prominent Americans. Becky Franks effused, "The [head]dress is more ridiculous and pretty than anything that ever I saw: great quantity of different coloured feathers on the head at a time, besides a thousand other things, the hair dress'd very high." These elaborate hairstyles were not, of course, either domestic or modest. Franks urged a friend to come to Philadelphia, for an "opportunity of rakeing as much as you choose, either at plays, balls, concerts, or assemblys."[3] Fashionable high hair was enticing because it provided an entrée into a libertine life of flirtation, entertainment, and excitement. Sallie Eve playfully argued that "w[h]ere a person thought the high heads beautiful and would like to weare there own so, but could not reconcile it to there conscience, that person merits prais altho we may wonder at, nay pitty the excessive tenderness of there conscience."[4] Eve's half-serious pity for the morally squeamish in 1773 was not an attitude that could be easily sustained in the later turmoil of revolution.

As war broke out, the debates about women's place in relation to luxury, fashion, and extravagance took on a heightened urgency. Elizabeth Drinker was appalled by the fashionable ("How insensible do these people appear, while our Land is so greatly desolated"), and the Rev. Henry Melchior Muhlenberg thought that "headdresses required . . . wool, false hair, oil, and quintessence of wheat etc., etc., without which the poorer families must supply their barest wants."[5] It seemed to many, particularly the revolutionaries, that the social order was in danger of being overthrown: women were superior to men, and the wealthy crassly robbed their dependents. It was bad enough that wealthy women adopted these fashions, but their example was spreading. The young woman known only as Poll "dressed her head in tip-top fashion" before absconding from her master.[6]

Patriotic women should avoid these excesses. In 1775, Sarah Mifflin helped define a female patriotism of sacrifice and work when she asserted, "All my sister Americans . . . have sacrificed both assemblies, parties of pleasure, tea drinking and finery to that great spirit of patriotism."[7] Most radicals agreed with her vision of revolutionary simplicity, ridiculing high hair as "a big pile of hay on a hayfork."[8] Particularly among the middling and lower sort, these extravagant fashions were considered to be dangerous, undermining the seriousness of the revolutionary cause and the hierarchical order of the family. These exorbitant fashions in hairdressing signaled a growing division of Americans along lines of wealth and privilege. High hair was absurd, promoted licentiousness, diverted goods from the needy, and was a British imposition on American manners.

The British army evacuated the city on June 18, 1778, but before they left, British officers threw a lavish ball and pageant for their commander called the Mischianza (or Meschianza). Local elite women, both Tories and Whigs, danced with and cheered British officers engaged in a mock combat that drew on images of both feudal and "oriental" despotism. These young women dressed their hair even more elaborately than usual and masqueraded in Turkish costumes that connoted the harem and a sensualized, captive, nonmonogamous womanhood. It was an extravagant display of elite pretension in the midst of wartime.

On June 19 the American army moved back into the city. Germans, Britons, Frenchmen, Americans, Loyalists, Whigs, radicals, moderates, conservatives, spies, turncoats, collaborators, trimmers, profiteers, traitors, heroes, refugees, unruly servants, self-liberated freedmen, and neutrals flowed in, around, and out of the city. Who was a friend, and who a foe? Because military men had controlled the city in 1777 and 1778, civilian authority was uncertain. A new government under the Articles of Confederation was about to be endorsed but had not yet been established—delegates from the independent states were gathering in Philadelphia to decide that very issue. Some of the new nation's most radical proposals—an expanded electorate, a weakened executive, the gradual abolition of slavery, the end of sanguinary punishments—were both gaining support and arousing opposition in the state assembly.[9] Inflation, fueled by a shortage of goods and by unstable currencies, was spiraling upward. Prices were seven to ten times the precrisis levels.[10] For those with little money, it was a disaster that meant being ill-fed and ill-clad; for those with goods to sell or hard cash, it was a windfall. The poor were suffering, and the nouveau riche were flaunting their wealth amid the confusion of war and revolution.

What seemed particularly new and unsettling in the early stages of the revolutionary war was the involvement of women in politics. Since 1769, rebellious politicians had called on women as consumers and arbiters of fashion to enforce the nonimportation and nonconsumption resolutions.[11] Patriot women were being asked to sacrifice pleasure and convenience, in spartan self-denial, and to take up textile and food production as they sent their men to fight for a righteous cause. The early use of economic weapons against the mother country incorporated both women and men, but the extent and meaning of female participation in political protest was uncertain once economic struggle was eclipsed by war.

During the war, elite women of fashion had been drawn into the political jockeying of the general staffs of both the British and the American armies. Through the medium of gossip, flirtatious intrigue, and requests for special favors, decisions that appeared to affect the war were sometimes being made during tea parties, balls, and formal visits. Sir William Howe granted Becky Franks permission to send gifts across enemy lines, and another woman reported that British officers "never failed collecting whig news for me."[12] In traditional wars, where the object of the conflict was the conquest of specific plots of land, socializing across lines was of little moment because war aims remained sharply defined. In a war based at least in part on the contrasting ideologies of monarchy and republicanism, imperialism and nationalism, mercantilism and free trade, the revolutionary cause was jeopardized by any conflation of purpose. "The Whigs of the City would have escaped many evils and calamities had it not been for those vile miscreants [single and married women] at the elbow of the General [Howe]," fumed John Thaxter in a letter to Abigail Adams.[13] In the eyes of the most radical of Americans, these fashionable women had become liminal figures who blurred the political dimensions of the conflict by consorting with and apparently influencing prominent and powerful men on both sides of the conflict. These women corrupted revolutionary virtue, winning personal and political favors by flaunting their seductive powers. In the summer of 1778 Philadelphia was divided, but not into neat opposition parties. The city and new nation were fragmented along scores of social, gendered, economic, religious, and political lines that were further blurred by the too-friendly social contacts of British officers and American women. The issues were nebulous and inchoate, as conditions changed at a dizzying pace. Yet for a brief moment, one issue crystallized these fears and uncertainties: women's hairstyles.

The details of July 4, 1778, are simple enough. On Independence Day morning, there was an official parade of celebration organized by General Benedict Arnold, the military commander in charge of the city. A group of white-clad men with liberty caps led the procession, followed by musicians, artisans, troops, and the newly adopted flag of the United States. Afterward, James Wilson delivered an oration at the countryside estate of Andrew Hamilton, where influential men toasted each of the thirteen states. Fireworks in the evening were designed to entertain the crowd, but in the afternoon the wealthy were assembling for an elegant supper and a ball hosted by Arnold at the City Tavern. Arnold had not participated in the morning's parade, but sat in state all day at the tavern, his wounded leg propped on a cushion, while guests were ushered into his presence as if he were the monarch. It was well known that prominent women who had socialized with the British during the occupation, including some Tories, were to be among those attending that evening's elegant repast, along with leading American and French officers.[14]

The common people were not willing to wait until evening for their entertainment—they made their own after the official parade. In the afternoon, then, a barefoot, ragged, dirt-smeared woman was marched through the streets accompanied by a drummer or drummers making a racket. She was neither forced nor manhandled: accounts indicate that she played her part with good humor. Her hair was elaborately dressed in a parody of current aristocratic styles that was instantly recognizable to the large, boisterous crowd that followed, laughing, cheering, and taunting. While this mock parade seemed spontaneous, it must have taken several hours and some planning, expense, and expertise to dress the woman's hair in so intricate a manner: "about three feet high and of a proportionable width, with a profusion of curls, &c, &c &c."[15] The spectacle ended under the second-story windows of the city tavern in order to impress on the guests, and especially the elite women who had adopted the current soaring, excessive, and expensive hairstyles, that they were no better than tramps or prostitutes. Tory women, Whig women who had socialized with the British army during the occupation, Whig women who simply imitated these corrupt "British" hairstyles—all were intended to be shamed by the raucous crowd's parody.

The use of rough music by the "lower sorts" contrasted with the contemporary cultivation of sensibility by the middling and upper ranks of society. Sensibility promoted restraint, sympathy, and empathy.[16] Rough music was harsh, merciless, and characterized by "unpitying laughter, and the mimicking of obscenities"—reasons rough music often degenerated from street theater into violence.[17] It was more usual in England and elsewhere to pillory an actual offender instead of using a proxy, as in Philadelphia. It might be argued that in the summer of 1778 the Philadelphia crowd remained deferential to their "superiors," unwilling to risk more than a hint of social inversion, or that the intent of this mockery was the symbolic humiliation of an entire class of offenders, rather than the disciplining of particular individuals.

But violence was never completely foreclosed as a possibility. Crowds could and did turn ugly. In earlier local episodes of rough music against female extravagance, the male organizers had persuaded the public hangman or his wife to participate, driving home the crowd's message, part of which was the threat of death for women who refused to submit to communal supervision. Stories of the politicized rape of enemy women abounded during the war, especially after the occupation of Philadelphia. A crowd had beaten one Philadelphia woman to death in 1776 on suspicion of witchcraft. Violence against property, tarring and feathering, and severe beatings were also meted out to men during the early stages of the Revolution, with or without the accompaniment of rough music.[18] The laughter on July Fourth was brittle, and the humor was serious. Violence was never far from the message of the day.

This travesty on elite culture attracted widespread support—the crowd included radical officers as well as the "rabble." It is likely, but not certain, that women were among the boisterous onlookers, although no surviving source indicates noise from the beating of pots and pans, the usual instruments used by women participating in rough music. The presence of a drummer was an indication of the soldiers' leading role in organizing the spectacle. The drummer probably beat the "Whore's March" or the "Rogue's March," which announced the expulsion of "idle" women from military encampments.[19] Quakers did not participate in the rough music, but we know that Elizabeth Drinker approved the spectacle privately, from the front room of her home: "A very high Head dress was exhibited thro the Streets, this Afternoon on a very dirty Woman with a mob after her, with Drums &c. by way of rediculing that very foolish fashion."[20] While mirth and rather gentle satire dominated that day, the incident raised anxieties, especially among the men gathered for the sessions of the Continental Congress. The fact that so many wrote to friends and family to prove their loyalty makes this an unusually well documented episode.[21] None of the known writers claimed to be a participant, but most signaled their approval. Wealthy women too sought to justify their behavior in the wake of this travesty on feminine virtue and patriotism.

If the details of the day's activities are clear, the meanings of the episode are less so. Steven Rosswurm discusses the political significance of this episode, especially as located in the social divisions of eighteenth-century urban America. The political targets of the rough music in Philadelphia were the British, their American supporters, and those moderate and conservative Whigs who practiced aristocratic or elitist "cultural politics," including high hair for women. The perpetrators were the more radical, rank-and-file Whigs who were identified in virtually all surviving sources as the "rabble" or "mob" or "crowd."[22] But this rough music can reveal more than a community divided between British and American combatants or between conservative and republican ideologies. Gender, religion, fertility, and race were also among the key issues at stake in 1778.

Like traditional rough music, the symbolic simplicity of this episode—a dirty woman in sumptuary headdress—embodied multiple and often contradictory meanings. All rough music combined elements of popular justice, parades, and public theater.[23] In both Europe and America, community control over women was frequently the motivation for crowd action. In early modern Europe, husband-beaters, scolds, adulteresses, and witches threatened "notions of hierarchy" because "the patriarchal ideal was shared by all" in the community.[24] In Europe and in previous American episodes, it was enough for men to regain physical control over women through assaults on women's bodies (dunkings, bridlings, whippings, and exposure). What was remarkable about the rough music of 1778 was its call for women to adopt patriotism, republican manners, and loyalty to the soldiery, or, as Richard Henry Lee hoped, to turn from the "Monstrous head-dress of the Tory Ladies [to] the bounds of reason."[25] These were ideological commitments, not just outward, physical obedience. The self-indulgence of elite women, their sensual pleasures and flirtatious manner, and their conspicuous consumption of scarce commodities were all considered immoral by rank-and-file radicals. Moreover, in socializing with both sides in the conflict, in considering personal loyalties above political ideology, in dressing extravagantly in times of economic hardship, such women had lost their political virtue.

But extravagant women were not the only targets of this rough music, for implicit in the message of the afternoon was a critique of elite masculinity. Men who tolerated such corruption among women were effete cuckolds pulled along by the illusory attractions of a corrupted sexuality and seduced by empty finery. The easy sociability of the elite and the polite but insincere manners that were then the mode were equated with the promiscuity of whores and the cupidity of their customers. The mostly male crowd, of course, enacted their disdain for such women by the loud drumbeat and their mockery as they paraded through town; their noise and derision distanced them from moral weakness. They were anything but polite, but they were righteous.

It was a message that would have been quite familiar to nearly all observers, for this incident was a secularized dramatization of Vanity Fair from John Bunyan's *Pilgrim's Progress.* Christian, the hero of *Pilgrim's Progress,* denounced both the desire for and the commodification of the worldly temptations that could be found at Vanity Fair. At the fair, honors, titles, lusts, pleasures, whores, bodies, and souls were all exhibited for sale, and consumers were expected to indulge. Unlike the avaricious men who patronized Vanity Fair, however, the heroic Christian was not seduced by deceptive fashions, but remained loyal to his mission and to an absolute truth of Christian self-abnegation.[26]

The vibrant language of Bunyan's allegory was already circulating in the city before July 4. Sergeant William Young had blasted Philadelphia's wartime culture: "The wickedness of this city cryes Loud for punishment. . . . If Debauchery and Profaneness among all Sorts of people is a crying sin, Jehovah will find it here." The Mischianza represented "Scenes of Folly and Vanity" to Elizabeth Drinker; "the seductions of vice, vanity, and luxury" to Josiah Bartlett; and the "Fair of vanity profound" to Hannah Griffitts.[27] On the day before the Fourth of July, when Samuel Adams wrote from Philadelphia bemoaning that even Boston had lost, "her manly Virtue, for Levity & Luxury and a Train of ridiculous vices," his prose testifies to the gendered confusion of the early revolution. He closed by insisting, "He is the best Patriot who Stems the Torrent of Vice."[28] The soldiers acted on that belief the next afternoon.

True morality in its revolutionary context lay in an uncompromised, monogamous loyalty to the Whig cause and in a simple and unpretentious dress that would obscure distinctions between rich and poor, that would free resources for the needy, and that would identify simple, republican sympathies. The self-restrained, honorable Christian and the self-restrained, honorable revolutionary were not far apart. It was men's responsibility to remain in control.

One message of the street theater was therefore that republican women did not flit from party to party or from man to man, nor did their husbands, fathers, and brothers permit it. A week after the rough music, Anthony Wayne extolled "those Virtuous Daughters of America who Cheerfully gave up ease and Affluence in a city for Liberty and peace of mind in a Cottage." He then he made sure that his correspondent knew that "Among which number is my Daughter."[29] Men should stand together, because politics and military service were becoming the universal attributes of manhood (rather than being privileges of a small property-holding elite). This was a political innovation that had only recently been embodied in Pennsylvania's radical constitution of 1776, which opened the franchise and office-holding to virtually all taxpaying men and their sons in the state. Women should be at home, modest, domestic, loyal to their husbands or fathers and to the cause of American independence, eschewing tea and imported fineries and making do with American products produced by themselves or by American working men.

Embedded in these messages was a dilemma. One strand posited a rational, free-thinking, committed womanhood, the other called for patriarchal authority over the behavior of wives and daughters. A solution for several spectators was respectable love. Love would bind men and women together and obviate authoritarian relationships, while at the same time preserving traditional inequities within marriage and the family. Before Timothy Pickering informed his wife of the new standards of dress, he effused: "So prudent, so good, so amiable, so affectionate—I cannot forbear to express thus explicitly my sense of your worth and my love." His injunctions on proper republican hairdressing were softened first by declarations of love and then by stressing his own retreat from fashionable dress, and finally by an aside on the important role of his wife, "when you have dressed me up," in his life and public appearance. Anna Young Smith, who had just returned from exile, exclaimed, "When forc'd by British Arms abroad to roam / Far from our humble Roof and Native home, / My Damons love each anxious fear repress't."[30] She then went on to advocate equal domestic responsibilities for her husband and herself, mixing male protectiveness and female vulnerability with shared love and roles within marriage. While rough music was harshly critical, some contemporaries saw companionate marriages and sympathy as the appropriate response. Those who might have argued for stronger patriarchal control in July 1778 did not leave an explicit defense of hierarchy.

A few women, however, imagined more substantive rewards for their patriotism and sacrifice. An anonymous Philadelphian suggested that in two weeks time she and her friend could, if given the opportunity, "settle the nation, as we are most profound politicians."[31] Esther deBerdt Reed proposed an institutional reward for female sacrifice to patriotic male superiority. "Shall we hesitate to wear a cloathing more simple; hair dressed less elegant, while at the price of this small privation, we shall deserve your benedictions?" she wrote in 1780, before calling for a shadow female government of "treasuresses" on the county, state, and national level.[32] Her plan for parallel governments of men and women was strikingly similar to the structure of Quaker men's and women's meetings for business and one indication that in 1778 radical republicans looked to the Quakers for a model of simple living. The gendered issues raised by the Revolution and played out in the rough music of Independence Day could not be resolved except through the symbolic drama in the street. Many who applauded the rough music saw no need to reconcile its ambiguous messages on women's conflicting responsibilities to fathers, husbands, and the state.[33]

It was common in Europe to blacken the face of the target of rough music, and that tradition was continued in Philadelphia in 1778, where the unknown organizers caused dirt to be smeared on the face and clothing of the woman at the center of their mummery. To be "dirty" was to imply a perverse sexuality, so the dirty woman in the street impugned the targeted fashionable elite for their failure to uphold community standards of unspotted morality and undefiled femininity.[34] The dirt was intended to bring shame and humiliation on the offender, besmirching reputations. The dirty woman in the street was symbolic of the entangling of the political virtue of women with their sexual virtue. In addition, men's political virtue rested in large measure on the behavior of their wives and daughters. The enforcement of sexual purity was among the messages of the afternoon's street theater.[35]

Positing an older connection, Peter Shaw argues that the blackened face recalled the soot resulting from the "ritual conflagrations of the earliest fertility ceremonies, . . . aimed at ensuring the fertility of the land by burning to death groups of condemned criminal and captured enemies, along with live animals."[36] Violet Alford and Natalie Davis also find fertility at the core of European rough music: the sexual offenders most commonly punished in the early modern period were women and men who threatened to reduce the fertility of the village and therefore its very survival.[37] The prime offenses were mismatched marriages of very old and very young spouses that were unlikely to produce children, or adulteries that were also assumed to interfere with reproduction. It was the oddly coupled individual who was the usual target of rough music, while, as Alford notes: "Low on the list of culprits [came] loose conduct in an unmarried girl."[38] But in

Philadelphia in 1778, it was an unattached woman who was paraded and mocked.

If Old World rough music targeted married women and men whose sexual activities threatened the reproduction of the community, Whigs in Philadelphia posited a different politics of fertility in 1778. Many commentators interpreted the crowd's judgment as a condemnation of pregnancy, not of infertility. That summer both married and single women were accused of consorting with the British in the absence of their Whig protectors. Their reputations were sullied by rumors of collaboration, seduction, and rape, while pregnancy was criticized as it had never been before. A Quaker woman warned in Meeting that parents "must accept what [those warriors] leave behind"; John Thaxter referred scathingly to "the vestiges of the British Army and traces of British violence"; and the *Boston Continental Journal* correspondent smirked at the "extraordinary natural weight which some of the ladies carry before them."[39] Pregnancy, legitimate or illegitimate, voluntary or forced, was linked to immorality, sensuality, and consumer excess—proof that women had prostituted themselves to afford these excessive fashions.

True Whig women were not voluptuaries but restrained and controlled, although whether by duty to family, by love of their husbands, or by rational self-interest was a matter of debate. The revolutionary critique of luxury, abundance, excess, and superfluity could be understood as a rejection of high fertility and an endorsement of restraint and rational planning. "Prudence" was to become closely linked to fertility control, just as "virtue" was linked to women's sexual restraint.[40] Certainly, the uneasy acceptance of the Quakers as an appropriate model for secularized, republican behavior promoted a group whose fertility rates were somewhat lower than those of other Philadelphians.[41] An old form of social protest accommodated a new social message by providing a political rationale for the fertility transition to fewer births and smaller families that had just begun in a series of private, personal decisions.

If rough parallels to Quaker practice emerged in the female government proposed by Reed and in changing attitudes on fertility, several men looked explicitly to the Quakers for models of republican simplicity in the wake of the rough music as they tried to set standards of clothing and their wives and daughters. Timothy Pickering told his wife that in Philadelphia only the Quakers dress "with a becoming simplicity," and continued: "You may easily imagine how much I look like one of the brotherhood . . .

in my greyish coat and brown hat, with my straight thin locks unpowdered. But be assured, my dear, I am not singular in my plainness."[42] An anonymous newspaper correspondent, perhaps the radical Charles Willson Peale, also turned to Quakers for inspiration: "So far as [fashions] concern the gentlemen, they appear to be principally confined to the hat, which is now amazingly broad-brimmed and cocked very sharp. Were they flapped after the manner of the people called Quakers, these brims would be useful in this hot weather, because they would afford an agreeable shade to the face, but in the present mode they serve only as an encumbrance to the blocks they cover."[43] No women expressed an interest in the Quaker model, but a Mrs. Hodgson remarked: "I'm perfectly old fashioned in my cloaths, and cannot be prevailed on to conform in any thing but the cuffs which I always preferd to ruffles." Quaker women's clothing was not so much unique as out-of-date.[44]

Religion, politics, and fashion were inextricably linked by revolutionaries. The latitudinarian attitudes of Anglican and some Presbyterian clergy accommodated the gentry's flaunting of the imported, ornate, rococo fashions of the mid-eighteenth century. The elites' acceptance of aristocratic pretensions in dress and deportment was popularly associated with the rise of a new class of war profiteers who spent lavishly while poorer people suffered hunger and deprivation, even though not all the "mushroom" elite were Anglican or Presbyterian. Meanwhile, radical Whigs, many of Lutheran, Methodist, or Baptist persuasion, were finding republican virtue in wartime simplicity of manners and dress—a simplicity whose most conspicuous model was Quaker.[45] Only three months earlier the American and Pennsylvania governments had released eleven prominent Philadelphia Quakers who had been imprisoned on vague charges of disaffection. The politics of fashion, as well as violent behavior of British troops during the occupation, may have aided a process of rapprochement between the officially neutral Friends and moderate and radical revolutionaries.

If this particular episode of rough music divided Philadelphians by gender, social status, behavior, religion, and ideology, it also held out the possibility of reconciliation. Another message embedded in this comic street theater was its call for a change of heart on the part of the frivolous. Muhlenberg described the street theater as "a public exhibition which cost less and was more profitable than the present day comedies of the more refined sort," succeeding where critics and even preachers had failed. Richard Henry Lee wrote, "It has lessened some heads already" and "Tory women are very much mortified." Josiah Bartlett told his family, "Head Dresses are now Shortning & I hope the Ladies heads will Soon be of a proper Size & in proportion to the other parts of their Bodies."[46] Many women had learned their lesson, and their heads and stature had been shrunk. Reformation through a change in behavior signaled that these humbled women and their men might potentially be reincorporated into the community of stalwart revolutionaries.

By and large, the rough music of July 4, 1778, served its purposes. The common soldiers and their supporters clearly established their moral opposition to the sumptuous dress and polite but insincere sociability of elite women and effete men, and warned their officers about condoning such behavior. Many individuals were moved to modify their behavior in light of this well-publicized incident. Quaker simplicity and republican simplicity and Christian and revolutionary moral certainty began to merge. It looked as if the officers who had allowed genteel women too much independence would adopt a republican patriarchy. Men would lead, either through authority or through affection, while women would choose to follow and support their menfolk. For the few women commentators, their sacrifice of fashion, their self-restraint, and their acceptance of more stringent control of their sexuality were contractual and would be rewarded with increased respect and a political status approaching equality.

By the 1780s and 1790s, hairstyles became simpler and women's dresses imitated lower-class styles in adopting polonaises (short jackets traditionally worn by servants) and aprons, shepherdess costumes in inexpensive muslin, and the classical draperies of republican Rome. In addition, women's outerwear became masculine as tailored collars and cuffs predominated on riding coats, with nary a ruffle, flounce, or bow in sight.[47] In symbolic prints and in portraits, women's dress expressed an antiaristocratic, more "rational," more "natural," and less frivolous aesthetic of republican taste. If anything, men's fashions underwent the more profound and lasting transition from the elegant fripperies of the eighteenth-century elite to Benjamin Franklin's pseudo-Quaker cum frontiersman garb in the Court of France. His improvised costume reflected the republican fashion politics of 1778's rough music. A few decades later, men would adopt the dark trousers (originally lower class) and coat, white shirt, and cravat that have been worn as a uniform by the middle and upper classes ever since.

As the immediate sting of laughter and humiliation faded away, and perhaps because the men and women in the street in 1778 did not have access to a print culture that might have fixed their intent for a wider audience, opposition to the lessons of rough music emerged and soon subverted the musicians' message. Over the summer and fall of 1778 and well into the nineteenth century, wealthier Americans sought to recast the meaning of the 1778 rough music in their correspondence and in publications. One of the first tactics was to eliminate the symbolism of the episode by shifting derision away from the original objects of satire, the elite women, and onto the dirt-besmeared woman herself. She quickly became the object of contempt rather than a representation of the contemptible. Within forty-eight hours of the rough music, male correspondents began to employ a veritable thesaurus of terms for degraded, sexualized femininity to describe the woman player: "woman of the town," "noted and infamous doxy," "trull," "depraved female," "noted strumpet," "a strumpet, I suppose," and "wench." By the end of August, the meaning of the rough music was again recast. Massachusetts Congressman Josiah Bartlett not only gave "gentlemen" credit for organizing the public display but also was the first to make the protagonist an African American.[48] It may have been his own invention, or it may have reflected a shift in the telling and retelling of the story through gossip, hearsay, and later embellishments.

Images of race and color had been loosely connected with high hair and fashion even before Bartlett's letter to his family. In April, a scurrilous travesty on African-British troops had been published in a local newspaper. According to the story, General Howe ordered the soldiers' hair cut "in order to supply the ladies of the court of Great Britain with wool [curly hair] sufficient for the present fashionable head-dress." Muhlenberg had compared the women with high hair to "apes," a comparison that had racial overtones in the eighteenth century, when some scientists were still claiming a link between apes and Africans. On August 22 another newspaper article suggested that Tories be dyed black for easier identification.[49] The move from sexualized white woman to sexualized black woman presaged the later course of racist thought in the country, and it was as "an old Negro wench," "a negro wench," and "a negress" that the woman satirist was remembered into the nineteenth century.[50] A sexualized female could not be simply blackened in the new nation; she must be black. And if black women were sullied, then white women must be virtuous. If the filth was within, then any opportunity for reconciliation was foreclosed. The few nineteenth-century accounts of the 1778 rough music concluded that "nothing could stop the progress of fashion." Both the intent and the influence of the rank-and-file soldiers and their supporters were written out of history, while white women were denied political partisanship in their mindless pursuit of fashion.[51]

In addition to absolving wealthy white women, the commoner's image of effete, easily seduced gentlemen was restricted in later versions to particular individuals, letting most wealthy men of fashion and leisure off the hook. General Howe filled that emasculated role, as chief of the "heavenly, sweet, pretty red Coats," through the late summer of 1778, but Benedict Arnold took his place by the fall of that year.[52] Arnold's later defection was in some measure the result of this persistent antagonism concerning his incorporation of elite Tory women into revolutionary society, and David Shields and Fredrika Teute have adroitly reconstructed the links between the Mischianza and Arnold's treason.[53]

Those women and men who renounced patriotic austerity and who were offended by the righteousness of the radicals embraced a defense based on liberality of sentiment. As one woman wrote, "You, my friend, I am certain, have liberality of sentiment, and can make proper allowances for young people in the bloom of life and spirits, after being so long deprived." General John Cadwalader defended Benedict Arnold on similar grounds, arguing that "every man who has a liberal way of thinking highly approve his conduct [with the ladies.]"[54] Radicals held to a stricter morality. Ann White Morris critiqued "our military gentlemen who are too liberal to make any distinction between Whig and Tory ladyes." The choices and sacrifices of patriot women, and the potential rewards for partisan women in the new nation, would be lost if liberality prevailed. Genteel liberality challenged the rigid moral righteousness of the crowd and would affect the later versions of the story.[55] The change from a popular disciplining of the frivolous elite through symbolic street theater to a limited and narrow burlesque of an invented black woman in the street and a corrupt general at a dance robbed the incidence of rough music of its meaning and of its social and political resonance. Completely eviscerated by elite writers in the nineteenth century, historians and readers lost interest. The playful street theater of 1778, and the people who created it, were forgotten as the history of the Revolution was drained of its revolutionary content.

The rough music of July 4, 1778, used traditional forms for new purposes. Competing visions of female manners—one complaisant, polite, liberal, and sociable, the other partisan, loyal, self-sacrificing, and domestic—were the polarities signaled by hairstyles around which ideological, political, social, and economic disagreements might be organized and made more comprehensible. The Quakers, previously tainted by neutrality and a presumably pro-British stance, were at least partially incorporated into the American cause through their beliefs in simplicity and restraint in dress and behavior. The elite, the trimmers, and the frivolous might disavow the taint of disloyalty through personal reformation. Commitment, not ethnicity, gender, or religion, should define political loyalties. In its later manifestations, however, inclusion was not offered to all. By reconstructing this incident of rough music to stress race rather than the seduction of the elite, blacks were clearly placed outside the category of partisanship, and conflicts between wealthier and poorer whites were at least temporarily submerged. Blackness was becoming a permanent, racialized sign of exclusion and sexual threat, rather than an occasional humiliation applied to the faces of those who offended the community. The confusions and complications of the postoccupation settlement had been simplified on a symbolic level in 1778, if not in actuality. The male supporters of the people and of the revolutionary republic could be easily identified, thanks in part to the rough music of the crowd, by their relationship to consumption, to women, and to fashion, as virtuous, simple, restrained, and self-controlled. By the nineteenth century, patriots apparently needed only to be white and male. Women were irrelevant if white, or immoral if black.

The ludicrous display on the afternoon of July 4, 1778, was documented and communicated so widely because it touched on fears and aspirations that the participants and observers were anxious to resolve. The reception of the rough music indicated that the emerging middle class and the evolving working-class largely agreed in finding manhood in the independent, involved citizen heading his own household and acting as the breadwinner. Womanhood could be found in the domestic, selfless, loyal wife, perhaps beloved, contributing her smaller-scale talents to the country's well-being. While the visual expression of these goals was clear in the way women and men presented themselves through fashion, the actual performance of these roles was uncertain. Among the thorny issues were the place of republican consumerism in a market economy, the definition of community in an increasingly divided and politicized world, and the consequences of women's choices in a revolutionary society. In adopting new meanings in 1778, a local episode of rough music touched a national nerve, but these new meanings would also signal the demise of rough music as a popular form of discipline. Its deepest purpose was to perpetuate the reproduction of the community, but fecund abundance was being replaced by an ideal of prudent restraint. Republican wives, idealized as intuitively, obediently, rationally, or lovingly responsive to their husbands' domestic interests, could no longer threaten the community. And it was not clear that there was a community of interests to be threatened. Later elite commentators undercut the original broad social message of the commoners by narrowing the focus to a few actors. Political, social, and gendered divisions, and the later emphasis on racial divisions, would make enforcement of community norms an increasingly elusive project. Individualism, domesticity, class, race, and partisan politics were eroding community consensus, and with it the practice of rough music, while the memory of a revolutionary moment was purged of its radical critique of the status quo, and with it an opportunity for a reevaluation of women's role in politics.

The author wishes to thank Greg Knouff, Karin A. Wulf, and Al Young for valuable advice.

Notes

1. This incident of rough music is discussed by Steven Rosswurm, *Arms, Country, and Class: The Philadelphia Militia and the "Lower Sort" During the American Revolution* (New Brunswick, N.J.: Rutgers University Press, 1987), 152–53, although he follows one of the later versions of the episode. It has been mentioned in passing by Linda Kerber as an example of women's presence in crowd activity, and as a "significant incident" by Mary Beth Norton. See Linda K. Kerber, *Women of the Republic: Intellect and Ideology in Revolutionary America* (Chapel Hill: University of North Carolina Press, 1980), 44; Mary Beth Norton, *Liberty's Daughters: The Revolutionary Experience of American Women, 1750–1800* (Boston: Little, Brown, 1980), 352 n. 48.

2. Karin Calvert, "The Function of Fashion in Eighteenth-Century America," in Cary Carson, Ronald Hoffman, and Peter J. Albert, eds., *Of Consuming Interests: The Style of Life in the Eighteenth Century* (Charlottesville: U.S. Capitol Historical Society / University Press of Virginia, 1994), esp. 263–65. Elite officers also used hair length in order to heighten distinctions of rank among Pennsylvania troops, demanding that "the hair of all the non-commissioned officers and privates . . . be cut short and alike." In Gregory T. Knouff, "The Common People's Revolution: Class, Race, Masculinity, and Locale in Pennsylvania, 1775–1783" (Ph.D. diss., Rutgers University, 1996), 125.

3. Jacob R. Marcus, *The American Jewish Woman: A Documentary History* (New York: KTAV Publishing / American Jewish Archives, 1981), 15–17.

4. Diary of Sallie Eve, p. 18, Manuscripts, Special Collections Department, William R. Perkins Library, Duke University.

5. Elaine F. Crane et al., eds., *The Diary of Elizabeth Drinker*, 3 vols. (Boston: Northeastern University Press, 1991), 1:306; Theodore G. Tappert and John E. Doberstein, eds. and trans., *The Journals of Henry Melchior Muhlenberg*, 3 vols. (Philadelphia: Muhlenberg Press, 1958), 3:171–72.

6. William Duane, ed., *Extracts from the Diary of Christopher Marshall* (1877; reprint, New York: Arno, 1969), 42–43, 230.
7. Her letter was published under the initials "C.S." See Henry Steele Commager, ed., *Chronicles of the American Revolution* (New York: Grosset & Dunlap, 1965), 172; the attribution is in Mary Heaton, "Bucks County Women in Wartime," *Papers: Bucks County Historical Society* 5 (1926), 135.
8. Tappert and Doberstein, *Journals of Henry Melchior Muhlenberg*, 3:171–72.
9. Gary B. Nash and Jean R. Soderlund, *Freedom by Degrees: Emancipation in Pennsylvania and Its Aftermath* (New York: Oxford University Press, 1991), 101.
10. Ann Bezenson, Blanch Daley, Miriam Hussey, and Marjorie Denison, *Prices and Inflation During the American Revolution, 1770–1790* (Philadelphia: University of Pennsylvania Press, 1936), 344.
11. J. E. Crowley, *This Sheba, Self: The Conceptualization of Economic Life in Eighteenth-Century America* (Baltimore: Johns Hopkins University Press, 1974), 139; Norton, *Liberty's Daughters*, 157–63; Kerber, *Women of the Republic,* however, downplays the influence of women during the boycotts, 36–45.
12. Marcus, *American Jewish Woman*, 15–17; Charles Campbell, ed., *The Bland Papers* (Petersburg, Va.: Ruffin, 1840), 1:91–92.
13. July 6, 1778. L. H. Butterfield and Marc Friedlander, eds., *Adams Family Correspondence* (Cambridge, Mass.: Belknap Press of Harvard University Press, 1973), 3:58.
14. A detailed account of the official celebration can be found in Ray Thompson, *Benedict Arnold in Philadelphia* (Fort Washington, Pa.: Bicentennial Press, 1975), 50–59, but the incident of rough music is not mentioned.
15. James Curic Ballagh, ed., *The Letters of Richard Henry Lee*, 2 vols. (1911–14; reprint, New York: Da Capo Press, 1970), 1:421.
16. See G. J. Barker-Benfield, *The Culture of Sensibility: Sex and Society in Eighteenth-Century Britain* (Chicago: University of Chicago Press, 1992); and Shirley Samuels, *The Culture of Sentiment: Race, Gender, and Sentimentality in Nineteenth-Century America* (New York: Oxford University Press, 1992).
17. E. P. Thompson, *Customs in Common* (New York: The New Press, 1991), 469.
18. See, for example, William Logan to John Smith (9 mo[nth] 14th [day] 1766), John Smith Correspondence, 1740–70, Historical Society of Pennsylvania (hereafter HSP), "a large Mob of People consistg chiefly of Sailors & such like passed my door this afternoon with a poor young fellow in tow with a rope round his middle & tard. I know not ye Pticular Cause. Tho Bond knows ye whole I believe, but I hear he is the Collectors son of your Salem who seized ye Irish Vesells, & Greatly misbehaved to some Captn & others where he could find nothing to seize. They say much too forward & beyond his Authority, & being met with to day They thus rewarded him, & when they had done with him some people put him on board a Boat & sent him over to yt Side, but so much abused as some think it may endanger his Life." The peak of politicized rough music against men occurred as the revolutionary committees became the de facto government; rough music was their judicial arm. See, for example, Duane, ed., *Diary of Christopher Marshall.* Crowd actions that resulted in the deaths of Philadelphia women are known to have occurred in 1776 and 1787. See Rosswurm, *Arms, Country, and Class,* 36; Thomas P. Slaughter, "Crowds in Eighteenth-Century America: Reflections and New Directions," *Pennsylvania Magazine of History and Biography* 115 (Winter 1991), 31–33; and Edmund S. Morgan, "The Witch and We, the People," *American Heritage* 34 (August–September 1983), 6–11.
19. Robert Fridlington, "A 'Diversion' in Newark: A Letter from the New Jersey Continental Line, 1778," *New Jersey History* 105 (Winter–Spring 1987), 76–77. The "Pioneers' March" was sometimes used as well.
20. Crane et al., eds., *Diary of Elizabeth Drinker*, 1:314 (July 4, 1778).

21. John Fanning Watson lists three similar incidents in Philadelphia but gives no dates. Two occurred in the colonial period: one criticized a prevailing fashion of red cloaks for women by having the hangman dress a female felon in one as she was hanged, another dressed the wife of hangman Daniel Pettitteau in sumptuous dress and paraded her around town to the accompaniment of "rude music." Neither of these episodes was reported in the *Pennsylvania Gazette*. The third episode purportedly took place during the Revolution, when a tall man was dressed in high hair and marched around town with a drum. This latter example may reflect yet another variant retelling of the July 4, 1778, incident, because I have found no other reference to such an event. John F. Watson, *Annals of Philadelphia, and Pennsylvania in the Olden Time* (Philadelphia, 1899), 1:184. The threat of violence is obvious in the first two incidents.

22. Rosswurm, *Arms, Country, and Class,* 152–53.

23. Violet Alford, "Rough Music or Charivari," *Folklore* 70 (December 1959), 505–6; Martin Ingram, "Ridings, Rough Music and the 'Reform of Popular Culture,' " *Past and Present* 105 (November 1984), 92.

24. Ingram, "Ridings, Rough Music," 96, 112; Alford, "Rough Music or Charivari," 505–6; D. E. Underdown, "The Taming of the Scold: The Enforcement of Patriarchal Authority in Early Modern England," in Anthony Fletcher and John Stevenson, eds., *Order and Disorder in Early Modern England* (New York: Cambridge University Press, 1985); Susan D. Amussen, "Gender, Family, and the Social Order, 1560–1725," in ibid., 196–217. On the transfer of these traditions, see Alfred F. Young, "English Plebeian Culture and Eighteenth-Century American Radicalism," in James R. Jacob and Margaret C. Jacob, eds., *The Origins of Anglo-American Radicalism* (London: Routledge, 1984), 184–212.

25. Ballagh, ed., *Letters,* 1:421.

26. John Bunyan, *The Pilgrim's Progress* (1678; reprint, New York: Signet, 1964), 84–85.

27. "Journal of Sergeant William Young," *Pennsylvania Magazine of History and Biography* 8 (Summer 1884), 278; Crane, ed., *Diary of Elizabeth Drinker,* 1:306 (May 18, 1778). Bartlett is quoted in John Sanderson, *Biography of the Signers to the Declaration of Independence* (Philadelphia, 1823), vol. 3, "Josiah Bartlett," by Robert Waln Jr., 159–60. See also "Letters and Communications addressed to John F. Watson on the subject of his Annals of Philada" (Manuscripts, scrapbook, HSP, c. 1824), 1:29.

28. Paul H. Smith, ed., *Letters of Delegates to Congress* (Washington, D.C.: Library of Congress, 1983), 10:219.

29. Charles J. Stille, *Major General Anthony Wayne and the Pennsylvania Line in the Continental Army* (Philadelphia, 1893), 153–54.

30. Timothy Pickering to Rebecca Pickering, July 8, 1778, Pickering Papers, Massachusetts Historical Society, microfilm of original, reel 1; "Sylvia [Anna Young Smith]," Thomas Coombe Papers, HSP. Attribution thanks to Susan Stabile.

31. Campbell, ed., *Bland Papers,* 1:91–92.

32. Ester deBerdt Reed, "Sentiments of an American Woman (Philadelphia: Dunlap, 1780), in Library of Congress, "American Memory, An American Time Capsule: Three Centuries of Broadsides and Other Printed Ephemera," <http://memory.loc.gov>. For the importance of Reed's proposals, see Norton, *Liberty's Daughters,* 177–88; Norton, "The Philadelphia Ladies Association," *American Heritage* 31, no. 3 (April–May 1980), 103–7; Kerber, *Women of the Republic,* 99–110; and forthcoming work by Owen Ireland.

33. For subsequent developments, see Rosemarie Zagarri, "The Rights of Man and Woman in Post-Revolutionary America," *William & Mary Quarterly* 55 (Spring 1998), 203–30.

34. Ingram, "Ridings, Rough Music," 98.

35. Ruth H. Bloch, "The Gendered Meanings of Virtue in Revolutionary America," *Signs* 13 (Winter 1987), 37–58.

36. Shaw, *Patriots and Rituals,* 215.

37. Alford, "Rough Music or Charivari," 505–18; Natalie Davis, *Society and Culture in Early Modern France* (Stanford, Calif.: Stanford University Press, 1975), 104–7, 124–27.

38. Alford, "Rough Music or Charivari," 518; Davis, *Society and Culture*, 104–7, 124–27.

39. L. H. Butterfield and Marc Friedlander, eds., *Adams Family Correspondence*, 3:58; "From a Late Philadelphia Paper," *Continental Journal & Weekly Advertiser* (Boston), July 30, 1778.

40. Susan E. Klepp, "Revolutionary Bodies: Women and the Fertility Transition in the Mid-Atlantic Region, 1760–1820," *Journal of American History* 85 (December 1998), 910–45; Bloch, "Gendered Meanings of Virtue," *Signs*, 37–58; Carroll Smith-Rosenberg, "Domesticating 'Virtue': Coquettes and Revolutionaries in Young America," in Elaine Scarry, ed., *Literature and the Body: Essays on Populations and Persons* (Baltimore: Johns Hopkins University Press, 1988), 160–84.

41. Susan E. Klepp, *Philadelphia in Transition: A Demographic History of the City and Its Occupational Groups, 1720–1830* (New York: Garland Press, 1989), 218, 341; Robert V. Wells, "Family Size and Fertility Control in Eighteenth-Century America: A Study of Quaker Families," *Population Studies* 25 (March 1971), 73–83.

42. Timothy Pickering to Rebecca Pickering, July 8, 1778, Pickering Papers, Massachusetts Historical Society, microfilm of original, reel 1.

43. "From a Late Philadelphia Paper" *Continental Journal & Weekly Advertiser* (Boston), July 30, 1778.

44. Mrs. Hodgson to Susan Livingston, November 2, 1778, Livingston II Papers, reel 8, Massachusetts Historical Society (my thanks to Judith Van Buskirk for this citation and for a photocopy of the original letter); Amelia Mott Gummere, *The Quaker: A Study in Costume* (Philadelphia: Ferris & Leach, 1901).

45. This might have signaled an attempt at rapprochement. Many with Loyalist tendencies were feeling betrayed by British actions during the occupation and abandoned by their retreat from the city in June.

46. Tappert and Doberstein, *Journals of Henry Melchoir Muhlenberg*, 3:171–72; Richard Henry Lee to Francis Lightfoot Lee, July 5, 1778, in Ballagh, *Letters of Richard Henry Lee*, 1:421; Frank C. Mevers, ed., *Papers of Josiah Bartlett* (Hanover, N.H.: University Press of New England, 1979), 214.

47. Diana de Marly, *Dress in North America*, vol. 1: *The New World, 1492–1800* (New York: Holmes & Meier, 1990), 131–72. The author notes that while American fashions originated in Europe, "by the 1770s America was itself becoming a fashion," introducing into Europe and then back to America simplified, less rococo women's clothing that did not require a maidservant's assistance in dressing (p. 115).

48. Ballagh, *Letters of Richard Henry Lee*, 1:421; Butterfield and Friedlander, *Adams Family*, 3:56; Tappert and Doberstein, *Journals of Henry Melchior Muhlenberg*, 3:171–72; "From a Late Philadelphia Paper," July 30, 1778; William Ellery, diary entry for late July 1778, in Paul H. Smith, ed., *Letters of Delegates to Congress* (Washington, D.C.: Library of Congress, 1983), 10:221–22; Mevers, *Papers of Josiah Bartlett*, 214.

49. Frank Moore, *Diary of the American Revolution from Newspapers and Original Documents*, 2 vols. (1858; reprint, York: Arno, 1969), 34, 87; Tappert and Doberstein, *Journals of Henry Melchior Muhlenberg*, 3:171–72.

50. Mevers, *Papers of Josiah Bartlett*, 214; Sanderson, *Biography of the Signers*, 3:159–60; Elizabeth F. Ellet, *The Women of the American Revolution*, 2 vols. (New York, 1848), 1:88.

51. Ellet, *Women of the American Revolution*, citing Sanderson, *Signers of Independence*, 1:88.

52. Stille, *Major-General Anthony Wayne*, 153–54.

53. David S. Shields and Fredrika J. Teute, "The Meschianza: Sum of all Fetes / The

Meschianza's Meaning: 'How will it sparkle—page the Future?' " paper presented at the annual meeting of the Organization of American Historians, March 28, 1996, Chicago, 30–39. My thanks to Fredrika Teute for sending a copy of this innovative examination of the gendered and civic meanings of the event.

54. Campbell, ed., *Bland Papers,* 91–92; Gen. John Cadwalader to General Greene, December 5, 1778, Lee Papers, Publications of the New York Historical Society (1873), 8:252; Ann White Morris to her mother, November 1778, quoted in Scharf and Westcott, *History of Philadelphia,* 2:899.

55. David S. Shields argues for the postwar triumph of elite politeness and civility, only slightly modified by republican simplicity, in republican courts and salons. See his *Civil Tongues and Polite Letters in British America* (Chapel Hill: University of North Carolina Press, 1997). For an extended study of the revolution and memory, see Alfred. F. Young, *The Shoemaker and the Tea Party* (Boston: Beacon Press, 1999).

Revelry

8

White Indians in Penn's City

The Loyal Sons of St. Tammany

Roger D. Abrahams

In late April 1786, Cornplanter, the beleaguered sachem of a band of Senecas, visited Philadelphia. Whether or not he was seeking to repair political relations with those who now called themselves Americans (and against whom they had fought), he was certainly making an effort to assert his claims for land, as well as to raise other equity issues. The entourage arrived dressed in full ceremonial regalia and received some notice. Far from being unusual, this sojourn was remarkable only in that in late April or early May Cornplanter's party was entertained by a group of Philadelphia burghers, the Sons of St. Tammany, who themselves were "authentically" dressed as Indians. They performed a ceremony of war and peacemaking together. Each took the other seriously, eating, making speeches, singing and dancing together in Indian style—and all quite in public.

With the ethnic sensibilities of our own age, how can we better fathom such an entertainment? How did the two groups understand what was transpiring, and what were they able to draw on in common that made that understanding possible? And what of the cultural apparatus brought to the event by the Philadelphia spectators and by the members of the host organization and guests?

This chapter calls attention to the strange and multivalent character of cultural transferal, as this process can be teased out of historical records. This investigation involves only commonsense notions. I seek only to look at events like treaties and visitations, festivities and public ceremonies, to reveal some of the cultural layering that goes on in such activities and to reveal how these high-intensity occasions are especially open to alternative cultural vocabularies, even those of strangers and enemies. As groups with different customs, habits, and sentiments have an encounter, each leaves traces on the skin of the other.[1]

In many cases, these encounters result in the most extreme forms of animosity. This was especially so in colonial America and after the War of Independence. The character of these negotiations differed, from one colony to another, and depended on the relationship between Britons and Indians in matters of agriculture and commerce. Questions of property and providence, of land and labor, of order and civility were under constant surveillance, especially as issues of dependence and independence were being negotiated.

The conquered always leave behind them lifeways that are adopted by the conquerors. To discuss the Indian "gifts" to American culture, from corn through cold medicines, is to stretch the very notion of gift-giving in our contemporary world. Such gifts are no longer part of the progressive argument for a more civilized world; rather, stories of gifts and exchange have become embedded as part of a nostalgized frame of mind, producing the lament for the lost tribes as a way of clearing the record and making ourselves feel better and worse at the same time. But my aim is less emotionally complicated: I seek to understand a little more fully the actualities of cultural transference at particular times and places.

Even in the midst of the most belligerent interactions, both sides are deeply affected by the other's presence. And once put into practice, these culturally transferred effects continue to ripple through the lives of those involved and of those who inherit the memory of these occasions. Once I studied this scene of the ceremonial encounter of the Cornplanter Seneca and the Sons of St. Tammany (or the Tammanies, as I shall call them) and attempted to understand how it might be interpreted, it became clear to me, as a native Philadelphian, that a foundational scene was being reenacted: Penn's Treaty with the Indians, a legend and a ceremony that were a part of my cultural memory, embedded in my own universe. The story of the imagining of Penn's "Peaceable Kingdom" was then deeply inscribed in the landscape of Greater Philadelphia; there were trails and contact points still in place when I was growing up in the 1930s and 1940s. Perhaps there still are.

Of course, the memories of local Indian culture were, and are, severely skewed by the legendary formations through which they are filtered. Through reports of the encounter between Cornplanter's band and the Tammanies, we are able to learn a great deal more about the loyal Sons of St. Tammany than about the Senecas. Nonetheless, it is useful to conjecture about how the Iroquoian "equipment for living" might have been drawn on by the Senecas on this occasion.

The scene first caught my interest because the ceremony involved whites imitating actual Indian practices in detail, and doing so before an audience that included Indians. Perhaps by disinterring some of the embodied meanings of the two groups as they dressed in what the public perceived to be an exotic manner and performed esoteric ritual songs and dances, some insights might be gathered regarding the ways in which everyday life in the 1780s was carried out in Philadelphia at the very time the Constitution was being negotiated.

I do not argue that the interaction between Philadelphia merchants and Indian warriors, and between the Tammanies and the Cornplanter Senecas was important, or even significant. Rather, it is an interesting event, not only for understanding early Americans in their relations with Indians but also for how they provided each other an audience. This task seems especially useful as cultural exchanges took place during a period in which the unique conditions of this New World nation began to develop a set of practices that provided the basis for a national culture that truly drew on the many traditions of its plural peoples. None was more important in forming American notions of self and national character than those in which Indians came together with colonists and former colonists.

As always, ritual and festival apparatus is especially rich in suggested meanings. The spectacle discloses a range of possible interpretations, as it establishes a frame of reference for objects of fear and desire—the calumet, the covenant chain, the cast-off weapons—to be trundled out and passed around. The task of the reporter and the critical commentator is to reveal as many of these alternative (and often contradictory) readings as possible, rather than attempting to discover the meaning, even in the most ceremonial and scripted display activity. I argue that from the perspective of an ethnography of performance, it is not possible to conceive of an event such as this in which cultural transference of many sorts does not take place.

In carrying out this effort, I argue as a folklorist, not as a historian. Folklore study distinguishes rituals, by which the life passage of an individual and a group are marked; calendar customs, activities that take place each year; and occasional ceremonies and celebrations, festivities arising from a specific temporal disruption in the life of a community. Elements of all these types of gatherings are superimposed on each other on the occasion of Cornplanter's visit.

The character of the event that brings together Philadelphia prominenti and the Senecas is complicated by the fact that both a calendar custom and an occasional festivity were being celebrated, both of them drawing on ritual apparatus as well, making this a generically hybrid activity. Thus, even though the event was hardly important in the lives of any of the participants or, as things turned out, in anyone's political positioning, the cultural work being carried out was enormously complicated.

The late 1780s and the early 1790s were a time of self-conscious change for all Americans, no matter what their culture. Emissaries of all sorts came to the new capital to work out new relationships. The celebratory apparatus— the fife-and-drum marching bands, the firing of rifles and cannons, the elaborate costuming and parading floats, the eating and toasting, and other kinds of salute—all these devices were adapted by these former British subjects to intensify the moment, much as they had been employed by the British at similar points of historical change. As David Cressy says, "no other nation employed the calendar as the English did to express and represent their identity."[2] These practices were maintained and elaborated as devices of shared experience in political resistance before the war and maintained well through the rest of the century.[3]

The encounter between Cornplanter's group and the Tammanies had local resonances for Philadelphians. Peacemaking was especially to be celebrated, given the Quaker attitude toward life, an attitude that is well remembered and often replayed in depictions of the practices of treaty-making attached by legend to William Penn. Yet the connection between the Senecas and the Sons of St. Tammany seems to have generated its own plural meanings, developed out of the experiences of Indians and whites in more recent negotiations and alliances of a political and commercial sort. The occasion apparently successfully provided fun for both groups. It also seems to have been regarded by the city spectators as appropriate to the opening of spring, a celebration made all the more intense because of the felt need for patriotic public occasions following the American Revolution.

Consider the two groups: the Seneca band that had come with serious political purpose to Philadelphia; and the Sons of St. Tammany, a fraternal order of merchants and craftsmen engaged in masking and merrymaking. Cornplanter's entourage brought along an elaborate apparatus for peaceful activities in an unusual public celebration of the pan-Iroquoian Condolence Ceremony. A member of one of the most important clans in Iroquoia, the ever-troubled Cornplanter carried with him worries about recent military and political defeats that, one can conjecture, caused him to welcome the opportunity to use these acts as a means to advertise himself and his people, and their deep traditions of peaceable rituals, and to advance the virtue of their political position with regard to the former British former colonists.[4]

These visits to the new nation's capital were far from rare. The later visit of the "near fifty chiefs" of the Six Iroquois Nations in March and April 1792 elicited much more official response, including a delegation from the city that marched with the chiefs into the city to the accompaniment of martial parade music and a ritual firing of cannons.[5] In addition, a political struggle between the commercial eastern part of the state and the settlers in western Pennsylvania had arisen, in which the Philadelphians found themselves in some sympathy with the Indians and at odds with the rambunctious whiskey-making backcountry folk.[6] Encounters between whites and Indians on the frontier, and especially Indian raids, strained the relationship between the Penn family as proprietors and the state legislature.[7] The Senecas were one of the Indian groups with whom both the British and the Americans had attempted to make alliances in the war; indeed, the Senecas chose the side of the vanquished and were surely in Philadelphia to repair their relations as well as work toward more equitable terms regarding their ownership of lands.

Both groups, the real Indians and the dressed-up "White Indians," operated with the understanding that they were on display to the general public, a public brimming with vigor in light of the victory in the Revolution but also weary of the sacrifices and suffering engendered by the war. Following the fashion of the times, the event involved young males from both groups. The Senecas headed by Cornplanter were his most trusted warriors. The Tammanies were a fraternal group that had come to life as one of many nonpolitical dining and drinking clubs in eighteenth-century Philadelphia. Exercising conviviality under the banner of an American "saint" when the time came, after the Stamp Act, for the colonists to initiate dissent against the British, St. Tammany provided them with a figure of a peace-seeking Indian warrior of legendary memory.

A number of customary activities commingled in this strange ceremony. The first was the customary Philadelphia parade and dispersal that had been observed for nearly a century at the opening of the fishing season on the first of May. A second involved the annual public performance by the Tammanies of their usually secret ceremony of peace-bringing, a ceremony that seems to have evolved from replaying the signing of "Penn's Treaty." Its reenactment had become the way in which the Tammanies had declared their uniqueness to one another and to the outside world, as embodied in their arcane fraternal ceremonies.

A third set of meanings emerges from Seneca tradition itself. To the Senecas, the ritual embodied a great range of their own unique esoteric meanings and historical memories. It bespoke centuries of Indian powwows that had developed independently of the settlements of whites—indeed, that were practiced before the colonial period. It also carried a special understanding of the ceremony and its attendant myth, one that must be thought of as an Iroquoian notion of progress: the development of the people from cannibalism and war-making to the more peaceable attitudes of the People of the Longhouse. More than this, for this band of Senecas the mid-1780s was an especially appropriate time for them to sue for amicable relations in new nation's capital.

Finally, the Tammanies themselves not only replayed their version of the Indian ceremony, but also replicated much of the ceremonial devices common to clubs and other voluntary associations that were also secret societies, such as the Freemasons. As Carl Bridenbaugh notes, "Philadelphia developed into a great club town as organizations of all sorts sprang up after 1725,"[8] and the Tammanies were one among them. These organizations commonly picked a day for marking their existence, sometimes just with one another, sometimes in public. The Tammanies did just this on one of the more common holidays: the Opening of the Fishing Season on May 1.

Tammany: The Titular Saint of America

In the years between the Stamp Act and the American Revolution, Americans invented an American saint in the figure of Tammany, the Indian chief identified by legend with the peaceful treaty he made with William Penn. They did so in playful confrontation with the national saints of Britannia. As the popular song sung during the Revolution celebrating his name had it:

> Of Andrew, of Patrick, of David, & George,
> What mighty achievements we hear!
> While no one relates great Tammany's feats,
> Although more heroic by far, brave boys,
> Although more heroic by far.[9]

Though Tammany lost out to Yankee Doodle in the popularity race for nicknaming Americans, his name was trumpeted throughout the colonies as a peaceable but honorable warrior embodying the genius loci. As patriots sought to distance themselves from the weight of British domination both symbolic and political, a number of figures, like the Columbus as reported in this collection by Matthew Dennis, or Yankee Doodle, were elevated to heroic status by popular acclaim. Tammany was one of them.

Though far from the most important Indian signatory of the treaties with the Penn family, "Tamanend" (the common spelling for this figure in official documents) achieved the legendary status denied the others. He was the representative "king" of the Lenni Lenape who initiated the creation of the "peaceable kingdom" on the Indian side.[10] Thus, in depictions of the signing of Penn's Treaty, and in reenactment of the signing in pageants and parades, he became William Penn's counterpart in the popular imagination.[11] He seems to have been so identified in the very popular painting by Benjamin West of Penn's Treaty.[12]

There is some irony in this elevation of Tammany, for as John Heckewelder, early chronicler of Lenni Lenape tradition, put it, "the Great Sachem Tamanend, is held in the highest veneration . . . of all the chiefs and great men [of] the Lenape nation." But Heckewelder also pointed out that "many fabulous stories are circulated" about Tammany, replayed only "among the whites," and that "but little of his real history are known."[13] Nonetheless, Tammany went from chief to king to saint in the popular imagination between the 1730s and the late 1760s. As Ebenezer Hazard exclaimed in 1784 while reminiscing about his childhood, "We used to talk of King Tammany then but it seems he has been canonized since the

Declaration of Independence and has now become a saint. He will make as good a one as any in the Calendar."[14]

Although it is difficult to determine the meanings attached to the Tammanies' annual commemoration for Philadelphians in general, given its coincidence with the opening of the fishing season, it is evident that for at least some carousers the event was enlivened by a remembrance of the legend of Penn's Treaty at Shackamaxon in which fishing and hunting rights purportedly were first given palpable form.[15] While we know the power of this chartering scene from the paintings by Benjamin West and Edward Hicks, the importance of the event creeps into the record in the toasts given during feasts of many fraternal organizations, pointing to the power of Penn's character and that of the other signatories of the treaty.

Many American colonies developed legends centering on Indians like Tammany who served as a cultural donor figures—that is, heroes who passes on indigenous traditions to the more powerful newcomers.[16] A great hunter and leader of men, Tammany was by legend revered by his people at least as early as the 1750s (as his story was told by Philadelphians), and undoubtedly earlier. As colonizers arrived, Tammany reportedly freely entered into peaceful alliances, ceding hunting and fishing rights to a territory, receiving both goods and honor for his efforts. He visited with the newcomers regularly to reinforce that bond, commonly partaking in a kind of feast of renewal featuring indigenous foods.[17] As he grew older, he retreated to his wigwam—which then burned, transporting his soul to heaven.[18]

This story is a parable of expansion and submission widely found in both the Old World and the New World as a local explanation of how "the civilizing process" and the land came to be subjected to "improvement." The donor figure representing the earliest inhabitants commonly maintains a mythical or magical power that is, however, kept in check by the continuing presence of the conquerors. Now epitomized as an animal, a monster, or a troglodyte (such as the many dragons, big heads, hobbyhorses, or bulls still found in local European festivities), as well as the exotic dark warrior chief, the figure remains embedded in the stories and festivities that have become a part of traditional annual holiday celebrations. At such festive events the conflict of cultures is often depicted first, followed by a scene in which peace and amity is established. By reemerging within the licensed context of a festive drama or a meal, the "presence" of the original inhabitants reinfuses the play world with the power inherent in the violence of conquest.[19]

Because power is accompanied by the fascination and the fear of the crowd during the festival, whoever is chosen to represent the original inhabitants has a special place within the festive proceedings. In the form of horses, bulls, rams, mules, the wildman, the uglyman, or the dragon, such figures are still conventionally associated with rites of renewal in many parts of the Old and New Worlds. They are deeply related to the "luck" of the celebrating group, bringing transgressive vigor into the occasion. Even when appearing in human form, such figures are notable for their departure from civil norms of body presentation.[20]

This dimension of self-representation became especially evident during Cornplanter's visit and in his involvement with the Tammanies. The mere presence of groups of Indians in ceremonial garb visiting the city was noteworthy, perhaps because of the display of characteristics Philadelphia saw as "antick and horrible." A local newspaper found the celebration especially interesting, for the Sons of St. Tammany too wore Indian ceremonial garb, playing at this grotesquerie for the moment of celebration. The reports of the revelry make it clear that there were members who went to some pains to dress, speak, and act as authentically Indian as possible; one "gentleman" appeared "in a complete powwow dress" described as "at once both ludicrous and terrible," and he proceeded to perform "the maneta dance"—a form of the Great Spirit dance found throughout the Confederation of Iroquois Nations. In the contemporary accounts, such as that of the *Philadelphia Independent* of April 22 and May 6, 1786, it is clear that the two groups saw an advantage to reinforcing each others' public identities. They renewed the old treaty forms of symbolic exchange; the carousing merchants assembled in the market areas of the oldest part of the city, met with the Indians, and paraded with them through the town, singing and dancing all the way out to their rural retreat in the woods above Spring Garden.

The Tammanies had also painted their faces and developed a method of speech-making, again in "Indian style," produced in theatrical broken English. After the orations they formed one large circle and passed the "great calumet of peace," and the chief poured a libation on the ground while making appropriate oratorical note of what he was doing. The two groups, now joined by the leaders of the local militia, proceeded to display themselves in a dance of war and a dance of peace.[21]

The Renewal of Claims for Natural Rights

As early as the spring of 1783, the Tammanies decided to reinstate their annual celebration marking the "joyful cessation of hostilities." They "dressed and distinguished [themselves] in buck tails and feathers very expressive of the occasion" and seized the day, passing legislation within their own ranks "to compel every man to do perfectly as he pleases during the day." Reminding themselves of the spirit in which the organization was founded, they also proclaimed that these liberties should not impinge on the doings of others and that "peace and good order be preserved."[22]

Many fraternal organizations involved in public festivities reflected the model of European craft guilds in developed ritual apparatus, election of officers, regular meetings, and public display in ritual dress. But whereas the British and other European craftworkers organized around the learning of the trade and the maintenance of the ancient wisdom associated with pursuing the craft, American seaboard communities seemed instead to reflect ethnic connections to some part of the Old World. No organization played a more central role in representing this new spirit than this offshoot of the Schuylkill Fishing Club, the Tammanies, in the decade before the Revolution.

The Colony on Schuylkill, later the Schuylkill Fishing Club, began early in the eighteenth century. Mercantile life had been disrupted somewhat during Pennsylvania's earliest years, as the rights of the Penn proprietorship were being questioned. With the reassertion of the proprietary power of the Penn family by 1727, those claiming connection to the Penns through their purported Welsh ancestry established "The Sons of Ancient Britons" and marked the turn of events by celebrating St. David's Day. This was certainly the objective of the group that constructed the rural "garrison" of Fort St. David, in which the Society of Fort St. David held their meetings. Soon they were joined by the "Colony on Schuylkill" on the next plot of land along the river, a group that Bridenbaugh called "the most interesting and exclusive of colonial clubs."

As the Schuylkill Fishing Club historian expressed it, the members left few "memorials of their proceedings," as the club existed "for the purpose of conviviality and exercise" and its meetings were intended to be "a delightful occasional relief from the stern cares and toil of business." The meetings were also instituted to "liberalize the mind and improve the manners" through "friendly social intercourse of man with his fellow man" and to "cherish and promote . . . the generous feelings of the human heart."[23]

Unlike the better-known voluntary groups, such as Franklin's Junto or the Tuesday Club of Annapolis, with its chronicler, Dr. Alexander Hamilton,[24] the Sons of St. Tammany left little record of their activities. But Frances A. von Cabeen has found in the historical record a good deal of journalistic evidence regarding the manner in which the group assembled and how the idea of a club dedicated to an American patron saint spread throughout the maritime areas of the Middle Colonies.[25]

One local chief carrying the name of Tammany, but clearly not the signatory of the Penn treaties, was apparently a visitor at one of the meetings of the Colony on Schuylkill, perhaps in the 1730s. At least as early as 1747 the Colony adopted this chief as an ancestral figure, for in that year they presented a cannon to the city, with the motto "Kawania che Keekeru," attributed to Tammany.[26] (But Kilroe notes that the nineteenth-century scholar of Iroquoia, Horatio Hale, "says the words are not of the Delaware language, but of Iroquois origin, and mean 'I am master wherever I am.' ") The motto was engraved on a thirty-two-pound cannon presented by the Schuylkill Fishing Club to the Association Battery for use in the defense of Philadelphia in 1747.

That this motto was being used that early in the history of the company suggests that the identification with Tammany and the stereotype of the Indian who made war and peace with honor antedates the adoption of the costume and the other emblems of membership. Some form of this motto remained attached to the Schuylkill Company; between the 1740s and the Stamp Act crisis, one group of members branched off from the Colony and developed a central ceremonial place for Tammany, his motto, and Lenni Lenape myth and ritual. These became embodied in an arcane set of ceremonies and practices that proved to be attractive and stable enough that they led to the formation of "wigwams" in other mercantile centers, such as New York and Annapolis.[27]

John Fanning Watson, chronicler of Philadelphia history and traditions, has noted: "It is said, traditionally, that some Indian chiefs of the Lenni Lenape or Delaware tribe, with whom Penn made his treaty on the Delaware, attended a council of the colonists held in the forest, and in the name of the tribe granted the right and privilege to hunt in the woods and fish in the waters of the Schuylkill forever."[28] At meetings of the various fishing clubs, the license for these rights and privileges was symbolically renewed.

As the fraternal organization of the Colony on Schuylkill was restricted to twenty-five members, a new group, with a somewhat altered and intensified perspective, seems to have emerged.[29] This new group, perhaps made up of the first American-born generation of young men, built a separate rural retreat (their "wigwam"), established a new set of officers, and created a founding myth that was considerably more extensive than that of its ancestral group. Whether the offshoot group took its theme from the Lenni Lenape presence at the signing of Penn's Treaty or from the earlier visit to the meetings of the Colony on Schuylkill, this new organization now cavorted in the name of Tammany.

As the membership increased, with increasingly nationalistic motives just before the Revolution, a hierarchy was put into place: thirteen sachems representing the thirteen states, each symbolizing a different "wigwam," each given a separate tribal designation. Members developed a set of arcane practices that gave them the sense of belonging to a secret society. They paraded regularly with other such organizations, displaying themselves hierarchically and always marching single file. They devised their own calendar, referred to the months as "moons," and conducted their meetings in a mock-Indian oratorical style derived from the stock descriptions of Indian peacemaking ceremonies. Indeed, they saw themselves as following in Tammany's footsteps as peace-bearers and treaty-makers, a role they were to play actively in the late 1780s and early 1790s when it became necessary for the new nation to make treaties with some of the contiguous East Coast Indian nations.

By extending the invitation to the visiting Senecas in 1786, then, the Sons of St. Tammany were in all probability operating within the sense of their own traditions as being hosts to important Indian chiefs. Moreover, given the fifty years and more between when Tammany is purported to have visited and the coming of Cornplanter, the Sons of St. Tammany may have wanted to use the occasion to signal a renewal of the symbolic coming-together of peoples. They thus reinforced their "rights" to wear Indian garb and to organize themselves through using Indian paraphernalia and terms expressing status.

Such "White Indian" groups were far from unique to the English colonies. Indeed, at several flashpoints in American history both before and after the Revolution, groups resisting metropolitan authorities took to calling themselves Indians and to dressing and acting in ways that called their rights to the attention of officials who seemed to be undermining them.[30] Their Indianness came to reside in the symbolism of the tomahawk and the blanket, although the devices that were even more characteristic of the Sons of St. Tammany were the calumet and the buck's tail. In fact, they were popularly known as "the buck-tail crew." Their motto, now spelled "Kwanio Che Keeteru," was assigned the meaning "This is my right. I will take it"[31] and was emblazoned on the buck-flag found in their lodge. The legitimacy of their Indianness, in retrospect, would seem to be severely tested by the presence of Cornplanter and his retinue.

The Tammanies drew on conceptions of a newly emerging regional and national pride by employing the most widely accessible popular model of the peaceable encounter in terms that were particularly appropriate for Philadelphians. The replaying of the treaty had special significance for Tammanies and for Indians. Both were making bids to inherit the powers of the early inhabitants, and both sought to be identified with an official program of peacemaking and bonding in what was then the capital of the United States.

As the colonies found themselves sharing certain political problems, vis-à-vis official action by the English, the Tammanies turned their activities more toward political commentary, and eventually to resistance. The more the group found itself reacting to political questions, the more it formalized the organization. The costumes and paraphernalia of membership were ever more self-consciously fashioned by actual observation of Indians, especially the behavior of Indians waging war and pursuing peace. By imitating so closely the ceremonial aspect of being identified with Indians, they went far beyond the usual masking used by the groups of young male carousers. Now Indian dress, stance, oratorical style, and ritual dances were not used only as disguises. While the Tammany's members were Philadelphia prominenti, there was also a good deal of regional and national pride attached to this local organization.

The seriousness of the organization was repeatedly referred to in the speeches given at their meetings, both during and after the Revolution. It had become a patriotic organization, the members reminded everyone, and patriotic they would remain, without becoming immersed in political squabbling. As one speaker put it in 1795, "This Society acknowledges neither political principles for its establishment, nor political objects for its pursuits; but is founded on the broad basis of natural rights and is solely designed to connect American brethren in the indissoluble bonds of Patriotic Friendship."

This patriotism was to be effected by "adopting Indian terms, customs, dresses and ornaments, . . . that the Order might eventually adopt a pattern for a distinctive national dress." This was intended to encourage greater commerce between the states and to ensure a society "whose membership was not gauged by wealth or class."[32]

Between the adoption of Indian dress in the 1750s and the use of such costume for patriotic purpose after the Revolution came a number of social and political shifts that are interesting to note. In 1784, Ebenezer Hazard recalled of his childhood twenty-five or thirty years before (1754–59) that Philadelphia had already "consecrated" the first of May to the memory of Tammany. Hazard followed fashion in wearing a buck's tail in his hat as well as a picture of an Indian shooting a deer with a bow.[33] He may have been describing the beginnings of the Tammanies, though that is far from clear. Certainly by the mid-1750s, May Day and playing Indian had become traditions in the community. An interesting notice of May Day 1755 in the area by a German visitor, Gottlieb Mittelfort, states: "On the first or second days of May there is . . . merrymaking in Pennsylvania. . . . All amuse themselves with games, dancing, shooting, hunting and the like. These unmarried people who are native born adorn their heads with a piece of the fur of a wild animal, together with a painting of any wild animal they choose. Thus decked out they go, lads walk around town shouting 'Hurrah, hurrah.' But only the native born may attach such decorations to their hats and they are called 'Indians.' "[34] Mittelfort's "native born" suggests that a generational sense had developed among Philadelphians that those born on this side of the Atlantic had a more profound proprietary right to mask as Indians. Whether this characterized the youth of Philadelphia, in general or only the Tammanies, is a matter of conjecture.

While these notices point to the beginnings of the Tammanies thirty years before the Revolution, the first firm indication of their existence and spread was provided by William Eddis in his notice of a ball given on May 1, 1771, not in Philadelphia but Annapolis. Eddis said: "The Americans on this part of the continent have . . . a saint who shares legendary status with St. George, St. Patrick, St. Andrew, and St. David," a status "lost in fable and uncertainty." May Day is dedicated "to the memory of Saint Tamina [*sic*] on which occasion the natives wear a piece of the buck's tail."[35]

With the Sons of St. Tammany, as with the tea-dumping Boston Mohawks and many others who had carried out vigilante or guerrilla activities, playing Indian provided a way for males to organize in bands proclaiming amity and a common purpose. Customarily, "White Indian" groups in other states organized in opposition to tax-collectors or rent-collectors, and at moments of confrontation delivered speeches in which they proclaimed the brotherhood and generally peaceable attitude of Indians.[36] But the Philadelphia Tammanies, begun as a social club, had a much more evolved ritual, costume, set of speeches, and set of offices, and a full-blown ritual taken from actual Indian performers and performances. By the mid-1760s the players had become involved in a controversy that extended far beyond local festive matters.

Printed toasts and songs of the Tammanies indicate that by the early 1770s they were already positioned to comment on affairs extending beyond their own interests to those of "the country" (that is, the colony of Pennsylvania). Their use of Indian paraphernalia and practices served their goal of promoting unity in the face of a perceived threat to common interests. By the opening of hostilities, as far as the rest of the colonies were concerned, the Tammanies and the Sons of Liberty were the same organization of patriots.[37]

A Voluntary Organization

In the convergence of the Seneca and the Tammanies there was a commingling of English and Indian vocabularies of celebration. Merchants and artisans took part in a serious civic celebration in which they deployed Indianness within the confines of an English-style display event. The English-style bonfire and bell-pealing,[38] the trooping of the colors, the programmatic organizing of the parading groups showing the hierarchy of elected leaders, flags arrayed and ceremonial firing of cannons—all were characteristic of civic pageantry found throughout the West. On the other side, the Tammanies parading in public adopted the march in "Indian style"— single-line Indian file. To this was close to practices adapted from Indian ceremonies, the ring-dance and song, the passing of the pipe, the burying of the tomahawk, and the extensive exchange of speeches.

Both the Tammanies and European fraternal orders were made up of men who self-identified as warriors and peacemakers. It is the differences that are perhaps more profound. The Tammanies were a voluntary association, and their Indianness was nothing more than a guise of the day. They were involved in the expansive assertion of liberty that had animated such groups since their beginnings in the second decade of the eighteenth century, a liberty that was signaled by the retreat to the woods and the building and inhabiting of the Tammanies' "wigwam" headquarters in the woods. They were patently inventing themselves and their organization as they went along. On the other hand, in certain ways the development of secret fraternal societies in early modern Europe should be counted as early evidence of the cultural process involving a self-conscious invention of tradition—that is, these secret societies were self-generated groups who provided themselves with markers of antique practices and foundational stories, all "distressed genres" in the sense that Susan Stewart develops the term.[39] This often calls for appropriation of a foundation story, a myth that gives both a rendering of a primordial founding moment and a sense of legitimacy to those with present membership. As a commercial class developed in cities on both sides of the Atlantic, joining clubs became a means by which these upwardly striving men could establish a sense of convivial community. Each club tended to develop its own cast of characters or oddly named officers. Meeting in taverns, the clubs were primarily opportunities for members to display and discuss together their emerging common interests.[40]

In the United States, as in Great Britain, these included clubs of "bucks and blades," who dressed and acted wildly; jocose clubs, made up of local wits who often prepared facetious entertainments for fellow members; eating and drinking organizations; ethnic pride groups, made up of immigrants with a sentimental allegiance to their homeland; and groups that focused on ideas and issues, whether they were secret societies, such as the Freemasons, or more open gatherings of thinking men, such as the Philadelphia Junto or the Boston Caucus. As Robert Micklus points out in discussing the Annapolis organization, "The Tuesday Club," it was "an age when clubbing was the thing to do, [and] being a Freemason was as much a part of the normal social fabric of eighteenth century life as being a member of any other club." Such organizations "provided the framework by which . . . all enlightened men sought to structure their lives."[41]

Gordon Wood's dictum concerning the impact of Freemasonry on American life seems to apply to the Sons of St. Tammany as well: "It not only created national icons that are still with us; it brought people together in new ways and helped fulfill the republican dream on reorganizing social relations."⁴² Metropolitan peoples on this side of the Atlantic discovered in such organizations "a major means by which they participated directly in the Enlightenment." Specifically, the orders and practices of the Freemasons encouraged the development of republican values by rejecting "the monarchical hierarchy of family and favoritism and creat[ing] a new hierarchical order that rested on 'real Worth and personal Merit.' " To be sure, the Tammanies had not shed their allegiances to the values of the merchant-elite. While outside Philadelphia they were sometimes confused with the Sons of Liberty, there is no record of any overt official political involvement of the group during the Revolution.⁴³

Clubs operated in both private and public arenas. While stressing the arcane character of their rituals, which were held within their inner sanctums, they played an ever-greater part in public civic enterprises, including parades and pageants. Although the proceedings of their meetings remained secret, the groups began to enter more and more fully into the development of a pulsing public life. The enthusiasm the clubs generated had a direct influence on the development of local, regional, and finally national patriotism.

Like the Freemasons and other groups that could trace their lineage back to the medieval guild system, the Tammanies had a hierarchy of offices, a set of symbols that embodied both the order and the values of the group, and certain arcane practices they used to articulate the values of mutual assistance and free discussion. They also "invested" individuals with a ritual set of offices and practices that engaged a shared sense of creative fun. Like the Masons, they created, for fun, an origin narrative, which in this case focused on the figure of Tammany instead of Hiram the Mason.

Bound together by shared and intense previous experiences and a vocabulary of group celebration, the Tammanies surely entered into this occasion with two short-term objectives: to remind themselves and their community of their symbolic connection to the founding of the state, now reinforced by their patriotic commitment to the nation; and to reinforce their own claims to a set of ancient rights that had been established by the Lenni Lenape and passed on both by virtue of Penn's Treaty and also in the symbolism of the Tammanies' annual retreat to the woods and everything "natural" that stood for. As this was a jovial crew, it is difficult to discern how seriously they took these claims, but the rationalization scheme is all in place in their ritual.

Cornplanter's Cultural Equipment

The ritual practices of the Iroquois were fully formulated and complex and, like those of the Tammanies, based on a profound set of historically derived meanings and mythically chartered beliefs.[44] Unlike the Tammanies and other such fraternal organizations, the authority of their chartering narrative was never questioned, and neither was the centrality of their ritual apparatus in maintaining their unique sense of order and value. Yet the practices of both groups brought to the fore the values of peace and the possibilities of friendship. Peacemaking provided the theme for the Tammanies and the Senecas both. But the cultural reservoir of peacemaking was quite different for members of the Iroquois League, including Cornplanter and his Seneca retinue, just as it surely had been with the meetings involving William Penn and his advisers with the Lenni Lenape a century earlier.

Pennsylvania had, through the idea of the Society of Friends, promoted a peace-seeking set of beliefs and practices; so too had the Iroquois Federation developed the "House of Peace" as a means of bringing about cessation of hostilities within their federation, and as a way of alleviating the pervasive sense that contaminating outside forces were threatening their existence. In one foundational moment, Hiawatha, their culture hero, "raised up a string of wampum and declared to the wizard Thadadaho, 'These are the Words of the Great Law. On the Words we shall build the House of Peace, the Longhouse, with the five fires that is yet one household. These are the Words of Righteousness and Health and Power.' "[45]

The details of the myth in which Hiawatha delivers these words are important to understanding what Cornplanter and company might have brought to the 1786 Philadelphia meeting. The ceremony focused on the figure of Deganawidah, who brought his white stone canoe of peace to Iroquoia perhaps as early as the mid-fifteenth century. With Hiawatha's assistance, Deganawidah drew his people away from cannibalism. He reconstituted Iroquois political organization, still based on traditional Iroquois kinship and domestic organization, but now built on this new set of rituals.[46]

Deganawidah had faced a world in which ritual practices of cannibalism were the focus. In the myth, Hiawatha draws water and cooks a stew made of human body parts, then, upon seeing his reflection in the pot, has a vision of himself in new terms, as one who rejects such cannibalistic practices and achieves wisdom, righteousness, and strength—a lesson brought him by Deganawidah: "It was not the face of a man who eats humans."[47]

Deganawidah brought other changes for Hiawatha's people. Together they consigned the ugly brew to the hole made by an uprooted tree, a tree that forever symbolized this new vision of comity. But their focus was never on the land they controlled, but rather on the food it produced and the ways in which that food was prepared. Facing recurrent problems of food scarcity, the cooking of venison symbolized the hunters' contribution to the subsistence of the group. Hunting and fishing themselves were recoded under this new regime, for now the men had to go into the woods in a ritually clean fashion, not in pursuit of other men but to hunt deer and other animals. Commenting on the subsequent importance of antlers as symbols of this peace, historian Matthew Dennis notes: "The antlers they borrowed to crown Iroquois sachems symbolized legitimate authority granted to men who would dedicate themselves to righteousness, justice and peace."[48]

The Mohawks, the Oneidas, the Cayugas, then the Senecas and finally the remainder of the Onondagas were joined together in a confederation housed metaphorically in one extended lodge. Deganawidah and the civil chiefs planted a great Tree of Peace at Onondaga, the settlement of Thadodaho. After their displacement from the eastern colonies, the Lenni Lenape lived on the lands of the Iroquois Confederation. Each of these developments drew deeply on the condolence ceremony as a means of signifying and solidifying this alliance.

Treaty-Making Played and Replayed

This condolence ceremony provided the basis for the Penn Treaty and for its reenactment by the Tammanies, but it also influenced all treaty occasions in the colonies and in the early republic, for it provided the basic symbols of amity. A series of incidents in early America involving a coming-together of white settlers or traders and delegations of American Indians have been unearthed or resurrected. The records show how each party attempted to imitate the other through activities of both formal display and licensed playfulness. These incidents show Europeans and Indians engaging in cultural exchanges that go beyond negotiations for real or personal property, that are actually developing customs that quickly became traditional for such events: powwows, treaties, ceremonies centered on the exchange of words and gestures and goods. Common sense reminds us that in all such highly charged encounters a good deal of accommodation to the very presence of others takes place. In addition, the behavior of both whites and Indians is constantly under scrutiny by all the participants, especially for signs of understanding or misunderstanding.

Such moments of exchange are always being evaluated in context, according to the kind of event is taking place. Is the encounter being held to pass trade-goods between the groups, in which case the rules of "buyer or seller beware" are in play? Or are matters involving the use of territory or "real property" being negotiated, in which cases the invocation, and sometimes the prestation (the giving of a symbolically coded gift, usually in a ceremony) of power-invested objects (like wampum or bolts of cloth), occurs? Especially murky are the questions arising from the power negotiations as viewed from each party to the exchange. Simply regarding a treaty as a political or economic act ignores what may have been the most important dimension of the practice—the experience of being in the same place together under the rule of peace and amity.

In all these scenes there is cultural imitation between the two (or more) groups, and it is useful to be reminded that this interaction commonly involves adapting traditional or customary practices of exchange. Each event, then, is surrounded by specific objects and gestures that initiate construction of a repeatable cultural event. A point of assembly is agreed upon—often a particular open spot that can be identified by a large tree, a rock, or some other point in the borderlands between the groups.

Food and drink are shared in a special, customary manner. Particular ways of dressing are deployed, and such adornments are often included as objects that are part of the exchange. Certain gestures, such as holding the hand up to demonstrate that it is not carrying a weapon, symbolize the peacefulness of the encounter. Proffering objects of ceremonial dress, whether of cloth, metal, shells, or beads, represents the passing of power, as well as valuable considerations, between the groups.

Each episode resists any simple interpretation. The process of trade, under any circumstance, takes place in the most volatile zones of social intercourse. This is especially so in situations where there are language differences as well as alternative forms of customary prestation among those involved in the trade. Bargaining, in fact, seems to arise only in cases where trade takes place over a period of time that is long enough for a gesture-system or a trade-language, pidgin, to develop. The two or more groups engaged in the exchange attempt to discover expressive features of each other that may be elaborated ceremonially. Each group presumes motives of self-interest on the part of others. Each has invested power in particular ritual objects.

Both the Tammanies and the Iroquois, then, drew on basic elements of festive celebration in giving voice to their sense of community. Both invoked powers and practices developed in the past that underscore the importance of male bonds. Both brought forth the most powerful symbols of display and ritual practice in dramatizing solidarity. In the meeting of 1786, the two vocabularies of celebration reinforced each other. Both were based on an indigenous notion of the chartering of the group. For this one moment of celebration, for whatever reasons, carousing, fun, and hilarious spectacle seem to have created a successful coming together of different people who had different experiences and political agendas.

Understanding Nonevents

While the opening of the fishing season in 1786 was hardly an important historical occasion, the visit of Cornplanter and his party provided an opportunity to revive the Tammanies' prerevolutionary practice of reenacting something like the Indians' portion of the legendary Penn's Treaty. By enlisting the Senecan presence, the club was clearly making a bid to reinforce legendary claims for their "native rights," at least as they operated within their clubhouse and the surrounding territory.

We must also assume that Cornplanter recognized an opportunity to repair his and his peoples' access to the power of the new federal government. They had allied themselves with the British during the Revolution, and they needed to mend their relationship with the American government. Facing political divisions among his people, Cornplanter had come to Philadelphia to attempt to recover whatever face he had before the Revolution, although historians of the period see his other visits as more significant in this endeavor.[49] Both sides saw an advantage to affirming a peaceful alliance. A peace-making set of festive gestures, and a generous passing of the bottle, energized the occasion.

An examination of the ways in which each group developed its own set of display techniques reveals layers of meanings accruing to each side over time. Although the miracle of mutual understandings emerging, for a moment, in this coming together sheds little light on the situations of either group, the range of imitations across what appear to be linguistic and cultural boundaries provides a glimpse into the way cultures on the move operate.

Drawing on Indian devices and practices in otherwise European power displays eventually produced a language of political/social celebrations that was uniquely American. And if Indians themselves were susceptible to becoming part of the festivities, the potentials for risk-inducing fun were that much more intensified. From a British and American perspective, accessing different styles and gestures of wonder-inspiring display were valued highly. "Native Naturalls," whether they came from the ancient repositories of older British life (Celts, borderers, the remnant of the old peasantry) or from more exotic sources, such as the Mediterranean, Africa, or the American colonies, were drawn on as stock figures in public entertainments throughout the land. The Tammanies were only one of many carousing groups borrowing from an otherwise feared set of characters. If they did so more extensively and with a greater attempt at authenticity, this reflected a particular moment in the development of local and then national identity.

Notes

1. This study parallels that of my earlier work, *Singing the Master* (New York: Pantheon Books, 1993), in which I discussed the interactive dialogue carried out between masters and enslaved peoples on the Southern plantation emerging from the autumnal cornshucking. Again, here in this chapter, I do not focus on the politics and social class of the individuals involved in the process of cultural transference, or even on the inequities between the participants. Rather, I take the actors to be representative of larger cultural patterns.

2. For the way the British employed such devices, see David Cressy, *Bonfires and Bells: National Memory and the Protestant Calendar in Elizabethan and Stuart England* (Berkeley and Los Angeles: University of California Press, 1989).

3. Simon P. Newman, *Parades and the Politics of the Street: Festive Culture in the Early*

American Republic (Philadelphia: University of Pennsylvania Press, 1997); Len Travers, *Celebrating the Fourth: Independence Day and the Rites of Nationalism in the Early Republic* (Amherst: University of Massachusetts Press, 1997); David Waldstreicher, *The Making of American Nationalism: Celebrations and Political Culture* (Chapel Hill: University of North Carolina Press, 1997). An earlier and still foundational study covering a later period is Susan G. Davis, *Parades and Power: Street Theater in Nineteenth-Century Philadelphia* (Philadelphia: Temple University Press, 1986).

4. Anthony F. C. Wallace, *The Death and Rebirth of the Seneca* (New York: Random House, 1969), 129–46.

5. Elizabeth Drinker Diary (typescript in the Historical Society of Pennsylvania), March 14, 1792; *Aurora*, March 15, 1792. See also Sarah Eve, "Extracts from the Journal of Sarah Eve written when Living near the City of Philadelphia," *Pennsylvania Magazine of History and Biography* 5 (1881), 19–36.

6. Daniel Richter discusses the negotiations going on at the time, not only with Cornplanter but also with other Indian groups. See Daniel Richter, "Onas, the Long Knife: Pennsylvania and the Indians, 1783–1794," in Frederick Hoxie, Ronald Hoffman, and Peter Albert, eds., *Native Americans in the Early Republic* (Charlottesville: University of Virginia Press, 1999). My thanks to Richter for sharing this material before its publication.

7. Lorette Treese, *The Storm Gathering: The Penn Family and the American Revolution* (University Park, Pa.: The Pennsylvania State University Press, 1992).

8. Carl Bridenbaugh, *Cities in the Wilderness* (New York: n.p., 1938), 440. See also Daniel L. Gilbert, "Patterns of Organization and Membership in Colonial Philadelphia Club Life, 1725–1755" (Ph.D. diss., University of Pennsylvania, 1952); Stephen C. Bullock, *Revolutionary Brotherhood: Freemasonry and the Transformation of the American Social Order, 1730–1840* (Chapel Hill: University of North Carolina Press, 1996); and David Shields, *Oracles of Empire: Poetry, Politics, and Commerce in British America, 1690–1750* (Chicago: University of Chicago Press, 1990), each of which surveys similar activities in mercantile centers throughout the colonies.

9. Francis Von A. Cabeen, "The Society of the Sons of Saint Tammany in Philadelphia," *Pennsylvania Magazine of History and Biography* 26 (1902), 218.

10. John Witthoft, "The Lenape as Peacemakers of the Forests," *Keystone Folklore* 4 (Fall 1992), 49–58. For a fuller description of the material and spiritual culture of the Lenape, see Herbert C. Kraft, *The Lenape: Archaeology, History, and Ethnography* (Newark: New Jersey Historical Society, 1986).

11. The bibliography concerning the symbolism of capitulation of various Indian groups in Colonial America is large and daunting. Works such as Philip J. Deloria's *Playing Indian* (New Haven: Yale University Press, 1998) and Jill Lepore's *The Name of War: King Philip's War and the Origins of American Identity* (New York: Knopf, 1998) provide an overview of the appropriation of the image of the Indian in literature and on stage. For Rayna Green's overview at an earlier juncture in the development of these ideas, see "The Tribe Called Wannabee: Playing Indian in America and Europe," *Folklore* 99 (1988), 35–36. I have benefited a great deal from discussions with Samuel Kinser, who has been engaged in a long-term study of the use of Indian costume and custom in both Old and New World festivities; see especially his *Carnival American Style: Mardi Gras in New Orleans and Mobile* (Chicago: University of Chicago Press, 1990).

12. The picture is described in detail by West's contemporary, Stephen de Ponceau, in his *Discourse on the History of Pennsylvania* (Philadelphia, 1826). For what we really do and do not know about the treaty, see J. William Frost, " 'Wear the Sword as Long as Thou Canst': William Penn in Myth and History," *Explorations in Early American Culture* 4 (2000), 13–45.

13. John Heckewelder, *History, Manners, and Customs of the Indian Nations* (1818; reprint, Philadelphia, 1876), 300.

14. Ebenezer Hazard, in Belknap Papers, 1:335 (Massachusetts Historical Society, Boston),

cited in Edwin Patrick Kilroe, *Saint Tammany and the Origin of the Society of Tammany; or Columbian Order in the City of New York* (Ph.D. diss., Columbia University, 1917), 75. Hazard was born in Philadelphia, January 15, 1744, and graduated from Princeton in 1762. He became a well-known classical scholar, antiquarian, and patriot.

15. Indians who played similar roles in other colonial areas include Massasoit and Squanto at the Plymouth Plantation and Pocohantas in Virginia. Shields, *Oracles of Empire,* 48, mentions Willigan in Pennsylvania and Tomochichi in Oglethorpe's Georgia. My concerns here are not in the larger politics of culture involved in the expropriation move invoked by "Playing Indian" as Deloria, Lepore, and Green have it. Rather, I am interested in them as symbolic cultural deployments of replayed Indian practices, by whites in Philadelphia, Pennsylvania, in the 1780s. Penn's symbolic legacy of interest and interaction with Indians needs to be taken into consideration before accepting the New England–inspired generalizations made by Lepore, *Name of War,* 191–226.

16. The pattern is best known and most commonly reenacted in the pageants and legends surrounding Thanksgiving. This reflects the continuing remembrance of the accord reached by Miles Standish, captain of the small band of "Muskitiers" in the Plimouth Colony, and Massasoit, leader of the Wampanoags; the description is given us in the document commonly called "Mourt's Relation" by William Bradford and Edward Winslow: *A Relation or Journall of the English Plantation setled at Plimoth in New England,* published in 1622. See also Karen Ordahl Kupperman, "Mirror Images: Language, Religion, and Relationships in Early America," paper presented to the McNeill Center for Early American Studies Seminar, January 22, 1999. Here, as elsewhere, the treaty reportedly turns on the salute between the two leaders, the mutual trading of kisses, the sharing of strong drink, all surrounding the speech-making, and followed by the ritual sharing of fresh meat.

17. The food differs from one area to another, but usually rests on one of the Indian preparations of corn, such as boiled green corn, roasted whole ears, or hominy. Kathy Neustadt has documented how the presence of the indigenous Indians of coastal Massachusetts have maintained clams at the center of the widespread local feast, the clambake: *Clambake: A History and Celebration of an American Tradition* (Amherst: University of Massachusetts Press, 1992).

18. Cabeen, "Tammany"; Kilroe, *Tammany;* Kenneth Silverman, *A Cultural History of the American Revolution* (New York: Columbia University Press, 1987), 311–13.

19. For further discussion of the festival dynamic in which such first inhabitant figures reside, see Dorothy Noyes and Roger D. Abrahams, "From Calendar Custom to National Memory," in Dan Ben-Amos and Liliane Weissberg, eds., *Cultural Memory and the Construction of Identity* (Detroit: Wayne State University Press, 1999).

20. Robert Blair St. George, *Conversing by Signs: Poetics of Implication in Colonial New England Culture* (Chapel Hill: University of North Carolina Press, 1998), 163–73, explores the complications of British and Early American notions of deformity as associated with Indians.

21. Cabeen, "Tammany," 443–45.

22. Ibid., 216.

23. William Milnor Jr. et al., *A History of the Schuylkill Fishing Company of the State in Schuylkill, 1732–1888* (Philadelphia, 1889), 13.

24. Robert Micklus, ed., *The Tuesday Club: A Shorter Edition of the History of the Ancient and Honorable Tuesday Club* (Baltimore: Johns Hopkins University Press, 1995), surveys this accomplishment in the introduction to his edited edition of Hamilton's record of the club.

25. Cabeen, "Tammany."

26. Kilroe, *Tammany,* 26, notes.

27. Cabeen, "Tammany"; Kilroe, *Tammany.*

28. John Fanning Watson, *The Annals of Philadelphia and Pennsylvania in the Olden Times,* 3 vols. (Philadelphia, 1900), 3:292.

29. See here Hazard in the Belknap Papers, 1755, 364, cited in Kilroe, *Tammany*.

30. These are surveyed in my "History and Folklore: Luck Visits, House Attacks, and Playing Indian in Early America, " in Michael Roth and Ralph Cohen, eds., *History And* . . . (Charlottesville: University of Virginia Press, 1995); and "Making Faces at the Mirror: Playing Indian in Early America, " in Dorothy P. Noyes, ed., *Facade Performances*, special issue of *Southern Folklore* 52 (1995), 121–36; Deloria, *Playing Indian*, 38–70, and the studies of particular colonies by Alan Taylor, *Liberty Men and Great Proprietors: The Revolutionary Settlement on the Maine Frontier, 1760–1820* (Chapel Hill: University of North Carolina Press, 1990); Rhys Isaac, *The Transformation of Virginia, 1740–1790* (Chapel Hill: University of North Carolina Press, 1982); Henry Christman, *Tin Horns and Calico: A Decisive Episode in the Emergence of Democracy* (New York: Holt, 1945); Thomas Slaughter, *The Whiskey Rebellion: Frontier Epilogue to the American Revolution* (New York: Oxford University Press, 1986), 256; Larry J. Gerlach, Prologue to Independence: New Jersey in the Coming of the American Revolution (New Brunswick, N.J.: Rutgers University Press, 1976), 198–200, 445; Dorothy Kubik, *A Free Soil—A Free People* (Fleischmanns, N.Y.: Purple Mountain Press, 1977); Charles W. McCurdy, *The Anti-Rent Era in New York Law and Politics, 1839–1865* (Chapel Hill: University of North Carolina Press, 2001); and the materials on the Mohawks at the Boston Tea Party in Benjamin Labaree, *The Boston Tea Party* (New York: Oxford Unversity Press, 1966). See also the important article by Alfred Young, "English Plebeian Culture and Eighteenth-Century American Radicalism," in Margaret C. Jacob and James R. Jacob, eds., *The Origins of Anglo-American Radicalism* (London: Humanities Press, 1984), 185–212; and E. P. Thompson, *Customs in Common: Studies in Traditional Popular Culture* (New York: The New Press, 1993).

31. Kilroe, *Tammany*, 138. The speech was given in the face of the establishment of the Society of the Cincinnati and its elitist perspectives.

32. Ibid., 138.

33. Hazard in Belknap papers, cited in ibid.

34. Gottlieb Mittelberger, *Journey to Pennsylvania* (1750–54), ed. Oscar Handlin and John Clive (Cambridge, Mass.: Harvard University Press, 1960), 55; the observation by Mittelberger is not about Philadelphia, though it is from eastern Pennsylvania. Thanks to James Merrill for this reference.

35. William Eddis, *Letters from America* (1792), ed. Aubrey C. Land (Cambridge, Mass.: Harvard University Press, 1969).

36. Rhys Isaac, *The Transformation of Virginia* (Chapel Hill: University of North Carolina Press, 1982), 252; Taylor, *Men of Property;* Christman, *Tin Horns and Calico*, summarized in Abrahams, "History and Folklore."

37. The record is not clear on whether one should give credence to this perception. Kilroe, *Tammany*, 108, surveys these reports without making further commentary. Certainly after the war, its members were associated with the ideas promulgated by those who became Democratic-Republicans.

38. Cressy, *Bonfires*.

39. Susan Stewart, *Crimes of Writing: Problems in the Containment of Representation* (New York: Oxford University Press, 1991), 66–101.

40. Peter Thompson, *Rum Punch and Revolution: Taverngoing and Public Life in Eighteenth-Century Philadelphia* (Philadelphia: University of Pennsylvania Press, 1999).

41. Micklus, ed., *Tuesday Club*, xx.

42. Gordon Wood, *The Radicalism of the American Revolution* (New York: Knopf, 1992), 223.

43. Thompson, *Rum Punch and Revolution*, 161, discusses how many of the Philadelphia clubs found themselves politically divided at the outbreak of hostilities. Thompson mentions the two fishing clubs. It is unclear whether the Tammanies were one of these. Kilroe, *Tammany*, 157,

argues that at least during the 1790s the Tammanies saw themselves as serving as a counterbalance to the growth of the elite Cincinnati.

44. Especially important here are William Fenton, ed., *Parker on the Iroquois* (Syracuse, N.Y.: Syracuse University Press, 1968); Daniel K. Richter, *The Ordeal of the Longhouse: The Peoples of the Iroquois League in the Era of European Colonization* (Chapel Hill: University of North Carolina Press, 1992); and Matthew Dennis, *Cultivating a Landscape of Peace: Iroquois-European Encounters in Seventeenth-Century America* (Ithaca, N.Y.: Cornell University Press, 1993).

45. Dennis, *Cultivating a Landscape of Peace*, 94, quoting Paul W. Wallace, *The White Roots of Peace* (Philadelphia University of Pennsylvania Press, 1946), 24.

46. Dennis, *Cultivating a Landscape of Peace*, 84.

47. Wallace, *White Roots of Peace*, 15.

48. Dennis, *Cultivating a Landscape of Peace*, 95. See also Richter, *Ordeal of the Longhouse*, 41–42.

49. A. F. C. Wallace, *Death and Rebirth of the Seneca*, 172–78.

9

The Eighteenth-Century Discovery of Columbus

The Columbian Tercentenary (1792) and the
Creation of American National Identity

Matthew Dennis

The public quincentenary commemorations of Columbus's Voyage of Discovery, observed in 1992, "made history." They did not alter social, economic, or political life, nor did they "recreate" the past, yet the various events did shape public memory and interpret America's past popularly. This recent episode in the history of American commemoration might challenge us to consider Columbus's place in earlier historical moments when identity and historical meaning were contested and shaped in the United States. In fact, Columbus has been at the center of American history and mythmaking for at least two hundred years, since the critical period following the American Revolution, as the new republic searched for and struggled to define its national identity. In the 1780s and 1790s, as in the 1980s and 1990s, the historical meaning of origins, citizenship, patriotism, and identity were being negotiated. This chapter examines that era and its "invention of tradition" generally. It suggests that Americans in the last decades of the eighteenth century believed they lived in a unique historical time, and it focuses on their use of Columbus and Columbianism to mold and mark that moment. If the birth of their nation-state represented an escape from the past, we need to consider the following questions: Toward what did they imagine they were escaping? What did they believe they were leaving behind, and what did they choose from the past to take with them?[1]

The answers to these questions are complex, and I can offer but a partial answer. I will suggest, however, that Americans came to believe that their new republic represented an escape from Europe (especially Britain) and history, and a venture into the West, republicanism, and the future. Columbus, the European explorer who became the first American, represented a link with European civilization but also a departure from its corruption. Representing the new nation as Columbia, the symbolic Columbus—a finder of new lands—stood not only for the realization of a new republican destiny in the present but also for the future promise of the American nation as an expanding Empire of Liberty. Columbus as hero, Columbia as symbol, and Columbianism as concept constituted, paradoxically, an ahistorical use of history, one that proved to be easily deployed and momentarily useful, if highly unstable in the end.

Christopher Columbus has been the emptiest—although among the most priceless—of American historical vessels, somehow available to be filled with a stunning variety of facts and interpretations, meanings, and moral lessons.[2] My focus here is less the history of Columbus the man and his early modern accomplishments or misdeeds, and more the public history of Columbus the hero and symbol. As eighteenth-century Americans sought to define themselves as a people, the persona of Columbus—"Columbia"—allowed them to imagine and represent their unique American national identity and purpose. Especially as partisanship burst into national politics in the 1790s, Columbus symbolism could be used to unite diverse white Americans, particularly behind the idea of the United States as an expanding republic. Looking west, rather than focusing on problems all around them, easterners could imagine nationalism and equate it with expansion.

Taking Columbus's story beyond the early national period, the hero reappeared as a champion for ethnic Americans—especially Irish, Italian, and (later) Hispanic Catholics—who could bypass the Anglo past of the United States as they raised up their patron Columbus, an ethnic founding father—indeed, America's first immigrant. The cacophony of celebration in 1892–93 was followed by slumbering interest in Columbus until the 1990s and the quincentenary. In essentially the same way as those who preceded them, Indians and other dissidents would find in Columbus the antihero a means to establish their identity, to challenge traditional ethnocentric narratives of American history, and to assert their legitimate, prior place in America, past, present, and future.³

American Columbianism in Colonial and Revolutionary America

Americans' appreciation of Columbus's voyage of discovery predated the founding of the United States itself. The prominent Massachusetts Puritan merchant, judge, and diarist Samuel Sewall was among the first English residents to designate the New World as "Columbina," a form of Columbia, land of Columbus. In his *Phaenomena qaedam Apocalyptica* (1697), he endorsed the endeavors of English cleric Nicolas Fuller "to do *Columbus* the Justice, as to eternalize his Honour, by engraving his Name upon the World of his Discovery." Sewall argued, "It is every where called America: but according to Truth, and Desert, men should rather call it *Columbina*, from the magnanimous Heroe *Christopher Columbus a Genuese*, who was manifestly appointed of GOD to be the Finder out of these Lands."⁴

For Puritans, who conceived of their American settlements in eschatological terms, as forming a New Jerusalem in which God's plan would be made manifest on earth, Columbus, rather vaguely at first, could fill the role of Moses, the divinely selected "Finder out of these Lands." America as "Columbina" linked New England directly to Columbus's discovery, making it the culmination of the providential process commenced by the Admiral, even if Columbus, Moses-like, could never himself enter the Puritans' New English Canaan. Few American colonists matched Sewall's modest interest in Columbus, however, as they ignored not only the bicentenary in 1692 (the year of Salem's witch trials) but also the two hundred and fiftieth anniversary that fell in 1742. Few besides Samuel Sewall noticed the yearly anniversary of the discovery that occurred each October 12.⁵

Not until the era of the American Revolution did Americans invoke Columbus with any frequency. By then, Columbus's part in the drama of American millennialism was expanding, in both its religious and its secular (or, rather, civic) versions. In mid-century, for example, Jonathan Edwards, the great Puritan minister, theologian, and philosopher, developed the millennialist theme of Sewall and others as he made sense of the Great Awakening and prophesied America's future amid the turmoil of the times: "This new world is probably now discovered, that the new and most glorious state of God's church on earth might commence there; that God might in it begin a new world in spiritual respect, when he creates the *new heavens and new earth*."[6] Others would secularize this vision, and, employing the historical and symbolic Columbus, they advanced the same sense of America as a new land of opportunity, possibility, and progress.

It is significant that this project was carried out in an emerging "public sphere," especially through the act of "publication." Print not only reached a larger audience for news, information, and ideas expressed by men (and sometimes women) of letters in America; it largely constituted that audience as public and autonomous (relative to the state). In contrast to "traditional cultures of print," the new republican print discourse "made it possible to imagine a people that could act as a people and in distinction from the state," argues Michael Warner. Such a reading public understood itself to be nearly limitless, yet, although individuals within this public could never actually assemble and encounter each other physically all at once, they could imagine themselves vitally connected through the common act of reading. Moreover, publication could reproduce and thus extend and allow the appropriation of experience itself. The reported public activities of subjects and then citizens—whether riots, parades, orations, banquets, or toasts—that spoke to Americans' search for a national identity could be read by others without being directly involved, and then incorporated as collective memories, vicarious but critical contributions to a developing American national consciousness.[7]

Thus we can see how a semipublic ceremonial act like a commencement address, reproduced and reaching a larger audience through publication, could help to constitute the American public as it addressed the subject of America's identity and destiny. And playing a prominent role in one such cultural and political work was Christopher Columbus. According to *A Poem, on the Rising Glory of America* (1771) by Philip Freneau and Hugh Henry Brackenridge, first delivered by Freneau to the College of New Jersey's graduating class, the progress of civilization begins with Columbus and ends with colonial Anglo-America and its utopian future. It was "the last, the best / Of countries," representing the cumulative improvement of humanity. Though still "sons of Britain," the poets nonetheless gave voice to a rising sense of American nationalism and sense of mission that would help fuel the colonial revolt against Great Britain and, later, American expansion to the Pacific and beyond.[8]

The Columbus myth continued to forge a sense of nationalism or peoplehood as it cast the Admiral as a latter-day American Moses. Joel Barlow, the American poet, patriot, and politician who returned often to the Columbus story, wrote in his *Columbiad* (1807):

> The bliss of unborn nations warm'd his breast,
> Repaid his toils, and sooth'd his soul to rest;
> Thus o'er thy subject wave shall thou behold
> Far happier realms their future charms unfold,
> In nobler pomp another Pisgah rise,
> Beneath whose foot thy new-found Canaan lies.
> There, rapt in vision, hail my favorite clime.
> And taste the blessings of remotest time.[9]

Yet ironically, before the 1770s, a mythic Columbus could figure as a symbol of the British Empire as easily as he would later represent American nationalism. Philip Freneau's vision of Columbus hardly differed from that of James Kirkpatrick (d. 1770), the Anglo-Irish doctor, writer, and poet laureate of Britain's commercial empire. For Kirkpatrick, whether on the Atlantic or in Charleston, South Carolina, he was in Britain. In Kirkpatrick's *The Sea-Piece: A narrative, philosophical and descriptive Poem* (1750), Columbus stands as a heroic visionary: "Bold was the Man, who dar'd at first to shew / From the old World the Passage to a new." And given Columbus's achievements, which somehow redounded to the credit of the British Empire, Kirkpatrick, like others before him, advocated renaming the continent for the American Aeneas, recommending "Columbona." Similarly, and ironically, Columbus's difficulties with his Spanish, Catholic monarchs qualified him as an opponent of superstition and a representative of Reformed Christianity and its imperial mission, despite the Admiral's clear Italian origins, not to mention his mysticism and his Catholic faith. Kirkpatrick knew that Britain's present and future greatness depended on the seas, and he naturalized Columbus, as a companion to Britannia, to represent the ancient origins of Britain's imperial, mercantile triumph.[10]

While Kirkpatrick lionized the mythic Columbus and incorporated him into the narrative of British imperial progress, some American writers initially found it more difficult to naturalize Columbus. In 1758, in Sylvanus Americus's [Samuel Nevill's] "The History of the Northern Continent of *America*," the first extended account of Columbus published in the colonies, the author associated Columbus with Spain and its Black Legend. Yet in contrast to this and later nationalist treatments, and congruent with

Kirkpatrick's heroic Columbus, the figure "Columbia" appeared regularly in American loyalist verse as late as 1761, as, for example, in a poem attributed to Thomas Hutchinson, lieutenant governor of Massachusetts, which celebrated the marriage and accession of George III: "Behold, Britannia! in thy favour'd Isle; / At distance, thou, Columbia! view thy Prince."[11]

During the revolutionary protests, and especially after independence was achieved, the use of Columbus's name proliferated as Americans fashioned his persona to satisfy the needs of an emerging new republic in search of a national identity. In the process, as they molded the Admiral into a national hero, Americans would conserve some of the imperial connotations of Kirkpatrick's Columbus and ultimately refashion him into a patron of their own new "Empire of Liberty."

All the while, references to Columbus became increasingly frequent. In the late 1760s, as colonists decried the tyranny of the Townsend Acts, Columbus began to appear in their "liberty songs" and "liberty poems." "Rusticus," in his poem *Liberty* (1768), had Columbus warn the colonists of Grenville's plans to "invade" their freedom: "On *Care* and *Union* your *Success* depends," the Mariner advised, and as their guardian and patron he took their case to the king. In *America: A Poem*, by Alexander Martin (1769), Columbus's discovery—so pregnant with promise—was compared to the hated Townsend Duties, with the question posed, "Was it for this?"[12] Among the reasons for the growing appeal of Columbus as an American patron saint was the fact that the Italian discoverer, who sailed for the Spanish Crown, was not British, despite the poetically licensed attempts by some British imperial writers to naturalize him. In Columbus, Americans found "a past that bypassed England," as historian Claudia Bushman so aptly puts it.[13]

By the 1770s, the colonies were more frequently being referred to as "Columba" or "Columbia," as in Mercy Otis Warren's "Poetical Reverie," published in the February 13, 1775, *Boston Gazette*; in Philip Freneau's *American Liberty: A Poem*, which appeared in April; or in a Phillis Wheatley poem addressed to "His Excellency, Gen. Washington" in October of the same year. Freneau was among the first literary figures to emerge in the cultural ferment of the revolutionary period, which began to produce, for the first time in America, a modern, Western, but nationally distinct culture. Like many of his contemporaries, Freneau turned to Columbus as a worthy American subject, beginning, as we have seen, with *The Rising Glory of America*. His 1772 poem "Discovery" celebrated the Mariner and his accomplishments, though not without a measure of doubt about the cost of colonization, anticipating the harsher criticisms that would emerge in the nineteenth and twentieth centuries:

> Alas! how few of all that daring train
> That seek new worlds embosomed in the main,
> How few have sailed on virtue's nobler plan,
> How few with motives worthy of a man!

For the moment, however, Columbus seemed to escape the stain of the Spanish Black Legend and represented the nobility of the American nation.[14]

By the 1780s, America as Columbia had become thoroughly conventional. New York City's institution of higher learning could not remain King's College after the Revolution, and in 1784 it became instead Columbia.[15] The allegorical, classic female figure "Columbia"—replacing the rude, unclothed, and supposedly uncultured Indian maiden as the symbolic representation of America—adorned coins struck by the Congress in 1785 and 1786. In 1786, Columbia became the new capital of South Carolina, and in Philadelphia *Columbian Magazine* began publication, in 1787 printing Timothy Dwight's song "Columbia," which served as an unofficial national anthem into the nineteenth century. Within fifty years of the American Revolution, versions of Columbus's name graced the titles of some sixteen periodicals, eighteen books, and a half-dozen scholarly societies.[16]

By 1789, the New York Tammany Society had diversified its name, becoming the Saint Tammany Society, or Columbian Order. Through the mythical Delaware Sagamore Tammany and Christopher Columbus, the Society could identify itself with the best of both Europe and America yet avoid any reference to British forebears. In 1791, Americans decided to seat their national capital on the Potomac River and to call it the Territory of Columbia. Washington, D.C., conjoined in its name the two greatest deities in America's republican pantheon. And in 1792, in the year of the tercentenary, Captain Robert Gray discovered and named the great river of the American Northwest, the Columbia, after his ship the *Columbia Rediviva*. The powerful course of the mighty Columbia seemed to embody the vision of westward expansion proclaimed in the works of nationalist poets Philip Freneau, Timothy Dwight, and Joel Barlow. Through such representations of Columbia, Americans sought to define their place in history, subdue the North American landscape, situate their republic in the world, and distinguish their nation from its tainted British origins.[17]

In short, Columbus proved central to Americans' practice of nationalism. Though intricately related, two facets of American Columbianism might be distinguished to illuminate the particular cultural and political work that the myth, image, and symbol of Columbus performed in changing revolutionary and early national America: Columbus as symbol of a republican national destiny, and Columbus as symbol of a rising American continental empire. Since the early eighteenth century, in the religious writing of Samuel Sewall, Cotton Mather, and then Jonathan Edwards, Columbus had symbolized American destiny. By the period of the American Revolution, that destiny seemed to entail the emergence of an independent republic in North America.

Columbus, abstracted and feminized as "Columbia," vaguely represented that Promised Land. Like other, European symbols of sovereign lands, the goddess Columbia was depicted as feminine. Lands—homelands—were conventionally feminized (that is, as Mother Earth and Motherlands), while political states were more often (though not always) represented as masculine (Fatherlands). In the early American republic, this female symbolism—imbued with notions of Republican Motherhood—achieved a particular potency. "Columbia" suggested more than the nation—it signified the subdued, domesticated space of the continent that had become, or was destined to become, part of the United States. More than the masculine figure Columbus, Columbia expressed the dignity and gentility of an emerging American civilization.[18] But the symbolic hero/heroine had little specific to say about the particular social and political arrangements that would develop in the new United States. In its vagueness, Columbianism promoted consensus among disparate Americans joined in coalitions to effect their independence from Great Britain. By the 1790s, amid the partisan battles that emerged to confound the republic, Columbus was sometimes reinvented and enlisted in factional struggles. But the abstractness and antiquity of Columbus, in contrast to the living, breathing Washington or Jefferson, made this hero less useful in partisan debate.

More important, Columbus proved to be a perfect symbol for America, not merely as a discrete republic but also as an expanding continental empire. A crisis of the West in the 1780s challenged the very notion and destiny of the union achieved by the Revolution. Western lands, placed under the control of Congress in the Articles of Confederation, were among the very few common possessions of U.S. citizens, most of whom were arrayed in separate states along the Atlantic Coast. Yet the fate of these lands remained ambiguous. Expansion of white Americans into such regions was a foregone conclusion, but would westerners' interest diverge from those of eastern Americans and create conflict and disunion? On what basis would such lands be incorporated into the Union? Indeed, could they be protected from the grasp of imperial powers that already had footholds in the American interior? Could political integration be effected without creating a new colonialism that recreated the evils of the British colonial system so recently rejected? Was it possible to maintain liberty and republicanism under the sort of centralized, energetic regime that apparently was required to govern so extensive a nation? If the Northwest Ordinance of 1787 was the practical solution offered for these problems, Columbianism was the cultural and symbolic response. By facilitating peaceful incorporation of new states in the West, not as colonies but as full members of the Union on a par with the original thirteen states, Congress avoided the mistakes of British imperial policy and designed an expansionism that was understood to be not colonial. Of course, the policy was both colonial and imperial, but Columbianism helped Americans justify the latter and ignore the former. Through Columbus imagery and place names, American could imagine that which at one time might have seemed oxymoronic: an Empire of Liberty. In a sense, the common reading of the West as America's destiny helped constitute the readers—that is, U.S. citizens, otherwise divided by different regional or class interests—as a nation, "Columbia."[19]

Columbianism and the Tercentenary

While an imperial Columbianism was taking shape, Columbus in his more vague manifestation, as a symbol of American destiny and the beginning point for national history, was appearing prominently in public, celebratory, and political demonstrations on the streets of the new republic. Following the drafting of the Constitution in Philadelphia in 1787, the symbolic Columbus was enlisted in the ratification debates. In New York in April 1788, for example, the American Company—a theatrical group—promoted "A Serious Pastoral . . . by Citizens of the United States, called

The Convention, or the Columbian Fathers," joining the Constitution with Columbus and suggesting implicitly that this frame of government was the natural culmination of America's founding process, which had begun in 1492. As state after state adopted the Constitution, citizens celebrated with public festivals—parades, public banquets, orations, poetry readings, concerts, and plays. Following the official announcement by Congress on July 2, 1788, that the Constitution had garnered the approval of the requisite nine states and was therefore enacted, spectacular demonstrations erupted, both to toast the new nation and to prod the states that had not yet ratified. In New York, a grand procession was held on July 23, while, upstate in Poughkeepsie, men still heatedly debated the Constitution; within three days New Yorkers joined the new union as the eleventh state to ratify.[20]

These events were designed to "make history," to shape the direction of the new nation and to interpret actively the meaning of America. As James Wilson noted explicitly in his oration following Philadelphia's Grand Federal Procession on July 4, 1788, such public actions "may *instruct* and *improve*, while they *entertain* and *please*. . . . They may preserve the *memory*, and engrave the *importance* of great *political events*. They may *represent*, with peculiar felicity and force, the *operation* and *effects* of great *political truths*. The *picturesque* and *splendid decorations around me*, furnish the most *beautiful* and most *brilliant* proofs, that these remarks are FAR FROM BEING IMAGINARY."[21] Among the national heroes displayed as portraits or effigies, along with Washington, was Christopher Columbus. Pictures, floats, and costumed figures were carefully arranged to form a long historical chain linking Columbus ultimately to the new federal Constitution, and to the future. Citizens were the producers as well as the consumers of such events, and they were participants as well as observers. As they "made history" they made themselves as Americans. In imagining—and making public—their local festival as the celebration of an extralocal community, they encouraged others to conclude as well that the nationalist sentiments expressed by men like Wilson were indeed "FAR FROM BEING [merely] IMAGINARY."[22]

The year 1792 offered Americans a rare opportunity to develop the Columbian theme, to define themselves, as all centenary years since have emerged as invitations to employ the symbolic Columbus in the service of particular notions of Americanism. A number of celebrations occurred throughout the republic, in Philadelphia and Baltimore, in Providence and

Richmond, and in smaller communities like Windsborough, South Carolina, marked typically with military parades, dinners, and toasts.[23] In Boston on October 23, in the first public lecture sponsored by the newly formed Massachusetts Historical Society, its founder the Rev. Dr. Jeremy Belknap delivered an oration, subsequently published as *A Discourse Intended to Commemorate the Discovery of America by Christopher Columbus* (Boston, 1792), that served as the centerpiece of a major civic event attended by Governor John Hancock, Lieutenant Governor Samuel Adams, and numerous other dignitaries. Following their quarterly meeting, the Society proceeded, accompanied by music, to the Brattle Street church, where they heard Belknap's address as well as prayers and an ode written for the occasion. Members and honored guests then adjourned to a lavish feast at the house of the Honorable James Sullivan, the society's president, where, according to newspaper reports, "the memory of Columbus was toasted in convivial enjoyment, and the warmest wishes were expressed that the blessings now distinguishing the United States might be extended to every part of the world he has discovered."[24]

Although it was organized by Boston's elite, the tercentenary celebration was intended nonetheless to have a wider impact. Attendance at the lecture and banquet was limited to Society members and notables, but the procession invited popular attention and at least vicarious participation. The vagueness and venerability of Columbus promoted such goals. As a newly constructed but ancient American hero, he was a bipartisan champion in an era of vicious partisan contention. Belknap's, and the society's, intention was not to function merely for their own edification. They sought to disseminate historical information broadly, to promote "useful knowledge," and in general cultivate a learned, virtuous, patriotic American citizenry. The Society therefore published Belknap's "public discourse" for popular consumption and advertised its sale in *American Apollo*, the Society's magazine.[25]

The New York City tercentenary celebration preceded and outshined the events in Boston. As one contemporary newspaper reported, "The 12th inst., being the commencement of the IV. COLUMBIAN CENTURY, was observed as a Century Festival by the Tammany Society, and celebrated in the style of sentiment which distinguishes this social and patriotic institution."[26] John Pintard, sagamore of the Tammany Society (or Columbian Order) in New York City, had been in correspondence with Jeremy Belknap on a number of matters and may well have been the first to suggest that the Massachusetts Historical Society celebrate the three-hundredth anniversary of Columbus's voyage. In New York, Pintard's Tammany Society staged a larger, less sedate, and more popular festival, the first ever held exclusively for Columbus in the Americas. In addition to their customary "Long Talk" and banquet, members erected an illuminated shaft or monument to the memory of Columbus, "ornamented by transparency with a variety of suitable devices."[27]

In the shape of an obelisk, the monument stood upward of fourteen feet in height and could be moved from place to place. From its base—a globe emerging out of clouds and chaos—a pyramidal shaft arose, depicting on its four sides mythologized scenes from the Admiral's life and emphasizing the themes of progress, science, commerce, the ingratitude and abuse of monarchs, and the ultimate triumph of freedom over despotism and knowledge over superstition. The "Genius of Liberty" ultimately appears before the dejected Columbus and cheers him—pointing to the Tammany monument itself, "sacred to his memory, reared by the Columbian Order," and allowing him to see the glorious legacy of his discovery, which America now embodied. The obelisk was exhibited "for the gratification of the public curiosity" preceding the tercentenary program, and at the close of the celebration it was placed in the Tammany Society's museum in a large room in the Exchange on Broad Street, where it attracted considerable attention. Thereafter, it was illuminated annually each October 12, a day sacred to the society's second patron, Columbus. The unusual monument figured prominently in the advertisements of the Tammany Museum, until the collection was sold, ultimately finding its way into the hands of P. T. Barnum. Like many of the museum's objects, the obelisk slipped into oblivion.[28]

The Tammany Society in New York, like those elsewhere, was "conceived in a spirit of festival and celebration," the movement's historian has observed; its purpose was both patriotic and recreational. Although its leader, John Pintard, shared many of the same aspirations that inspired Jeremy Belknap and the members of the Massachusetts Historical Society—indeed, Pintard was instrumental in founding the New-York Historical Society and was the driving force behind the Tammany Museum—the New York Tammany Society had more populist inclinations. And along with other Tammany societies in Pennsylvania, New Jersey, Maryland, Virginia, the Carolinas, and Georgia, it exhibited a strong social and nationalistic character. Their principal holiday, Saint Tammany Day, fell traditionally on May 1, the beginning of the sporting season, which clubs would inaugurate with raucous celebrations and plenty of strong drink. In the context of American opposition to Britain, the societies had become more clearly political—and they would remain so following independence—but they refused to abandon their commitment to frivolity and amusement, even when they aspired to greater gentility and respectability.[29]

Early Tammany spokesmen committed the Society to nationalism, patriotism, liberty, charity, and brotherly love. It spoke out against local and class prejudices; its membership was not based, at least theoretically, on caste, wealth, or ethnicity. Like the plebeian society that apparently supplied much of its membership and enjoyed its festivals, it embraced a democratic vision.[30] In the Columbian tercentenary celebration—its impact magnified by its popular and festive appeal—we see the Tammany Society in the act of "making history," "inventing traditions" that would define and promote the new American republic as a nation dedicated to liberty, equality, and fraternity. Through direct participation, as they viewed the Society's portable monument or took part in its parades, illuminations, and songs, its Columbian odes, feasts, and toasts, celebrators helped to constitute an American people while they shaped popular perceptions of America's national identity and destiny.

Amid the "rational amusements" that filled up the evening's entertainment, members of the Tammany Society toasted "the discoverer of *this* new world" and "the United *Columbian* States." Revelers expressed the dream that their world would forever enjoy peace and liberty, escape "the vices and miseries of the old," and provide "a happy asylum for the oppressed of all nations and of all religions." They raised their cups hoping that this might "be the last Century Festival of the Columbian Order that finds a slave on this globe." They toasted George Washington, Thomas Paine, the Rights of Man, and Lafayette and the French Nation.[31] Through the mythic persona of Columbus, constructed in their own image, these patriots found a means to legitimize their particular national vision and supply it with an ancient, sacred pedigree. They imbued the great mariner and his exploits with meaning—he stood for bold independence, initiative and persistence, triumph over Old World tyranny and oppression, freedom, and economic, political, and religious liberty, their odes and speeches tell us—and then they, as the American Sons of Columbia, enlisted the Columbus they had made as their direct ancestor, patron, and inspiration. For neither the first time nor the last, the malleable Columbus proved useful as Americans fashioned their identity and crafted a national purpose.

Only in retrospect, perhaps, is it ironic that orations and toasts, in Boston as well as in New York, would read Columbus out of the Black Legend of Spanish colonization, dissociating the Admiral from slavery and the slave trade.[32] Almost immediately following the tercentenary, such indiscrete mixing in toasts—to Washington and to Paine, to the Rights of Man, or to the French Nation—would become impossible in the charged partisan climate that pit Jeffersonians against Hamiltonians, and enthusiastic supporters against alarmed critics of the French Revolution in the United States.[33] Nonetheless, Columbus somehow remained an untarnished and popular hero.

Later in the 1790s, the Tammany Society became involved in other festive promotions of Columbus, as in its sponsorship of the opera written by Mrs. Anne Julia Hatton, titled *Tammany, or The Indian Chief,* which somehow managed to feature Columbus in a prominent role. Little remains of the opera; apparently only the prologue was printed, and the plot is only barely sketched in the hostile reviews of the Federalist dramatist William Dunlap, who called the play "a melange of bombast," "seasoned high with spices hot from Paris, and swelling with rhodomontade for the sonorous voice of Hodgkinson." Dunlap admitted that the play was "received with unbounded applause," but he denigrated the audience as being composed of "the poorer class of mechanics and clerks." Columbus shared with Tammany the audience's acclaim. The opera subsequently played successfully in Philadelphia and Boston. In September 1797, Morton's play *Columbus, or The World Discovered,* first performed at London's Covent Garden in 1792, ran successfully in New York and later at the Boston Haymarket, where it was the hit of the season, further attesting to the popularity of the hero Columbus. In 1798, William Dunlap put on his play, *Andre,* a sympathetic treatment of the British major John Andre, who was hanged in 1780 for his part in the conspiracy arranged by Benedict Arnold to hand over West Point to the British. Andre himself was an engaging sort who played a prominent role in British military theatricals during the war. But American audiences apparently were disappointed by the play's "lack of patriotic fervor," according to historian Jared Brown, and the Federalist Dunlap "was forced to rewrite his play as a patriotic pageant entitled *The Glory of Columbia* in order to attract audiences."[34]

In the 1790s, Columbus became increasing important as a Tammany Society patron; as Tammany members deemphasized their Indian saint and elevated Columbus, their actions mirrored those occurring nationally in the iconography of the United States. As early as July 4, 1782, a Philadelphia Tammany Society poem had remarked, "While mimic Saints a transient joy impart, / That strikes the sense but reaches not the heart, / Arise Columbia!—nobler themes await." These sentiments seemed designed to denigrate not only the Indian "Saint Tammany," but also his newest, immigrant rival, Saint Patrick.[35]

But Indians as symbols proved to be a growing liability for the Society and the nation. As John Higham has suggested, after the Revolution the conventional Indian maiden as symbol for America seemed to concede "the cultural inferiority of the New World." Americans needed symbols that would connect them with the civilized world while yet declaring their separation. Perfectly suited to the task was the new spirit of America, the goddess "Liberty," or "Columbia," a reworking of the Roman goddess "Britannia." If the patronage of the ancient sagamore Tammany, safely buried, helped assert claims of white Americans to the North American landscape, the memory of real Indians, like those who mauled Generals Harmar and St. Clair in the Ohio Country before their defeat at Fallen Timbers, undermined the effectiveness of such "savage" native people as legitimate American icons. The broadside *The Columbian Tragedy,* for example, which appeared late in 1791, depicted two rows of coffins above its headlines, pictures of a "BLOODY INDIAN BATTLE" and the slain Major General Richard Butler, and "A PARTICULAR AND OFFICIAL ACCOUNT of the Brave and Unfortunate Officers and Soldiers, who were Slain and Wounded in the Ever-Memorable and BLOODY INDIAN BATTLE." When the broadside called the battle "perhaps the most shocking that has happened in AMERICA since its first Discovery," it menacingly linked Columbus to an unacceptable American destiny.[36]

To the extent that Indians could be naturalized as American ancients and assigned a place among the American natural antiquities, which some argued rivaled those of Greece or Rome, they could be useful components in the new republic's nationalism. Imposing classical names on the landscape (and later building Greek and Roman Revival structures) similarly might assert an American nationalism based simultaneously on distinctiveness from Europe (at least from Great Britain) and identity with Western civilization. Another effective means was to Columbianize the American landscape. Referring to the continent as Columbia at least discursively claimed and subdued it and legitimated the possession of it by whites, in the present and the future. Faulting the goddess symbol Americans created for its remoteness and abstraction, historian John Higham has written: "Naming her Columbia scarcely began to bring her down to earth." Yet in a sense it did precisely that. Columbia, not simply the goddess but the place, *was* the American earth, and the hero Columbus had given it to Americans. The mythic Columbus had discovered the New World and, unlike the conquistadors of the Black Legend, "endeavored as far as possible to treat [the natives] with justice and gentleness," Jeremy Belknap told his compatriots. Columbus's example seemed to promise, as did the vanishing of the sagamore Tammany and the appropriation of his legacy by Tammany Society members who dressed up like Indians, an American expansion with honor.[37]

In 1790, addressing a visiting Creek delegation, New York Tammany Grand Sachem Dr. William Pitt Smith informed his guests:

> Although the hand of death is cold upon their bodies, yet the spirits of two great Chiefs are supposed to walk backwards and forwards in this great wigwam and to direct our proceedings—Tammany and Columbus. Tradition has brought to us the memory of the first. He was a great and good Indian chief, a strong warrior, a swift hunter, but what is greater than all, he loved his country. We call ourselves his sons. Columbus was a famous traveller and discoverer . . . , the first white man that ever visited this western world. But history makes it known that because he wished to treat the Indians with kindness, friendship, and justice, he was cruelly used. Brothers—Tammany and Columbus live together in the world of spirits in great harmony, and they teach us to cultivate like friendship and reciprocal good offices with you and all Indians.[38]

The spirits of Tammany and Columbus together, as lovers of the American land and as fathers, peacefully consigned the American landscape to the early republic's white citizens, and, having made his bequest, the sagamore faded into the shadows.

Philip Freneau's important poem "The Indian Burying Ground" (1787) can be read as just such an expression of the Vanishing Indian myth and the ways that the Indian past could be imagined (simultaneously with conquest) and naturalized. While Freneau interred Indians, Tammany Society members like New York's John Pintard helped to transform Indian subjects into objects of antiquarian interest through their efforts to found and maintain museums. Yet Ignoble Savages continued to exist in tandem with "Noble Savages"—the latter treated nostalgically because they were gone, and the former treated with disdain as all too alive and menacing. Nonetheless, white Americans seemed prepared to claim their continental legacy and domesticate the landscape, whether through peaceful means or by warfare. With the War of 1812, playing Indian became untenable; both western Indians and Great Britain merited American wrath, as each failed to yield gracefully. Thus an anti-British cartoon linked evil Britain, again threatening the republic, with malicious Indians, depicted scalping American soldiers being paid for the trophies by a British officer. Rhyming lines provided the following caption:

> Arise Columbia's Sons and forward press,
> Your Country's wrongs call loudly for redress,
> The savage Indian with his scalping knife
> Or tomahawk may seek to take your life.
>
> By bravery aw'd, they'll in a dreadful fright
> Shrink back for refuge to the woods of flight.
> Their British leaders then will quickly shake
> And for those wrongs shall restitution make.[39]

As the American landscape was cleared of native people and classicized, it was Columbianized. In New York State alone rose the new cities of Troy, Utica, Ithaca, Sparta, Syracuse, and Rome. Yet Columbus would give his name to more places in the United States than anyone except Washington himself, a heroic figure often paired with the goddess Columbia. In the Old Northwest, in the process of being tamed, Cincinnati, Ohio, so named by Governor Arthur St. Clair in 1788, incorporated an earlier town named Columbia. In 1812, after the initial conquest but in a time imperiled by new threats from the British and Indians, the Ohio state legislature sought to reimpose the heroic eponym on their landscape and directed Joel Wright to plan a new capital city on the bend of the Scioto River named Columbus. The name Columbus thus marked conquest but also represented that aggrandizement as legitimate and benevolent. Western Columbias and

Columbuses, whether new towns or counties or rivers, represented the triumph of an expanding American republic. Such place names implicitly linked the rising glory of America with the intrepid explorer Columbus who ventured west to find new lands and claim them for Christendom. In some cases, latter-day explorers, like those reconnoitering the Columbia River, would carry Columbia-Washington medals west to distribute to native peoples. Such medals, literally representing the currency of Columbus and the potency of his symbolism when paired with Washington, and minted to celebrate the opening of trade with Canton and the Pacific Northwest, depicted the ships of discovery named after the two great American heroes.[40]

Expansion itself became a national ritual, a means of constituting the nation (literally and imaginatively) and celebrating it through westward movement. These events and experiences were marked and reproduced in texts and illustrations, not just in the published accounts of explorers and travelers, but also in maps. Place names themselves, then, could function as national monuments for residents, as local expressions of national history and identity. And seeing those names on maps could encourage those in other parts of the United States to imagine that they, along with other residents throughout their far-flung republic, shared a single national community and identity as Americans. If this was the case, the practice of expansion, inscribed in text and disseminated through publication, could in turn produce a national way of thinking and practice. Geographical description became national prescription. The land Columbia became a monument to the nation itself, a place inspired and guided by its eponymous hero, Columbus. For Americans as early as the 1790s, looking west and celebrating the "Rising Glory of America" thus became among the most potent rites of ascent and "rites of assent."[41]

Notes

1. On memory and history, and their popular construction in America, see the work of Michael Kammen, esp. *Mystic Chords of Memory: The Transformation of Tradition in American Culture* (New York: Knopf, 1991). See also John Bodnar, *Remaking America: Public Memory, Commemoration, and Patriotism in the Twentieth Century* (Princeton: Princeton University Press, 1992); David Glassberg, *American Historical Pageantry: The Uses of Tradition in the Early Twentieth Century* (Chapel Hill: University of North Carolina Press, 1990); John R. Gillis, ed., *Commemorations: The Politics of National Identity* (Princeton: Princeton University Press, 1994); Eric Hobsbawm and Terence Ranger, eds., *The Invention of Tradition* (Cambridge: Cambridge

University Press, 1983); and Pierre Nora, "Between Memory and History: *Les Lieux de Mémoire*," *Representations* 26 (Spring 1989), 7–25.

2. A number of recent works have reexamined Columbus, the man as well as the myth. Among the most significant on an ever-growing list are the following: Felipe Fernandez-Armesto, *Columbus* (New York: Oxford University Press, 1991); William D. Phillips Jr. and Carla Rahn Phillips, *The Worlds of Christopher Columbus* (Cambridge: Cambridge University Press, 1992); Paolo Emilio Taviani, *Columbus: The Great Adventure, His Life, His Times, and His Voyages* (New York: Orion Books, 1991); Kirkpatrick Sale, *The Conquest of Paradise: Christopher Columbus and the Columbian Legacy* (New York: Knopf, 1990), the exemplary anti-Columbus history; John Noble Wilford, *The Mysterious History of Columbus: An Exploration of the Man, the Myth, the Legacy* (New York: Knopf, 1991); Claudia L. Bushman, *America Discovers Columbus: How an Italian Explorer Became an American Hero* (Hanover, N.H.: University Press of New England, 1992). See also the *Columbian Encounters* special issue of the *William & Mary Quarterly*, 3d ser., 49, no. 2 (April 1992), esp. Delno West, "Christopher Columbus and His Enterprise to the Indies: Scholarship of the Last Quarter Century," 254–77; and David B. Quinn, "Columbus and the North: England, Iceland, and Ireland," 278–97.

3. This chapter is part of a chapter on centenary commemorations of Columbus and of American Columbus Day in my larger, forthcoming study *Red, White, and Blue Letter Days: Identity, History, and the American Calendar* (Ithaca: Cornell University Press, 2002). For a somewhat different analysis of this topic, see Thomas J. Schlereth, "Columbia, Columbus, and Columbianism," *Journal of American History* 79 (December 1992), 937–68.

4. Samuel Sewall, *Phaenomena quaedam Apocalyptica Ad Aspectum Novi Orbis configurata; or Some few lines toward a description of the New Heaven, As It makes to those who stand upon the new earth* (Boston, 1697), 47; see also 49. See also M. Halsey Thomas, ed., *The Diary of Samuel Sewall, 1674–1729, newly edited from the manuscript at the Massachusetts Historical Society*, 2 vols. (New York: Arno Press, 1973), 2:630, 960, 1039.

5. Thomas, ed., *Diary of Sewall*, 2:960: on October 11, 1720, Sewall wrote, rather awkwardly and obscurely, to the widow he was courting, "I thank you for your Unmerited Favours of yesterday; and hope to have the Happiness of Waiting on you tomorrow before Eight a-clock after Noon. I pray GOD to keep you, and give you a joyfull entrance upon the Two Hundred and twenty ninth year of Christopher Columbus his Discovery."

6. Jonathan Edwards, "Thoughts on the Revivals in 1740," *The Works of President Edwards, in Ten Volumes* (New York: S. Converse, 1829–30), 4:129. Beginning part 2, section 2, "The Latter-Day Glory is probably to begin in America," Edwards wrote: "It is not unlikely that this work of God's Spirit, so extraordinary and wonderful, is the dawning, or at least a prelude of that glorious work of God, so often foretold in scripture, which, in the progress and issue of it, shall renew the world of mankind" (128). See also Delno C. West and August Kling, "Columbus and Columbia: A Brief Survey of the Early Creation of the Columbus Symbol in American History," *Studies in Popular Culture* 12, no. 2 (1989), 48.

7. Michael Warner, *The Letters of the Republic: Publication and the Public Sphere in Eighteenth-Century America* (Cambridge, Mass.: Harvard University Press, 1990), quotation at xiii. On the original concept of the "public sphere," perceptively applied and reworked by Warner and others, see Jürgen Habermas, *The Structural Transformation of the Public Sphere: An Inquiry into a Category of Bourgeois Society*, trans. Thomas Burger (Cambridge, Mass.: Harvard University Press, 1989 [orig. 1962]). On the idea of nationalism, the place to begin is Benedict Anderson, *Imagined Communities: Reflection on the Origins and Spread of Nationalism*, rev. ed. (London: Verso, 1991); see also David Waldstreicher, *In the Midst of Perpetual Fetes: The Making of American Nationalism, 1775–1820* (Chapel Hill: University of North Carolina Press, 1997). Jay Fliegelman, *Declaring Independence: Jefferson, Natural Language, and the Culture of Performance* (Stanford, Calif.: Stanford University Press, 1993), esp. 25–26, emphasizes the performative

aspect of "publishing" in revolutionary America. Thus, not only did texts recapitulate events not witnessed by readers, but some, like the Declaration of Independence, could *produce* events. On July 4, 1776, the Continental Congress ordered the distribution of copies of the Declaration so that it could be "proclaimed in each of the United States." The document itself sought to "publish and declare," that is, in the contemporary sense "to announce formally and publicly" America's independence. The subsequent public readings (sometimes to large crowds, as in Philadelphia) made the Declaration "an event rather than a document" (25). Moreover, Fliegelman suggests, some who expressed concern about the inadequacies of the pen relative to the tongue sought both to improve public speaking and to preserve "the special character of the spoken voice in written composition" (26). To the extent that such efforts proved successful, reading could begin to simulate experience and fabricate memory.

8. Philip Freneau [and Hugh Henry Brackenridge], *A Poem, on the Rising Glory of America* (1771), in *Poems Written Between the Years 1768 and 1794*, a facsimile reproduction (Delmar, N.Y.: Scholars' Facsimiles and Reprints, 1976), 36–46. See also Kenneth Silverman, *A Cultural History of the American Revolution: Painting, Music, Literature, and the Theatre in the Colonies and the United States . . .* , *1763–1789* (New York: Crowell, 1976), 232–34. In pointing out Freneau's and Brackenridge's "nationalism," I do not mean to suggest that nationalism generally was necessarily the cause of the American Revolution. As John M. Murrin, "A Roof Without Walls: The Dilemma of American National Identity," in Richard Beeman et al., eds., *Beyond Confederation: Origins of the Constitution and American National Identity* (Chapel Hill: University of North Carolina Press, 1987), 333–48, argues persuasively, nationalism was a gradual product, rather than a chief precipitating factor, of the American Revolution and revolutionary settlement. The "community," or nation, that these poets and others typically "imagined" before 1775 was Great Britain. For a description of the public rituals and the crowds attendant at the College of New Jersey commencements of the era, see Thomas Jefferson Wertenbaker, *Princeton, 1746–1896* (Princeton: Princeton University Press, 1946), 109–11.

9. Joel Barlow, *Columbiad* (1807), book 1, lines 176–84. The complete poem, in facsimile reproduction of the enlarged and revised 1825 edition, is in *The Works of Joel Barlow* (1825), 2 vols. (Gainesville, Fla.: Scholars' Facsimiles and Reprints, 1970), 2:371–866.

10. David S. Shields, *Oracles of Empire: Poetry, Politics, and Commerce in British America, 1690–1750* (Chicago: University of Chicago Press, 1990), 26–32. Others have noticed and analyzed brilliantly the British and imperial origins and sometimes ironic redeployment of many public and festive rituals practiced by revolutionary and early national Americans. See Simon P. Newman, *Parades and the Politics of the Street: Festive Culture in the Early American Republic* (Philadelphia: University of Pennsylvania Press, 1997), esp. 11–43; and David Waldstreicher's provocative "Rites of Rebellion, Rites of Assent: Celebrations, Print Culture, and the Origins of American Nationalism," *Journal of American History* 82, no. 1 (June 1995), 37–61, as well as his *In the Midst of Perpetual Fetes*.

11. Sylvanus Americus [Samuel Nevill, ed.], "The History of the Northern Continent of America," serialized in *The New American Magazine* (Woodbridge, N.J., 1758). On Nevill's history and loyalist verses, see Bushman, *America Discovers Columbus*, 28–30, 42–43.

12. Silverman, *Cultural History of the American Revolution*, 116–17.

13. Bushman, *America Discovers Columbus*, 41. See also Philip J. Deloria's brilliant *Playing Indian* (New Haven: Yale University Press, 1998). Deloria argues that use of the Indian as a symbolic embodiment of America, which was acted out quite literally when white Americans (like members of Philadelphia's Tammany Society) dressed up as Indians, similarly resulted from an urgent need among Americans of the revolutionary generation to define themselves as something new, different, and non-English. In a complex process, colonists—then citizens—employed the symbolism and guise of Indians to forge a new, multiple identity—American—"that was aboriginal and European and yet neither" (36). By the 1790s, however, Tammany

societies, like other white Americans, moved away from Indians and toward Columbus as a national symbol. The activities of real Indians, defending homelands against white encroachment, and their representation as savage in the U.S. press, made identification with Indians problematic (see Deloria, *Playing Indian,* esp. 51–54). On the role of Indian images in the symbolic representation of America in the late colonial, revolutionary, and early national periods, see also John Higham, "Indian Princess and Roman Goddess: The First Female Symbols of America," *Proceedings of the American Antiquarian Society* 100 (1990), part 1, 45–79.

14. Mercy Otis Warren, "A Political Reverie," first published in the *Boston Gazette,* and subsequently in *Poems, Dramatic and Miscellaneous by Mrs. M. Warren* (Boston, 1790), reproduced in facsimile in Benjamin Franklin V, comp., *The Plays and Poems of Mercy Otis Warren* (Delmar, N.Y.: Scholars' Facsimiles and Reprints., 1980), 188–97. Phillis Wheatley, "His Excellency, Gen. Washington," written at Providence, Rhode Island, October 26, 1775, later published in the *Pennsylvania Magazine* (see Julian D. Mason Jr., ed., *The Poems of Phillis Wheatley* [Chapel Hill: University of North Carolina Press, 1966], 87–90]). On these poets, see Bushman, *America Discovers Columbus,* 41–42, 46, 48–50, 62–75; see also Silverman, *Cultural History of the Revolution,* 227, 284–85, 320. The Yale poets Timothy Dwight and Joel Barlow, described in ibid., 402–3, and in Bushman, *American Discovers Columbus,* 50–53, 75–80, similarly deployed the idea of "Columbia" in their popular, nationalist works. Doubts similar to those voiced in Freneau's *Discovery* (1772) would be elaborated in Europe by Cornelius De Pauw in the 1790s and inspire the Abbe Raynal's famous essay contest to determine if the discovery of America had been useful or harmful to mankind. See J. H. Elliott, *The Old World and the New, 1492–1650* (Cambridge: Cambridge University Press, 1970), 1–5; Durand Echeverria, *Mirage of the West* (1957; reprint, Princeton: Princeton University Press, 1968), where the titles of known essays are listed on p. 157. See also David Brion Davis, *The Problem of Slavery in Western Culture* (Ithaca, N.Y.: Cornell University Press, 1966), esp. 15, on Raynal's judgment that European expansion into the New World "was characterized from the beginning by unbelievably cruelty, slaughter, and despotic slavery." Rather than hope and redemption, America represented for Raynal and other *philosophes* a place of unlimited exploitation. Remarkably, however, Columbus generally managed to escape being tarred by the same brush that painted Spanish colonization as a Black Legend, as Freneau's lines above illustrate.

15. David C. Humphrey, *From King's College to Columbia, 1746–1800* (New York: Columbia University Press, 1976), 270–72.

16. See Sale, *Conquest of Paradise,* 338–39; West and Kling, "Columbus and Columbia," 52–54; and Bushman, *America Discovers Columbus,* 54–55. On the goddess Columbia, see Deloria, *Playing Indian,* 51–53; Higham, "Indian Princess and Roman Goddess"; E. McClung Fleming, "The American Image as Indian Princess, 1765–1783," *Winterthur Portfolio* 2 (1965), 65–81; and Fleming, "From Indian Princess to Greek Goddess: The American Image, 1783–1815," *Winterthur Portfolio* 3 (1967), 37–66.

17. See Edwin Patrick Kilroe on *Saint Tammany and the Origin of the Society of Tamman; or Columbian Order in the City of New York* (New York: By author, 1913). See also Deloria, *Playing Indian,* 38–70, as well as Roger D. Abrahams, "White Indians in Penn's City: The Loyal Sons of St. Tammany," in the present volume. Edward G. Porter discusses "The Ship *Columbia* and the Discovery of Oregon," *New England Magazine* 6 (June 1892), 370–71. The ship *Columbia,* a replica of that three-masted windjammer that Captain Gray sailed in 1792 along the Oregon coast and into the Columbia River, now rides in the shallow lagoon at Disneyland; there it functions as a sort of postmodern monument to generic American greatness.

18. On the meaning and implications of gendered symbolism of America, see Higham, "Indian Princess and Roman Goddess," 45–79, esp. 56–58; Deloria, *Playing Indian,* 53; Fleming, "American Image as Indian Princess," 66. The dual-gendered Columbia (feminine) / Colum-

bus (masculine) became a multivocal symbol expressing almost simultaneously stability and passivity, on the one hand, and dynamism and expansion, on the other.

19. On the Northwest Ordinance, see Peter S. Onuf, *Statehood and Union: A History of the Northwest Ordinance* (Bloomington: Indiana University Press, 1987). Of course, the denial that expansion of white Americans into the American interior was colonial required a willful disregard of native peoples and their occupation of these lands. The myth of the Vanishing Indian in the Old Northwest became a self-fulfilling prophecy, the realization of which came only at great trouble, expense, and loss of life. It is also clear that this "common reading" of the West as destiny was, in fact, exclusive, leaving out, for example, African Americans, most of whom remained slaves. For provocative analysis of the potent intersection of nationalism and regionalism, especially western regionalism, see Waldstreicher, *In the Midst of Perpetual Fetes*, 246–93. See also Edward L. Ayers et al., *All Over the Map: Rethinking American Regions* (Baltimore: Johns Hopkins University Press, 1996).

20. Silverman, *Cultural History of the American Revolution*, 576, 579, 585.

21. *Account of the Grand Federal Procession, Philadelphia, July 4, 1788, To which are added, Mr. Wilson's Oration, and a letter on the Subject of the Procession* (Philadelphia, 1788), 17.

22. As Silverman, *Cultural History of the American Revolution*, 580, puts it, "those [parade participants] who witnessed and who comprised the flowing visions of a past tied inexorably to the present were not merely the arguers but also the argument, not merely the spectators but also the actors, observing themselves in the process of defining themselves." If such an event as the Grand Procession can be read as a text, the reverse seems also true: the published account read by nonparticipants, in a sense, might produce an event, an experience of nationalism for its readers. Susan G. Davis, *Parades and Power: Street Theatre in Nineteenth-Century Philadelphia* (Philadelphia: Temple University Press, 1986), a pathbreaking study of festive culture in early America, perceptively examines this and similar events in early national Philadelphia.

23. Edward F. De Lancey, "Columbian Celebration of 1792: The First in the United States," *Magazine of American History* 29, no. 1 (January 1893), 12; Charles T. Thompson, "Columbus Day One Hundred Years Ago," *The Chautauquan: A Monthly Magazine* 16 (n.s., vol. 7) (November 1892), 192–93. Philadelphia's commemoration may have been celebrated publically only in print, with the publication of a "Columbia edition" of Dunlap's *Daily American Advertiser*. In nearby Princeton, Philadelphia patriot Joseph Reed delivered a celebratory oration on Columbus, which was reproduced in Dunlap's paper. Near Baltimore, on his private estate, Charles Francis Adrian le Paulmier, Chevalier d'Anmour, French consul and American patriot, dedicated an obelisk, some twenty-eight feet tall, to the sacred memory of Columbus. See William Eleroy Curtis, "The Columbus Monuments," *The Chautauquan: A Monthly Magazine*, (November 1892), 138–39; J. M. Dickey, comp., *Christopher Columbus and His Monument Columbia* (Chicago and New York, 1892), 73–78. See also Bushman, *America Discovers Columbus*, 92–94, on the Baltimore monument.

24. *The Independent Chronicle, and the Universal Advertiser* (Boston), October 25, 1792. See Massachusetts Historical Society, *Proceedings*, vol. 1 [1791–1835] (Boston, 1879), 28–29, 31, 44–46; Louis Leonard Tucker, *Clio's Consort: Jeremy Belknap and the Founding of the Massachusetts Historical Society* (Boston: Massachusetts Historical Society and Northeastern University Press, 1990), 134–35. See also "The Last Columbian Centuary Anniversary," *Harper's Weekly*, August 17, 1889, 655; De Lancey, "Columbian Celebration of 1792," 2–5; and Thompson, "Columbus Day One Hundred Years Ago," 190–91. See also Bushman, *America Discovers Columbus*, 81–97, esp. 88–91. The ode, oration, and toasts occasioned by the event used the opportunity to proclaim support, among other things, for the *Rights of Man*. Whether such partisanship was contested by those hostile to the French Revolution is unclear (and in any case, the French Revolution itself was just beginning to emerge as a matter of great controversy in America, following the August 10 insurrection in Paris and the suspension of the king). In general, orga-

nizers of the celebration focused on Columbus and seemed intent on promoting consensus and nationalism rather than pressing partisan divisions.

25. Tucker, *Clio's Consort,* 134–35.
26. *New York Journal & Patriotic Register,* October 17, 1792.
27. Ibid.
28. On the Tammany monument to Columbus, see ibid. See also Kilroe, *Saint Tammany,* 184–86, and, on the Tammany Museum, see 173–77. See also De Lancey, "Columbian Celebration of 1792," 6–11; Thompson, "Columbus Day One Hundred Years Ago," 189–90. Other, more permanent Columbian monuments were described in William Eleroy Curtis, "The Columbus Monuments," *The Chautauquan* (November 1892), 138–46.
29. See Kilroe, *Saint Tammany,* 84–87; the appendixes, 209ff., list the various Tammany societies in the colonies and United States, their celebrations, and their orations, dating from 1771. See also, on the Tammany societies, Deloria, *Playing Indian,* esp. 38–70, and Abrahams, "White Indians in Penn's City," in the present volume. Deloria carefully distinguishes the New York Tammany Society from the Philadelphia Tammany Society, the latter conceived in the very different terms required by postrevolution America (47–50). On the rituals of the New York Tammany Society, see also Alfred F. Young, *The Democratic Republicans of New York: The Origins, 1763–1797* (Chapel Hill: University of North Carolina Press, 1967), 398–99. Young argues that the strength of the Society "lay in the fact that it remained essentially a fraternal order replete with paraphernalia, ritual, and rich symbolism" (399). Its membership, composed of some five hundred men, mostly artisans and tradesmen, had not yet committed fully to the Republican cause or transformed themselves into an electioneering club.
30. Ironically, pledges to inclusiveness notwithstanding, the New York Tammany Society exhibited a strong anti-Catholic, anti-Irish sentiment in its early years and worked to keep "foreigners" out. Needless to say, women and blacks—free or otherwise—were similarly excluded. The Irish came to dominate the Tammany Society in Pennsylvania; the collision between these immigrants and older members, filled with ethnic, nativist prejudices, caused the fragmentation and demise of most older Tammany Societies. Later, the New York society too would be dominated by Irish immigrants and their descendants; see Kilroe, *Saint Tammany,* 142–46; Deloria, *Playing Indian,* 45–47.
31. *New York Journal & Patriotic Register,* October 17, 1792.
32. See, for example, Belknap's *Discourse,* as well as his treatment of Columbus in his *American Biography; or An Historical Account of those Persons Who Have Been Distinguished in America* (Boston, 1794–98), 123–28. Blacks in the urban North suffered continued exclusion, even with abolition and the enlargement of the public sphere. See esp. Waldstreicher, *In the Midst of Perpetual Fetes.* See also Shane White, " 'It Was a Proud Day': African Americans, Festivals, and Parades in the North, 1741–1834," *Journal of American History* 81 (June 1994), 13–50; on the slow and troubled process of abolition in New York, see Shane White, *Somewhat More Independent: The End of Slavery in New York City, 1770–1810* (Athens: University of Georgia Press, 1991); on slavery, abolition, and race in New England, see Joanne Pope Melish, *Disowning Slavery: Gradual Emancipation and "Race" in New England, 1780–1860* (Ithaca, N.Y.: Cornell University Press, 1998).
33. On the impact of the French Revolution in the United States, see Newman, *Parades and the Politics of the Street,* esp. 120–51.
34. On *Tammany; or The Indian Chief,* see George O. Seilhamer, *History of the American Theatre: New Foundations* (Philadelphia, 1891), 85–86, quotation at 86. On Morton's play *Columbus; or The World Discovered,* see ibid., 366; George C. D. Odell, *Annals of the New York Stage, Volume One [to 1798]* (New York: Columbia University Press, 1927), 463–64; *Diary of William Dunlap (1766–1839), Collections of the New-York Historical Society for the Year 1929,* 62 (New York,

1930), 146–47. On William Dunlap's play, *Andre: The Glory of Columbia*, see Jared Brown, *The Theatre in America During the Revolution* (Cambridge: Cambridge University Press, 1995), 169.

35. Poem quoted in Francis Von A. Cabeen, "The Society of the Sons of St. Tammany of Philadelphia," *Pennsylvania Magazine of History and Biography* 27, no. 1 (1903), 36.

36. Higham, "Indian Princess and Roman Goddess," 57, 63. See also Deloria, *Playing Indian*, 38–70. The Indian problems of the 1790s, and their resolution through successful conquest and peace (and expansion) "with honor," can be surveyed concisely in John K. Mahon, "Indian-United States Military Situation, 1775–1848," in Wilcomb Washburn, ed., *Handbook of North American Indians: Indian-White Relations*, vol. 4 (Washington, D.C., 1988), 149–52; *Columbian Tragedy*, illustrated at 151; see also Reginald Horsman, "United States Indian Policies, 1776–1815," in ibid., esp. 32–35.

37. See Paul Semonin on " 'Nature's Nation': Natural History as Nationalism in the New Republic," *Northwest Review* 30, no. 2 (1992), 6–41; Deloria, *Playing Indian*, 44–45, 50, 58; Higham, "Indian Princess and Roman Goddess," 66; Belknap, *American Biography*, 128.

38. Reported in *New York Journal & Patriotic Register*, August 10, 1790; see Deloria, *Playing Indian*, 54–55.

39. Philip Freneau, "The Indian Burying Ground" (1787). The 1812 anti-British cartoon (drawing probably by William Muldaux, possibly published in a Pennsylvania newspaper) is illustrated in Horsman, "United States Indian Policy," 38.

40. John W. Reps, *The Making of Urban America: A History of City Planning in the United States* (Princeton: Princeton University Press, 1965), 225, 227; see 229, fig. 135 for plan of Columbus, Ohio. Generally, on "Columbianization" of the landscape, see George R. Stewart, *Names on the Land: A Historical Account of Place-Naming in the United States* (New York: Random House, 1945). See Anne E. Bentley on "The Columbia-Washington Medal," *Proceedings of the Massachusetts Historical Society* 101 (1990), 120–27.

41. This word-play is inspired by David Waldstriecher's use of the concept "ruling rites of assent" (see "Rites of Rebellion, Rites of Assent," 38, 38 n. 5), which he distinguishes from Sacvan Bercovitch's *The Rites of Assent: Transformations in the Symbolic Construction of America* (New York: Routledge, 1993).

10

American Women and the French Revolution

Gender and Partisan Festive Culture in the Early Republic

Susan Branson and *Simon P. Newman*

Women seldom appear on the pages of most of the political histories of the early American republic. In their studies of voting, party formation, and political leadership, historians have concluded that because women were unable to participate in these vital elements of political life they had no meaningful role in the public world of politics.¹ Both political and women's historians suggest that the most that even educated women of means achieved was republican motherhood, a role that celebrated female virtue by relegating women to the home, where they might inculcate civic virtues in the next generation.²

Women were, however, active and significant participants in the public world of politics in the new republic. Politics transcended the letters and speeches of partisan leaders, the process of voting, or the practice of elective leadership. For many Americans, politics was all about the partisan badges they wore and the songs they sang, the parades they attended, the feasts they enjoyed, and the celebrations and ceremonies that filled their calendar. Women were important actors in these rich and colorful events, and as such they were active players in their political world during the bitterly partisan years when the nation's first political parties emerged.

Such annual celebrations as Washington's Birthday and Independence Day were extremely partisan events, and supporters of the Federalist administrations of Washington and Adams, and the emerging Republican opposition, joined in political battle to contest the form and content of these festive rites. However, French revolutionary feasts, festivals, and parades, which dominated American popular political culture during Washington's second term, were somewhat different. Virtually all who identified with the Federalist administrations of Washington and Adams refused to participate in any events that celebrated the French Revolution. As a result, these parades, feasts, and festivals lacked the legitimacy that would have been conferred by the participation of members and supporters of the Federalist government. They acquired, however, an entirely different kind of legitimacy through the enthusiastic support of a great many ordinary American men and women. Between the fall of 1792 and the fall of 1795, the presence and participation of large numbers of citizens in celebrations from Maine to Kentucky to Georgia gave a popular validity to French revolutionary celebrations that were profoundly political and partisan in their opposition to the policies and goals of the Federalist government.[3]

By the late 1790s, however, Federalists had regained the initiative. Public support for France diminished in the second half of the 1790s as deteriorating Franco-American relations encouraged a sharp change in opinion about the Revolution. By the end of the decade, the political and economic issues that entwined the fates of Britain, France, and the United States provoked a very different public response. The partisan politics and competing visions of government, which generated competition between Federalists and Republicans to shape the meaning of political ceremonies and celebrations, assumed a strongly Federalist cast.[4] By 1798, men and women of anti-Gallic opinions, many of them Federalist-minded, claimed the public political stage.[5]

Both the pro-French and anti-French celebrations of the 1790s allowed, and indeed were dependent on, levels of female participation and initiative unknown in the rather more nationalist festive culture of Independence Day and Washington's Birthday. Those who supported and then those who attacked France sought female support to validate their positions, and women responded with enthusiasm, molding their participation in order to articulate their partisan positions. Perhaps more than anything else, America's French ritual culture of the 1790s demonstrated how ready and able women were to appear on the public political stage.

* * *

During the early to mid-1790s it was the supporters of the French Revolution who dominated festive political culture. Lacking the legitimacy conferred by the participation of members and supporters of the Federalist government, they employed a language of unity to legitimate the "civic festivals," "civic balls," and "civic feasts" held throughout the United States.[6] The emerging Republican party was not slow to employ these events to its own partisan advantage. But by seeking out and employing the popular sanction of the community at large, Republicans enhanced the political significance of those who often were left on the margins of early national politics. More than in any other popular celebrations and festivals of this era, ordinary women joined men and took an uncommonly active role in these French revolutionary parades, feasts, and festivals. Such participation allowed people to express partisan allegiances and their own political beliefs, objectives, and identities.

Women's participation in the popular politics of French revolutionary festive culture provides further evidence that the boundaries between the idealized separate spheres of a private world of women and a public world of men were remarkably fluid. Jürgen Habermas argued that the male public sphere could "articulate and validate processes that promote open discussion among a wide spectrum of social actors on a wide range of concerns." Thus, the eighteenth-century public sphere had the "capacity to bring citizens together to rationally present, discuss, and reach a consensus about the general good."[7] Anyone "with access to cultural products," be they "readers, listeners, and spectators," could enter the public sphere, but Habermas could envision this as only a male population.[8] For decades, historians compounded this impression by arguing that women found fulfillment and a degree of power within a separate, domestic sphere; using women's magazines, novels, and private correspondence, these historians have charted the coalescence of an ideal of domesticity as the separate sphere of women.[9]

More recently, feminist scholars have complicated Habermas's definitions, showing that public space was in fact composed of such competing "counterpublics" as "nationalist publics, popular peasant publics, elite women's publics, and working-class publics."[10] Late-eighteenth- and early-nineteenth century society consisted of a multiplicity of public arenas, often intersecting, overlapping, and even enveloping one another. It is true that the classical republican ideology of the early national United States envisioned a male, propertied, and white public sphere, defined in opposition to the ostensibly female characteristics of dependence, weakness, and effeminacy found within a private sphere. Yet this was far from a description of social and political reality. Women's celebrations of the French Revolution played a vital role in creating a new public space. In the context of the gradual democratization of American politics, American women who participated in French revolutionary festive culture opened up public spaces with new forms of female political participation. Women's presence in spaces traditionally designated as public, and therefore male, helped to regender public political space in the early republic. But this was by no means an easy process, for public space was contested and defended as a male province, and Federalists were not slow to criticize both women and the Republicans for regendering popular political activity, even though the Federalists themselves were more than ready to foster women's participation in political culture when it suited their purpose.

While the vagaries and intricacies of French politics often confused Americans, they were enthralled by the French Revolution.[11] Easily identifiable epochal events such as the fall of the Bastille, the execution of the king, and major military victories captured the popular imagination, which was sustained by newspaper reports of French constitutional debates, arguments over the monarchy, wars between the new French republic and foreign aggressors, and a host of related issues.[12]

Such events as these challenged the "distinctions between active/passive, male/female citizens and the public/domestic spaces where citizenship could be acted upon," in ways that may have resonated for American women who participated in their own, albeit less violent celebrations of the French Revolution.[13] Among the most tangible expressions of the popularity of the French Revolution were the widespread and large-scale celebrations of the new French republic that permeated the American festive calendar. These fell into four main categories: commemoration of the anniversary of the Franco-American alliance of 1778; the achievement or anniversaries of major constitutional reforms in France; the battlefield victories of the French republic; and the arrival in the United States of leading French officials and citizens. All these celebrations fueled a particularly intense form of popular politics and furnished many men and women with far greater opportunities for participation in popular politics than domestic festive occasions afforded. Throughout the middle years of the 1790s, citizens regularly gathered in large public meetings "to fix on some plan to express their joy" at events in France, issuing invitations to "every class of Citizen patriots" to participate in their festivities.[14] All who felt "an interest in the glorious cause of liberty" were welcome to join in a Bastille Day celebration in Philadelphia; in New London the town crier cheered "Liberty" and "Equality" and invited "*all* citizens" to a celebration of French victories in Holland; and in Charleston all "*friends of Liberty and Equality*" were welcomed to a celebration of the naval victories of the French warship *L'Embuscade*.[15]

Women were not slow to participate as spectators in many of the celebrations of the French Revolution, nor were they slow to take advantage of Republican invitations to attend and participate in this festive culture. The single largest and best reported French revolutionary celebration took place in Boston on January 24, 1793, when the whole town came together to celebrate the French military victory at Valmy. This event depended for its success on the enthusiastic participation and support of the townspeople as a whole, but there were clear risks involved in enlisting "all classes and persons without discrimination" in this celebration of radical democratic revolution.[16] The town's Republicans had welcomed the participation of "every class of Citizen patriots" in their partisan celebration, promising that social rank would be "abolished by the title of Citizens" and hoping to draw a crowd large enough to cow their Federalist opponents.[17] These partisan leaders envisioned a celebration of Valmy premised on the rhetoric of liberty and equality that would give them temporary control of public space and demonstrate the depth and extent of popular support for their pro-French and, by implication, anti-Federalist sentiments.

The women of Boston did indeed watch and participate in this celebration of Valmy, viewing the parade either from the "balconies and middle stories of the houses" or from the streets themselves, and then crowding into State Street for a grand civic feast. Throughout the 1790s it was unusual for Republican leaders to seek or recognize more than the enthusiastic spectatorship of women, but women were quick to transcend passive spectatorship and assume a meaningful role in the proceedings for themselves. Boston, after decades of war and out-migration, was a city in which adult women outnumbered adult men, and the fierce politicking of partisan leaders and their desperate search for communal support and sanction involved the participation of thousands of women, many of whom wore tri-colored cockades to indicate publicly their support for the French Revolution and its ideals as they interpreted them.[18] To a significant degree, the success of Boston's Valmy festival was contingent on both the passive and active participation of "bevies of our amiable and beautiful women."[19] Newspapers as far away as Pennsylvania reported how some Boston women took advantage of this to demand equal status with male citizens participating in political culture, with the appropriate label "citess."[20]

Federalists who felt threatened by these festivals were quick to seize on these female incursions into the male realm of politics in order to condemn their partisan opponents who had made such actions possible by their sponsorship of the inclusive Valmy festival. After complaining about Boston's celebration, John Adams protested that "Cit and Citess is to come instead of Goffer and Gammer, Gooder and Gooden, Mr. and Mrs."[21] Other criticisms of female politicization were of far greater consequence. The rites, symbols, and language of Boston's Valmy celebration implied a very real leveling within the political community, an equality that did not sit well with Federalist conceptions of deferential female activities within an orderly and hierarchical polity. One satirical poem in the *Connecticut Courant* attacked "every *Citizen* and *Citess*" who had worshiped the stump of the liberty tree "like heathen folks," with seemingly savage "*Indian talk*."[22] Another Federalist, also from Connecticut, derisively dismissed the "citesses in Boston" by applauding a local woman who had just given birth to "FOUR equality citizens" and by condemning another who had taken the rhetoric of liberty and equality to heart and decided "that her husband ought not to be the sole occupant of her; that all men have an equal right—and that she is determined to keep open hours."[23]

This was a clear condemnation of women who transcended the domestic and subservient role of wife and mother. Such criticism was taken a stage further in a poem that made explicit the criticism that women who ventured too far into the male domain of the public sphere were no better than prostitutes:

> No citess to my name I'll have, says Kate,
> Tho' Boston lads about it so much prate,
> I've asked its meaning and our Tom, the clown,
> Says, darn it, 't means a woman of the Town.[24]

All around the country, Federalist men sought to exploit the discomfort of Republican men over this kind of female political activity. Yet Republicans, in an effort to garner public approval of their nascent political party, continued to encourage women's support for their French revolutionary celebrations. One proponent of Boston's Valmy celebration commented that the town's women "did honor to the 'RIGHTS of WOMEN' by rejoicing in the vindication [of] the 'RIGHTS of MAN.'" This author was attempting to limit female participation to a supportive role, but by linking Paine and the ideology of the American and French Revolutions that was a bedrock of the Republican party with Mary Wollstonecraft's seminal *A Vindication of the Rights of Woman,* he succeeded only in drawing attention to the radical potential of female attendance and participation.[25]

In the decidedly partisan milieu of these Valmy celebrations, with Republicans eagerly seeking the support and sanction of many different members of their communities, the women who chose to participate were occasionally able to create their own unique celebrations and political stands. In Menotomy, Massachusetts, for example, some fifty women assembled at the home of Mrs. Willington to mount their own celebration "of liberty and equality" and "to felicitate their sisters in France upon the happy revolution in their nation."[26] They, and the women of Portsmouth, New Hampshire, "wore upon their caps the national cockade," and a woman from the latter group made clear her "patriotic disposition" by calling for "the democratic dance Ça Ira."[27]

Male Republicans were troubled by such displays of female agency in public spaces and by Federalist attacks on female politicization. Though they wanted female support to strengthen their festive political culture, they sought to control and direct women's activities. In the toasts that followed the all-male civic feasts that were often integral to French revolutionary celebrations, these men struggled to acknowledge and applaud the female support they needed, while trying to limit it by reference to women's appropriate private and domestic sphere. In Alexandria, Virginia, for example, men feasting in celebration of Valmy toasted "the Rights of Women," saying, "May the Ladies ever obtain a due share in the administration of family government." In Baltimore a year later, the men present echoed this attempt to consign women to the safety of republican motherhood by raising their glasses to "the American and French ladies": "May they early inspire their children with the love of the law." At Oeller's Hotel, a few hundred feet from where the federal Congress sat in Philadelphia, another group of men drank to "the Fair of France and America": "May each weave a cap of liberty for a husband." To these men, the only legitimate political existence for a woman was as supporter of her husband and educator of his children.

However, having learned of the active role French women were taking in popular politics, and after accepting Republican invitations to participate in and support their partisan celebrations of revolutionary France, some American women proved less than willing to accept the role prescribed for them by men. On occasion, women secured prominence in French revolutionary celebrations, which they were then able to refashion into protofeminist events. In 1793, for example, two widows in Charleston, South Carolina, one French and one American, were publicly "married" to each another. According to the *City Gazette,* "after having repudiated their husbands on account of their ill-treatment, [they] conceived the design of living together in the strictest union and friendship . . . in order to give a pledge of their fidelity, requested that their striped gowns should be pinned together, that their children should be looked upon as one family, while their mothers shewed them an equal affection."[28] A Mr. Lee officiated, and explained the "reciprocal obligations" of the two women. A militia unit fired its guns to signal completion of the contract, while the soldiers and spectators shouted "thousands of huzzahs." Each woman had a male representative: the American was a Mr. Samuel Prioleau, while the French consul M. A. B. Mangourit represented his countrywoman by urging the spectators to celebrate the Carmagnole and to sing the "Ça Ira."[29]

In another case, in December 1792, Philadelphians assembled to articulate their opposition to the British government and its francophobe policies. The local Pennsylvania Republican leader Blair McClenahan headed an unusual procession of citizens to the home of the British minister, dominated by a large number of girls and young women who, dressed in white and wearing tri-colored ribbons, led the way.[30] Contemporary notions of gender etiquette meant that neither a horrified Federalist government nor an annoyed British ambassador could act against or ignore this female deputation: Republicans thus benefited from an event that had given primacy to women.[31]

On another occasion, women assumed the principal role in what were most likely male-organized events. Taking place near the center of Philadelphia, this march to and protest at the British Minister's house would have been witnessed by many Philadelphians—some supportive of, some indifferent to, and others angered by the political opinions displayed. None could have ignored the fact that Philadelphia women legitimated and even empowered the event by their very presence in the public political sphere.[32]

Many of the women who watched this and other public displays of support for France wore their own tri-colored ribbons, usually shaped into a simple cockade, on their hats, dresses, or coats. Simple rosettes fashioned from silk or a cheaper fabric, cockades were more than familiar to contemporaries. In the years after the Battle of Yorktown, the soldiers and officers of the Continental Army proudly sported the black cockades they had worn during the War for Independence as emblems of this patriotic service.[33] Later, during the early years of the French Revolution, Americans read in their newspapers about the French patriots who stormed the Bastille wearing "the cockade of Union, white rose, and blue"[34] and about the subsequent symbolic battles between royalists wearing white cockades and republicans wearing the tri-colored "national" cockade.[35]

Shortly thereafter republican French sailors and privateers first introduced these simple yet striking tri-colored cockades into American port communities. American men and women who favored the cause of the revolutionaries took to making and wearing these badges themselves, and soon the red, white, and blue ribbons were in evidence all over the nation, "the men with it in their hats, the women on their breasts." Almost "all the little boys" in Morristown, New Jersey, had "a tri-colored French ribbon on their hats"; many Philadelphians chose to "put on the national cockade"; the "tri-colored cockade was generally worn" in Charleston; and women in Boston wore "upon their caps the national cockade."[36]

Tri-colored cockades, however, could have meanings and significance to those who wore them that transcended mere support for the French Revolution. To women who had taken an active role in the American Revolution, and who had read in their newspapers about the activities of French women in their own revolution, these cockades may have represented a good deal more than unquestioning support of the rights and freedoms of the white male citizenry. They may have read with interest the accounts of female politicization in France, as when "4,000 citizen wives" assembled in Bordeaux "with the national cockade in their breasts," publicly affirming their intention to "bring up their children in the principles of the new constitution."[37] This was a version of republican motherhood that was far more public and decidedly more assertive than anything to be found in America at the time. American women were more than able to grasp the implications of the extension of revolutionary republicanism for their own situation. Employing the familiar model of female discussion of political issues in a *salon*, a woman who signed herself "C" published a "conversation," as part of a letter to the editor of the *Philadelphia Aurora*, in which Roxana longed for "the glorious day . . . when our sex shall be delivered from an ignominious slavery of 6000 years," and "Thalestris" answered that there must be "100,000 sisters in the United States" who supported this proposition and anticipated "the glorious day when American ladies shall be Commanders, Presidents of Congress, Ambassadors, Governors, Secretaries of State, Professors, Judges, Preachers."[38]

Abigail Adams was typical of many elite and well-educated women in that she sympathized with the political conservatism of her husband. John Adams was committed to a Federalist conception of an ordered and structured society led by the "better sort," and Abigail Adams joined her husband in condemning the leveling radicalism of the French Revolution. Yet she and many women or her class were beginning to develop their own ideas about women's political rights, and the signs, songs, and symbols of French revolutionary political culture played a role in their evolving ideas of the right of women to discuss and participate in politics.

It was more common, however, for nonelite women and girls actually to wear the national cockade. Hundreds of lower and middling sort women in Boston thus exhibited "their patriotic enthusiasm"[39] during one French revolutionary festival, just as a group of young Philadelphia women wore tri-colored cockades when they escorted French mariners to the home of the French consul.[40] The impoverished women of Philadelphia's Northern Liberties who warned their neighbor that her windows would be broken if she did not remove the English flag hanging from her house well understood the power of female-controlled symbols. Their actions recalled those of women during the early stages of the war for independence, when the "Daughters of Liberty" often played as large a role as men in enforcing resistance through nonimportation and nonconsumption.[41]

It is difficult to gauge the meaning of red-white-and-blue cockades to impoverished women who were unable to secure a sufficient income to survive independently. Such women relied on the wages of husbands, fathers, and sons, many of whom worked as sailors or in the various industries that supported seafaring commerce. When the wars of the French Revolution broke out, the British government began a series of devastating attacks on American commerce and renewed the practice of impressing

American sailors, policies that had a real effect on the lives of tens of thousands of poor American women. The unwillingness of successive Federalist administrations to respond to these British affronts may well have encouraged many women of the lower orders to adopt the tri-colored cockade as an emblem of their opposition to government policies they deeply resented, policies supported by merchants who were thriving while these women and their families suffered. Moreover, these cockades may have served as badges of their support for the French revolutionaries in their war against Britain and its counterrevolutionary assaults on American commerce.[42]

One of the largest French revolutionary festivals, and certainly the most frightening to Federalists, was Philadelphia's "Feast of Reason," held on Monday August 11. Again, the influence of French festive culture was apparent, for this event was more like a Parisian festival than anything else ever staged in America, uniting a broad cross-section of Philadelphians in a celebration of radical revolution and popular liberty that took place a stone's throw away from the homes and work spaces of the members of the Washington administration. The *Aurora* advertised a public meeting at Oeller's Hotel, open to all "friends of the French republic,"[43] at which detailed arrangements for this extraordinary event were worked out and then published in advance.[44]

The day began in traditional fashion, with a cannonade, but rather than the usual federal salute, twenty-two cannons were fired in honor of the date "so dear to all true friends" of France. At eight o'clock another salute "called the citizens to meet at the center square." No estimate of the number of participants survives, but the fact that it took two hours to organize the paraders suggests the large scale of this event, particularly when one considers that many spectators joined the parade after watching it pass.[45]

It was a grand but unusual procession, given that the organizers strove for the gravity of a Parisian festival by demanding that the "dignity of the people" be expressed by "the strictest order and a most profound silence."[46] This was no rabble-rousing demonstration in the nation's capital, but rather a well-ordered and powerful exhibition of popular support for the French Revolution and the Republicans. Two cannons with French and American crews led the way, followed by drummers, long rows of American and French citizens, four men bearing a large obelisk surrounded by young girls dressed in white, a member of the French National Guard in full uniform, and local and visiting dignitaries, with "an immense number of citizens of both nations arm in arm" bringing up the rear. Such a large procession was certainly witnessed by many more Philadelphians, with white men of all ranks, black men, and black and white women of the lower orders participating as spectators along the sides of the streets, while elite and middling white women watched from windows and balconies.[47]

The obelisk that formed the centerpiece of the parade was carried by four American and French citizens, each wearing a militia or military uniform and a liberty cap. The obelisk itself was "surmounted by a Liberty cap," and on its four sides were written mottoes commemorating "*immortality*," the French republic, "*liberty, equality and fraternity*," and a warning to "*tyrants*." The young girls in white who skipped and danced around this monument wore tri-colored ribbons and carried baskets of flowers. The procession made its way through the streets of the American capital before ending in the gardens of French Minister Jean Antoine Joseph Fauchet. In the center of the garden "was erected an altar to liberty, with an elegant statue of the goddess of liberty on it." The young girls and the musicians took up positions around the altar, and after a short speech by citizen Dubois Chotard and a response by Fauchet, the band struck up the "Marseillaise and other patriotic hymns." The girls cast their flowers on and around the altar, and Fauchet and the French citizens present "swore to uphold the republic, to live free or die."[48]

Having watched these ceremonies with great interest, the assembled spectators then began their own celebration, dancing to the "Carmagnole" and other patriotic airs performed by the band, enjoying refreshments, and then crowding out onto Market Street a few hundred yards west of both Congress and Washington's residence, where they proceeded to burn the British flag. While these ordinary folk thus celebrated the French republic, "about 500" more elite partisans of France feasted at Richardet's Tavern, drinking toasts that reflected the sentiments of the day, which ended with "a beautiful exhibition of fire works."[49]

In France, political theater such as this was a deliberate attempt to reshape the history of the French nation; no longer were monarchs and princes, or religious icons like the Virgin Mary, the centerpieces of ritual. As Lynn Hunt describes it, the new political ideology called for visual, "transparent" representations of Reason, Liberty, and Nature in which male and female citizens took part. In Philadelphia and elsewhere, this French symbolism assumed an American form. Young women became central performers who not only expressed the political opinions espoused by male Republicans but also asserted their right of access to the public political arena. Participation extended beyond the young women who were part of the festival. Their mothers, who had decorated those white costumes with tri-color ribbons, sanctioned and encouraged their daughters' political identities and at the same time displayed their own.

The French orations meant little to many present, but the monuments to liberty, the tri-colored ribbons and liberty caps, the young women dressed in white, the secular altar, and the affirmations of devotion to liberty were rites and symbols that were readily accessible to most of the American men and women present. Thus, when thousands danced to the "Carmagnole" in the gardens of the French minister, they were taking part in a ritual affirming the goals and the ideology of the French Revolution. They were also demonstrating their opposition to the policies of Washington's government that were steering the nation away from France and toward the counterrevolutionary nation of Great Britain. For American women, such ceremonies enabled them to center themselves within public political space. They could truly claim, as "Cornelia" did in 1792, that women as well as men were responsible for shaping political expression: "That we direct the fashions is incontrovertible. Now there are fashions in opinions as well as dress. Am I not just in the inference that we form your political characters; that we can hold out liberty or slavery to you . . .[?] It is a trite saying that a man must ask his wife if he will be rich; I will extend this idea a little further and say, that a man must ask our sex if he shall be free."[50] Again, republican motherhood assumed political form: women held the key to the safety and well-being not just of their individual families, but of the nation as a whole.

The "Carmagnole" and other French revolutionary songs and music played a vital role in the festive culture of the 1790s. Throughout 1793 and 1794, American newspapers printed translations of the leading French revolutionary songs, and Americans were as quick to learn French songs as they were to assume French cockades. Once again these French imports were favored by Republican partisans: while "Yankee Doodle" was a patriotic air favored by Federalists and Republicans alike, only those who supported France and the Republicans adopted the imported "Ça Ira" or the "Marseillaise" as political anthems.

The songs of the French Revolution were enormously popular during the first half of the 1790s. Both John Francis and Alexander Anderson remembered male and female New Yorkers singing and dancing the "Carmagnole."⁵¹ In Philadelphia, John Watson was only one of the many Americans who "had caught many national airs." He recalled that "the streets by day and night, resounded with the songs of boys, such as these: 'Allons enfants de la patrie, le jour de gloire est arrivé!' &c.—'Dansons le carmagnole, vive le sang! vive le sang!' &c.—'A ç'ira, ç'ira,' &c. Several verses of each of these and others were thus sung."⁵²

The politicization of music also inspired the creation of new songs in the United States. A Mrs. Marriot penned "On the Revolution in France," while a "Young Lady" of New York City published "The Rights of Woman," to be sung to the tune of "God Save the King." Firmly critical of the fact that "man boasts the noble cause" while women lie "in base obscurity," this songwriter championed women's "equal rights" and Mary Wollstonecraft, beginning and ending with the rousing chorus "Woman is Free!" Although the song may never have enjoyed a public performance, it was reprinted in newspapers around the country, thus reaching a wide audience of both men and women.⁵³ When Sarah Bache wrote to her son Benjamin Franklin Bache and requested "the music and words" of several of the popular political songs of the early 1790s, she illustrated that such material was as much within women's domain as men's. Politics could be performed in the parlor as well as out in the street.

While on one level French tunes served to delight and entertain, it was all but impossible for contemporaries to ignore their political nature. Popular in the truest sense of the word, they allowed all Americans who so desired to learn, articulate, and perhaps even rework a variety of political sentiments. Within the context of domestic partisan politics, either singing or applauding the singing of French revolutionary songs generally indicated support for the Republicans and opposition to the ostensibly pro-British policy of neutrality maintained by Washington's administration. But these songs could say and mean much more, including support for the cause of the French Revolution, outrage at British attacks on American shipping and their impressment of American sailors, and protest against what some Americans perceived as the counterrevolutionary policies and personnel of the Federalist government. Perhaps songs of revolution had even deeper resonance among those for whom the American Revolution had done little, including black Americans, white women, and the urban and rural poor. Thus a poor washerwoman who wore a tri-colored cockade and sang the "Marseillaise" while walking through the streets was able to articulate an unmistakably political comment with a variety of possible meanings. Once again the political culture of the French Revolution had enabled the voiceless to find a new voice.[54]

Popular support for the French Revolution began to diminish after 1795. The Jay Treaty between the United States and Great Britain succeeded in improving Anglo-American relations, while sending Franco-American relations into a downward spiral that ended with an undeclared quasi-war between the countries at the end of the decade. Moreover, the increasing radicalism and violence of the French Revolution worried Republican leaders, who sought to distance themselves and their supporters from France. By the end of Washington's second term, French revolutionary celebrations had all but disappeared in the United States, tri-colored cockades had fallen out of favor, and theater audiences were calling for American songs and anthems.

Though relatively short-lived, French revolutionary festivals had played a vital role in the creation of a popular political culture in the new republic. A quarter-century before the advent of Jacksonian Democracy, the French Revolution mobilized a broader cross-section of American society than any other event, and in their tens of thousands Americans joined in or watched these events. Relying on newspaper accounts from all over the nation, the arch-Federalist editor William Cobbett estimated that during 1795 the French conquest of Holland had prompted "twenty-two grand civic festivals, fifty-one of an inferior order, and one hundred and ninety three public dinners." According to his estimation, more than twenty thousand people had participated in these events, while countless more had cheered with enthusiasm from the sidelines.[55]

American foreign policy issues, and the commercial problems attendant on political disharmony, fostered a sharp change in opinion about the French Revolution and that nation's foreign policies by the mid-1790s.[56] The treaty with Great Britain, concluded by John Jay in 1795, precipitated a series of conflicts between France and the United States. By April 1798 these conflicts culminated in the announcement by President Adams of the XYZ Affair and the failure of negotiations with the French. A backlash against France and American supporters of France spread quickly though the United States, encouraging Federalists to seize the initiative and the active role in popular political culture.[57]

Having condemned Republicans for encouraging female politicization, the Federalists were quick to adopt similar strategies to illustrate that

American men and women were united in their support of the Adams administration. Reports of Federalist celebrations and festivals emphasized the patriotic zeal with which men and women came to the defense of their country and of Federalist attacks on allegedly unpatriotic Republicans.[58] Many Federalists had never been happy about the French Revolution, which challenged constituted authority and privilege. Federalists had long criticized the Revolution's power to undermine order, fearing the consequences of such an ideology in their own country. In this climate of anxiety and accusation, Federalist women articulated their condemnation of the French. As one woman wrote in William Cobbett's *Porcupine's Gazette,* France was the "enemy," a nation "divested of every principle of morality and virtue."[59] Another woman privately expressed her fervent wish to see "every French *Demo,* at the bottom of the Sea or anywhere else in this world."[60] Elizabeth Hewson, expecting her brother's return to the United States after an extended residence abroad, told him of her hope that "the French party will not be those whom you most associate with. I should be very sorry indeed to have you in the Democratic society."[61]

Beginning in the summer of 1798, and continuing throughout the autumn, women helped create a new political ceremony that was integral to this Federalist resurgence. As the Federalists assumed greater prominence in the public arena, they marshaled opinion against France by stirring citizens to patriotic defense of the nation. With Federalist propagandists insisting that a French invasion was imminent, men and women gathered to support the militia groups mobilized to defend American shores. Women were central to these vehemently patriotic events, giving a virtuous blessing to the militia units formed to protect the nation. Often this took the form of a ritual presentation of an emblematic flag (sometimes fashioned by the female presenters themselves). This role of women as exhorters was hardly new, and a generation earlier newspapers such as the *Massachusetts Spy* had applauded the "daughters of liberty," who urged men to support the tea boycott in Boston.[62] Just as with the Republican women of the mid-1790s, the Federalist women of the late-1790s were not only visible participants in public rites but also a necessary and prominent part of them.[63]

There was a high degree of ritual conformity within these events. Usually one but occasionally several women presented a new standard to the militiamen in a formal setting, often adding a partisan civic blessing. In 1797 the First Troop of Philadelphia City Calvary, under Captain Dunlap's command, wrote to ask Elizabeth Willing Powel, widow of the former

Federalist mayor, to present them with a new standard. Citing her age and infirmity, Powel declined, but she did send them a standard, which she begged they would accept "as Evidence of her confidence in their valor and Patriotism." Powel and her family were entrenched within Philadelphia's Federalist leadership and was thus a very appropriate choice for the Federalist militia company.[64] Zilpah Wadsworth of Portland, Maine, presented a flag to the Federal Volunteers of Portland in 1799.[65] Wadsworth wrote of the "innumerable" number of spectators present, in addition to the group of young women who joined with her in presenting the flag. She had been somewhat reluctant about playing such a public role, fearing that newspapers would record the event, handing her name about "so publicly." Although this demonstrates that not all women were eager to participate in the public political sphere, it also illustrates how well women understood the public nature of women's partisan performances.[66]

During most of these militia presentations, groups of women were represented by one of their number who spoke to the assembled militiamen. Zilpah Wadsworth, for example, spoke for the "young ladies of Portland," while in Philadelphia Mrs. Joseph Hopkinson, wife of a Federalist congressman, spoke and presented an emblematical painting to MacPherson's Blues on behalf of the city's Federalist women.[67] The rhetoric of such presentations always emphasized American women's patriotism, drawing attention to their desire, like that of a Roman matron, to encourage the troops. As Mrs. Abigail Lyon claimed in her presentation to the Worcester, Massachusetts, Volunteer Cadet Infantry company, "While the delicacy of our sex excludes us with propriety from the cabinet or field, permit me to observe, that our influence in the domestic department is great. While the tear of distress awakens the tender feeling of sympathy in the breast of sensibility, the fortitude of a Roman Matron inspires true courage, and urges on to glory. Suffer me, then, to address you in the style of Spartan virtue." She reminded the men that the "defenseless sex, recline [upon you] for safety and protection."[68] On this occasion in Worcester, the newspaper noted that "a number of ladies together with a number of Misses from ten to fourteen years of age, uniformly dressed in white frocks and blue sashes, were marshaled before the house at the delivery of the standard." By carefully coordinating their physical appearance, these women publicly emphasized their united stance, just as other women had demonstrated their shared support for revolutionary France.

Militia presentations also included songs and toasts. On one occasion, after delivering the militia colors, men and women together sang the Federalist song "Adams and Liberty." They then gave several appropriate toasts. One Federalist newspaper claimed with satisfaction that the female breast, "swells with just resentment at the recent insults offered to our country, and glows with patriotic ardor to aid in repelling every hostile attempt of its enemies. What more liberal encouragement can the cause of Columbia have, than the sanction of her fair daughters. Even they are roused to expressions of political sentiment, which bear the plausible stamp of Federalism."[69]

The rhetoric of the presentation speeches also embodied the sentiments of republican motherhood. Like Mrs. Lyon, many women spoke of "Spartan virtue," claiming for themselves "the fortitude of a Roman Matron" that would "inspire true courage" in their men. In turn, the militia commanders accepted the standards as emblems of "female patriotism and independence."[70]

Militia presentations were innovative in a number of ways. Women were the leaders of these occasions, with men following behind or acting in concert. Thus, men and women frequently drank toasts *together* after the ceremonies. Although framed in opposition to earlier celebrations of the French Revolution, these presentations were equally significant in helping women attain a share of public political space. Women were no longer restricted to expressing their politics in their homes, gazing from windows and balconies, gracing male proceedings "with their smiles." In a more active role, they had assisted at male-directed Republican ceremonies, such as Philadelphia's "Feast of Reason," and then in the militia presentations.[71]

In addition to taking part in militia presentations, women played a role in reenergized celebrations of Independence Day. As tensions grew between the United States and France over ship seizures, Federalists regained control over some of the nation's July Fourth festivities.[72] In what seems to have been an instance of particularly strong female political assertion, one group of women in Middletown, Connecticut, drank toasts to liberty, freedom, Mrs. Adams, Mrs. Washington, and, finally, to "The daughters of America—May their applausive smiles reward the patriotic youth who step forward in defense of their country, and their frowns appall the traitor or coward who dares to betray or desert it." These women were then joined by a group of men, and then, after more toasting, the two eldest women present led the entire group in a procession "through the principal street, to a liberty tree."[73]

While illustrating innovative female public behavior, Federalist festivities of the late 1790s retained elements of older ceremonies. The Liberty Tree, for example, harkened back to the American Revolution, and Federalist women recreated a political role that women had played during the War of Independence. In the 1770s, women had encouraged men to remain true to the Patriot cause, and they had publicly shamed those they identified as traitors. Federalist women adopted a similar stance in 1798. As the Connecticut women expressed it, "when the Fair exhibit such a spirit in their country's cause, who that is not a recreant, but would blush, to remain inactive."[74] The public circumstances of such events conducted by women (with men participating under female direction) added a new, gendered element to American political culture. The ceremonies and parades of the 1790s were "public dramas of social relations." As such, these occasions illustrate the conditions under which women entered public political space.[75]

The partisan nature and significance of women's participation in popular politics throughout the 1790s was confirmed by the tone of newspaper accounts of such events. Newspaper editors offered partisan reports of women's activities, supporting or attacking female participation, not in and of itself but according to its political content and their own partisan allegiances.[76] However, whether supported or attacked by male editors, American women performed an important political function, for they offered the possibility of a heightened degree of civic and social harmony for whichever party they supported.[77] Women's public presence helped assert competing notions of national identity: women were welcomed into public political space by one party when they were required to reinforce the position and principles of that party over its opponents. As a result, partisan opponents criticized women for their public political activities.

The result was a high degree of fluidity within the public political sphere, a fluidity that required female participation while simultaneously affording these women a public political role and an increased degree of agency. However, female political participation remained bounded by traditional notions of gender. Though innovative in terms of *what* women did, the reasons for such action can still be explained by the republican conception of the relationship between family and the state. What had been true during the American Revolution remained true in the 1790s: a republican ideology lay at the root of female political participation. Women's activism was possible because "eighteenth-century thought located family and state on a single continuum of society, rather than separating them into public and private realms." This ideology gave women "a peculiar popular access to public time that nineteenth-century citizenship would not encompass and that liberalism would reformulate and, in some instances, actively counter."[78]

By 1801, the resolution of the diplomatic crisis with France removed the French Revolution from the arena of popular political culture in America. Americans took note of Napoleon's rise, his foreign policies, and his eventual downfall, together with the larger situation in France and the rest of Europe. But France no longer occasioned public ceremonies and displays of women's political support in the United States, and the era of American public responses to France lasted less than a decade. During these years, however, as readers, spectators, and participants, American women first tested the boundaries of republican motherhood, and the very existence of separate spheres. They did so by recreating roles from the American Revolution, but also through the invention of new female-focused political rituals based on or in reaction against the French Revolution.

The public presence of women was one of the defining features of popular politics during the 1790s, setting women on a series of paths leading toward greater economic and political autonomy in the century ahead. Historians interested in the development and expansion of women's public role in nineteenth-century America would do well to look to the foundations established in the 1790s, for it was during these years that American women began developing a collective identity that led to early nineteenth-century female organizations and further female political activities. Early nineteenth-century benevolent organizations, such as the Orphan Asylum Society New York (1806), provided women with institutional legitimacy in the public sphere. Taking their cue from the Ladies' Association in 1780, nineteenth-century women created permanent organizations, with "uniquely female" mandates that encouraged the transformation of private female activities into public, and often political, roles. Moreover, there were direct political legacies from the eighteenth century. Women's participation in electioneering and party events such as public processions, the presentation of standards, picnics, and balls during the Whig campaign of 1840 were all grounded in the precedents established in the female popular politics of the 1790s.[79]

Notes

1. Recent political histories that all but ignore women include James Roger Sharp, *American Politics in the Early Republic: The New Nation in Crisis* (New Haven: Yale University Press, 1993); Stanley M. Elkins and Eric L. McKitrick, *The Age of Federalism: The Early American Republic* (New York: Oxford University Press, 1993); and Gordon S. Wood, *The Radicalism of the American Revolution* (New York: Alfred A. Knopf, 1992).

2. The major work on republican motherhood remains Linda K. Kerber, *Women of the Republic: Intellect and Ideology in Revolutionary America* (Chapel Hill: University of North Carolina Press, 1980).

3. For further discussion of French revolutionary festivals, see Simon P. Newman, *Parades and the Politics of the Street: Festive Culture in the Early American Republic* (Philadelphia: University of Pennsylvania Press, 1997), 120–51.

4. Details of the foreign policy issues directly affecting relations with France and Britain are lucidly presented in James Sharp, *American Politics in the Early Republic: The New Nation in Crisis* (New Haven: Yale University Press, 1993), and in Stanley Elkins and Eric McKitrick, *The Age of Federalism: The Early American Republic, 1788–1800* (New York: Oxford University Press, 1993), 303–75. For Philadelphia in particular, see Albrecht Koschnik, "Political Conflict and Public Contest: Rituals of National Celebration in Philadelphia, 1788–1815," *Journal of the Early Republic* 68 (July 1994), 209–48.

5. For details on the difficulties of the United States with both France and Britain in the 1790s, see Jerald A. Combs, *The Jay Treaty: Political Battleground of the Founding Fathers* (Berkeley and Los Angeles: University of California Press, 1970); and Alexander DeConde, *Entangling Alliance: Politics and Diplomacy Under George Washington* (Durham, N.C.: Duke University Press, 1958).

6. "Civic Festival," *Gazette of the United States* (Philadelphia), May 3, 1794; "*Civic Ball—*At Portsmouth," *Massachusetts Mercury* (Boston), February 5, 1793; "Civic Feast at Harris's Hotel," *Columbian Herald* (Charleston), March 19, 1794.

7. Jürgen Habermas, "The Public Sphere: An Encyclopedia Article (1964)," *New German Critique* 5, no. 2 (1974), 49–55.

8. Craig Calhoun, introduction to *Habermas and the Public Sphere* (Cambridge, Mass.: MIT Press, 1992), 13; Jürgen Habermas, *The Transformation of the Public Sphere*, trans. T. Burger and F. Lawrence (Cambridge, Mass.: MIT Press, 1989), 37.

9. Barbara Welter first described this new definition of gender roles, which developed in the early nineteenth century, know as separate spheres ideology, in "The Cult of True Womanhood, 1820–1860," *American Quarterly* 18, pt. 2 (1966), 151–74. See also Nancy F. Cott, *The Bonds of Womanhood: "Woman's Sphere" in New England, 1780–1835* (New Haven: Yale University Press, 1977). For recent thoughts on how historians should move beyond this conceptual framework, see Linda Kerber et al., "Beyond Roles, Beyond Spheres: Thinking About Gender in the Early Republic," *William & Mary Quarterly* 3 (July 1989), 565–85.

10. Nancy Fraser, "Rethinking the Public Sphere: A Contribution to the Critique of Actually Existing Democracy," in Calhoun, ed., *Habermas and the Public Sphere*, 116.

11. The most comprehensive study of American reactions to the French Revolution remains Charles Downer Hazen, *Contemporary American Opinion of the French Revolution* (Baltimore: Johns Hopkins University Press, 1897).

12. These newspapers reached many Americans: in 1790 there were more than one hundred newspapers serving a population of some four million. By 1800 the number of newspapers had more than doubled, giving the United States the highest ratio of newspapers to population of any nation on earth. James D. Tagg, *Benjamin Franklin Bache and the Philadelphia Aurora*

(Philadelphia: University of Pennsylvania Press, 1991), 90–97; Donald H. Stewart, *The Opposition Press of the Federalist Period* (Albany: State University of New York Press, 1969), 16; Beatrice F. Hyslop, "American Press Reports of the French Revolution, 1789–94," *New York Historical Society Quarterly Bulletin* 42 (October 1958), 329–48; and "The American Press and the French Revolution of 1789," *Proceedings of the American Philosophical Society* 104, no. 1 (1960), 54–85; Kurt Beerman, "The Reception of the French Revolution in the New York State Press, 1788–1791" (Ph.D. diss., New York University, 1960); Huntley Dupre, "The Kentucky Gazette Reports the French Revolution," *Mississippi Valley Historical Review* 26 (September 1939), 163–80.

13. Darline G. Levy and Harriet B. Applewhite, "Women, Radicalization, and the Fall of the French Monarchy," in Harriet Branson Applewhite and Darline G. Levy, eds., *Women and Politics in the Age of the Democratic Revolution* (Ann Arbor: University of Michigan Press, 1990), 90.

14. "Glorious and Interesting Advices," *The Carlisle Gazette and the Western Repository of Knowledge* (Carlisle), December 19, 1792; "Civic Feast," *Massachusetts Mercury* (Boston), January 17, 1793.

15. "French Revolution," *General Advertiser. Aurora* (Philadelphia), July 7, 1792; "New-London, April 27, 1795," *Gazette of the United States* (Philadelphia), June 4, 1795; "Patriots!!!" *Columbian Herald; or The Independent Courier of North-America* (Charleston), August 27, 1793.

16. "Boston, Monday, January 14," January 14, 1793. One Bostonian noted that rank "is abolished by the title of Citizens" and hoped that "a numerous collection" would assemble for "this republican entertainment." See "Civic Feast," *Massachusetts Mercury*, January 17, 1793.

17. "Civic Feast," *Massachusetts Mercury*, January 17, 1793.

18. For discussions of women's presence, participation, and wearing of cockades, see "Civic Festivals," *Columbian Centinel*, January 30, 1793; "Celebration of the Feast of Liberty and Equality," *The Independent Chronicle*, January 31, 1793. In 1790 the Boston population totaled 18,038, which included 7,701 males and 9,576 females. See *Return of the Whole Number of Persons*. For more on this subject, see Kulikoff, "The Progress of Inequality." Alfred F. Young has explored the role of Boston women in America's revolutionary struggle in "The Women of Boston: 'Persons of Consequence' in the Making of the American Revolution, 1765–76," in Harriet B. Applewhite and Darline G. Levy, eds., *Women and Politics in the Age of the Democratic Revolution* (Ann Arbor: University of Michigan Press, 1990), 181–226.

19. "Civic Festivals," *Columbian Centinel*, January 30, 1793.

20. *Pittsburgh Gazette*, February 23, 1793.

21. John Adams to Abigail Adams, Philadelphia, January 31, 1793, *Letters of John Adams, Addressed to His Wife*, 2:123.

22. "On the Meeting of the *Citizens of Boston* round the *Liberty-Stump* in the late Procession," *Connecticut Courant*, February 11, 1793.

23. "Extract of a letter from a gentleman in Connecticut, to his friend in this town," *Pittsburgh Gazette*, March 30, 1793.

24. Citess, *Columbian Centinel*, March 16, 1793. The practice of using "citess" was surprisingly widespread; see Susan Branson, " 'Fiery Frenchified Dames': American Women and the French Revolution," unpublished paper delivered at the annual meeting of the American Historical Association, 1991. Men's practice of labeling women who ventured too far out into the male-dominated public sphere has a long history. See Glenna Matthews, *The Rise of Public Woman: Woman's Power and Woman's Place in the United States, 1630–1970* (New York: Oxford University Press, 1992), 3–8. Perhaps the most famous case occurred in May 1862, when Major General Benjamin Butler used the same tactic of branding oppositional women as prostitutes in his infamous General Order Number 28. See Mary P. Ryan, *Women in Public: Between Banners and Ballots, 1825–1880* (Baltimore: Johns Hopkins University Press, 1990), 2–4, 130–32.

25. "Celebration of the Feast of Liberty and Equality," *Independent Chronicle,* January 31, 1793.

26. "Rights of Women," *New-York Journal,* May 1, 1793.

27. "Civic Ball—at Portsmouth," *Massachusetts Mercury,* February 5, 1793.

28. *City Gazette & Daily Advertiser* (Charleston, S.C.), July 20 1793. Our thanks to Robert Alderson for sharing this remarkable source with us. His dissertation, " 'This Bright Era of Happy Revolutions:' M.-A.-B. de Mangourit in Charleston, S.C., 1792–1794," University of Georgia, forthcoming, details the experiences of the French refugees in that city.

29. *City Gazette,* July 20, 1793.

30. *National Gazette,* December 26, 1792. See also John F. Watson, *Annals of Philadelphia, and Pennsylvania, in the Olden Time,* ed. Willis P. Hazard (Philadelphia, 1884), 1:179–80.

31. The inclusion of young girls in public ceremonies and festivities invites us to reevaluate the boundaries of female political activism in this era. These examples of public politics give sharper definition to the concept of civic virtue as it was prescribed for women in postrevolutionary America.

32. This occasion was reminiscent of public punishments during the American Revolution, where women did their share of pelting or jeering at the target of their anger. In the 1790s, women continued to demonstrate their political opinion in the street. Young, "The Women of Boston," 192.

33. John R. Elting, ed., *Military Uniforms in America: The Era of the American Revolution, 1755–1795* (San Rafael, Calif.: Presidio Press, 1974), 70–98; Minor Myers Jr., *Liberty Without Anarchy: A History of the Society of the Cincinnati* (Charlottesville: University of Virginia Press, 1983), 33–34.

34. "Paris, July 30," *Gazette US,* September 26, 1789.

35. See, for example, *Boston Gazette,* October 19 and December 7, 1789; *Gazette US* December 12, 1789; *Virginia Gazette or Advertiser,* September 14, 1791; *Massachusetts Mercury,* July 27, 1798. For a discussion of cockades in Revolutionary France, see Aileen Ribeiro, *Fashion in the French Revolution* (New York: Holmes & Meier, 1988), 53–56.

36. Henry Wansey, *Henry Wansey and His American Journal, 1794,* ed. David John Jeremy (Philadelphia: American Philosophical Society, 1970), 175, 76; John F. Watson, *Annals of Philadelphia, and Pennsylvania, in the Olden Time,* ed. Willis P. Hazard (Philadelphia, 1884), 2:179–80; Charles Fraser, *Reminiscences of Charleston, Lately Published in the Charleston Courier, and Now Revised and Enlarged by the Author* (Charleston, 1854), 39; *Massachusetts Mercury,* February 5, 1793. See also John W. Francis, *Old New York; or Reminiscences of the Past Sixty Years* (New York, 1866), 115–16; Theophile Cazenove, *Cazenove Journal 1794: A Record of the Journey of Theophile Cazenove Through New Jersey and Pennsylvania,* ed. Rayner Wickersham Kelsey, Haverford College Studies 13 (Haverford: Pennsylvania History Press, 1922), 10; Watson, *Annals of Philadelphia,* 2:179.

37. "Paris, July 3," *Virginia Gazette or Advertiser,* September 14, 1791.

38. C., Letter to the Editor, *Aurora,* January 20, 1791. For more on the political culture of women's literary salons and networks, see Susan Stabile, " 'By a Female Hand': Letters, Belles Lettres, and the Philadelphian Culture of Performance, 1760–1820" (Ph.D. diss., University of Delaware, 1996).

39. *Massachusetts Mercury,* February 5, 1793.

40. Watson, *Annals of Philadelphia,* 1:179–80.

41. "English Flag," *Porcupine's Gazette,* May 3, 1798.

42. For further discussion of the politics of seafaring patriotism in the early republic, see Simon P. Newman, "Eagles, Hearts, and Crucifixes: The *Mentalités* of Philadelphia Seafarers in the New Republic," paper presented at the Philadelphia Center for Early American Studies, January 1994.

43. "Birth-Day of the French Republic," *Aurora,* August 1, 1794.

44. "Arrangements for the Festival of the 10th of August which is to be celebrated on Monday 11th instant," *Aurora,* August 9, 1794.

45. *Aurora,* August 28, 1794.

46. "Arrangements for the festival of the 10th of August which is to be celebrated on Monday 11th instant," *Aurora,* August 9, 1794.

47. *Aurora,* August 28, 1794.

48. Ibid.

49. Ibid.

50. *National Gazette,* Wednesday, December 26, 1792.

51. John W. Francis, *Old New York,* 115–16; Alexander Anderson, Diary, 1793–99, Manuscripts Copy, from Manuscript Original in Library of Columbia College, NYHS.

52. John F. Watson, *Annals of Philadelphia,* 1:179–80.

53. "Ode on the Revolution of France," *Gazette of the United States,* October 1,1794. This article reported that Mrs. Marriot's "Ode" was performed by her spouse "at the Old American Theatre" in Philadelphia. "Rights of Woman," *Weekly Museum,* April 25, 1795; see also "Rights of Woman," *Philadelphia Minerva,* October 17, 1795. The song was most recently performed by a group of early American historians in 1991, in the library of the American Philosophical Society.

54. Laura Mason, " 'Ça Ira' and the Birth of the Revolutionary Song," *History Workshop: A Journal of Socialist and Feminist Historians* 28 (Fall–Winter 1989), 22–38.

55. Porcupine, *A Bone to Gnaw,* 50–51.

56. Details of the foreign policy issues directly affecting relations with France and Britain are lucidly presented in James Sharp, *American Politics in the Early Republic: The New Nation in Crisis* (New Haven: Yale University Press, 1993), and in Stanley Elkins and Eric McKitrick, *The Age of Federalism: The Early American Republic, 1788–1800* (New York: Oxford University Press, 1993), 303–75. For Philadelphia in particular, see Koschnik, "Political Conflict and Public Contest."

57. For details on the difficulties of the United States with both France and Britain in the 1790s, see Jerald A. Combs, *The Jay Treaty: Political Battleground of the Founding Fathers* (Berkeley and Los Angeles: University of California Press, 1970); Alexander DeConde, *Entangling Alliance: Politics and Diplomacy Under George Washington* (Durham, N.C.: Duke University Press, 1958).

58. Newspapers noted the dangers of women associating with Democrats and French men. Edward G. Everette, "Some Aspects of Pro-French Sentiment in Pennsylvania, 1790–1800," *Western Pennsylvania Historical Magazine* 43 (1960), 25 n. 8.

59. *Porcupine's Gazette,* October 22, 1798. Now Federalists feared a wild Jacobin joining the Irishman under every bed. For a discussion of the anti-French attitudes prevailing in late 1790s the following are useful: Alexander De Conde, *The Quasi-War: The Politics and Diplomacy of the Undeclared War with France, 1797–1801* (New York: Charles Scribner's Sons, 1966); Newman, *Parades and the Politics of the Street,* chap. 7.

60. Mary Ridgely to Henry M. Ridgely, Philadelphia April 27, 1798. Mabel L. Ridgely, ed., *Ridgelys of Delaware and Their Circle: What Them Befell in Colonial and Federal Times: Letters 1751–1890* (Portland, Me.: Privately printed, 1949), 118.

61. Elizabeth Hewson to Thomas Hewson, Bellemeade, June 5, 1797. Microfilm 103, frame 65, American Philosophical Society.

62. Alfred F. Young, "The Women of Boston: 'Persons of Consequence' in the Making of the American Revolution, 1765–76," in Harriet Branson Applewhite and Darline G. Levy, eds., *Women and Politics in the Age of the Democratic Revolution* (Ann Arbor: University of Michigan Press, 1990), 203.

63. Across the Atlantic, where a French invasion was a more realistic possibility than in the

United States, British women participated in similar militia presentations. When war broke out between France and Britain in 1793, women began sewing and presenting flags and banners to the troops. They also organized collection drives for money and clothing reminiscent of those conducted by American women in the 1770s. There were at least ninety presentations in Britain between 1798 and 1800. Linda Colley, *Britons: Forging the Nation, 1707–1837* (New Haven: Yale University Press, 1992), 260.

There is some precedent for these female militia presentations from the early eighteenth century and the American Revolution. The *Pennsylvania Gazette* reported a presentation on January 12, 1748. Ellet mentions only one Revolution case: "The wife of Col. Barnard Elliott presented to the second regiment, . . . a pair of richly embroidered colors, wrought by herself. They were planted, three years afterwards, on the British lines at Savannah, by Sergeant Jasper, who in planting them received his death wound." Elizabeth F. Ellet, *Domestic History of the American Revolution* (New York, 1850), 45. A few other instances are discussed in Edward W. Richardson, *Standards and Colors of the American Revolution* (Philadelphia: University of Pennsylvania Press, 1982). What stands out in the 1790s presentations is the publicity accorded the events, and especially the quite extensive transcriptions of the women's speeches on these occasions. Laurel Thatcher Ulrich describes Maine female presenters between 1799 and 1805 in " 'From the Fair to the Brave': Spheres of Womanhood in Federal Maine," in Laura Fecych Sprague, ed., *Agreeable Situations: Society, Commerce, and Art in Southern Maine, 1780–1830* (Kennebunk, Me.: Brick Store Museum), 215–25.

64. Elizabeth Powel to Captain Dunlap, March 16, 1797. Powel Collection, Elizabeth Powel Papers, Outgoing Correspondence, Box 1, folder 2, 1788–99. See Richardson, *Standards and Colors of the American Revolution*, 177, 240, 321–22.

65. Quoted in Ulrich, " 'From the Fair to the Brave,' " 223.

66. Ibid.

67. *Philadelphia Gazette*, July 9, 1798: an "offering to Patriotism." Emily Mifflin Hopkinson (1773–1856) married Federalist Congressman Joseph Hopkinson (1770–1842) in 1794. For another examples of these presentations, see *Country Porcupine*, October 23 and 24, 1798. The Federalists' appropriation of Fourth of July festivals in 1798 is discussed in Newman, *Parades and the Politics of the Street*, chap. 4; and in Len Travers, *Celebrating the Fourth: Independence Day and the Rites of Nationalism in the Early Republic* (Amherst: University of Massachusetts Press, 1997), chap. 5.

68. *Country Porcupine*, October 23 and 24, 1798, reporting Mrs. Abigail Lyon's presentation to the Worcester Volunteer Cadet Infantry Company.

69. Ibid. Linda Kerber has remarked that the Republican newspapers of the decade were receptive to women in politics, while the Federalist press was not. This was clearly not the case in 1798. See *Women of the Republic*, 279.

70. *Country Porcupine*, October 23 and 24, 1798.

71. For a discussion of the redefinition of political space, see Mona Ozouf, *Festivals and the French Revolution*, trans. Alan Sheridan (Boston: Harvard University Press, 1988), chap. 6.

72. Newman, *Parades and the Politics of the Street*, chap. 5; and Travers, *Celebrating the Fourth*, chap. 4.

73. "Female Toasting," *Porcupine's Gazette*, July 14, 1798. Travers, *Celebrating the Fourth*, 135–41, discusses women's participation in July Fourth celebrations.

74. Young, "The Women of Boston: 'Persons of Consequence' in the Making of the American Revolution, 1765–76," 192; *Porcupine's Gazette*, July 14, 1798.

75. Susan G. Davis, *Parades and Power: Street Theater in Nineteenth-Century Philadelphia* (Philadelphia: Temple University Press, 1986), 6; Dominique Godineau, "Masculine and Feminine Political Practice During the French Revolution, 1793–Year III," 73–75; Joan Wallach Scott, "French Feminists and the Rights of 'Man': Olympe de Gouges's Declarations," *History Work-*

shop Journal 28 (Fall–Winter 1989), 1–21; Lenora Cohen Rosenfield, "The Rights of Women in the French Revolution," *Studies in Eighteenth-Century Culture* 7 (1976), 117–37; Jane Abray, "Feminism in the French Revolution," *American Historical Review* 80, no. 1 (February 1975), 43–62.

76. Koschnik, "Political Conflict and Public Contest," 231.

77. David I. Kertzer, *Ritual, Politics, and Power* (New Haven: Yale University Press, 1988), 12.

78. Barbara Clark Smith, "Food Rioters and the American Revolution," *William & Mary Quarterly* 51 (January 1994), 30.

79. Ronald J. Zboray and Mary Saracino Zboray, "Whig Women, Politics, and Culture in the Campaign of 1840: Three Perspectives from Massachusetts," *Journal of the Early Republic* 17, no. 2 (Summer 1997), 278–315; Elizabeth R. Varon, "Tippecanoe and the Ladies Too: White Women and Party Politics in Antebellum Virginia," *Journal of American History* 82 (September 1995), 494–521.

11

African American Festive Style and the Creation of American Culture

William D. Piersen

African Americans across North America took advantage of whatever antebellum holidays were open to them to celebrate their own communal awareness. The diversity of occasions did not inhibit celebrations by blacks, because it was easier for arrivals from hundreds of separate African nationalities to create new American festivals mixing a variety of African and European-American elements than to maintain more specialized, and far narrower, Old World holidays. These new festival traditions were not imitative or flawed copies of European-style holidays, but purposefully African American and multicultural constructions. In fact, the similarities among black celebrations across the Americas suggest that the generalized aesthetic of African cultural expression was as important in shaping these celebrations as the particular Euro-American occasions that served as their pretexts.

The major slave festivals in what is now the United States were Negro Election Day in New England, Pinkster in New York and New Jersey, Jon Koonering[1] in southern Virginia and North Carolina, corn huskings almost everywhere, and Christmas Day throughout the South. There were also various local black festivities in most urban areas, notably in New Orleans, Mobile, and Philadelphia. Because all these celebrations took place in tandem with white regional holidays, historians have typically emphasized the connection between black and Euro-American occasions. Unfortunately, however, such cultural and geographical parochialism obscures more interesting and important connections among African American holidays throughout the hemisphere. Indeed, analyzing African American festivals with a lens focused on European and Euro-American political boundaries exaggerates local variations and hides the extensive interrelationship of all African American life. Thus, while all major black celebrations were framed within particular Euro-American holidays, black styles of revelry nonetheless soon became dominant in each region, whatever the original holiday traditions of each area's white population.

Why did nominally ascendant forms of Euro-American holidays so quickly give way before African American styles of celebration? To what degree did these African-influenced festive styles shape later holiday traditions of whites? What do the differences between African American and Euro-American styles of celebrations suggest about the interrelationship between the individual and the community in both black and white America? How do the early festive traditions of both groups shape our understanding of their cultures? To answer these questions, it is best to start by examining some specifics of the black festive style.

Musical parading activities strutted to the center of most antebellum African American festive occasions. While whites commonly interpreted such raucous processions as being black imitations of more dignified Euro-American political or mumming activities, so many features of the African American parades occur throughout the Americas that their similarities argue far more strongly for an African essence.[2]

African American parades typically featured boisterous, improvised music and back-and-forth interaction between male and female spectators and parade performers. Neither feature was typical of white parades or processions of the era, but both prevailed in black rites in West Africa and the Caribbean. Certainly, the "showy" Negro Election parades of eighteenth-century New England, to take one example, did not try to approximate the region's Euro-American regard for ordered uniformity. Typically, a group of slave musicians dressed in "somewhat fantastic" unmatched articles of clothing escorted the region's black kings and governors. Sometimes parade participants were even more outlandishly bedecked with ribbons and feathers. The musicians carried whatever assortment of banjos, brass horns, tambourines, drums, fifes, fiddles, clarinets, and "sonorous metals" they could find to serenade the accompanying crowd of revelers.[3]

In early New England, the features that distinguished black processions escorting black governors and kings from parallel white escorts for the region's incumbent white governors were the random firing of salutes, the raucous style of music, and the playfulness of the black paraders. It is interesting that the region's African Americans developed the first American inaugural parades. The compromise with solemnity that followed in their wake came to mark the American political parades of whites.[4]

In New England as elsewhere in the Americas and West Africa, observers noted a preference of blacks for the noisy and random firing of holiday gunpowder salutes. According to Philip Fithian's journal entry of December 24, 1773, in Westmoreland County, Virginia, "Guns are fired this Evening in the Neighborhood and the Negroes seem to be inspired with new life."[5] Firing weapons around Christmas continued in the South and eventually expanded northward.[6] The cracks of gunfire that punctuated New England Election Day parades were also heard during the Christmas festivals in the Bahamas and Jamaica.[7] By the middle of the nineteenth century, fireworks had become an emblem of most West Indian Christmas celebrations.[8]

African American processions in the South marking other holidays nonetheless displayed a parade style much like New England's. In the Jon Koonering masking celebrations of the eighteenth century, for example, about a half-dozen secondary performers typically followed in the train of the principal actors. Much like some of the New England musicians of the same era, these celebrators were described as "arrayed fantastically in ribbons, rags, and feathers, and bearing between them several so-called musical instruments." The makeshift Jonkonnu bands were followed by noisy, cheering crowds of black spectators of all ages who constantly interacted with the processions as they moved from house to house.[9]

It was reported in Edenton, North Carolina, in 1824 that the "John Canno" festival was "a sport common in this part of the state with slaves on Holy-days," with blacks "serenading and exhibiting" until late at night on Christmas Eve.[10] Similar Jonkonnu traditions were also widespread in the West Indies. The accompanying forms of the pageant had antecedents throughout West Africa.[11]

Activities similar to those normally associated with "Jon Koonering" also appeared, but without the principal African-style maskers, in eighteenth-century funeral "plays" and the nineteenth-century Christmas activities on southern plantations. As James Murray reported from Cape Fear, North Carolina, in 1755, "all the Negroes . . . are at a great loss this Christmas for want of a death to play for."[12] Large groups of blacks attended African American funeral rites, parts of which they treated as festive occasions, or "plays," in honor of the deceased's triumphal entry into the world of ancestral spirits. The Jonkonnu rites that have been associated with ancestral maskers typical of West African secret societies may therefore be only specific forms of an already ongoing and widely diffused institution.[13]

Black festivals or "plays" required both free time and an excuse for merrymaking. New England's Election Day provided this; in the South it was often funerals or Christmas holidays.[14] But the activities were much the same. Consider the street dancing, so similar to Jon Koonering, that appeared in New Orleans in the 1820s. Timothy Flint reported that slaves there were given the liberty to "dance through the streets" as "merry Bachanaliars" whose antics "convulsed even the masters of the negroes with laughter." At these events the central character, whom Flint called a "king," wore "a series of oblong, gilt-paper boxes on his head, tapering upwards, like a pyramid," from which hung two huge tassels. These parades strongly suggest the Jonkonnu ceremonies of the West Indies in the style of the masks, the role of a festive "king," and the associated humorous processional activities.[15] All the characters that followed the performers were said to have "their own peculiar dress, and their contortions. They dance, and their streamers fly, and the bells that they have hung about them tinkle."[16]

Jonkonnu-like processions, such as those that wandered the streets of New Orleans, were also probably far more common during the Christmas holidays in the South than we have previously thought. Consider the black parade observed in Saint Mary's, Georgia, on December 27, 1843, which incorporated aspects of Election Day, Pinkster, Jon Koonering, and the Mardi Gras of Mobile, Alabama. The blacks paraded during the last day of their feast "with a corps of staff officers with red sashes, mock epaulets & goose quill feathers, and a band of music." They were followed by others, "some dancing, some walking & some hopping, others singing, all as lively as lively can be." With "music enough to deafen" observers, the black merrymakers went about "levying small contributions on all the whites," who in turn appeared as maskers in their own right on the next day.[17]

Similarly, the first so-called "Mardi Gras" activities in Mobile among whites took place in 1830 on Christmas Eve. The drunken Michael Krafft appeared in Jonkonnu-like garb and was followed on New Year's Day by fifty "Cowbellion de Rakin' " maskers who made up "as weird as they could." These white maskers who boisterously roamed the streets, shouting and singing and making a rowdy spectacle, stopped to serenade at the houses of certain important citizens, who furnished them with liquid refreshment just like so many Jon Kooners. It seems unnecessary to search far afield for white sources for these events in unrecorded Celtic Southern mumming or obscure Nova Scotian or Pennsylvania German masking when so many similar African American processions were to be found along the Gulf Coast and the nearby Caribbean.[18]

In early New York, where Pinkster became the holiday of choice, African American style again quickly asserted itself. In Albany, "a motley group of thousands" was said to have followed the local black "king" as he and his attendants wandered the streets "calling at one door after another and demand[ed] tribute, which demand he enforce[d] by . . . a horrid noise and frightful grimaces."[19] This ceremony recognizing local authorities has often been interpreted in the Jonkonnu festival as an imitation of European-style mumming, but we have few, if any, examples of white English or Celtic-style mumming groups "queting" (begging for small gifts) throughout the Americas. On the other hand, there were African American examples (including the grimaces). It seems more reasonable to connect the house-to-house "queting" for gifts and liquor featured at Pinkster in Mobile, on the North Carolina coast, and in the Caribbean, to West African holiday traditions. Kenneth Little describes one: "[A] spirit, escorted by a number of attendants and followers, usually visits every big man in town and squats in various grotesque poses in front of his house. It then proceeds to parade about the town attracting spectators and causing amusement wherever it goes. Bystanders with a position of social standing to maintain hand over a 'dash' of money to the spirit's followers."[20]

Similar "dashing" or "queting" traditions were found across West Africa and were also ubiquitous in the West Indies at Christmas time. It should thus not be surprising that they appeared in a less exotic guise, without the central masker, in the "Christmas gift" activities of the southern United States. What looked to southern whites like a simple feudal homage of peasants and slaves to masters, or an African form of wassailing, was in reality for the blacks a syncretized African-style custom that cut two ways. It alternated apparent praise of important white folk who gave generously with veiled social criticism of those who did not.

Crucial to the humor of the African American celebrations was the role of black spectators who both observed and participated. In 1829, Edward

Warren recorded just such an audience-performer interchange between the two central characters in the Jon Koonering festivities in Washington County, North Carolina. A "motley crowd of all ages, dressed in their ordinary working clothes, which seemingly comes as a guard of honor to the performers," followed them.[21] When the central Jonkonnu masker improvised a song asking a white worthy for a gift, "the whole crowd joined in the chorus, shouting and clapping their hands in the wildest glee."[22]

This interaction between performer and audience is an essential part of African American festive style. We might call this the principle of the second line. In New Orleans, the term "second line" has traditionally referred to "the friends and neighbors who dance with the [black Mardi Gras Indians or funeral society bands] along the streets and sidewalks."[23] As trumpeter Bunk Johnson described those who followed the jazz funeral bands: "We would have a second line there that was most equivalent to King Rex parade—Mardi Gras Carnival parade. The police were unable to keep the second line back—all in the street, all on the sidewalks, in front of the band.... We'd have some immense crowds following. They would follow the funeral up to the cemetery just to get this ragtime music comin' back."[24]

Audience and performers also interacted when bands of African American musicians played for white militias in the antebellum South. As northern schoolteacher Emily Burke noted in her journal of life in 1840s Georgia, "this performance [of the black musicians] also calls out all the servants that can obtain permission to attend the training, and it is not a few of them that not only follow but go before the companies whenever they march. They are excessively fond of such scenes, and crowds of men, women, and children never fail of being present on all such occasions, some carrying their master's children on their heads and shoulders."[25]

Early reports of black parades in North America usually did not spell out clearly what was going on between performers and audience, but the probable style of interaction can be illuminated by reference to more detailed observations of African American dance. African American dancer Katherine Dunham observed a similar interactive exchange between a black audience and performers in Haiti. In 1937 she described the back-and-forth feedback: "[The crowd] may stop to watch the dance of competition, cheering the more agile and ridiculing the loser, or they may go into a frenzy of dancing alone or with random partners."[26] African American spectators never remained passive observers either in processional second lines or as members of the dance circle.[27]

Samuel Kinser offers a suggestive trope in his analysis of the dance structure of New Orleans Mardi Gras "Indians." He compares blacks' dance interaction with the musical improvisations and exchanges of jazz:

> Each performer when he gets the feeling takes a riff, struts, moves to the center and does his stuff. That will stimulate somebody else, they may play then together. But it's all done with a guiding rhythm. . . . A challenge is a break in the rhythm, making strong dance moves, getting the tambourines to follow your moves, stopping the rap of the other. . . . As the confrontation gathers, people who are standing around, letting their bodies move with the tambourines, start throwing up fists, flail their arms, open wide their bodies, go away and go back toward the conflict. . . . Challenge is talking about yourself, boasting. You talk 'till you're cut.[28]

Similarly, folklorist Roger Abrahams has pinpointed the uniqueness of the black style of audience/performer interaction in his detailed study of corn huskings in the American South. When whites began to imitate black dance styles they took up the competitive "showing off," but they failed to duplicate, or even appreciate, the important interactive role of the "second line": "Through this imitation, whites seized license to dance alone, each dancer simply responding to the rhythms of the music. This is a white interpretation of the 'apart-playing' of the slave ring play or dance, without adopting or recognizing the black convention in which the dancer at the center of these show-off occasions relied on the support of the circle of dancers."[29] To avoid being cut from the circle, black dancers had to win the active and interactive support of their audience and fight off the challenges of the competitors. Those who were best also forced changes in the beat of the music, for the musicians in black dance, as in black parades, responded to and interacted with both spectators and fellow performers.[30]

It is useful to compare Andrew Burnaby's description in the mid-1770s of a white but African American influenced Virginia jig, which he felt lacked the method and regularity of European dancing, with black examples. In the white imitation, "a gentleman and a lady stand up, and dance about the room, one of them retiring, the other pursuing, then perhaps meeting in an irregular manner. After some time, another lady gets up, and then the first lady must sit down, she being, as the term is, cut out; the second lady acts the same part which the first did, till somebody cuts her out. The gentlemen perform in the same manner."[31] Black dances of this type were both competitive and suggestive. Nicholas Cresswell reporting black dancing in Virginia at the same period put it this way: a "couple gets up and begins to dance a jig (to some Negro tune) others comes and cuts them out." The effect of these dances was "more like a Bacchanalian dance than one in polite company."[32]

More modern observers have stated these points more explicitly. In viewing a Trinidadian dance, Katherine Dunham observed: "The [dancers] would shuffle again, and spurred by remarks from the sidelines, the center couple would come closer and the emphasis would move from the feet well into the central torso, becoming unmistakably sexual in intention."[33] As Roger Abrahams explained in the context of ring play dancing: "Each player is encouraged to show off in some way, either through some kind of individualized dance step ('show me your motion'), or through strutting, teasing, flirting, and wiggling, with everyone else clapping, commenting, and joking in support. This is the point. For while the player is at the center he or she is never alone; rather there is constant commentary and support by the ring."[34]

African American festive audiences appreciated satirical takeoffs. For example, in many antebellum celebrations the central target for African American humor was the pretentiousness of the master class. The use of satire directed against people in power had long been traditional during holiday festivities in West African societies, where song lyrics in general targeted moral and ethical pretensions in whatever forms these unsociable qualities appeared. Such critical songs came to serve the same purpose in America as they had in Africa: to mobilize and affirm the ultimate authority of community values.[35]

Less formal occasions for lampooning members of local communities also used the same mechanism. African satire typically involved both physical humor and accompanying song lyrics. Consider the experiences of early nineteenth-century European visitors to West Africa: René Caillié and Thomas Edward Bowditch. The Mandingo, said Caillie, "ridiculed my gestures and my words, and went about the village mimicking me."[36] The Ashanti, bemoaned Bowditch, "used to entertain themselves with mimicking our common expressions and our actions, which they did inimitably."[37]

Throughout the Americas, as in Africa, whites quickly became the favorite targets for black humor.[38]

Such satiric entertainment appeared in the informal gatherings called plays[39] by the slaves, as well as on more formal festive occasions like corn huskings, elections, parades, and militia training. Typical of the satirical plays is the example noted by the *South Carolina Gazette* in 1772 where a local black entertainment was described as being opened "by men copying (or taking off) the manners of their masters, and the women their mistresses, and relating some highly curious anecdotes, to the inexpressible diversion of that company."[40]

Black militias that trained and paraded in the early nineteenth century also featured satirical performances. Pointed humor appeared as part of the New England Negro Election festivities. It was said that "masters did not interfere until the utmost verge of decency had been reached, good-naturedly submitting to the hard hits leveled against themselves, and possibly profiting a little by some shrewd allusion."[41] When black "Governor" Eben Tobias of Derby, Connecticut, drilled his escort, his troops responded to the command "Fire and fall off!" literally, sprawling comically to the ground.[42] English visitor James Boardman understood that the black militiamen wearing a set of motley uniforms to their Fifth of July parade, the day after white New Yorkers' Fourth of July festivities, were "a parody upon the shopkeeper colonels of the previous day."[43] William Cullen Bryant had noticed the same phenomenon in the South, where "from the dances [of the blacks] a transition was made to a mock military parade, a sort of burlesque of our militia trainings, in which the words of command and evolutions were extremely ludicrous."[44]

One of the aspects of African American festivities that most annoyed Euro-Americans was the indefatigable nature of the celebrations. This was as true at a funeral ("At a half past five I was dressed and out. The hymns of the Negroes, which had continued through the night, were still to be heard on all sides"[45]) as at a play ("The party at Pierce's continued their jollification until broad daylight, when I returned to my master's house, somewhat wearied with the loss of rest"[46]) and as at a formal holiday event ("The [Christmas Day] entertainment was kept up till nine or ten o'clock in the evening . . . [when the blacks] at last retired, apparently quite satisfied with their saturnalia, to dance the rest of the night at their own habitations"[47]).

Celebrations in West Africa ran far into the night, in part to avoid stultifying daytime heat in the tropics.[48] But white Americans whose cultural roots were adapted to cooler climes found such late celebrations too much for themselves. Similarly, the noise level of black festivities, customarily held outdoors in Africa, was excessive for Euro-American sensibilities.[49]

Scholars of early African American festivals, noting the humorous role reversals common in the holiday festivities, remind us that many European festivals also centered on symbolic representations of class differentiation, such as carnival, featuring lords of misrule, who reversed and parodied the class structure. African-centered performance styles also attacked social barriers, but in the cultural world of blacks the suppressed aggression was channeled into the interaction and shifting focus between the apparently dominant performers and the actually controlling, and often majority female, audience. This exchange was purposefully subversive to artificial distinctions of power and prestige.

Nevertheless, attempting to disentangle activities that were primarily African in inspiration from those that imitated European traditions is complicated. By now, the theory of E. Franklin Frazier and Richard Dorson that little African cultural influence survived the brutal filter of the slave trade seems way overstated.[50] Probably most scholars would feel more comfortable proposing that African American festive style resulted from cultural blending—to one degree or another—of both African and Euro-American traditions. Among current writers, Sterling Stuckey and Roger Abrahams lean, as I do, toward emphasizing African influence.[51] To one degree or another, Shane White, Samuel Kinser, and Genevieve Fabre remind us not to neglect European precedents.[52] Among the Africanists, Stuckey emphasizes the Yoruba heritage that shaped western Nigeria and nearby Dahomey. My own work gives as much attention to the lower Windward Coast and the festive traditions of the Senegambia as to Nigeria. For his part, Roger Abrahams prudently uses a more generalized West Africa as the source culture.

To demonstrate European influences on African American festive culture, Genevieve Fabre offers interesting and suggestive speculation as to the origins of Jonkonnu ceremonies found across the West Indies and on the North Carolina coast. Her Eurocentric ideas can serve as a case study of the difficulties of separating out the African and European components within a particular ceremony. Fabre is well aware that Jonkonnu existed in a multicultural setting. She concedes to the theories of earlier scholars that the feast bore the name of a resident of the Gold Coast, John Coony, and that it continued to memorialize him. But she also emphasizes that in North Carolina the festival was clearly associated with the European holidays of Christmas and New Year's. More important, the key rites were also European; the slaves, Fabre says, "appropriated the [English] mumming tradition of visiting wealthy houses, setting themselves on an equal footing with their masters and white neighbors, [and] demanding gifts as a just retribution, deriding in songs those not generous enough to accede to their requests." Fabre believes that "this reinterpretation of mumming, of the Roman Saturnalia custom of masters serving their slaves during the festival, and of the visiting and gift-giving rituals enabled the slaves to make statements of their condition as well as claims to greater social justice." For Fabre, the slaves' costuming was "in mock imitation of the European masquerading tradition, the rags reminiscent of jesters' garments," and the whip was "both a magical instrument, and, in mock imitation of the driver's lash, a tool to chastise and enforce order."[53]

Yet African American parades in colonial Cuba on the Day of Kings also featured parallel queting processions, and were certainly not derived from Celtic mummers. As the Cuban scholar Fernando Ortiz notes: "The Day of Kings was when the transplanted African groups allowed their secret society maskers, described as 'little devils,' to be seen on the streets of Havana."[54] According to F. W. Wurdeman's 1844 observations:

> The central object in the group was an athletic negro, with a fantastic straw helmet, an immensely thick girdle of strips of palm-leaves around his waist, and other uncouth articles of dress. Whenever they stopped, their banjoes struck up one of their monotonous tunes, and this frightful figure would commence a devil's dance, which was the signal for all his court to join in a general fandango, a description of which my pen refuseth to give. Yet when these parties stopped at the doors of the houses, which they frequently did to collect money from their inmates, often intruding into the very passages, the ladies mingled freely among the spectators.[55]

None of the Cuban observers thought they were watching an imitation of European customs.

Ortiz writes that an associated dance, called "Kill the Snake," "was very popular among the negroes, so much so that the writers of the day say that it was 'the dance of the mob.' One dancing group of negroes jumping, dancing and singing, carried on their shoulders a huge artificial snake several meters long through the streets of Havana, stopping in front of the large houses where they gave them gifts. [On] the Day of Kings, after traveling through all of Havana, such a pantomime was done in the patio of the captain generals, before the supreme authority."[56] In analyzing these activities, Cuban scholars have not felt the compelling need of their English and French counterparts to look first to Europe for parallels for what seemed clearly to contemporary observers to be essentially African-style practices.

Similarly, it is plausible to argue that the Jonkonnu maskers of North America were also modeling their performances on West African maskers from both hunting and ancestral societies. The anthropologist Martha Beckwith was told by a West Indian Myal priest, a specialist in counteracting the evil magic of obeah, that the key Jonkonnu mask was essentially an ancestral spirit object:

> Before building the house-shaped structure worn in the dance, a feast must be given consisting of goat's meat boiled without salt, together with plenty of rum. As the building progresses other feasts are given. On the night before it is brought out in public, it is taken to the cemetery, and there the songs and dances are rehearsed in order to "catch the spirit of the dead," which henceforth accompanies the dancer until, after a few weeks of merriment during which performances are given for money at the great houses and at village crossroads, it is broken up entirely. For "as long as it stays in the house the spirit will follow it."[57]

On mainland North America, on the other hand, the secular elements of the so-called Jonkonnu ceremonies quickly displaced the more spiritual aspects.

Whatever such holidays' ultimate origins, the aesthetic design of the performances displays the essential patterns that differentiate Afro-cultural from Euro-cultural elements and emphases.[58] Black music and dance have emphasized improvisation and competitive personal stylization within a rhythmically complex dialogue between artist and audience sometimes described as a "call-and-response" effect. In both music and dance, performer and musician must see beyond the apparent multiplicity of beats to an unstated but unifying rhythmic center. The black artistic tradition fosters its individual improvisation within a communal tradition and a collective setting. Competitive personal stylization such as "apart playing" is a crucial mark of excellence, but it always operates within a communally approving context.

Early African American performances typically occurred in permeable circular formations that reflected the communal, interactive, and nonliterate nature of African-style performance. Sterling Stuckey has seen African American dance as symbolic of the very circle of African American culture.[59] Certainly, black artistic performers were usually infused with a joyful communal spirit even while they moved away from their own improvised commentary on the shared realities of their life in America.[60]

Such generalizations about an African American aesthetic illuminate many of the characteristics that mark the festive style for blacks in antebellum North America. Certainly, most black celebrations can be characterized as long, loud, satirical, and joyful. Typically the central celebrators or performers interacted with a participatory audience of both sexes. When the events took place in a stable location, the spectators usually circled the action, and the principal performers would move into and out of the circle on the basis of both personal initiative and audience feedback. When the celebrators were moving, as in a parade, there was usually special costuming for at least some of the male central performers, and the interacting audience moved along with the procession, forming a kind of second line.

Performers at African American festive occasions usually also competed as individuals for audience approval. Improvisation and stylistic embellishment were the necessary marks of artistry. Yet the individual performers had to stay within the social bounds of audience approval.

To be sure, black parades of the various urban societies in the nineteenth-century North became more bourgeois and European. They sought to appeal both to white observers and to the black elite. In 1828 *Freedom's Journal* caught the widening class and cultural divisions within African American society as it castigated the older African forms of a march in Brooklyn, New York: "Nothing is more disgusting to the eyes of a reflecting man of colour than one of *these grand processions,* followed by the lower orders of society."[61] That is, nothing was more disgusting than the controlling effect of the second line that required individual, elitist antisocial pretensions to be punctured and only communally approved showmanship to be flaunted.

By the nineteenth century, the circle of culture was coming full round as blacks took up Euro-American styles. At the same time, however, blackface minstrel shows, the mummers' parade in Philadelphia, and the festive performances of Mardi Gras showed that whites were also drinking deeply of long-established African American patterns of performance. It was becoming more and more difficult in America to say where one ethnic culture began and another ended.

Notes

1. The spelling of the name of this festival varies, it seems, with almost every observer. The first North Carolina account from Edenton called the celebration "John Canno," and six years later the term as used in Somerset was "John Koonering"; Marvin L. Michael Kay and Lorin Lee Cary, *Slavery in North Carolina, 1748–1775* (Chapel Hill: University of North Carolina Press, 1995), 183–84. Other references from rites both in the Caribbean and in the United States have used the terms "John Connú," "Jon-canoe," "JonKanoo," "Jon-konnu," and "John Kunering." For consistency I use John Koonering and Jonkonnu, without getting into the argument over which should be the standard term.

2. The extreme importance of music within the West African culture of the Senegambia region was clearly described by Richard Jobson in the early seventeenth century: "There is without doubt, no people on the earth more naturally affected to the sound of music than these people; which the principal persons do hold as an ornament of their state, so as when we come to see them their music will seldom be wanting; wherein they have a perfect resemblance to the Irish rhyme, sitting in the same manner as they do upon the ground, somewhat remote from the company; and as they use singing of songs unto their music, the ground and effect whereof is the rehearsal of the ancient stock of the King, exalting his ancestry, and recounting over all the worthy and famous acts by him or them hath been achieved: singing likewise extempore upon any occasion is offered whereby the principal may be pleased; wherein diverse times they will not forget in our presence to sing in the praise of gratification. Also if at any time the Kings or principal persons come unto us trading in the River, they will have their music playing before them, and will follow in order after their manner, presenting a show of taste." Richard Jobson, *The Golden Grade; or A Discovery of the River Gambia and the Golden Trade of the Aethiopians* (London, 1623), 105–26.

3. William D. Piersen, *Black Yankees: The Development of an Afro-American Subculture in Eighteenth-Century New England* (Amherst: University of Massachusetts Press, 1988), 121–22.

4. Ibid., 122.

5. Philip Vickers Fithian, *Journal and Letters of Philip Vickers Fithian, 1773–1774: A Plantation Tutor of the Old Dominion*, ed. Hunter Dickson Farish (Williamsburg, Va.: Colonial Williamsburg Foundation, 1957), 39.

6. Ibid., 244 n. 79.

7. Anonymous, "Characteristic Traits of the Creolian and African Negroes in Jamaica, & c &c.," *Columbian Magazine*, April–October 1797, as quoted in Roger D. Abrahams and John F. Szwed, eds., *After Africa: Extracts from British Travel Accounts and Journals* . . . (New Haven: Yale University Press, 1983), 233.

8. See, for example, L. D. Powles, *The Land of the Pink Pearl; or Recollections of Life in the Bahamas* (London, 1888), 147; and William G. Sewell, *The Ordeal of Free Labor in the British*

West Indies (London, 1862), 216–17, as quoted in Abrahams and Szwed, eds., *After Africa*, 271, 319.

9. Kay and Cary, *Slavery in North Carolina*, 185–86.

10. Elizabeth A. Fenn, " 'A Perfect Equality Seemed to Reign': Slave Society and Jon Konnu," *North Carolina Historical Review* 65 (April 1988), 130–33.

11. Kay and Cary, *Slavery in North Carolina*, 184–85.

12. James Murray, Cape Fear, to "Sister Clark," December 26, 1755, as quoted in Sylvia R. Frey, *Water from the Rock: Black Resistance in a Revolutionary Age* (Princeton: Princeton University Press, 1991), 41.

13. Martha Warren Beckwith, *Black Roadways: A Study of Jamaica Folk Life* (Chapel Hill: University of North Carolina Press, 1929), 151.

14. Early black funerals in New England probably were close in style to their southern cousins, but we do not have as much evidence; see Piersen, *Black Yankees*, 77.

15. See, for comparison with the New Orleans mask, a very similar West Indian mask or crown pictured in J. M. Belasario, *Sketches*, reprinted in Lynne Fauley Emery, *Black Dance in the United States from 1619 to 1970* (New York: Books for Libraries, 1972), 31. On the role of the black "king" as a central character in early John Canoe rites, see Robert Dirks, *The Black Saturnalia* (Gainesville: University of Florida Press, 1987), 174–75.

16. Timothy Flint, *Recollections of the Last Ten Years, Passed in Occasional Residences and Journeyings in the Valley of the Mississippi* . . . (Boston, 1826), 140.

17. Lester B. Shippee, ed., *Bishop Whipple's Southern Diary, 1843–1844* (Minneapolis: University of Minnesota Press, 1937), 51. On the red ribbon as an African American holiday marker, Solomon Northrup noted that Christmas morning was "the happiest day in the whole year for the slave. . . . The time of feasting and dancing had come. . . . That day the clean dress was to be donned—the red ribbon displayed." See Solomon Northrup, *Twelve Years a Slave* (Cincinnati, 1853), as quoted in Eileen Southern, ed., *Readings in Black American Music*, 2d ed. (New York: W. W. Norton, 1983), 101.

18. On this subject, compare the hypothesis for European origins developed by Samuel Kinser, *Carnival American Style: Mardi Gras at New Orleans and Mobile* (Chicago: University of Chicago Press, 1990), 80–81, 88–89, with the African American emphasis given by William D. Piersen, *Black Legacy: America's Hidden Heritage* (Amherst: University of Massachusetts Press, 1993), 121–31.

19. *Albany Centinel*, as quoted in Shane White, "Pinkster: Afro-Dutch Syncretization in New York City and the Hudson Valley," *Journal of American Folklore*, 102, no. 403 (January–March 1989), 70. King Charley's accompanying drummers were also described as displaying "uncouth and terrifying grimaces"; see Shane White, *Somewhat More Independent* (Athens: University of Georgia Press, 1991), 97. On the grimace as an African performance mannerism, see Thomas Edward Bowditch, *Mission from Cape Coast Castle to Ashantee* (London, 1819), as quoted in Eileen Southern, ed., *Readings in Black American Music*, 14; and Lydia Parrish, *Slave Songs of the Georgia Sea Islands* (1942; reprint, Athens: University of Georgia Press, 1992), xxxii. Sterling Stuckey, *Going Through the Storm: The Influence of African American Art in History* (New York: Oxford University Press, 1994), 61–63, suspects that King Charley's grimaces and demands for tribute were not historical descriptions but the fevered imaginings of a racist creed that was intended to destroy the holiday. It is true that the original 1803 description came from a biased observer, but I believe the description is not one of "extortion" and insinuated "rape," but more simply typical African American festive queting.

20. Kenneth Kittle, "The Role of the Secret Society in Cultural Specialization," *American Anthropologist* 51 (June 1943), 208–9.

21. Edward Warren, *A Doctor's Experiences on Three Continents* (Baltimore, 1885), 201.

22. Ibid., 202.

23. The direct quotation here comes from Samuel Kinser's description of the second line among Mardi Gras Indian tribes, *Carnival American Style*, 213.

24. Album notes, "New Orleans Parade," American Music Records, nos. 101–3, as quoted in Marshall W. Stearns, *The Story of Jazz* (New York: Oxford University Press, 1956), 61. While the second line is most noted in New Orleans, its presence was nearly ubiquitous in Afro-America; as noted about early twentieth-century Harlem, "A brilliant parade with very good bands is participated in not only by the marchers in line, but also by the marchers on the sidewalks. For it is not a universal custom of Harlem to stand idly and watch a parade go by; a good part of the crowd always marches along, keeping step to the music." James Weldon Johnson, *Black Manhattan* (1930; reprint, New York: Atheneum, 1968), 168–69. On the African American influence on New Orleans Mardi Gras parades, see Piersen, *Black Legacy*, 121–36.

25. Emily Burke, *Pleasure and Pain: Reminiscences of Georgia in the 1840s* (Savannah, Ga.: Beehive Press, 1978), 26–27, as quoted in Roger D. Abrahams, *Singing the Master: The Emergence of African American Culture in the Plantation South* (New York: Pantheon, 1992), 193.

26. Katherine Dunham, *Dances of Haiti* (New York, 1937), 34, as quoted in Kinser, *Carnival American Style* (Los Angeles: Center for Afro-American Studies, 1983), 227.

27. Jacqui Malone, *Steppin' on the Blues: The Visible Rhythms of African American Dance* (Urbana: University of Illinois Press, 1996), 10.

28. Kinser, *Carnival American Style*, 185–88.

29. Abrahams, *Singing the Master*, 139.

30. Malone, *Steppin' on the Blues*, 5, reminds us that "competitive interaction" is the driving force behind African American dance, music, and song.

31. Andrew Burnaby, *A Concise Historical Account of All the British Colonies in North America* (Dublin, 1776), 213.

32. Nicolas Cresswell, *The Journal of Nicolas Cresswell, 1774–1777* (1924; reprint, Port Washington, N.Y.: Associated Faculty Press, 1968), 52–53. The "cutting contest" was a crucial feature of the African American aesthetic and was widely featured in contested speech events like the dozens in early jazz performances; see, for example, Samuel A. Floyd, *The Power of Black Music* (New York: Oxford University Press, 1995), 138–39.

33. Katherine Dunham, "Ethnic Dancing," *Dance Magazine* 20 (September 1946), 34.

34. Abrahams, *Singing the Master*, 104.

35. John Miller Chernoff, *African Rhthym and African Sensibility: Aesthetics and Social Action in African Musical Idioms* (Chicago: University of Chicago Press, 1981), 71, as quoted in Abrahams, *Singing the Master*, 112. See especially the chapter on satire in Piersen, *Black Legacy*, 53–73.

36. Réné Caillié, *Journal d'un voyage à Tembucto et à Jenne dans l'Afrique Centrale* (Paris, 1830), as quoted in Christopher Hibbert, *Africa Explored: Europeans in the Dark Continent, 1769–1889* (1924; reprint, New York: W. W. Norton, 1983), 169.

37. T. Edward Bowditch, *Mission from Cape Coast Castle to Ashantee*, 292.

38. Piersen, *Black Legacy*, 60–73.

39. The African American term "play" did not mean drama but something far closer to the more modern term "play party."

40. *South Carolina Gazette*, September 17, 1772, as quoted in Peter H. Wood, *Black Majority: Negroes in Colonial South Carolina from 1670 Through the Stono Rebellion* (New York: W. W. Norton, 1974), 342; likewise, see Marshall Stearns and Jean Stearns, *Jazz Dance* (New York: Macmillan, 1979), 22; Kinser, *Carnival American Style*, 73; and the many similar examples from around the Americas cited in Piersen, *Black Legacy*, 63–64.

41. James R. Newhall, *The History of Lynn* (Lynn, Mass., 1883), 236, as quoted in Piersen, *Black Yankees*, 139. Compare Newhall's description with that of the associated satire of the Christmas "gombayers" in Jamaica in 1826: "The slaves sang satirical philippics against their

mater, communicating a little free advice now and then; but they never lost sight of decorum." Cynric R. Williams, *A Tour Through the Island of Jamaica* (London, 1826), as quoted in Abrahams and Szwed, *After Africa*, 250.

42. Jane de Forest Shelton, "New England Negro: A Remnant," *Harper's New Monthly Magazine* 88 (March 1894), 536, as quoted in Piersen, *Black Yankees*, 138.

43. James Boardman, *America and the Americans* (London, 1833), 310, as quoted in Shane White, " 'It Was a Proud Day': African Americans, Festivals, and Parades in the North, 1741–1834," *Journal of American History* 81 (June 1994), 45–46.

44. William Cullen Bryant, *Letters of a Traveler* (New York, 1850), as quoted in Abrahams, *Singing the Master*, 194.

45. Fredricka Bremer, quoted in Southern, *Readings in Black American Music*, 106.

46. Solomon Northrup, *Twelve Years a Slave* (Cincinnati, 1853), as quoted in Southern, *Readings in Black American Music*, 102; similarly, see Charles Ball, *Slavery in the United States: A Narrative of the Life and Adventures of Charles Ball, a Black Man, Who Lived Forty Years in Maryland, South Carolina, and Georgia as a Slave* (New York, 1837), 201: "[On Saturday night] Our quarter knew but little quiet. . . . Singing, playing on the banjoe, and dancing occupied nearly the whole community, until the break of day."

47. Williams, *A Tour Through the Island of Jamaica*, 21–23. This could be compared with a sympathetic white like Randolph Jefferson, who "used to come out among the black people, play the fiddle and dance [only] half the night." This recollection of Jefferson by Isaac, a Monticello slave, is quoted in Dena J. Epstein, *Sinful Tunes and Spirituals: Black Folk Music to the Civil War* (Urbana: University of Illinois Press, 1977), 122.

48. See, for example, such typical African references as Richard Burton's: They "sing, drum, and dance all the day. . . . [They] seem hardly to take natural rest; the drum and dance may be heard until dawn." Richard Burton, "*A Mission to Gelele, King of Dahome*," in Frederick E. Forbes, *Dahomey and the Dahomans, Being the Journal of Two Missionaries, 1849–1850* (reprint, New York: Frank Cass, 1966), 196, 215; or Richard Jobson, *The Golden Trade*, as quoted in Southern, *Readings in Black American Music*, 3: "For both day and night, more especially all the night the people continue dancing until he that playes be quite tyred out."

49. On the noise level at black festivals, see M. G. Lewis's typical observations from Jamaica: "In the negro festivals . . . the chief point lies in making as much noise as possible." Matthew Gregory Lewis, *Journal of a West India Proprietor* (London, 1834), 27. Similarly, see Charles William Day, *Five Years Residence in the West Indies* (London, 1852), 1:289; and James Kelly, *Voyage to Jamaica* (Belfast, Northern Ireland, 1838), 20–21.

50. E. Franklin Frazier, *The Negro in the United States* (New York: Macmillan, 1957); Richard M. Dorson, *American Negro Folktales* (Greenwich, Conn.: Fawcett, 1967).

51. Sterling Stuckey, *Slave Culture, Nationalist Theory, and the Foundations of Black America* (New York: Oxford University Press, 1987); Roger Abrahams, *Singing the Master;* William D. Piersen, *Black Yankees;* idem, *Black Legacy*.

52. Shane White, "Pinkster"; Samuel Kinser, *Carnival American Style;* Genevieve Fabre, "Festive Moments in Antebellum African American Culture," in Werner Sollors and Maria Diedrich, eds., *The Black Columbiad: Defining Moments in African American Literature and Culture* (Cambridge, Mass.: Harvard University Press, 1994).

53. Fabre, "Festive Moments in Antebellum African American Culture," 58–62.

54. Fernando Ortiz, *Los Bailes y el Teatro de los Negros en el Folklore de Cuba* (Havana: Editorial Letras Cubanas, 1951), 195.

55. F. W. Wurdeman, *Notes on Cuba* (Boston, 1844), 83–84.

56. Ortiz, *Los Bailes y el Teatro de los Negros en el folklore de Cuba*, 192.

57. Beckwith, *Black Roadways*, 151.

58. For scholarly efforts to come to grips with the African American aesthetic, Gena Dagel

Caponi, "The African American Aesthetic in African American Expressive Culture" (unpublished), suggests a reading of John Miller Chernoff, Olly Wilson, Samuel A. Floyd, and Portia Maultsby in music; Henry Louis Gates Jr., Houston Baker, and Toni Morrison in literature; Robert Farris Thompson in visual arts and dance; Marshall Stearns in dance; and to Caponi's suggestions I would add Roger Abrahams and John Michael Vlach in folklore, and Sterling Stuckey and Lawrence Levine in history.

59. Stuckey, *Slave Culture,* 3–97.

60. I am expanding here on the insights of scholars who have emphasized the coded messaging of African American verbal performance to suggest that most festive performances were also "signifying." For an introduction to this topic, see Theophus Smith, *Conjuring Culture* (New York: Oxford University Press, 1994), 148–52.

61. *Freedom's Journal,* July 11 and 18, 1828, as quoted in White, " 'It Was a Proud Day,' " 40.

12

The Paradox of "Nationalist" Festivals

The Case of Palmetto Day in Antebellum Charleston

Len Travers

> The first of June, the British Fleet
> Appeared off Charleston Harbor;
> The 28th attacked the Fort,
> And wounded Young the Barber.
>
> Sir Peter Parker, foolish man
> To put himself in danger;
> Don't you think they served him right
> To treat him like a stranger?
> —"Revolutionary Ditty,"
> *Charleston Courier*, June 28, 1845

In June 1776, open hostilities between Great Britain and its American colonies were more than a year old. After months of debate, the colonial governments stood poised for the decisive vote that would turn an armed uprising into an outright war for independence.

And off the coast of South Carolina, a British invasion force commanded by Admiral Sir Peter Parker prepared to take that fledgling state out of the fight in one fell blow, by capturing its capital and vital seaport, Charleston. At the southern tip of Sullivan's Island, where Charleston harbor meets the sea, American rebels worked feverishly to bar the British warships with a low, square fortification (subsequently named for its commander, Colonel William Moultrie). The fort was a makeshift affair of beach sand ramparts faced with logs from locally available palmetto trees. General Charles Lee, continental general for the Southern Department, considered the fort a death trap and advised abandoning the position, but local commanders insisted on its defense. On June 28, with the vote for independence less than a week away, the blow fell. The fort's rear was still unfinished, but a British amphibious assault on that position fell behind schedule, leaving the assault troops cut off from the fort by a high tide. The fate of Charleston now depended on a shooting match between the outgunned battery and the Royal Navy. British gunnery was heavy and accurate, but instead of shattering the fort's protective log sheathing, which then would have collapsed the sand walls, the solid iron cannonballs sank ineffectually into the spongy palmetto wood. Stout rebel resistance, coupled with the loss of one of the warships on a sandbank opposite the fort, persuaded Sir Peter to call off the attack.

For the next fourscore years, Charlestonians remembered June 28 as "Palmetto Day," in honor of the humble native tree that had saved their city from the enemy. In the years immediately following the victory, they commemorated Palmetto Day with a popular civic festival of renewal to the patriot cause. After the war, however, Palmetto Day steadily lost favor. Local boosters eager to place June 28 in the calendar of national red-letter days faced not only a curiously unresponsive local public but also stiff competition from Independence Day, unquestionably the most successful and enduring nationalist festival to come out of the Revolution. Over the course of forty years, despite the best efforts of dedicated individuals, the celebration of Palmetto Day in Charleston languished and all but died. Then, as the revolutionary generation faded away and the "rising generation" took its place, Palmetto Day underwent an ominous revival. Initially, the old festival's revitalization echoed a reaffirmation of South Carolina's significance in the national saga of American Independence. Increasingly, however, the anniversary became a focal point for Carolinians professing a different sort of nationalism entirely: Southern nationalism.

The evolution of Palmetto Day from revolutionary festival to secessionist rally exemplifies the difficulty, if not impossibility, of arranging patriotic public ceremonies in any strict taxonomy of ritual behavior. Historians (this one included) who have grown accustomed to regarding revolution-inspired commemorations as "nationalist" events run into the problem of explaining their ambiguity and multiplicity of messages. Even defining "nationalism," or, more important, determining how the subjects of historical study understood the notion, must necessarily be burdened with qualifications. Precise definition is elusive because nationalism is not an objective, empirically measurable entity of which one is either possessed or deficient. Even the term itself was not much in use before the middle of the nineteenth century; Americans generally employed the terms "patriotism" or "national spirit" instead.[1] Given such an elusive concept, flexibility is the best policy. For the purposes of this chapter, nationalism is best understood simply as a belief in and, more important, an emotional attachment to, membership in a parent society.

In the case of the young United States, creation of a national community of continental dimensions from a number of discrete colonial societies required an expansion of what James Kettner has styled the essentially local personal "community of allegiance."[2] As a consequence of the British imperial crisis and the war that followed, the usually insular colonies/states tentatively embraced unfamiliar localities and their people to create a new geopolitical "national state." But because the American colonies created the United States first and foremost to fight a war for independence, and not out of an overwhelming sense of kinship with one another, the nationalism resulting from the Revolutionary War was more a by-product of that experience; it was, in the words of John Murrin, "an unexpected, impromptu, artificial, and therefore extremely fragile creation."[3] The core of American nationalism, as it was understood in the early republic, was formed from this common heritage of the revolutionary union and, after 1789, a commitment to its codification in the U.S. Constitution.[4] This national identity did not exclude regional or local identities. Indeed, formed as it was from a sometimes grudging consensus, it left plenty of room for alternative allegiances, even outright sectionalism, for "so long as a national government is able to embrace and preserve diverse interests—whether those interests be sectional, class, ethnic, political, social, or economic—it will retain the loyalties of the various elements in its population. Provided that local and national goals can be coordinated, local allegiances can reinforce nationalism."[5] In the case of Palmetto Day, the "nation" that the day presumably celebrated seems particularly elusive—or, as we shall see, particularly adaptable.

Rituals of nationalism have received considerable attention in recent years, and with good reason.[6] Patriotic performances, staged at historically significant moments or in historically significant space, have the power to plant, nurture, and promulgate the myths that bind societies together: stories of cultural unity, of social continuity, of unchanging tradition, of shared belief. In addition, they can motivate or initiate desirable behavior and reinforce a society's most hallowed values.[7] As such, patriotic holidays are touchstones for students seeking insight into the shared—and contested—beliefs and aspirations of Americans in the early republic. Palmetto Day reconnected antebellum Charlestonians with a legendary moment in their civic past, a signal victory that shattered their former allegiance to Britain and defined them as resolute opponents of tyranny. Far removed from the main theater of the war in the North, Charleston's successful defense in 1776 appeared to be an exclusively local achievement. And coming as it did a week before the Congress made American independence official, the gallant (and fortuitous) stand at Fort Moultrie asserted a prior claim on the imaginations of patriotic Charlestonians.

Palmetto Day's first observance was in 1777, one year after the dramatic event. Most of what occurred during the first celebrations of Independence Day in coastal towns a week later reflected spontaneous, unscripted expressions of festive behavior. But in Charleston, on this first anniversary of Fort Moultrie's victory, little was left to the whim of crowds. The Palmetto Society, an alliance of artisans, mechanics, and well-connected gentlemen formed expressly to commemorate the victory, carefully worked out the day's schedule of events. Pealing bells in church steeples and cannon fire from the harbor batteries greeted the dawn. At noon, South Carolina legislators gathered at the State House at the center of town to receive and review the two volunteer companies that had defended the fort the year before. These "heroes of the 28th of June" then publicly renewed their "oath of allegiance to the cause of Independence," received the cheers of their fellow townsfolk, and fired three volleys of musketry. Next came the formal dinners. The colonel commanding the two companies treated his officers, while the Palmetto Society hosted an "elegant entertainment" at Valk's Long Room for the state president, the vice-president, the council, and some three hundred others. To make sure no one had trouble finding the place, Society members flanked the gate to the establishment with two palmetto trees festooned with fireworks. The Congress, with some militia officers, remained at the State House and probably ate best of all; according to one witness, they enjoyed "food . . . in abundance, and even in profusion," although, he discreetly added, "without much pomp and without much etiquette." Cheers and thirteen-gun salutes from cannons in the square just outside punctuated the many patriotic toasts. Sundown and a final salute from the harbor forts closed the daytime ceremonies, but the celebration continued in the center of town, where, in the relative cool of the summer evening and under a canopy of their beloved palmetto trees, the noncommissioned officers and privates attended a collation "provided for them by the Ladies." Fireworks in several places throughout the town and an unprecedented illumination of houses and public buildings capped the night's activities.[8]

For the two years following the first anniversaries of the battle and of independence, Charlestonians continued to celebrate both Palmetto Day and the Fourth of July, but a comparison of newspaper accounts suggests that, of the two, Palmetto Day garnered more local interest.[9] In 1778, a young Loyalist woman and her family left inhospitable Charleston the day before the second anniversary of the Fort Moultrie battle, perhaps to avoid the Tory-baiting that inevitably intensified on patriotic holidays. In what must have appeared as a secular version of a Catholic Palm Sunday, Louisa Wells noticed that "many boats were employed in carrying up Palmetto trees and boughs to celebrate, in Town, the Anniversary of the ever inglorious 28th of June 1776!"[10] Of limited economic or aesthetic value, palmetto trees had disappeared from the town long before the Revolution; Wells's observation suggests that Charleston's patriots were willing to make strenuous efforts to honor June 28 with the appropriate focal symbols. A friendlier observer noted that there were no fewer than three "public celebrations" in the town, where no doubt the palmetto boughs cut previously and brought into the town received prominent display.[11] In contrast, the Independence Day program of 1778 appears to have been a slightly scaled-down version of the previous year's.

Anyone who has read accounts of the British king's birthday celebrations in prerevolutionary America will find the celebratory forms employed for Charleston's first Palmetto Day familiar: guns, bells, parades, lavish dinners, fireworks, illuminations, and generous supplies of alcohol. None of these practices was particularly new; in fact most were ancient, harkening back centuries.[12] The Revolution quickly destroyed the royalist associations of the old rites, but instead of immediately creating entirely new public rituals, Americans retained familiar forms of commemoration and celebration while constructing new meanings for them.[13] Indeed, the facility with which so many Americans grafted assertive and politically regicidal associations onto traditional, conservative rituals of submission suggests that "monarchical culture" may not have run very deep in eighteenth-century America after all.[14]

Certainly Charleston's creation of Palmetto Day was unique on several counts. Most former colonies could point to a moment predating July 4, 1776, when their "patriots" had unambiguously positioned themselves in open and violent defiance of British authority. Massachusetts, of course, could claim the first shots fired in actual combat at Lexington, Concord, and Bunker Hill, but there were others. Virginia could point to the ouster of its governor, Lord Dunmore, in June 1775, and North Carolinians to the clash between that colony's patriot and loyalist forces at Moore's Creek Bridge the following February. But unlike Charleston, none of these communities chose regularly to celebrate these dramatic, decisive moments until after the war, and in some cases not until well into the nineteenth century.[15] In addition, unlike Independence Day, which at first received almost no official encouragement, Palmetto Day was carefully choreographed, with elaborate dinners and military review. Last, whereas July Fourth celebrators throughout the rebelling states commemorated a sublime political act belonging to no one state or locale but ostensibly the work of all, Palmetto Day recalled a spectacular victory against the odds that was Charleston's alone.

Charlestonians responded to Palmetto Day with unique civic pride. Most of those who took an active part in the defense of the harbor fort were still quartered there or somewhere in town. The citizens who had watched the distant struggle in day-long suspense and fear and who had heard the fearsome thunder of the bombardment could share vicariously in the moment. It is not that Americans in Charleston and in other urban centers did not grow enthusiastic on July Fourth—quite the contrary—but Charlestonians had reason for a more personal response to the annual recurrence of June 28. Palmetto Day possessed an immediacy and a significance that Independence Day could not match; the annual re-remembering of their victory dedicated them to a struggle whose issue was still in doubt.

Instantly successful as it was, Palmetto Day would almost certainly have continued unabated in popularity, and perhaps have eclipsed Independence Day throughout the era of the early republic but for the fortunes of war. The British returned to Charleston in force four years after their first attempt, and they did not make the same mistakes a second time. After a brief siege, they compelled a mixed force of militia and Continental Army units to surrender the town in May 1780. Not until the war's end would Charlestonians again have the opportunity to express their patriotism openly. When that day came, depressed economic conditions, political instability, and the lingering humiliation of occupation all but doused demonstrative patriotism; only the Palmetto Society (which had now become a veterans' aid society) regularly marked the day with a meeting and a members-only dinner.[16] In proffering a toast to the company, one member hoped that "the victory obtained on this day" would be "ever remembered by our posterity," but signs of that were not encouraging. With independence won, Palmetto Day's message of armed resistance to imperial oppression seemed redundant. Any notion of celebrating June 28 as a day recalling deliverance from the enemy would have been painful mockery, given subsequent events. In its place, growing slowly in popularity, was Independence Day, whose celebration of nationhood was less emphatically militaristic and more forward-looking. While continuing to be honored by dawn bell-ringings and artillery salutes from the harbor forts, Palmetto Day was virtually suspended as a public celebration, finding expression chiefly in the private dinners of the Palmetto Society.[17]

There were periodic attempts to reawaken public interest in commemorating the event, but they came to little. In 1808, "a number of amateurs" offered a patriotic "serenade on the water" as an evening entertainment. A year later, the Palmetto Society resolved to follow the example of Independence Day practices and sponsor a public oration "delivered annually on this anniversary . . . in order that a memorable event in our late Revolution may be more effectually known to the rising generation."[18] A better opportunity for revival came with America's second war with Britain in 1812. Fort Moultrie had been allowed to decay in the peacetime years, but with Charleston as vulnerable to seaborne invasion as it ever was, a frantic rebuilding program returned the historic battery to a defensible condition. Enlisting Charlestonians' patriotism as well as their historical memory, builders put out the call for "600 PALMETTO Logs, best quality" to restore the venerable fort.[19]

As they labored, the people of Charleston must have hoped that the Royal Navy would make a second try at forcing the harbor entrance, and allow them to repeat the victory of 1776. That opportunity never came, but Palmetto Day did enjoy a brief wartime revival. The Palmetto Society attracted more auditors for its annual oration; the members' processions to the church building where these recountings were held had formerly been of modest dimensions, but increased in 1813 to include members of the patriotic '76 Association and members of the city council, all escorted by the Cadet Light Infantry. After-dinner toasts praised "The Day! Glorious in our Country's annals," and hoped that the "Sons of the Fathers of the Revolution" would "emulate the patriotic virtues of their progenitors, by an invincible perseverance in the just cause of their country."[20]

Sadly, perhaps, the sons remained untested. With something like an anticlimax, Charlestonians resumed their prewar routine in 1815. After that, events of local significance fell more and more behind in importance as Charlestonians were caught up in the wave of nationalist sentiment that swept the country after the war and captivated by the supposed achievement of a "national character."[21] At the height of this period of nationalist euphoria, one old Charleston patriot who remembered the attack on Fort Moultrie more than three decades earlier lamented: "The memorable days of our Revolutionary history do not now bring with them, in their annual recurrence, those lively feelings which they formerly did. The grateful associations they once excited have nearly yielded to the impressions of subsequent events." Referring to Palmetto Day, he could "scarce realize the apathy that is now manifested at its anniversary. It is numbered with the days before the flood." Acknowledging the inevitable eclipse of his own generation, the writer concluded that Charlestonians' patriotic amnesia came about because "new connections arise, and new views display themselves, identified with interests for which we are more zealous."[22] Some years later, another survivor of the Revolution asked incredulously: "Can it be possible that Carolinians should ever forget a Victory, which was no less important to the general success of the Revolution, than it was highly favorable to the patriotism and valor of their Native State?"[23]

Apparently it was. But the honeymoon with American nationalism was short-lived. Beginning in 1819, regional and national events progressively convinced white Charlestonians that their distinctiveness from the rest of the nation was perhaps of greater consequence than the bond of national character. The Panic of 1819, followed by more than a decade of economic decline in the city, stung the residents smartly.[24] The more industrialized and capital-rich northern states were able to recover relatively quickly, partly, as in the case of New York, by taking over Charleston's shipping needs. The Missouri Compromise debates of 1820 served notice to Charlestonians, as to southerners everywhere, that their political economy, which was based on slavery, was anathema to a growing number of Americans in the North.[25] Adding still more to the growing sense of isolation and distinctiveness, the Denmark Vesey insurrection scare of 1822 reminded white Charlestonians of the dangers inherent in their "peculiar institution"—an institution that forced them to be constantly on guard against the black majority within (South Carolina and Mississippi were the two states in which blacks outnumbered whites) while combating antislavery assaults from without. The defensiveness and insecurity bred by this succession of events accelerated Charleston's transformation to an inward-looking "closed society" that regarded "national interest" as interpreted by northerners with instant suspicion.[26]

It was in this context that the long-ignored Palmetto Day showed signs of making a comeback. Interest in the old revolutionary holiday revived as Charlestonians turned to their past for inspiration and reassurance in the troubling times after 1819. Feeding the public's desire for local heroes, Alexander Garden produced his *Anecdotes of the Revolutionary War* in 1822. This "key work in South Carolina hagiography" brought back to heroic life the deeds of Colonel Moultrie, Francis Marion, and the intrepid Sergeant Jasper, a hero of the attack on Fort Moultrie.[27] Inspired perhaps by Garden's history, a "native genius" thrilled Charlestonians in 1825 with a re-creation of the battle in miniature, complete with floating, firing models of the British ships of the line, in the harbor waters just off the popular Bathing House.[28] That same year some patriotic citizens revived the Palmetto Society, which had quietly faded into oblivion years before, "for the express purpose of commemorating the glorious deeds of the heroes" of that encounter. As in old times, they marched in procession to one of Charleston's meetinghouses to hear an oration and met afterward for a formal dinner, toasting the memory of that battle, which "for cool and determined courage ranks in the struggles of American liberty, second only to the battle of Bunker Hill."[29] A year later, taking inspiration from Massachusetts' recently begun monument to this last-named battle, members of the Society used the 1826 jubilee celebration of July 4 to drum up donations for a similar memorial to Charleston's proudest moment.[30]

Still, Palmetto Day did not sustain the interest of Charlestonians beyond its own jubilee event that same year. The reconstituted Palmetto Society, apparently abandoning philanthropy in favor of sheer patriotic commemoration, still contained a core of veteran members who envisioned little more than annual paeans to the past, and genteel rites of devotion to the old heroes. But Independence Day already did much the same thing, and did it better. So little did Palmetto Day impress the imaginations of Charleston that the editors of the *Charleston Mercury* let the fiftieth anniversary of the event pass without acknowledgment, admitting later that it simply "did not occur to us."[31]

After 1828, that was not going to happen again. In that presidential election year, supporters of Andrew Jackson framed a congressional bill intended to embarrass incumbent John Quincy Adams. Known to southerners as the "Tariff of Abominations," it heavily favored New England manufacturers while penalizing import-dependent consumers in the South. As expected, the tariff produced a storm of angry protest from southern legislators, including those of South Carolina, who denounced the tariff as unconstitutional. Vice-President John C. Calhoun, a native of South Carolina, anonymously published an essay promoting "nullification" as a remedy for the South's ills. According to this doctrine, any state could void or "nullify" a federal law within its own borders until three-quarters of the states agreed the law was constitutional—an argument that emphasized the preeminence of "states' rights."

Charleston nullifiers found the perfect vehicle for publicly venting their frustration and for publicizing their views. On June 28, 1828, while members of the Palmetto Society doggedly performed their lackluster commemoration in town, a large party of prominent Charlestonians and states' rights proponents crossed the harbor to Fort Moultrie by steamer. There they joined the citizens of Moultrieville (which had grown up near the fort) for a commemoration with a decidedly more stimulating theme. Following religious services, "a very energetic Oration" was delivered by none other than Alexander Garden himself, the champion of South Carolina's revolutionary saga. Recalling "in a very animated manner" the battle that had raged close by, Garden compared the British invasion to that of Xerxes, whose mighty Persian host had likewise been roughly handled by a small band of determined patriots. "He then adverted to the present condition of the country, to the oppression inflicted on the Southern section of it, and observed, that the time for argument had passed away." As was customary, the sumptuous dinner was followed by toasts, but these were not the well-worn formulas of former times. Praising southern statesmen and castigating New England in particular, celebrators advocated a belligerent defense of "States' Rights [and] Southern Policy—The Constitution for its text—Native talent for its advocate—Sovereign States for its arbiters—

Palmetto Logs and Cotton Bags for its Bulwarks." Moving quickly past mere policy, the toasts grew increasingly bellicose, as when Charles Cotesworthy Pinckney (a nephew of his famous revolutionary namesake) compared "the battle of 28 June and the Tariff of June 28—Let New England beware how she imitates the Old," and when William Carson offered a glass to June 28, "the day on which forbearance and patience cease to be virtues."[32]

No one could mistake the confrontational sentiments. Palmetto Day's original message of active resistance to tyranny dovetailed neatly with the fears and anger of Charlestonians who were frustrated with national politics and the perceived assault on their economic and political culture. Their antifederal rally at Sullivan's Island symbolically linked them with the patriots who also had stood up to misguided authority in 1776. Moreover, the "holy ground" they occupied at the island, together with their invocation of the hallowed cause of liberty, justified and indeed sanctified the rhetorical broadsides they hurled at the foe. At the house where they ate dinner, they were surrounded by the old revolutionary symbols—the palmetto and the laurel of victory—and the toasts breathed the old spirit of defiance.

Back in Charleston proper, the Palmetto Society celebrated "in a very appropriate and patriotic manner." In complete contrast to the fiery bombast across the harbor, the Society's orator, William G. Simms Jr., "avoid[ed] the party feeling of the day." Obviously aware of the sentiments guiding the observance at Sullivan's Island, Simms, "advantageously known to the public as a poet," tried to steer the interpretation of Palmetto Day into moderate channels, dwelling "upon the patriotic devotion of those who stood forth manfully in defense of the country in its hour of trial," and hoped "to stimulate the rising generation to imitate their virtues." Although the orator refused to wax political openly, other members were not so bound, and at dinner unionist John Ward offered a toast that was more of a curse to "the advocates of Disunion—Palsied be the arm and withered the heart of him who would attempt to destroy this fair fabric of liberty."[33]

In this tale of two patriotic celebrations, we see almost the moment of transformation when Palmetto Day went from a ritual memorializing a historic event, to a ritual in which the past was brought forth to inform present concerns. Whatever the merits of the arguments of either side, there can be little doubt about which Palmetto Day observance appealed to Charlestonians' imaginations more. The pilgrimage across the harbor, the reverence for historic locale, the silent but puissant language of symbols, and the bold oratory, all gave the ceremonies at Sullivan's Island a vitality and a connectedness with Charleston's revolutionary past that the Palmetto Society could not deliver. In vain did one Society member offer a toast to "States' Rights—if infringed, moderate and judicious remonstrance will ensure their security."[34] Such tame language did little to soothe political tension and invited comparisons with the arguments of Loyalists a half-century before. Unlike the Palmetto Society, the celebrators at Sullivan's Island were interested in Palmetto Day not so much as a commemoration but, more like its original context, as a call to action.

Some members of the Palmetto Society apparently felt that if the original message of Palmetto Day was to be perverted by applying it to modern political agendas, the anniversary was better left alone. After the success of the 1828 Sullivan's Island celebrations, they suggested, according to the editors of the *Charleston Mercury,* "that the political commemoration of this sacred day should be discontinued—that the orations usually delivered on that occasion are mere partisan effusions, tending rather to evil than to good." No longer did Palmetto Day operate "to enlighten or instruct the mind, or to inculcate rational principles of freedom." Instead, they claimed, "the ordinary modes of celebration" debased and undermined republican principles.

Not so, cried the dissenters. By defending the preeminence of the federal government, they said, conservatives like those of the Palmetto Society turned their backs on "the spirit of liberty" that was so fundamental to the meaning of Palmetto Day. Far from denying or discouraging "effusions," the new patriots countered that if ever "the recurrence of that day shall excite no popular emotion, or be received without any . . . popular enthusiasm," the people of Charleston will have "exchanged a political religion . . . for a miserable and debasing mental thraldom."[35]

More ominous tidings were to come, as were more explicit shifts in "political religion." The Nullification crisis inspired the first loud cries for outright secession in South Carolina, and Palmetto Day was fast becoming a rival to July 4 for the hearts and minds of Charlestonians. Scornful unionists referred mockingly to the Island activities as "The Feast of Nullification" and railed against "the fanatics in Southern institutions," but increasingly their voices were drowned out by the enthusiastic rhetoric of nascent southern nationalism.[36] On Palmetto Day the "States' Rights Party" sponsored orations "particularly replete with sound Southern sentiments," cheered toasts that blasted South Carolina's "oppressors," declared that "Consolidation and corruption are synonymous," and warned northerners to "beware [South Carolina's] sting." They especially applauded the pronouncement of "Our true allegiance—Allegiance to our native state."[37]

As radical Charlestonians' devotion to federal union diminished, they grew increasingly expansive regarding the significance of the historical event that had inspired Palmetto Day. Early writers and orators had been content to regard the 1776 battle as locally important, certainly, and as one of a number of conspicuous early revolutionary events, but little more. This was probably the context for one 1805 celebrant's toast to "The Day—One of the corner stones on which was erected the fabric of our glorious Independence."[38] In the attempts to revive Palmetto Day in the 1820s, however, writers after Alexander Garden's heart amplified the consequence of the battle, comparing it to the famous last stand of the Spartans at Thermopyle. Up to this time, it was Bunker Hill that had been referred to popularly as the "American Thermopyle" (and because the Massachusetts soldiers technically lost, the comparison was apt), but, after 1826, Charlestonians appropriated the metaphors of classical antiquity for local application. Colonel Moultrie became a second Leonidas, his soldiers became "a Spartan band," and the fort itself "another Thermopyle" and "the Thermopyle of the South," defended against "a foe more formidable than the Persian host."[39] Indeed, Charlestonians seem to have suffered from a kind of Bunker Hill envy, noting the prominent place American history texts gave to the Massachusetts battle, while giving the defense of Fort Moultrie short shrift.[40] Proponents of a monument (which never materialized) continually made comparisons with the progress of the Massachusetts effort and exhorted Charlestonians to do as much. "This is our Bunker's Hill," declared one correspondent. "Let us make for Moultrie a shaft equal in eminence to that with which Massachusetts marks her Thermopyle. . . . Are we to excuse ourselves from these performances, which all other nations . . . deem so essential to patriotism?"[41]

It even seemed to some Charleston patriots that there was a conspiracy among academics to deny Palmetto Day—indeed, the entire South—its rightful place in the revolutionary saga, a connivance that mirrored their fears of northern domination of the union. In one of its frequent updates on the Bunker Hill project, the *Charleston Mercury* reported a rumor that "amongst the inscriptions on the monument, are suitable notices of every important battle during the war of the Revolution, except those which occurred in South Carolina. Can this really be true?"[42] "The Revolution in South Carolina," explained another, "was peculiar in many respects, and these peculiarities have been too often overlooked. . . . We have left our battlefields, and our trophies, and the tombs of our prophets, sages, and heroes too much to the care and regards of others." The author insisted, "Had such an action as that we this day commemorate marked a strait or sound, or island fortress, near the rock-bound coast of another section [plainly an allusion to New England], its anniversary would have excited impulses and interests that would have vibrated throughout the country."[43]

If former writers were willing to accept that the defense of Fort Moultrie had been second in importance to that of Bunker Hill, the new patriots were not. Charlestonians, insisted one writer, ought to be "as proud of [June 28, 1776] as Boston is of the 17th of June, 1775."[44] The defense of Fort Moultrie, a local patriot wrote, "ranks among the first actions of that war, for valor and skill."[45] Another went further, and declared that June 28, 1776, had been "the first decisive victory of the American Revolution" and, more important, "a proud memorial of what South Carolina was— and a cheering token of what she will be, whenever called upon to defend her rights, her interest, and her honor."[46] Still another agreed that June 28 "occupies the same place in our calendar of glory, as the days of Lexington and Bunker Hill do in that of old Massachusetts."[47] Nevertheless, decades later, the supposed neglect of South Carolina's contributions to the Revolution had not been addressed to general satisfaction. A southern patriot complained, "Those who have learned and loved to believe that all great events of American history were projected and executed within the shadow of Bunker Hill . . . have not seen much great or noteworthy in the defense of Fort Sullivan, conducted as it was by South Carolinians, without, or rather against, the Continental authority."[48]

This last point—whether South Carolina acted in its own behalf or on that of a nation of united colonies—was of vital importance to nullifiers and secessionists eager to justify and legitimize their positions. South Carolina patriots argued that because the attack on Fort Moultrie occurred four days before the Second Congress passed the resolution for independence, and six days before approval of the Declaration of Independence, the state was independent by dint of its own initiative before Congress assumed federal preeminence. Thus, instead of Charleston's greatest moment laying the foundation for a strong federal government, the defense of Fort Moultrie set South Carolina free to determine its own course. Indeed, the argument continued, the cart was very much before the horse, and it was rather Moultrie's victory that "animated the confederated colonies of America to the bold declaration and the great and glorious work of united independence."[49] "The Congress of 1776," concluded another Charleston revisionist, "felt their immortal resolve sanctified by the victory of 28th June."[50] Consequently, they reasoned, Palmetto Day was much more of an Independence Day for South Carolina than the Fourth of July was.

More moderate Charlestonians conceded that the battle was a "precursor and harbinger of the Declaration of our National Independence," which followed. However, they maintained that the "bond of union did then exist," if not in the strictly legal sense, then in a virtual and spiritual regard, and that " 'more perfect union' . . . should be the prayer, not the apprehension, of every patriot's heart."[51] They realized that the defeat of the British fleet was a "sectional triumph" but that Palmetto Day was "best celebrated by the immolation of sectional feeling—its value is to be best appreciated, by regarding it as a title to the common heritage of American glory—as a bright link in the chain of an indissoluble Union."[52]

But Fort Moultrie represented "the first scene of the first act of Carolina opposition to unconstitutional taxation," according to states' rights advocates and southern separatists, who added, "The drama is not yet closed."[53] The drama became more intense in 1846, when the United States went to war with Mexico. Sectional differences at first seemed moot, as Charlestonians were caught up in the patriotic zeal and expansionist opportunities that the war engendered. The war's successful conclusion in 1848, however, renewed and intensified the rift between North and South over the question of slavery in the newly won territories. After that, Palmetto Day was an occasion for focused castigation of federal authority.

Especially so, since in the 1850s possession of Fort Moutrie's "holy ground" brought on an annual confrontation between the U.S. Army and some indignant Charlestonians. After the War of 1812, Fort Moultrie passed into federal hands, to be more regularly maintained and garrisoned than the state had done heretofore. In 1844, the garrison commander allowed the Palmetto Day celebrators to conduct their ceremonies and eat their convivial dinner on the fort grounds, "on the very spot where the victorious thunder of American cannon silenced the battle ships of haughty Britain." Naturally, they were delighted to move their usual observances from nearby Moultrieville to the "hallowed ground of our wave-washed fortress." They were even more honored when the steamer that took them across the harbor was met at the dock on Sullivan's Island by the soldiers of the garrison, brightly uniformed and formed for escort duty. The soldiers displayed every mark of respect, leading the way from the protected cove to the fort entrance, where they stood at attention facing the Moultrie Guards, a militia group from the city, on the other side of the way, while the civilians and dignitaries entered first. Once inside, the citizens found the fort "tastefully arranged for their reception," with galleries erected and tables set for dinner.[54] The event was such a success that it was repeated the next year, and the year after that, quickly becoming "traditionalized" in the repertoire of Palmetto Day activities.

Unfortunately, the goodwill between the federal military and citizenry in Charleston did not long survive the Mexican War. In the bitter political debate over the captured territories that erupted before the war was even over, sectional wounds reopened and, predictably, resurfaced in subsequent Palmetto Day observances. At the 1850 dinner in the fort compound, angry and saber-rattling toasts indicated that the secessionist solution to South Carolina's pique was as fashionable as ever. One of the Moultrie Guards revived the Thermopyle theme, declaring: "The North will find a Salamis and Platra beyond." Another blasted "Northern demagogues" and "Northern Jacobinism," suggesting that the Southern Convention become a Southern Congress. Other participants elaborated the theme, easily finding contemporary relevance for the long-ago battle: "It was fought for Independence then, we are ready to strike for Independence now"; "Revolution—the Resort of freemen under oppression"; "The Day . . . a warning to tyrants and Oppressors."[55] This was too much for the fort's commander, one Colonel Irving, and the next year he denied Charlestonians the use of the fort, "on the ground that he, as an officer of the Federal Government, could not permit such language, as had been used at the last celebration, to be uttered again within the precincts of the Fort."

Irving was to hear far worse. Infuriated at being denied the use of the "sacred ground" they considered rightly theirs, and by a representative of the very federal establishment they railed against, the arrangements committee for the Sullivan's Island celebrators determined to make this Palmetto Day a particularly pointed and well-publicized protest. Because they could not hold their ceremonies inside the fort, they built a fifty-two-foot-square pavilion, which alone accommodated some three hundred people, just outside it, virtually "under the shadow of the Fort." It was "prettily decorated" with leaves of the venerated palmetto, and instead of the stars and stripes under which they had formerly celebrated, the committee surmounted the pavilion with their own banner, "a white flag, on which was neatly inscribed a single star and a Palmetto Tree."

The featured orator did not mince words. For him, the 1776 battle was "the first act in the Drama which had led to the formation of that Constitution, under which [South Carolina] had, from the commencement of the present century, been suffering." Now, "plundered of her commerce, and her wealth by partial and protective legislation, she is taunted with her weakness and poverty, and as if to bring the burning sense of shame and degradation to our very hearts and homes, we are this day excluded by Federal soldiers, from the spot, which has been stained with the best blood of the State." All this, because South Carolinians had dared to oppose "the unconstitutional and insulting Legislation of the usurping government whom they [the garrison] serve"—ironically, he might have added, on a spot that had made opposition glorious. He reminded his listeners that their "ancestors gathered and fought under the sovereign banner of South Carolina," not that of the United States, and that it was high time to do so again. It was his sincere conviction, he concluded, "that the only method to be resorted to, was the dissolution of the Union" as soon as possible. As for the federal government, represented by the garrison soldiers who were undoubtedly listening to all this, "our little state can make it a dangerous thing to invade her, and a costly experiment to insult her."

The oration was seconded at dinner by the most belligerent toasts yet addressed on Palmetto Day. "Surrendered for our defense," cried one in a salute to the fort, "our defense requires that it should be surrendered back again. Let the State order, and it shall be done." Another declared, "The time has now arrived when it becomes her to throw off the shackles of an oppressive and tyrannical government." Three cheers went up for "the flag that waves over us," not the flag of the United States, but to the palmetto-and-star emblem of their regional pride and allegiance. "We once loved the Stars and Stripes, when they were the symbol of freedom," confessed a participant, but it was now "the emblem of an infamous and degraded Tyranny." Stoking the already palpable indignation over the alleged violation of sacred space, an indignant patriot reminded his fellows that some of the defenders killed in action seventy-five years earlier were buried on the other side of the fort wall. "The North has stolen the very graves of our dead Warriors," he railed, "and we are bound to avenge the act."[56]

After six years of this sort of vitriol, a new fort commander worked out a compromise with Charleston citizens that reopened the fort for the purpose of accommodating the orations, but the dinners (with their inflammatory toasts) had to take place back in the city. As a consequence of being excluded from the historic fort, Charleston's growing number of volunteer militia units were forced to look elsewhere for places to celebrate. In the process of gathering and marching to the Citadel, Hibernian Hall, Mount Pleasant, and various other places in and around the city on Palmetto Day, the militia formed colorful parades with marching bands that recaptured something of the public participation of revolutionary times.[57]

By the end of the 1850s, Palmetto Day had come full circle, from an active revolutionary festival, to a commemoration, to virtual oblivion, then to rebirth as regional saga, political rally, and finally once again as a revolutionary festival. From an important but much-overlooked act of resistance in 1776, Charleston patriots had transformed the event in their minds to "the opening action of the Revolution," "the longest fought, most worthy and most brilliant engagement of the Revolution" and "the first victory of the Revolution," which by and of itself constituted "a practical declaration of American Independence."[58] As far as Charlestonians were concerned, the earlier military actions at Lexington, Concord, Bunker Hill, and Moore's Creek, and the political act of July 4, 1776, might never have happened; for them, the successful defense of Fort Moultrie on June 28, 1776, was "the dawn of American Freedom."[59]

Thus claiming to have initiated the fight for American liberty, Charlestonians also maintained that their modern sentiments and actions were consistent with the original values of the republic. Remaining vestiges of respect and allegiance to the union quickly fell away. When Charlestonians laid the cornerstone for their grandest monument in 1858, dedicated to their nearly deified defender of states' rights, John C. Calhoun, they chose Palmetto Day, not July 4, for the ceremonies. The latter holiday, which had supplanted Palmetto Day so many years ago, was now in its death throes in South Carolina.[60] Palmetto Day was Charleston's premier patriotic holiday now, the day when its citizens raised their glasses to "The Southern Confederacy—The only union to which the sons of the Palmetto will own allegiance."[61]

Palmetto Day in 1861 found Charleston reliving its imagined revolutionary past. Two months previously, Fort Moultrie had again fired its guns in anger at a symbol of oppression and tyranny, and Charleston was again the scene of an opening act of revolution. As "a hostile fleet" once more threatened Charleston, its citizens celebrated "this truly Southern Jubilee" with enthusiastic public demonstrations and cessations of business not seen since the Revolution. Bells rang, cannons thundered, and flags broke out from the public buildings and many private residences—the palmetto flag of South Carolina and the new flag of the Confederate States.[62]

As Palmetto Day demonstrates, nationalist festivals based on revolutionary events present the paradox of ostensibly nation-building rites that carried with them potentially nation-wrecking messages. The events they celebrated were originally acts of spectacular defiance of authority. Restraining the seditious message implicit in these kinds of nationalist rituals became the problem of the new authority, which had to decide what kind of political or social resistance, and how much, would be legitimate in the new regime. Ideally, commemorative events like Palmetto Day and Independence Day serve as "structuring" rituals, building and reinforcing people's membership in a national community. For reasons specific to Charleston's history, Palmetto Day did not function that way—or rather it did, but not in the way originally intended. By their very nature, nationalist festivals involve a certain degree of ambiguity and tension. Their purpose is to convince people of their kinship with thousands or even millions of other citizens that is physically impossible for them to experience genuinely. Nationalism becomes thus a mass act of faith in an immense, hypothetical "extended family" that frequently competes with the narrower, personally experienced "community of allegiance."

South Carolina's attachment to a federal government may well have been conditional from the beginning, as one historian has argued; American nationalism may have been more fragile and more tenuous there than in other states.[63] The uncertainty of South Carolina's political loyalties may well help to explain why early efforts to work Palmetto Day into an American national calendar failed. But Palmetto Day succeeded brilliantly on a different level when, in the middle of the nineteenth century, the "nation" it spoke to and South Carolina's community of allegiance corresponded more closely. Palmetto Day may have failed as commemoration, even at the local level, but it survived, or rather was revived, by those who adapted its radical message to contemporary concerns. A new generation of South Carolina patriots rediscovered the original, revolutionary messages of Palmetto Day: defiance of authority, and repudiation of outworn allegiances. For them, the 1776 battle did not so much presage the creation of an indissoluble union as it justified the dissolution of a "tyrannous" union, by force if necessary. Thus, finally, instead of drawing Charlestonians into the master American cultural fiction *e pluribus unum*, Palmetto Day buttressed a belief in a unique South Carolinian destiny, in which attachment to a national state was unnecessary and irrelevant.

The author wishes to extend particular thanks to C. Patton Hash at the South Carolina Historical Society in Charleston for sharing much of his own Palmetto Day research.

Notes

1. In 1844 a contributor to *Fraser's* magazine waggishly defined nationalism as "another word for egotism." *Oxford English Dictionary* (New York: Oxford University Press, 1971).

2. James H. Kettner, *The Development of American Citizenship, 1608–1870* (Chapel Hill: University of North Carolina Press, 1978), 3.

3. John Murrin, "A Roof Without Walls: The Dilemma of American National Identity," in Richard Beeman, Stephen Botein, and Edward C. Carter II, eds., *Beyond Confederation: Origins of the Constitution and American National Identity* (Chapel Hill: University of North Carolina Press, 1987), 344.

4. John McCardell, *The Idea of a Southern Nation: Southern Nationalists and Southern Nationalism, 1830–1860* (New York: W. W. Norton, 1979), 6.

5. Ibid., 5.

6. For examples, see Lynn Hunt, *Politics, Culture, and Class in the French Revolution* (Berkeley and Los Angeles: University of California Press, 1984); Sean Wilentz, *Rites of Power: Ritual and Politics Since the Middle Ages* (Philadelphia: University of Pennsylvania Press, 1985); Susan G. Davis, *Parades and Power: Street Theater in Nineteenth-Century Philadelphia* (Berkeley and Los Angeles: University of California Press, 1986); David Proctor, *Enacting Political Culture: Rhetorical Transformations of Liberty Weekend 1986* (New York: Praeger, 1991). Most recently, a trio of monographs, all published within the same year, focused on ritual and nationalism in the early American republic: Simon Newman, *Parades and the Politics of the Streets: Festive Culture in the Early American Republic* (Philadelphia: University of Pennsylvania Press, 1997); Len Travers, *Celebrating the Fourth: Independence Day and the Rites of Nationalism in the Early Republic* (Amherst: University of Massachusetts Press, 1997); and David Waldstreicher, *In the Midst of Perpetual Fetes: The Making of American Nationalism, 1760–1820* (Chapel Hill: University of North Carolina Press, 1997).

7. For examples, Christian "mystery plays" or early modern civic processions, see Charles Pythian-Adams, "Ceremony and the Citizen: The Communal Year at Coventry, 1450–1550," in Peter Clark and Paul Sack, eds., *Crisis and Order in English Towns 1500–1700: Essays in Urban History* (London: Routledge & Kegan Paul, 1972), 57–85.

8. See *Gazette of the State of South Carolina,* June 30, 1777, and Elmer Douglas Johnson, trans., "Frenchman Visits Charleston in 1777," *South Carolina Historical and Genealogical Magazine* 52 (April 1951), 89–92, for first Palmetto Day exercises. On the makeup of the Palmetto Society, see Richard Walsh, *Charleston's Sons of Liberty: A Study of the Artisans, 1763–1789* (Columbia: University of South Carolina Press, 1968), 116. Walsh implies that the Society was made up exclusively of artisans and tradesmen, but I believe there were some professionals and merchants involved as well; certainly this was the case after the British occupation of the city.

9. It is tempting to imagine the period from June 28 to July 4 as a week-long patriotic festival in Charleston, with Palmetto Day kicking off observances that climaxed on Independence Day, but such does not appear to have been the case.

10. Louisa Susannah Wells, *The Journal of a Voyage from Charleston, S.C., to London Undertaken During the American Revolution by a Daughter of an Eminent Loyalist in the Year 1778 and Written from Memory Only* (New York: New York Historical Society, 1906), 2.

11. *Gazette of the State of South Carolina,* July 8, 1778.

12. David Cressy argues that the origins of modern nationalist festive style, in England at any rate, date to the sixteenth century, although the forms of celebration are much older than that. David Cressy, *Bonfires and Bells: National Memory and the Protestant Calendar in Elizabethan and Stuart England* (Berkeley and Los Angeles: University of California Press, 1989).

13. Peter Shaw, *American Patriots and the Rituals of Revolution* (Cambridge, Mass.: Harvard University Press, 1981); Waldstreicher, *In the Midst of Perpetual Fetes,* chap. 1.

14. Richard L. Bushman describes "monarchical culture" in prerevolutionary America in *King and People in Provincial Massachusetts* (Chapel Hill: University of North Carolina Press, 1985).

15. For example, Concord held its first public commemoration of the action at the Old North Bridge in 1823.

16. For the philanthropic mission of the Palmetto Society, see *South Carolina Weekly Gazette,* July 5, 1783; and *South Carolina Gazette & Public Advertiser,* June 2, 1784. For the toast, *South Carolina Gazette & Public Advertiser,* June 29, 1785.

17. A significant exception is the performance, in 1794, of "The Attack on Fort Moultrie" at the City Theater. This historical play was obviously written to be performed on or about June 28 and featured some stirring rhetoric, an excerpt of which appeared in the *Columbian Herald,* July 4, 1794. However, I have been unable to find any other part of the script, and it appears never to have been printed or performed again.

18. *Charleston Courier,* June 29, 1808; June 28, 1809.

19. *Charleston Courier,* June 26, 1812.

20. *The Investigator* (Charleston, S.C.), June 29, 1813.

21. For example, postwar revelers in Charleston raised their glasses to "The Late War," saying, "It has brightened the character of the nation, and made every American feel he had a country." *Southern Patriot,* July 5, 1815.

22. *Charleston Courier,* June 29, 1818.

23. *Charleston Mercury,* June 28, 1823.

24. Charles S. Sydnor, *The Development of Southern Sectionalism, 1819–1848* (Baton Rouge: Louisiana State University Press, 1966), 111.

25. Ibid., 132; Glover Moore, *The Missouri Controversy, 1819–1821* (Lexington: University of Kentucky Press, 1953).

26. George C. Rogers Jr., *Charleston in the Age of the Pinckneys* (Norman: University of Oklahoma Press, 1969), 135–45.

27. Alexander Garden, *Anecdotes of the Revolutionary War* (Charleston, S.C., 1822); Rogers, *Charleston in the Age of the Pinckneys,* 150–51.

28. *Charleston Mercury,* June 28, 1825.

29. *Charleston Courier,* June 16, 1825; *Charleston Mercury,* June 29, 1825.
30. *Charleston Mercury,* July 4, 1826.
31. *Charleston Courier,* July 29, 1818; *Charleston Mercury,* July 28, 1823; June 29, 1826.
32. *Charleston Mercury,* June 30, 1828.
33. *Charleston Mercury,* June 30, 1828; *Charleston Courier,* June 30, 1828.
34. *Charleston Mercury,* June 28, 1828.
35. *Charleston Mercury,* July 7, 1829.
36. *Charleston Mercury,* June 28, 1830; *Charleston Courier,* June 30, 1830.
37. *Charleston Mercury,* June 28, 1831; June 30, 1830.
38. *Charleston Courier,* July 2, 1805.
39. *Charleston Courier,* June 30, 1826; June 28, 1831; June 28, 1847; *Charleston Mercury,* June 28, 1828.
40. And still do, incidentally.
41. *Charleston Courier,* June 29, 1853.
42. *Charleston Mercury,* July 4, 1829.
43. *Charleston Courier,* June 28, 1855.
44. *Charleston Courier,* June 28, 1836.
45. *Charleston Courier,* June 28, 1821.
46. *Charleston Mercury,* June 30, 1828 (italics in the original)
47. *Charleston Courier,* June 28, 1847.
48. *Charleston Courier,* June 28, 1861.
49. *Charleston Courier,* June 28, 1845.
50. *Charleston Mercury,* June 28, 1828. In fact, eighteenth-century communications being what they were, Congress did not learn about the British repulse at Charleston until the following July 19—three weeks after the event and more than two weeks after declaring independence. See *Journals of the Continental Congress, 1774–1789* (Washington, D.C.: U.S. Government Printing Office, 1906), 5:593; *Pennsylvania Gazette,* July 24, 1776.
51. *Charleston Courier,* June 28, 1836; June 28, 1833.
52. *Charleston Courier,* June 28, 1836; June 28, 1833.
53. *Charleston Mercury,* June 30, 1834.
54. *Charleston Courier,* June 27, 28, and 29, 1844.
55. *Charleston Courier,* June 29, 1850.
56. The preceding account of the 1851 proceedings is from the *Charleston Courier,* June 29, 1851.
57. According to one correspondent, these displays were especially gratifying to "the usual representatives of 'Young Carolina' and 'Young Africa.'" The latter, he explained, "seem to enjoy the lion's share of all our festive days, and if anyone wished to verify by observation the happiness, mirth and quiet contentment of the race, in its appropriate and natural relationship to a master-race of protectors and guardians, the streets of Charleston, on any public day, would afford abundant opportunities." *Charleston Courier,* June 29, 1855.
58. *Charleston Courier,* June 28, 1860; *Charleston Mercury,* June 30, 1856; *Charleston Courier,* June 30, 1859.
59. *Charleston Mercury,* June 29, 1855. South Carolina patriots discovered an ingenious explanation for the demoralizing loss of Charleston to the British in 1780: the defending American army was led by General Benjamin Lincoln, a Massachusetts man, and by other "commanders not native to the soil and not acquainted with the genius of its sons." *Charleston Courier,* June 28, 1858.
60. A. V. Huff Jr., "The Eagle and the Vulture: Changing Attitudes Toward Nationalism in Fourth of July Orations Delivered in Charleston, 1788–1861," *South Atlantic Quarterly* 73 (Winter 1974), 10–22.

61. *Charleston Courier*, June 29, 1854. Curiously, the toast was followed by a rendition of "The Star Spangled Banner."
62. *Charleston Courier*, June 28 and 29, 1861.
63. Mark D. Kaplapnoff, "How Federalist Was South Carolina in 1787–1788?" in David R. Chestnutt and Clyde N. Wilson, eds., *The Meaning of South Carolina History: Essays in Honor of George C. Rogers Jr.* (Columbia: University of South Carolina Press, 1991), 67–103.

Contributors and Acknowledgments

ROGER D. ABRAHAMS was most recently the Hum Rosen Professor of Folklore and Folklife and Director of the Center for Folklore and Ethnography at the University of Pennsylvania. His most recent publications concern the intersection of folklore, culture, and history, especially in Renaissance Europe and Early America.

SUSAN BRANSON is Assistant Professor in American history at the University of Texas at Dallas. She has recently published *"These Fiery Frenchified Dames": Women and Political Culture in Early National Philadelphia*, published by the University of Pennsylvania Press in 2001.

MATTHEW DENNIS is Associate Professor of History at the University of Oregon. He is the author of *Cultivating a Landscape of Peace: Iroquois-European Encounters in Seventeenth-Century America* (1993) and *Red, White, and Blue Letter Days: Identity, Public Memory, and the American Calendar* (2001), both published by Cornell University Press.

THOMAS J. HUMPHREY is Assistant Professor at Cleveland State University. He has written several essays on rioting in eighteenth-century New York and is currently writing "This Land Is Our Land: Rioting and Revolution in New York's Hudson Valley, 1753–1797."

SUSAN E. KLEPP is Professor of History at Temple University and chair of the executive council of the McNeil Center for Early American Studies. Her other publications include *The Infortunate: The Voyage and Adventures of an Indentured Servant*, with Billy Smith (Penn State Press, 1992).

BRENDAN McCONVILLE is Associate Professor of History at SUNY-Binghamton. He is the author of *"Those Daring Disturbers of the Public Peace": Agrarian Unrest and the Struggle for Political Legitimacy in New Jersey*, published by Cornell University Press in 1999.

SIMON P. NEWMAN is Director of the Andrew Hook Centre for American Studies at the University of Glasgow. His most recent book is *Parades and the Politics of the Street: Festive Culture in the Early American Republic*, published by the University of Pennsylvania Press in 1997. His next book, *Embodied History: Reading the Bodies of the Poor in Early National Philadelphia*, will appear in 2002.

WILLIAM PENCAK, Professor of History at The Pennsylvania State University, edited *Pennsylvania History* from 1994 to 2002 and edits *Explorations in Early American Culture: The Annual Journal of the McNeil Center for Early American Studies*. Other books he has edited with Penn State Press include (with John Frantz) *Beyond Philadelphia: The American Revolution in the Pennsylvania Hinterland;* (with William Alan Blair) *Making and Remaking Pennsylvania's Civil War;* and (with Daniel K. Richter) *Friends and Enemies in Penn's Woods* (forthcoming).

The late WILLIAM D. PIERSEN, Professor of History at Fiske University, was the author of *From Africa to America: African-American History from the Colonial Era to the Early Republic*, published by Twayne Publishers in 1996; *Black Legacy: America's Hidden Heritage*, published by the University of Massachusetts Press in 1993; and *Black Yankees: The Development of an Afro-American Subculture in Eighteenth-Century New England*, published by the University of Massachusetts Press in 1988.

STEVEN J. STEWART resides in Chalfont, Pennsylvania, with his wife, Terry. They have started a company that manufactures scale model trains. His co-authored book on the Pennsylvania Railroad was published by Carstens Publications in the fall of 2001.

LEN TRAVERS is Assistant Professor of History at the University of Massachusetts at Dartmouth. He is the author of *Celebrating the Fourth: Independence Day and the Rites of Nationalism in the Early Republic*, published by the University of Massachusetts Press in 1997.

* * *

We thank Peter Potter, editor-in-chief of Penn State Press, whose efforts were essential in bringing the volume to publication. We also thank our copyeditor Peggy Hoover and indexer Mary Mortensen for their superb efforts. In addition, Anthony Cutler persuaded us to make the book more appealing to anthropologists and folklorists, hence Roger Abrahams's introduction, and Richard S. Dunn deserves our greatest thanks for his wise advice and encouragement.

Index

abolitionists, 9
Abrahams, Roger, 261, 262, 264
Adams, Abigail, 159, 238
Adams, John
  Boston Massacre trial, 129–30
  on "citesses," 234
  on French Revolution, 238
  as president, 230, 243, 244
  pseudonyms, 131
  on Stamp Act, 138
Adams, John Quincy, 282
Adams, Samuel, 4, 131, 138, 151–52, 163, 215
"Adams and Liberty," 246
adultery
  legal punishments, 96
  punished with rough music, 47–48, 49–50, 52–56, 62–63, 90, 109, 110
Africa
  cultural influences on African American festivities, 257, 259, 262, 263–64, 266
  festivities, 257, 259, 263–64
  music, 268 n. 2
  satires of white visitors, 262
African American festivities
  African cultural influences, 257, 259, 262, 263–64, 266
  Christmas, 255, 257–58, 263
  corn huskings, 255, 261, 263
  costumes, 256, 265, 267
  dances, 260–62, 266, 267
  differences from European celebrations, 256–57, 266–67
  European cultural influences, 119–20 n. 2, 259, 264–65, 267–68
  funeral plays, 257, 258, 263
  guns fired in, 257
  humor in, 259–61, 262–63
  influence on white celebrations, 259, 261–62, 268
  Jon Koonering, 255, 257, 258, 260, 264–65, 266

Mardi Gras, 258–59, 260, 261
militia training, 263
Negro Election Day, 255, 256–57, 258, 263
nighttime, 263–64
noise level, 264
parades, 256–58, 259–61, 267
Pinkster, 119–20 n. 2, 255, 259
plays, 263
requests for gifts, 259, 265
satires of whites, 262–63
similarities across locations, 255–56, 257
slave festivals, 255, 258, 263
spectators' roles, 259–61, 262, 264, 267, 270 n. 24
styles, 256, 266–67
African Americans. *See also* slaves
  exclusion from public sphere, 15–16
  musicians, 260, 266
  participation in protests, 5
  as scapegoats for violence, 51
  violence against, 9
  voting rights, 9
African-British troops, 169
Albany (New York)
  African American festivities, 259
  Stamp Act riots, 111–14
Alexandria (Virginia), 235
Alford, Violet, 43, 165
Allison, Mary, 49, 79
Allison, William, 49
America: A Poem (Martin), 210
American Apollo, 215
American Company, 213–14
American Liberty: A Poem (Freneau), 210
American Revolution. *See also* Boston protests; Palmetto Day
  battle commemorations, 278
  British in Charleston, 273, 274, 278–79
  Bunker Hill, 135, 278, 281, 285–86
  crowd violence during, 8–9
  nationalism resulting from, 275

American revolution (cont'd)
  plays about, 218
  roles of crowds, 5, 8–9, 16
  rough music during, 6
  songs, 130, 141–48, 151, 185
  women's participation, 247
Anderson, Alexander, 241
Andre, John, 218
Andre (Dunlap), 218
Anglican churches, 93, 138
Annapolis (Maryland), 192, 194
Appleby, Joyce Oldham, 150
Arnold, Benedict, 159, 160, 170, 218
Articles of Confederation, 158, 213
Ashanti people, 262
Attleborough (Massachusetts), rough music episodes, 6, 54–56, 79, 96
Attucks, Crispus, 134
Avery, John, Jr., 128
Avery, Joseph, 67

Bache, Benjamin Franklin, 242
Bache, Sarah, 242
Bahamas, 257
Baltimore, French Revolutionary celebrations, 235
Bangs, Edward, 148
Banks, Mary Ogden, 95
Barlow, Joel, 208–9, 211
Barnum, P. T., 216
Bartlett, Josiah, 163, 168, 169
Beckwith, Martha, 266
Belknap, Jeremy, 215–16, 220
belsnicklers. *See* mummers
Bernard, Francis, 134
Bewell, Samuel, 65
Bickerstaff's *Almanac*, 131
Billings, Williams, 130
Birdsall, Benjamin, 74–76
Boardman, James, 263
Boords, John, 89
Bordeaux (France), 237
Boston. *See also* Boston protests
  anti-Catholic violence, 9
  commemorations of Columbus's voyage, 215–16
  Committee for Tarring and Feathering, 133
  customs commissioners, 134, 140, 146
  destruction of Hutchinson's house, 16, 129, 132, 138
  French Revolutionary celebrations, 233–34, 235, 238
  hostility toward British soldiers, 133, 140–41
  Liberty Tree, 132, 133, 136, 137, 140, 142, 145
  "Mohawks," 34, 130
  Pope's Day processions, 99, 106 n. 63, 130, 132, 133–34
  riots, 57
  rough music episodes, 6, 44, 47–48
  sex ratio of population, 233
  Sons of Liberty, 130, 137
  Stamp Act resistance, 99, 128, 131–32, 137
  tricolor cockades worn, 237, 238
Boston Continental Journal, 166
Boston Gazette, 130, 133, 135, 146, 210
Boston Massacre, 5, 141
  annual commemorations, 134–35
  boys involved, 129–30
  songs about, 141–43
  trial, 129–30
Boston protests
  boys involved, 128–29, 130
  creation of festivities, 133–35
  deaths, 130
  disguises, 130
  against impressment, 3–4, 51, 138, 144
  mock punishments, executions, and burials, 131–33, 136
  officials and crowds, 137–41
  playful elements, 127–28, 129–30, 149
  pseudonyms used, 130–31
  replacement of traditional authority symbols, 136
  sarcasm in, 135–36
Boston Tea Party, 130
Boswell, James, 154 n. 45
Bound Brook (New Jersey)
  Regulators, 98
  rough music episodes, 87, 89–90, 95, 96, 98
Bowditch, Thomas Edward, 262
boys
  involved in protests, 128–29, 130
  women dressed as, 109
Brackenridge, Hugh Henry, 208
Bradley, Richard, 48–49, 78
Brattle, William, 133, 150
Bridenbaugh, Carl, 184, 188
Brinkerhof, Stephen, 58
Brisby, James, 63–64

Index

Britain. *See also* American Revolution
  Columbus symbolism, 209–10
  craft guilds, 188
  festivities, 193
  "Heart of Oak," 143–44, 146, 154 n. 45
  immigrants from, 104–5 n. 39
  impressment of sailors, 238–39
  Jay Treaty, 243
  militia presentations by women, 253 n. 63
  political protests, 121 n. 8
  popular culture, 88, 104–5 n. 39
  Riot Act, 83 n. 37
  rough music in, 43, 44, 45–46, 88, 160
  Royal Navy, 3, 51, 144, 274
  Sherwood Forest, 125
  songs, 142–44
  War of 1812, 221, 279–80
  wars with France, 143, 236, 238
British army. *See also* Boston Massacre
  African soldiers, 169
  in Boston, 133, 140–41
  in Charleston, 273, 274, 278–79
  in Philadelphia, 158, 159, 160, 163, 170
  punishments, 104 n. 39
  rough music used against, 104 n. 39
  social contacts with Americans, 159, 160, 162, 166
  songs about, 141, 142
  suppression of land riots, 116
Brooklyn (New York), African American festivities, 267
Brown, Jared, 218
Bryant, William Cullen, 263
Brynson, Daniel, 92
Brynson, Frances, 92
Bunker Hill battle, 135, 278, 281, 285–86
Bunyan, John, 163
Burke, Emily, 260
Burnaby, Andrew, 261
Burr, Esther Edwards, 92, 93, 95
Burrowes, Edwin, 130
Bushman, Claudia, 210
Bute, Lord, 132
Butler, Richard, 219

Cabeen, Frances A. von, 189
Cadwalader, John, 170
Caillie, Rene, 262
Calhoun, John C., 282, 290
Calvinism, 88, 90

Canada, rough music episodes, 8, 44
Cape Fear (North Carolina), 257–58
Carson, William, 283
Catholics, violence against, 9
celebrations. *See* festivities; holidays
charitable organizations, 248
charivari, 43, 48. *See also* rough music
Charleston Mercury, 282, 284, 285–86
Charleston (South Carolina). *See also* Palmetto Day
  British assault, 273, 274
  British occupation, 278–79
  divisions from North, 280–81, 287
  Fort Moultrie, 273–74, 276, 279, 282, 285–88, 290, 291
  Fourth of July celebrations, 277, 279
  French Revolutionary celebrations, 233
  "marriage" of women, 236
  tricolor cockades worn, 237
Charleton, John, 63
Chatfield, Henry, 65, 73
Chatfield, John, 66, 68
Chester County (Pennsylvania), 46–47
children. *See* boys
Chotard, Dubois, 240
Christie, John, 49
Christmas, African American celebrations, 255, 257–58, 263
Cincinnati (Ohio), 221
cities
  crowd violence in, 78–79
  rough music in, 8, 14, 47–48, 49–50
City Gazette (Charleston), 236
Civil War
  draft riots, 9
  states' rights debate, 282–85, 287–92
Clarke, Elizabeth, 57–60
Clarke, Jonathan, 54
Clarke, William, 57–59
class conflict. *See also* land riots
  increase in, 158
  in legal system, 123 n. 18
  moral differences, 8
  overcome in prerevolutionary America, 149–51
  in Philadelphia, 167
  in rough music, 8, 160–62, 170–71
  satires of women's hairstyles, 156
Clay, Henry, 10–11

clothing. *See also* costumes
  men's, 166–67, 168
  plain, 163, 164, 166–67, 168
  related to politics and religion, 163, 164, 166–67, 168
  women's fashions, 167, 168
clubs. *See also* Sons of St. Tammany
  men's, 194–95
  secret societies, 184, 194
Cobbett, William, 243, 244
Colden, Alice, 53
Colden, Cadwallader, 53
Cole, Elisha, 115
Colman, George, 143
Colony on Schuylkill, 188, 189
Columbiad (Barlow), 209
"Columbia" (Dwight), 211
Columbia (female figure), 211, 212, 219, 221
Columbian Magazine, 211
The Columbian Tragedy, 219
Columbia Rediviva (ship), 211
Columbia River, 211, 222
Columbia (ship), 225 n. 17
Columbia (South Carolina), 211
Columbia University, 211
Columbus, Christopher
  commemorations of voyage, 205, 206, 214–16, 217–18
  as ethnic hero, 206
  Indians' views of, 206–7
  monuments to, 216, 226 n. 23
  name used in New World, 207, 211, 213, 220, 221–22
  as nationalist symbol, 206, 208–9, 210–14, 217, 219–20
  poetic references, 208, 209, 210–11
  Puritans' view of, 207
  symbolism, 207–8, 209–10
Columbus, or The World Discovered (Morton), 218
Columbus (Ohio), 221
communities
  moral consensus in, 79, 172
  rough music used for social control, 7–8, 88, 90, 108, 111, 162
  symbolic systems, 28–29
Conestoga Indians, 8–9
Conklin, Jacob, 68
Conklin, Jeremiah, 67, 68
Conklin, Nathan, 65, 66

Connecticut
  legal system, 92
  rough music episodes, 45, 77, 122–23 n. 17
Connecticut Courant, 234
Constitution, U.S., 213–14, 275
Continental Army, 104 n. 39, 158, 159, 237
Continental Congress, 161
Coram Committee of Safety, 73
corn huskings, 255, 261, 263
Cornplanter, 179, 183, 190, 196, 199–200
costumes
  in African American festivities, 256, 265, 267
  materials, 23
  of outsider figures, 29
  of White Indians, 187, 190, 192, 193
Courtlandt's Manor, 50, 79
craft guilds, 188
Crannel, V., 48
Creek Indians, 220
Cresswell, Nicholas, 262
Cressy, David, 182
Cromwell, Oliver, 131
Cronkheight, George, 50
crowd activities. *See also* festivities; parades; protests; riots; rough music
  in colonial America, 4–5
  costumes, 23
  noise, 22
  objects and props used, 22–23, 181, 191
  risks, 23
  scholarship on, 14, 21–22, 26–28, 29–32, 34–35
  violence, 8–9, 17
Cuba, Day of Kings, 265–66
cultural critique, 31
cultural donor figures, 186–87
cultural transference
  activities, 179–80
  in African American festivities, 259, 264–65, 267–68
  customs of conquered peoples adopted by conquerors, 180
  between Europe and America, 88, 104–5 n. 39
  between Europeans and Indians, 198–99, 200

dances
  African American, 258, 260–62, 266, 267
  French Revolutionary, 235, 236, 240, 241–43

Iroquois, 187
West Indian, 260, 262
Daniel, William, 96
Darnton, Robert, 31
Daughters of Liberty, 238
Davis, John, 66
Davis, Natalie Zemon, 5, 21, 43, 48, 165
Davis, Susan G., 12, 28
Dawes, T., 137
Dayton, Cornelia Hughes, 110
Dayton, Daniel, 68
Dayton, Ebenezer
  activities during Revolution, 73–74
  business, 64–65
  money lost, 67, 69–70
  prosecution of rough music perpetrators, 68–73, 80
  rough music against, 65–68
Dayton, Henry, 66, 71
Dayton, Jeremiah, 66
Dayton, Phebe Smith, 73
Dean, Elijah, 51
Deganawidah, 196–97
democracy. *See also* political parties
  groups excluded from, 15–16
  reform movements, 10
Democratic Party, 10–11, 12
Demos, John, 76
Dening, Greg, 32
Dennis, Matthew, 197
"Derry Down," 142, 143
Dickinson, John, 144–46, 150
Discovery (Freneau), 210–11
District of Columbia, 211
domestic violence. *See* spouse abuse
Dorson, Richard, 264
Douglass, William, 3–4
Drinker, Elizabeth, 157, 161, 163
Drinkwater, William, 45, 77
Dunham, Katherine, 260, 262
Dunlap, William, 218
Dunlap (Captain), 244–45
Dutchess County (New York), land riots, 114–18
Dutch immigrants, 119–20 n. 2
Dwight, Timothy, 211

East Hampton (New York), rough music episode, 64–73, 78, 79
East India Company, 130

Eddis, William, 192
Edenton (North Carolina), 257
Edes and Gill, 147
Edwards, Jonathan, 53, 207–8, 212
Election Day. *See* Negro Election Day
Elizabethtown (New Jersey)
  Regulars, 87, 96, 98
  rough music episodes, 89–90, 93, 95, 97, 98
England. *See* Britain
Essex County (Massachusetts), 101 n. 12
ethnic groups
  clubs, 194
  Columbus as hero, 206
  discrimination against, 227 n. 30
  rituals celebrating ancestry, 188
Europe. *See also* Britain; France
  craft guilds, 188
  cultural influences on African American festivities, 119–20 n. 2, 259, 264–65, 267–68
  fascination with New World, 33–34
  mummers, 29
  parades, 23–24
  patriarchy, 162
  public sphere, 14–15
  rough music, 108–9, 165
  women's roles, 110
Eve, Sallie, 157
evolution, anancastic and cataclasmine, 126

Fabre, Genevieve, 264–65
Fauchet, Jean Antoine Joseph, 240
"Feast of Reason" (Philadelphia), 239–41
Federalists
  criticism of French Revolution, 230, 238, 244
  holiday celebrations, 12, 229–30, 246–47
  popular political culture, 243–47
  relations with Britain, 239
  songs, 246
  views of political parties, 10
  views of women's political participation, 232, 234
  women, 244, 245
fertility, 165, 166
festivities. *See also* African American festivities; French Revolutionary celebrations; holidays; parades
  adoption of Constitution, 214
  in colonial America, 277

festivities (cont'd)
  commemorations of Columbus's voyage, 205, 206, 214–16, 217–18
  conventional figures, 29
  distinction from rituals, 182
  in early United States, 182, 277–78
  English styles, 193
  formal, 23, 26, 28
  gender roles, 247
  historical memory and, 26, 27
  Indian styles, 193
  militia presentations, 244–46
  nationalistic, 11, 14, 133–35, 217, 275–76, 291
  outsider figures, 29, 30
  rituals, 34
  social meanings, 26, 33, 34
  spontaneity, 26, 28
Fishkill (New York), 57–61, 78, 79
Fithian, Philip, 257
Fithien, David, 66
Flaherty, David H., 44, 76–77, 78
Fliegelman, Jay, 130
Flint, Timothy, 258
folktales, 90
Fort Wilson incident, 7
Foucault, Michel, 123 n. 18, 126, 127
Fourth of July celebrations. *See also* Philadelphia, July Fourth rough music
  in Charleston, 277, 279
  decline in South, 290
  early, 276, 277, 278
  of Federalists, 246–47
  longevity, 274
  partisanship in, 12, 229–30
  Philadelphia parade, 159–60
France. *See also* French Revolution
  charivari, 43, 48
  relations with United States, 230, 243, 246
  wars with Britain, 143, 236, 238
  women's participation in politics, 237
Francis, John, 241
Franklin, Benjamin, 149, 168
Franks, Becky, 157, 159
Frazer, James George, 26–27
Frazier, E. Franklin, 264
Freedom's Journal, 267
Freemasons, 184, 194–95
French Revolution
  American reactions, 232
  American support, 217, 218, 230, 231, 236–37
  cockades worn, 237
  critics in United States, 230, 238, 244
  political theater, 240
  Reign of Terror, 15
  Rights of Man, 217, 235
French Revolutionary celebrations
  in Boston, 233–34, 235
  categories, 232
  dances and songs, 235, 236, 240, 241–43
  decline of, 243, 248
  feasts, festivals, and parades, 230, 231, 232–33, 239–41
  rituals and symbols, 241
  tricolor cockades worn, 233–34, 235, 237, 238–39, 243
  women's participation, 231, 232, 233–34, 236–37, 240–41
Freneau, Philip, 208, 209, 210–11, 220–21
Fries's Rebellion, 9
Fuller, Nicolas, 207

Gabriel's Rebellion, 9
Garden, Alexander, 281, 282, 285
Gardiner, Abraham, 66, 67, 68
Garrick, David, 143, 146
gender relations. *See also* marriages; patriarchy
  in civic festivities, 247
  in colonial New England, 90–91
  criticism of elite men, 162–63
  criticism of women's political participation, 231, 234
  effects of changes in consumption, 94
  in politics, 247–48
  Puritan views of roles, 90, 110
  in Revolution, 164–65, 168, 171
  separate spheres, 231–32
Gênet, Edmond, 11, 12
George III, King, 117, 147, 210
Georgia, African American festivities, 258, 260
Gilje, Paul, 5, 9
Goldstone, Jack, 151
Goodrich, Peter, 46
Gray, Robert, 211
Great Awakening, 6, 93
Greenberg, Douglas, 78–79
Greene, William, 54
Greenland, Henry, 91–92
Grenville, George, 132, 210
Griffitts, Hannah, 163
Gross, Robert, 14

Habermas, Jürgen, 14–15, 139, 231
hairstyles
  of elite women, 156–58, 164, 168, 169, 170–71, 174 n. 21
  men's wigs, 157
Haiti, 260
Hale, Horatio, 189
Hamilton, Alexander, 10
Hamilton, Alexander, Dr., 189
Hamilton, Andrew, 159–60
Hancock, John, 131, 134, 150, 215
Harlequin's Invasion, 143
Harrison (customs commissioner), 140
Hatton, Anne Julia, 218
Hausbrook, Daniel, 61
Hays, James, 63–64
Hazard, Ebenezer, 185–86, 192
"Heart of Oak," 143–44, 146, 154 n. 45
Heckewelder, John, 185
Hedges, Daniel, 65–66
Hedges, Henry, 73
Hedges, Jeremiah, 65, 66
Hedges, Steven, 66
Hempstead (New York), rough music episode, 74–76, 79
heterotopias, 127
Hewson, Elizabeth, 244
Hiawatha, 196, 197
Hicks, Edward, 186
Hicks, Thomas, 68
Higby, James, 58, 60, 61
Higginbotham, Joseph, 50
Higham, John, 219, 220
Hodgson, Mrs., 167
Hoeder, Dirk, 5, 99
Holdridge, Hezekiah, 52–53, 77, 107–8
holidays. *See also* Christmas; festivities; Fourth of July celebrations; Palmetto Day
  partisanship in, 12, 229–30
  Washington's Birthday, 12, 229
Holmes, Jonathan, 89, 94–95
homeless, violence against, 51–52
Hopkinson, Mrs. Joseph, 245
Howe, Sir William, 159, 169, 170
Howel, Jehiel, 67, 71
Hughson, George, 115, 116
Hughson, Robert, 115
Huizinga, Johan, 8, 126, 127
humor
  in political protests, 131–32

  sarcasm, 135–36, 142
  satire, 24, 148, 156, 262–63
Humphrey, Thomas, 7
Humphrey, William, 60–61, 78
Hunt, Jeremiah, 48
Hunt, Lynn, 240
Hutcheson, Samuel, 66–67, 69, 71
Hutchinson, Thomas
  British soldiers and, 141
  caricatures of, 131
  destruction of house, 16, 129, 132, 138
  lack of support for Stamp Act, 137, 139
  opposition to, 134, 137–39
  poetry, 210
  sons, 133

Ide, Abigail, 56
Ide, Benjamin, Jr., 55, 56
imitation, 32–33
Independence Day. *See* Fourth of July celebrations
Independent Advertiser, 4, 138
The Indian Burying Ground (Freneau), 220–21
Indians. *See also* Iroquois people; Seneca people; White Indians
  battles with Americans, 219
  Europeans' encounters with, 197–99
  festivities, 193, 199
  land disputes, 114, 117
  legends about, 186–87
  massacres of, 8–9
  myth of vanishing, 220–21
  Penn's Treaty, 180, 182, 184, 185, 186, 191, 197
  relations with British settlers, 180, 183
  seen as savages, 219, 221
  stereotypes of, 189
  symbolism, 219, 224–25 n. 13
  treaties with United States, 190, 197
  views of Columbus, 206–7
individuals, relationship to society, 127
Iroquois people. *See also* Seneca people
  Condolence Ceremony, 183, 197
  confederation, 197
  dances, 187
  importance of peacemaking, 196
  rituals, 183, 196–97
  visits to Philadelphia, 183
Irving (Colonel), 288

Isaacs, Aaron, Jr., 65, 66, 67, 68
Isaacs, Aaron, Sr., 67

Jackson, Andrew, 10–11, 282
Jackson, Jacob, 74
Jackson, James, 49
Jackson, Samuel, 75
Jamaica, 257
Janse, Peter, 59
Jasper (Sergeant), 281
Jay, John, 75, 243
Jay Treaty, 243
jazz, 260, 261
Jefferson, Randolph, 271 n. 47
Jefferson, Thomas, 10
Jeffersonian Republicans, 10
John Canno festival. *See* Jon Koonering (Jonkonnu) festival
Johnson, Bunk, 260
Johnson, Peter, 58, 61
Johnson, Rachel, 52
Jones, David, 61–62
Jones, Howard Mumford, 33
Jones, Samuel, 73
Jon Koonering (Jonkonnu) festival, 255, 257, 258, 260, 264–65, 266
Jordan, Winthrop, 130
Joyce Jr., 106 n. 63, 133
July Fourth. *See* Fourth of July celebrations

Kempe, John Tabor
  Dayton case, 67, 68–73
  investigations of rough music, 51–52
  letters to, 60–61
  prosecutions of rough music perpetrators, 58, 78, 117
  records of rough music, 6
  Seaman case, 75
Kempe, William
  letters to, 50–51, 52–53, 60
  prosecutions of rough music perpetrators, 49, 50, 78
Kettner, James, 275
Kevelson, Roberta, 125–26, 127, 150
Kilroe, Edwin Patrick, 189
Kinser, Samuel, 261, 264
Kirkpatrick, James, 209
Kniffin, Ebenezer, 52–53
Knowles, Charles, 3
Knowlton, Mr., 63, 64

Krafft, Michael, 258–59

Ladies' Association, 248
Lafayette, Marie Joseph Motier, Marquis de, 217
land riots, 9, 48, 62, 111, 114–18
Latin American revolutions, 150
law enforcement. *See also* legal system
  in colonial America, 76, 77, 78
  punishment of spouse abuse and adultery, 91–92, 96, 103 n. 22
  rough music as substitute for, 42, 44, 76–77, 79–80, 96–97, 107–8
Lawton, Andrew, 44
lawyers, professional, 92
Lee, Charles, 274
Lee, Richard Henry, 162, 167–68
legal system
  confrontations between classes in, 123 n. 18
  expenses of prosecution, 50, 73, 78
  judges, 61–62
  lack of authority, 8
  mock trials, 115–16
  of New Jersey, 91–93, 96, 103 n. 22
  of New York, 123 n. 18
  playful protests against, 125–26
  power of elite in, 116–17, 118, 123 n. 18
  prosecutions of rough music perpetrators, 48–50, 59–61, 63, 66, 68–73, 78, 79
  rights of women, 92
  social functions, 118
Lemisch, Jesse, 5
Lenni Lenape people, 185, 189–90, 195, 197
Lent, Abraham, 59
Lent, Abraham, Jr., 60
Lent, Isaac, 60, 61
Lewis, Micah, 63–64
Liberty, goddess of, 219
Liberty Boys, 99, 130
"Liberty Hall," 142
Liberty (Rusticus), 210
"Liberty Song," 144–46, 150
Liberty Tree
  in Boston, 132, 133, 136, 137, 140, 142, 145
  symbolism, 247
Lillie, Theophilus, 129
Little, Kenneth, 259
Livingston, James, 114
Livingston, Robert, Jr., 117

Livingston, Robert L., 61–62
Livingston, Robert R., 111, 117
Livingston family, 62
Lockwood, Ephraim, 49
"Lodgings for Single Gentlemen," 143
London, rough music episodes, 45–46
Louisiana, rough music in, 44
lower classes. *See also* class conflict
   exclusion from public sphere, 15
   participation in rough music, 160–61
   political participation, 14
   protests, 5, 12
   social and moral differences from upper class, 8
   victims of rough music, 51–52
loyalists
   in Boston, 131, 132
   hostility toward, 136
   on Long Island, 73–74, 75
   poetry, 210
   rough music against, 6, 8, 64
   violence against, 16
Ludeman, John, 95
Ludlow, A., 58
Lynd, Staughton, 5
Lyneall, Barbara, 63–64
Lyon, Abigail, 245

Mackensie (homeless man), 51–52
Mackintosh, Ebenezer, 131, 133–34, 137, 150
Mackintosh, Pasquale Paoli, 131
MacPherson's Blues, 245
Madison, James, 17
Maier, Pauline, 4–5, 9
Maine
   militia presentations, 245
   White Indians, 34
Mandingo people, 262
Mangourit, M. A. B., 236
Mardi Gras, 258–59, 260, 261
Maring people, 149
Marion, Francis, 281
Marks, Isaac, 48
marriages. *See also* adultery; spouse abuse
   companionate, 164
   women's mock, 236
Marriot, Mrs., 242
Martin, Alexander, 210
Marx, Karl, 149

masks and masquerading. *See also* White Indians
   in Boston protests, 130
   Jon Koonering festival, 257, 258, 266
   meanings, 30, 33
   West African, 266
Masons. *See* Freemasons
Massachusetts. *See also* Boston
   administrative elite, 138–39
   Anglican churches, 138
   Bunker Hill battle, 135, 278, 281, 285–86
   land bank crisis, 6
   laws against rough music, 55
   legislature, 136, 139–40
   Plymouth Plantation, 24
   rough music episodes, 6, 54–56, 79, 96, 101 n. 12
   Shays' Rebellion, 4, 152
Massachusetts Calendar, 131
Massachusetts Historical Society, 215–16
Massachusetts Spy, 244
Mather, Cotton, 131, 212
McClenahan, Blair, 236
McLean, John, 71–72
measles, 64–65, 71–72
Mein, John, 131, 132
men. *See also* gender relations; spouse abuse
   clothing, 166–67, 168
   clubs, 194–95
   control of violent, 91–92
   criticism of elite, 162–63
   masculinity, 162–63, 170, 171
   political roles, 231
   proportion of New England population, 91
   views of women's political participation, 235
   wigs, 157
Menotomy (Massachusetts), 235
Mexican War, 287, 288
Mick, Andrew, 59, 60, 61
Micklus, Robert, 194
Middletown (Connecticut), Fourth of July celebrations, 246–47
Mifflin, Sarah, 157
militia presentations, 244–46, 253 n. 63
militias
   African American, 263
   protests against service in, 12
millennialism, 207
Miller, Johannes, 50
Mischianza, 158, 163, 170

Mittelfort, Gottlieb, 192
Mobile (Alabama), African American festivities, 255, 258–59
Moger, Isiah, 71
Moger, James, 70–71
monarchies, 23–24
monuments
  Bunker Hill, 281
  to Columbus, 216, 226 n. 23
morality
  class differences, 8
  community consensus, 79, 172
  laws, 76
  linked to patriotism, 163
  Puritan, 96
  rough music as enforcement mechanism, 7–8, 42, 44, 76–77, 79–80, 96–97, 107–8, 162
Morgan, Edmund S., 16–17, 137
Morris, Ann White, 170
Morris, Richard, 73
Morristown (New Jersey), 237
Morton (playwright), 218
motherhood
  criticisms of pregnancies, 166
  nationalistic metaphors, 130, 212
  republican, 235–36, 237, 241, 246
Moultrie, William, 273, 281, 285
Moultrieville (South Carolina), 282, 288
Muchlowain, Mary, 50
Muhlenberg, Henry Melchior, 157, 167, 169
Muirson, George, 68–69
Mulford, Anamias, 65, 66, 68
Mulford, Barnabas, 65, 68
Mulford, David, 71
Mulford, Elisha, Sr., 65–66
Mulford, Ezekiel, 66, 67, 68, 71
Mulford, Job, 66, 67
mummers, 29, 259, 265
Murray, James, 257–58
Murray, John, 70, 132
Murrin, John, 9, 275
music. *See also* songs
  African American, 260, 266
  jazz, 260, 261
  West African, 268 n. 2
Myers, Korah, 60, 61
My Night Gown and Slippers, 143

Napoleon Bonaparte, 15, 248
Nash, Gary, 99

national identity, in early America, 10
nationalism
  classical symbols, 219, 221
  Columbus as symbol, 206, 208–9, 210–14, 217, 219–20
  creating in public celebrations, 11, 14, 133–35, 217, 275–76, 291
  creation of American, 275
  definitions, 274–75
  female symbols, 211, 212, 219, 221
  patriarchal and matriarchal metaphors, 130, 212
  repression of dissent, 16
nationalist holidays. *See* Fourth of July celebrations; Palmetto Day
Negro Election Day, 255, 256–57, 258, 263
Nevill, Samuel, 209
Newark (New Jersey)
  Disciplinarians, 96, 98
  laws, 91
  Liberty Boys, 99
  religions of residents, 93
  rough music episodes, 62, 87, 89–90, 93, 95, 96, 98–99
new cultural history, 27, 31
New England
  crowd violence, 9
  gender relations, 90–91
  Negro Election Day, 255, 256–57, 258, 263
  rough music episodes, 6
  sex ratio of population, 91
New Hampshire
  French Revolutionary celebrations, 235
  riots, 6
New Haven (Connecticut), rough music episodes, 122–23 n. 17
New Jersey
  Anglican churches, 93
  conflicts over property rights, 92–93, 95–96, 98–99
  gentry, 97–98
  land riots, 9, 48
  legal system, 91–93, 96, 103 n. 22
  migrants from New England, 91
  Pinkster holiday, 255
  religious polarization, 93
  rough music episodes, 7, 62, 63, 87–88, 89–90, 92–96
New London (Connecticut), 233
New Milford (New York), 45

New Orleans
  African American festivities, 255, 258, 260
  Mardi Gras Indians, 260, 261
New York City
  African American parades, 270 n. 24
  commemorations of Columbus's voyage, 215–16
  Conspiracy of 1741, 6
  draft riots, 9
  French Revolutionary celebrations, 241–42
  New Year's Eve celebrations, 10
  parades, 214
  rough music episodes, 49–50, 62–63, 79, 96, 109–10
  Tammany Society, 211, 215–19, 220, 227 n. 30
New York (colony and state)
  ethnic groups, 6–7
  landlords, 116–17, 118, 123 n. 18
  land riots, 9, 48, 62, 111, 114–18
  legal system, 123 n. 18
  Pinkster holiday, 255, 259
  prosecutions of rough music perpetrators, 48–49
  rough music episodes, 6–7, 48–53, 57–61, 62–73, 74–76, 78, 79, 107–8
  Supreme Court, 48
New-York Historical Society, 216
New York Weekly Journal, 45–46, 47
New York Weekly Post Boy, 87
Nietzsche, Friedrich, 127
nonimportation agreements, 129, 133, 158–59, 238
North Carolina
  African American festivities, 257–58
  American Revolution in, 278
  Jon Koonering festival, 255, 257, 260, 264–65
  Regulators, 8
Northwest Ordinance, 213
nullification doctrine, 282, 286

Oliver, Andrew, 128, 132, 137–38
Oliver, Peter, 140
"On the Revolution in France," 242
operas, 218
Orphan Asylum Society New York, 248
Ortiz, Fernando, 265–66
Osborne, David, 68
Otis, James, 131, 132, 136, 144

Paine, Thomas, 135, 136, 217, 235
Palmer, Bryan, 8, 43, 44, 80

Palmetto Day
  declining interest in, 280, 281–82
  differing interpretations, 282–85
  evolution, 274
  first observance, 276–77
  meaning, 276
  nationalism in, 275, 285–87, 288–91
  observances in Fort Moultrie, 287–88
  popularity, 277, 279
  postwar celebrations, 279–80
  revival, 281, 282–85, 291–92
  states' rights represented in, 282–85, 287–92
  uniqueness, 278
Palmetto Society, 276, 279, 281–82, 283, 284, 293 n. 8
parades
  on adoption of Constitution, 214
  African American, 256–58
  in Europe, 23–24
  Fourth of July, 159–60
  nationalistic, 11
  as political protests, 12
  Pope's Day, 99, 106 n. 63, 130, 132, 133–34
  Sons of St. Tammany (Philadelphia), 187
Parker, Peter, 273, 274
"The Parody," 146–47
"The Parody Parodied," 147–48
Parsons, Henry, 65, 68
Parsons, Merry, 65
Parsons, Samuel, 66
patriarchy, 97
  in Europe, 162
  metaphors, 130, 212
  in revolutionary period, 168
  women's roles, 110
Patrick, Saint, 219
patriotism. *See also* nationalism
  displays of, 11
  moral implications, 163
  of women, 157, 158–59, 162, 163–65, 166
Patterson, Elizabeth, 62–63
Patterson, James, 62
Paxton Boys, 8–9
Peale, Charles Willson, 167
Peirce, Charles S., 126, 150
penitentiaries, 10
Penn family, 183, 188
Penn's Treaty, 180, 182, 184, 185, 186, 191, 197
Pennsylvania. *See also* Philadelphia
  conflicts between Indians and Europeans, 8–9, 183

Pennsylvania (cont'd)
  constitution, 164
  Fries's Rebellion, 9
  Quakers, 6
  rough music episodes, 7, 46–47
  state politics, 7, 183
  Whiskey Rebellion, 9
  Wyoming Valley, 9
Pennsylvania Gazette, 95
Perkins, Samuel, 63–64
Pernah, Luce, 101 n. 12
Perry, Isaac, 115
Peters, Samuel, 115–16
Philadelphia. *See also* Sons of St. Tammany (Philadelphia)
  African American festivities, 255
  British army ball, 158, 163, 170
  British army in, 159, 160
  City Tavern, 160
  class divisions, 167
  clubs, 184
  criticisms of women's fashions, 174 n. 21
  economic conditions during Revolution, 158
  election of 1742, 6
  Fort Wilson incident, 7
  French Revolutionary celebrations, 233, 235, 238, 239–41, 242
  Grand Federal Procession, 214
  hairstyles of elite women, 156–58
  July Fourth parade, 159–60
  march to British minister's home, 236–37
  May Day celebrations, 192
  memories of Penn's Treaty, 180
  militia presentations, 245
  militia protests, 12
  Oeller's Hotel, 235, 239
  rough music episodes, 160–61, 174 n. 21
  tricolor cockades worn, 237, 238
  violence against African Americans, 9
  visits of Indians, 183, 187
  witchcraft accusations, 7, 161
Philadelphia, July Fourth rough music, 156
  approval of other citizens, 161
  effects, 168
  gender relations, 170–71
  gender roles, 165
  later interpretations, 169–70, 172
  parody of hairstyles, 160
  participants, 161, 165, 169
  political significance, 161–64
  symbolism, 162, 165, 167–68, 169

Philadelphia Aurora, 238, 239
Philadelphia City Cavalry, 244–45
Philadelphia Independent, 187
Philipse, Frederick, 114, 115, 116, 117, 118
Pickering, Timothy, 164, 166–67
Pilgrims' Progress (Bunyan), 163
Pinckney, Charles Cotesworthy, 283
Pinkster holiday, 119–20 n. 2, 255, 259
Pintard, John, 215–16, 221
Pitt, William, 151
play
  definitions, 126
  elements in Boston protests, 127–28
  relationship to political protest, 125, 127, 134, 148–49
  rituals, 126
  songs about America as space for, 141–48
plebeian culture. *See* popular culture
Plymouth Plantation, 24
A Poem, on the Rising Glory of America (Freneau and Brackenridge), 208
poetry, Columbus symbolism, 208, 209, 210–11. *See also* songs
political parties
  holiday celebrations, 12, 229–30
  legitimate opposition, 10–11
  second-party system, 10–11
politics. *See also* protests; women's political participation
  activities, 229–30
  popular culture of, 243–47
  relationship to fashion, 163, 164, 167
Pope's Day processions, 99, 106 n. 63, 130, 132, 133–34
popular culture. *See also* plebeian culture
  in colonial America, 89
  English customs in America, 88, 104–5 n. 39
  political protests, 22, 99
  of politics, 243–47
  Puritan influence, 90–91
Porcupine's Gazette, 244
Portland (Maine), 245
Portsmouth (New Hampshire), 235
Poughkeepsie (New York)
  constitutional debates, 214
  rough music episodes, 48–49, 79
  trial of rebels, 116, 117
Powel, Elizabeth Willing, 244–45
Prendergast, William, 115, 116–18
Prime, Nathaniel S., 73

Prioleau, Samuel, 236
property rights. *See also* land riots
  violent conflicts, 92–93, 95–96, 98–99
protests. *See also* Boston protests; riots
  in colonial America, 6
  debates on, 3–4
  Indian costumes used, 193
  by lower classes, 5, 12
  network analysis, 150
  popular culture of, 22, 99
  in revolutionary period, 5, 7
  against Stamp Act, 111–14
  against taxes, 9
publications in early America, 208
public sphere, 208. *See also* women's political participation
  exclusion of African Americans, 15–16
  female roles, 15, 248
  as male domain, 231, 234
  multiplicity of arenas, 231–32
  rise of, 14–15
Puritans
  authority of churches, 93
  gender relations, 90, 110
  morality, 96
  view of Columbus, 207

Quakers
  beliefs, 171
  business meetings, 165
  clothing, 166–67, 171
  conflicts with other groups, 6
  importance of peacemaking, 182, 196
  imprisoned, 167
  in Philadelphia, 161
  political dominance of Pennsylvania, 7
Quebec, rough music, 44
Quincy, Josiah, 131

race. *See also* African Americans
  blackface, 51, 63, 165
  meanings of blackness, 171
Reed, Esther deBerdt, 164–65
reform movements, 10, 248
Regulators, 8, 94, 98
religion. *See also* morality; Puritans; Quakers
  Anglican churches, 93, 138
  anti-Catholic violence, 9
  Calvinism, 88, 90
  relationship to politics and fashion, 167

republican motherhood, 235–36, 237, 241, 246
Republican party, 231, 232, 233, 234–36, 242
Revere, Paul, 141
revolutions. *See also* American Revolution; French Revolution
  Latin American, 150
  sources, 151
Rhode Island, rough music episodes, 6, 54, 96, 98
Richards, Leonard, 63
Richardson, Ebenezer, 129, 130, 140
Ridgefield (Connecticut), 45, 77
rights. *See also* property rights
  of women, 92, 235, 238, 242
"The Rights of Woman," 242
riots. *See also* land riots; protests; rough music
  in Boston, 57
  in colonial America, 9
  draft, 9
  in early America, 9–10
  fatalities, 9
rituals
  distinction from festivities, 182
  of ethnic clubs, 188
  of European-Indian meetings, 198–99
  festive, 34
  French Revolutionary celebrations, 241
  Iroquois, 183, 196–97
  nationalistic, 275–76
  objects involved, 181
  of play, 126
  Seneca, 184
Robin Hood ballads, 125, 151
Robinson, Beverly, 114, 115, 116
Robinson, David, 49, 50
Robinson, Jane, 50
Robinson (customs commissioner), 140
Roe, Nathaniel, Jr., 70
Rosswurm, Steven, 161–62
rough music. *See also* Philadelphia, July Fourth rough music
  arrival in America, 44
  behaviors, 5–6, 108–9
  blackface in, 51, 63, 165
  in Britain, 43, 44, 45–46, 88, 160
  against British officials and loyalists, 6, 8, 64
  as challenge to authority, 97, 118–19
  in cities, 8, 14, 47–48, 49–50
  class conflict in, 8, 160–62, 170–71
  comparison of England and America, 88–89

rough music (*cont'd*)
  condemnation of, 97–98
  deaths during, 55, 96, 98
  decline of, 171–72
  efforts to curb, 56–57
  episodes, 6–7
  in Europe, 165
  evidence of in colonies, 42, 44
  examples, 45–76
  as extralegal means of social control, 42, 44, 76–77, 79–80, 96–97, 107–8
  against female extravagance, 161, 162
  frequency in colonial America, 6, 8, 76
  goals, 43, 80
  increase in, 104–5 n. 39
  justifications of, 53
  lack of prosecution, 50–52, 78, 79
  laws against, 55, 83 n. 37
  meanings, 97
  in nineteenth century, 43
  politicization, 14, 42, 99–100, 111, 116
  poor victims, 51–52
  potential violence, 160, 161
  prosecutions of perpetrators, 48–50, 59–61, 63, 66, 68–73, 78, 79
  punishment of adultery, 47–48, 49–50, 52–56, 62–63, 90, 109, 110
  punishment of sexual offenses, 42, 63–64, 165
  punishment of spouse abuse, 45–47, 62, 87, 90, 94–95, 96
  related to property disputes, 95–96, 98–99
  during Revolution, 6
  in rural areas, 8, 14, 77
  social control motive, 7–8, 88, 90, 108, 111, 162
  stages, 43
  victims, 42, 43–44, 77, 80, 109
  whitecapping, 8
  women's participation, 7–8, 45–48, 49, 62–63, 109, 110, 161, 169
rural areas
  crowd violence in, 78–79
  rough music episodes, 8, 14, 77
Russell, Samuel, 65
Russell, Steven, 65
Rusticus, 210
Rye (New York), rough music episodes, 52–53, 78, 79, 107–8

sailors, 3–4, 5, 51
St. Clair, Arthur, 221
Saint Mary's (Georgia), 258
satire
  in colonial America, 24
  of Washington, 148
  of whites, 262–63
  of women's hairstyles, 156
Schama, Simon, 24
Scheffer, Phillip, 50
schools, mandatory attendance, 10
Schooner, Jonas, 61
Schuylkill Fishing Club, 188–90
scolds, 88, 91, 101 n. 12
Scott, John Morin, 117
Seaman, Bean, 74
Seaman, John, 74–76
Seaman, Martha, 75
Seaman, Mary, 75
Seaman, Zebulon, 74
The Sea-Piece: A narrative, philosophical and descriptive Poem (Kirkpatrick), 209
second line, 260, 261
secret societies, 184, 194
Seneca people
  alliance with British, 183, 199
  land claims, 179
  rituals, 184
  visit to Philadelphia, 183, 187, 190, 196, 199–200
Sewall, Samuel, 207, 212
sexual offenders. *See also* adultery; morality
  rough music against, 42, 63–64, 165
  tolerance of, 44
Shaw, Peter, 99, 165
Shays' Rebellion, 4, 152
Sheppardson, Jonathan, Jr., 54–56, 77
Shields, David, 170
Shirley, William, 51
Shrewsbury (New Jersey), 63
Simms, William G., Jr., 283
Simpson, Able, 48
skimmington, 42–43. *See also* rough music
Slaughter, Thomas, 7, 8
slavery debate, divisions between South and North, 280–81, 287
slaves. *See also* African Americans
  economic role, 16–17
  festivals, 255, 258, 263
  population, 281
  revolts, 6, 9, 281
Smith, Anna Young, 164

Smith, Gilbert, 68, 69, 71, 72
Smith, Hugh, 69
Smith, Isaiah, 69
Smith, John, 53
Smith, Joseph, 50
Smith, Josiah, 69
Smith, Silas, 75
Smith, William, 71
Smith, William, Jr., 117
Smith, William Pitt, 220
Society for the Propagation of Gospel in Foreign Parts (SPG), 93
Society of Friends. *See* Quakers
songs. *See also* "Yankee Doodle"
  African, 262
  America as "play space," 141–48
  of American rebels, 130, 141–48, 151, 185
  Federalist, 246
  French Revolutionary, 235, 236, 240, 241–43
  "Heart of Oak," 143–44, 146, 154 n. 45
  "Liberty Song," 144–46, 150
  outlaw ballads, 125–26, 151
  parodies, 142–43, 146–48
  popular, 24–26
  references to Columbus, 210, 211
  responses to Boston Massacre, 141–43
  Robin Hood ballads, 125, 151
  satirical, 262
  on St. Tammany, 185
Sons of Ancient Britons, 188
Sons of Liberty, 130, 137, 193, 195
Sons of St. Tammany. *See also* Tammany Society (New York)
  association with Columbus, 211, 218–19
  nationalism, 216–17
  political activities, 217
  spring rituals, 217
  wigwams in various cities, 189, 192
Sons of St. Tammany (Philadelphia)
  activities, 183–84, 189, 190, 193, 195
  association with Columbus, 219
  ceremonial objects, 191
  ceremony for Cornplanter's visit, 179, 181, 182, 187, 190–91, 193, 195–97, 199
  differences from Indians, 193–94
  formation, 190
  immigrant members, 227 n. 30
  Indian costumes, 187, 190, 192
  parades, 187
  political activities, 191–92

public performances, 184
speeches, 187, 190
spring rituals, 182, 184, 186, 188, 192
structure, 190, 195
South Carolina. *See also* Charleston
  Columbia, 211
  relationship to federal government, 291
  secession debate, 284, 286, 288
  slave revolts, 6
South Carolina Gazette, 263
Southern United States. *See also specific states*
  divisions from North, 280–81, 287
  Fourth of July celebrations, 290
  nullification doctrine, 282, 286
  rough music episodes, 6
  states' rights, 282–85
Spain, New World colonies, 211, 218
SPG. *See* Society for the Propagation of Gospel in Foreign Parts
spouse abuse
  condemnation of, 90–91 .
  increase in, 92, 93–94
  legal punishments, 91–92, 103 n. 22
  punished with rough music, 45–47, 62, 87, 90, 94–95, 96
Stamp Act
  Hutchinson's views of, 137, 139
  provisions, 111
  resistance in Boston, 99, 128, 131–32, 137
  riots in Albany, 111–14
Standish, Miles, 24
states' rights, 282–85, 287–92
Stevens, George Alexander, 142
Stewart, Steven, 5, 15
Stewart, Susan, 194
Stono slave revolt, 6
Strongham, Samuel, 51
Stuckey, Sterling, 264, 267
Sullivan, James, 215
Suydam, Hendrick, 49
Swart, Dirck, 123 n. 18
Sylvanus Americus, 209

Tammanies. *See* Sons of St. Tammany
Tammany. *See also* Penn's Treaty
  as American saint, 184–86
  association with Columbus, 211, 218, 220
  association with Schuylkill Fishing Club, 189

Tammany (cont'd)
　legends about, 186
　symbolism, 184
Tammany, or The Indian Chief (Hatton), 218
Tammany (chief in 1730s), 189
Tammany Museum, 216
Tammany Society (New York), 211, 215–19, 220, 227 n. 30
Tappan, Lewis, 60
tarring and feathering, 22, 133, 136
taxes, protests against, 9
temperance movement, 10
Teute, Fredrika, 170
Thatcher, Peter, 135
Thaxter, John, 159, 166
theater
　opera, 218
　references to Columbus, 213–14, 218
Thompson, B. F., 73
Thompson, E. P., 5, 8, 17, 21–22, 44
Thompson, Samuel, 71
Tillinghast, Samuel, 54
Tilly, Charles, 21
Tilly, Louise, 21
Tobias, Eben, 263
Tocqueville, Alexis de, 17
Tongue, Dorothy, 62–63
Tongue, William, 62, 63
Tories. *See* loyalists
Towner, Samuel, 115
Towner's Tavern, 115
Travers, Hezekiah, Jr., 50
Travers, James, Jr., 50
Trinidad, 262
Turner, Nat, 9

Ulster County (New York), 63–64
Underdown, David, 5, 44
"Unhappy Boston," 141
U.S. Army, 287–88
upper class. *See also* class conflict
　administrative elite of Massachusetts, 138–39
　celebrations, 14, 16, 23
　condemnation of rough music, 97–98
　duels, 9
　judges, 61–62
　legal power, 116–17, 118, 123 n. 18
　masculinity, 162–63
　opposition to Stamp Act, 111, 137, 139
　political participation, 14
　social and moral differences from lower classes, 8
　social contacts with British army, 159, 160, 162, 166
　victims of rough music, 70, 98
　women's hairstyles, 156–58, 164, 168, 169, 170–71, 174 n. 21
utopianism, 208

Valmy, 233–34, 235
Vandervort, Benjamin, 57–58
Vandervort, Jacob, 57, 58
Vandervort, John, 57
Vandewater, Lanah, 61
Van Gennep, Arnold, 26–27
Vanity Fair, 163
Van Schaak, Henry, 111–14
Van Tollinsel, Ernest August Jacobus Printz, 50
Van Vleck, John, Jr., 61
Van Wyck, Richard, 59
Vermont, land riots, 9
Vesey, Denmark, 9, 281
Vincent, Ambrose, 48
Vincent, Michael, 48
violence. *See* riots; rough music
Virginia
　African American festivities, 257, 262
　American Revolution in, 278
　Jon Koonering festival, 255
　politics, 14
　slave labor, 17
Vischer, John, 112

Wadsworth, Zilpah, 245
Waldstreicher, David, 12
Wallace, Michael, 130
Walsh, William S., 44
Wappinger Indians, 114, 117
Ward, John, 283
Warner, Michael, 208
War of 1812, 221, 279–80
Warren, Edward, 259–60
Warren, Joseph, 130, 134–35
Warren, Mercy Otis, 131, 210
Warwick (Rhode Island), 54
Washburn, Simeon, 55
Washington, D.C., 211
Washington, George
　birthday as holiday, 12, 229

as national hero, 214, 217, 221, 222
Philadelphia residence, 240
as president, 229–30, 241, 242
satires of, 148
supporters, 229–30
tours of country, 12
in Virginia politics, 14
Washington County (North Carolina), 260
Watson, Jacob, 70
Watson, John Fanning, 189–90, 242
Wayne, Anthony, 163–64
wedding customs, 89
Wells, Louisa, 277
West, Benjamin, 185, 186
Westchester County (New York)
land riots, 114–18
rough music episodes, 51–53, 78, 107–8
West Indies
dance in, 260, 262
festivities, 257, 258, 259, 264–65, 265–66
Wheatley, Phillis, 210
Whigs, 10–11
clothing, 167
divisions among, 162
festivities, 248
in Philadelphia, 166
rough music episodes, 99, 162
Whiskey Rebellion, 9
White, Shane, 13, 264
whitecapping, 8
Whitefield, George, 53
White Indians. See also Sons of St. Tammany
Boston "Mohawks," 34, 130
in early America, 190–91
meanings of costumes, 192
objects used, 191
in Philadelphia, 192
political activities, 193
purposes of disguises, 34
symbolism of Indians, 224–25 n. 13
whites
festivities influenced by African American customs, 259, 261–62, 268
satires of, 262–63
Wickham-Crowley, Timothy, 150
Wiggins, Daniel, 68
Wilks, John, 50
Willet, Job, 68
Willett, Isaac, 53
Willett, William, 53

Williams, Allison, 109
Williams, David, 50
Williams, Thomas, 112
Williams tavern (Albany), 112–13
Willington, Mrs., 235
Wilson, Gertrude, 49, 50, 109–10
Wilson, James, 159, 214
Wing, Mehitabel, 117
witches, suspected, 7, 161
Wollstonecraft, Mary, 13, 235, 242
women. See also gender relations; spouse abuse
fashions, 167, 168
hairstyles of elite, 156–58, 164, 168, 169, 170–71, 174 n. 21
legal system and, 92
moral roles, 110
participation in rough music, 7–8, 45–48, 49, 62–63, 109, 110, 161, 169
patriotism, 157, 158–59, 162, 163–65, 166
position in American republic, 12–13
pregnancies, 166
proportion of New England population, 91
republican motherhood role, 235–36, 237, 241, 246
rights of, 92, 235, 238, 242
scolds, 88, 91, 101 n. 12
symbolism of female figures, 211, 212, 219, 221
victims of rough music, 49, 50, 57–60, 62–63, 88, 101 n. 12, 109–10
women's movement, 10
women's political participation
in Boston, 233
in charitable organizations, 248
discouraged, 231, 234
in early United States, 229, 248
economic motives, 239
encouraged by Republicans, 234–36
exclusion from public sphere, 15
Federalist festivities, 244–47
in France, 237
in French Revolutionary festivities, 231, 232, 233–34, 236–37, 240–41
interest in, 237–38, 241
limits to, 247–48
militia presentations, 244–46, 253 n. 63
partisanship in, 247
in revolutionary period, 158–59, 247
speeches, 245, 246

Wood, Gordon, 194–95
Woolsey, Mary, 50
Woolsey, Matthew, 50
Worcester (Massachusetts), Volunteer Cadet Infantry, 245
Wright, Joel, 221
Wright, William, 69–70
writers, pseudonyms, 130–31
Wurdeman, F. W., 265

Yamomamo people, 149
"Yankee Doodle," 24–25, 133, 148, 151, 241
Yates, Abraham, 111
Yoruba people, 264
Young, Alfred F., 5, 21, 22, 99
Young, William, 163
"You Simple Bostonians," 142–43

Zuckerman, Michael, 14, 78, 79

www.ingramcontent.com/pod-product-compliance
Lightning Source LLC
Chambersburg PA
CBHW031545300426
44111CB00006BA/179